ANALYZING
PUBLIC POLICY

ANALYZING PUBLIC POLICY

Concepts, Tools, and Techniques

Dipak K. Gupta

San Diego State University

CQ PRESS

A Division of Congressional Quarterly Inc.
Washington, D.C.

CQ Press
A Division of Congressional Quarterly Inc.
1414 22nd St. N.W.
Washington, D.C. 20037

(202) 822-1475; (800) 638-1710

www.cqpress.com

⊗ The paper used in this publication meets the minimum requirements of the American National Standard for Information Sciences—Permanence of Paper for Printed Library Materials, ANSI Z39.48-1992.

Figure 3.5 (page 52) is from *Public Policy: An Evolutionary Approach*, 2d ed., by J. P. Lester and J. Stewart, Jr. © 2000. Reprinted with permissionn of Wadsworth, an imprint of the Wadsworth Group, a division of Thomson Learning.

Analyzing Public Policy was designed and typeset by Impressions Book and Journal Services, Inc.

Cover design: Rich Pottern

Printed and bound in the United States of America

05   04   03   02   01   5   4   3   2   1

Library of Congress Cataloging-in-Publication Data

Gupta, Dipak K.
    Analyzing public policy : concepts, tools, & techniques / Dipak Gupta.
      p. cm.
    Includes bibliographical references and index.
    ISBN 1-56802-555-6 (pbk. : alk. paper)
    1. Policy sciences—Statistical methods.   2. Policy sciences—Mathematical models.   I. Title.

H97.G868 2001
320′.6′0727—dc21   2001025543

To Chitra and Samar Das

CONTENTS

TABLES, FIGURES, AND "A CASE IN POINT"

TABLES

FIGURES

"A CASE IN POINT"

PREFACE

A noted journalist, having visited India, remarked that any general statement about the country would be both true and false. What is true of a huge and complex nation is also true of the ways in which the vast field of public policy analysis is taught.

At the beginning of this project, CQ Press conducted a survey of instructors in the field to determine how the typical policy analysis course is taught. The results confirmed our belief that there is no universal approach to the pedagogy of public policy analysis. Ready access to the survey data proved too much of a temptation for this policy researcher. I performed a factor analysis of the results and discovered that courses are organized along three broad and overlapping strands—what I call concepts, tools, and techniques.

THE APPROACH

Some teach public policy analysis by emphasizing concepts, or the foundations of public policy analysis. They concentrate primarily on the process of policy formation and the role of an analyst within the political system and the bureaucratic structure. Others stress quantitative methods of data analysis and approach the subject from a more technical standpoint. They use the tools of statistical research, including descriptive statistics, probability theory, and various forms of hypothesis testing and analysis of variance. Still others emphasize the techniques of management, such as forecasting, cost-benefit analysis, decision analysis, and so on. The available textbooks on the market quite predictably follow these three general approaches.

The survey revealed the need for a book that provides an integrated perspective. Most students encounter policy analysis for the first time in the pages of their textbooks. Recognizing this opportunity to plant seeds in the minds of those who will work in government, business, or academia, this book tries to present a comprehensive picture, in which policy analysts maintain their professional, ethical, and technical integrity while submerged in a world of subjective perceptions and political considerations. Therefore, a consistent theme permeates the wide-ranging topics covered in *Analyzing Public Policy*. This theme resonates with an image proposed by Karl Popper, the philosopher of science, who views scientific theories as a collective "structure above the swamp." In our analyses we do not attempt to reach the *terra firma* of absolute truth—we are not sure that it exists. Instead, we build a structure that is stable, logically consistent, and clear about its underlying assumptions. A structure built on these premises may not represent the last word on an issue, but it will provide decision makers with a firm foundation on which an edifice of public policy can be constructed. In the final analysis the answer to a complex policy issue is less about finding the optimal solutions and more about reaching a well-reasoned balance among the conflicting needs of society and its many constituents.

Like most terms in the social sciences, "concepts," "tools," and "techniques" cannot be placed in hermetically sealed containers. Therefore, this book is divided into three somewhat overlapping sections. The first four chapters cover what I would describe as the concepts of public policy analysis. These chapters define public policy within the political, historical, and organizational contexts. In this section I discuss the role of a public policy analyst in a mixed economic system, with government and the private sector acting as full partners. The section ends with a discussion of critical thinking, the essence of objective analyses. The following four chapters describe the basic tools of statistical analysis and data organization. These tools include descriptive statistics, probability theory and hypothesis testing, survey design, and the presentation of data. Chapters 9 through 14 explore the techniques of efficient management, techniques designed to answer questions that confound a decision maker in a public organization: How can we predict the future course of a particular event or policy? How can we manage uncertainty? How do we choose the best project or course of action? Finally, chapter 15 puts the preceding chapters in perspective.

In this book I have discussed a number of quantitative techniques of management. However, due to space restrictions, I have not included less frequently used techniques, such as Markov's Chain, PERT networks, queuing theory and simulation, and linear and integer programming. Our survey indicated that those topics are of interest to many instructors. If you are teaching a course that covers these subjects and you would like to use my chapters about them, I would be pleased to send you the chapters by e-mail. I can be reached at dipak.gupta@sdsu.edu or through my homepage, http://www-rohan.sdsu.edu/faculty/dgupta/.

UNIQUE FEATURES

Every book makes its own claim to uniqueness. This one is no exception. I believe that professionals in the field will find the combination of topics in this volume different from that in other available books. I have discussed tools and techniques that vary widely in complexity, including technically involved multiple regression analysis and relatively simple predictions based on a causal variable or the growth rate of a single period. The guiding principle for including a technique in the book has been its actual or potential use in the world of a practicing policy analyst. For example, a great deal of policy analysis is done with clever graphic techniques of data presentation. Yet most textbooks exclude these techniques, regarding them as too simple. In this book I have taken great care to explain how numerical information can be presented in different ways, leading to a different conclusion each time. The same is true of single-factor projection techniques. A perusal of government documents, from in-house memos to consultants' reports, will convince anyone of the wide use and critical importance of these simple tools of analysis.

Another unique feature of this book is that it covers judgmental, or nonquantitative, methods of prediction, such as subjective assessment of probability. Advances in social psychology have revealed many of the hidden pitfalls of objective reasoning. I have brought some of these findings to students' attention in my discussions of subjective forecasting and subjective probabilities.

When it comes to the use of quantitative techniques, a deep chasm in the field of policy analysis separates the faithful from the agnostic. Critics such as Charles Lindblom advocate decisions based on "ordinary knowledge" over those grounded strictly in statistical reasoning. Others see in these quantitative techniques the answer to human frailty. In this enduring debate *Analyzing Public Policy* takes the middle ground.

When explaining the concepts of public policy analysis, this book draws extensively on case studies. In contrast, books that cover only quantitative techniques often do not forge a direct link to actual public policy issues. I have sought to make the discussions relevant and interesting to students by using real-world policy examples throughout the book. These examples cover a wide range of subjects, from criminal justice to environmental issues, urban planning to pure politics. A boxed feature, "A Case in Point," highlights particularly compelling policy dilemmas and gives students additional opportunities to apply the skills they have learned. I hope that students will find the examples engaging, often amusing, and always helpful in clarifying how the tools and techniques discussed in the book are used in public policy analysis.

CLASSROOM USE

Since *Analyzing Public Policy* covers wide-ranging topics, some instructors may choose to spend more than a week on each chapter. Keeping flexibility in mind, an instructor, making slight adjustments, should be able to fit the book's fifteen chapters into an academic semester or quarter.

Those who wish to emphasize concepts and tools can ignore some of the more involved techniques of regression analysis. Those with different goals can spend several weeks on regression models and cost-benefit analysis. To help instructors, each chapter ends with a list of key terms and offers many exercises.

Books do not dream, but their authors do. In this book I have made every effort to present the material in a way that is easy to understand and that grabs students' interest. If students find that this book delivers more than it demands, my dreams will be fulfilled.

ACKNOWLEDGMENTS

A number of my friends and colleagues have contributed to this book. Until his untimely death, Marco Walshok was a constant partner in discussions that clarified many ideas for me. I also gratefully acknowledge the help of Glen Sparrow, Jim Gazell, and Celeste Murphy, and I thank Louis M. Rea, director of the School of Public Administration and Urban Studies at San Diego State University, for his continuing support. Over the years many students of my graduate-level quantitative analysis class have helped me sharpen my arguments and suggested ways to make my explanations more accessible to them.

I also would like to take this opportunity to thank my reviewers. Among them, my intellectual debt runs particularly deep to Daniel J. Alesch of the University of Wisconsin at Green Bay, Lynn C. Burbridge of Rutgers University at Newark, Jeffrey Greene of the University of Montana, Florence Heffron of the University of Idaho, David J. Houston of the University of Tennessee at Knoxville, Nancy Marion of Akron University, Edward Miller of the University of Wisconsin at Stevens Point, Juliet Musso of the University of Southern California, Michelle Piskulich of Oakland University, John M. Strate of Wayne State University, and Paul Teske of the State University of New York at Stony Brook. Their thoughtful comments have contributed significantly to the quality of this book.

It must have been my good karma that brought CQ Press acquisition editor Charisse Kiino to my office for an unscheduled meeting. Since then, it has been both a pleasure and a privilege to know and work closely with Charisse and Senior Editor Christopher Karlsten. If there are special wish lists for authors at their reincarnations, the top item on my list would be the desire to work with CQ Press and its thoroughly caring and professional staff.

I cannot end the book without acknowledging the gifts of my family. My wife Munia and our children Shalini and Rohan gave me the peace of mind that allowed me to complete this arduous task. I also was fortunate to have my mother, Kanika, visit us during the crucial period of writing. Her presence was a source of great repose to me. Without my family's help, this book would not have been completed—not in this life, and perhaps not even in the next.

CHAPTER

1

INTRODUCTION

Oh, dear Lord!" cries Tevye the milkman, the central character of the hit Broadway musical-turned-movie *Fiddler on the Roof*. While sharing his story with the audience he describes life in Anatevka, the tiny Jewish village of turn-of-the-century Russia. In the opening song, "Tradition," he introduces the rabbi as the most important person in the village: "[The rabbi] tells us what to eat, when to eat, how to dress, when to pray." The audience wonders about this distant land and its alien customs. Life in this Russian village seems so different from life in our own country; here, no one tells us how to live. Or do they? Upon reflection, we realize that an outsider shapes practically every aspect of our lives. It intrudes far more than does the respected village rabbi of *Fiddler on the Roof*. In the modern world the government regulates almost everything we see, breathe, touch, use, ride, inject, or ingest, from our birth to our death. The government sets air and water quality standards and criteria for serving food and administering drugs. It levies taxes, circulates currency, makes education policy, and resolves questions of our personal welfare. The government tries to protect us by keeping law and order. It maintains a military to keep us safe from attack. It even passes laws affecting the most personal aspects of our lives, including laws regulating sexual behavior. State

1

governments determine the age of consent, prohibit or permit same-sex marriages, and define acceptable sexual practices. It would be difficult, if not impossible, to list all the government regulations and standards to which we must adhere in our daily lives.

Consider, for example, the birth of a baby. The hospital must follow strict rules and regulations governing medical equipment, medicines, and medical personnel. The parents must register the child's birth. When they leave the hospital and get into the family car, they cannot simply place the newborn on the mother's lap. In many states, the infant must be strapped into an approved car seat.

Similarly, when we die, many government regulations tell us how our family may dispose of our remains. Imagine how long the list would be if you wrote down all the ways government policies have touched your life since you got out of bed this morning.

The government does not make public policies in a vacuum. Its control over its citizens depends on several factors that determine what are and what are not acceptable domains of public policy. These factors include the nation's norms, values, culture, history, traditions, constitution, and technological sophistication. Together, these factors form the environment in which public policies are made. In the United States and other Western nations, the rights of the individual reign supreme; citizens challenge immediately any policy that impinges on these rights. Therefore, policy makers seek to uphold individual rights. In contrast, in collective societies ruled by a national religion or communism, lawmakers value the needs of the group more highly than the rights of individuals. In making public policy, such societies seek to uphold not the rights but the duties of citizens. Some countries arrest those who do not pray during specified times of public prayer, or impose fines for violating the sabbath. Other countries severely curtail the right of political expression. Although most Western countries consider property rights sacred, other nations balance these rights against competing national goals, such as eliminating poverty or meeting society's general needs, as defined by the political elite.

The extent to which government intrudes in the lives of its citizens is partly determined by technology. As technology advances, so does society's need for regulations. A simple agrarian society requires minimal government intervention. However, today's complex world, characterized by rapid changes in technology—from the Internet to genetically altered food, from the possibility of cloning animals and humans to the specter of global warming caused by unrestrained industrial activities—demands regulations with ever-increasing urgency.

In the wide-open field of public policy analysis the analyst performs a high-stakes balancing act. Going back to our opening analogy, we see that like the fiddler perched precariously on the roof, playing his fiddle, public policy analysts ply their trade by balancing a number of competing demands.

THE STUDY OF PUBLIC POLICY

The field of public policy is so vast that those who study it may be compared to a group of blind people who have been asked to describe an elephant: some people describe it by its trunk, some by its tusks, some by its large belly, some by its large, floppy ears or by its thin tail. According to the University of California's electronic library catalog, no fewer than 4,586 books with the words "public policy" in their titles have been published during the past ten years. This evidence indicates that there are many ways of studying public policy.

While some students of public policy focus on the political, cultural, and judicial contexts in which policies are made, others study how policies are adopted. Political scientists, for example, typically are most interested in the interaction in the policy process between the political system and interest groups. Scholars with backgrounds in public administration study the role of the bureaucracy in public policy. Economists concern themselves primarily with the effects of policies, while operations researchers examine the management policies that promote efficient delivery of services in public organizations.

If you define the study of public policy as advising those who govern, the field has a long history.[1] If, on the other hand, you define it as a systematic, objective, and institutionalized approach to improving the art of government, then policy sciences has a short past. Let us keep in mind both definitions as we discuss the evolution of the profession and the tools developed by policy analysts.

Four Models of Policy Making

The framers of the Constitution minimized the role of the government, particularly at the federal level. However, as the new nation took on greater responsibilities, government officials recognized the need for true professionals to run the government and make its policies. In the early years the administration and politics were inseparable, and elected politicians hired their own supporters to fill administrative positions. However, as the government grew more complex, untrained professionals drew criticism for mismanagement and corruption, prompting a public call for change.

The first serious study of public administration and the role of the bureaucracy began three years after the passage of the *Pendleton Act* (1884), which sought to reform the civil service by instituting merit-based selection procedures. The author of the study, a young political scientist named Woodrow Wilson, stressed the importance of a strict separation between elected officials and nonelected bureaucrats.[2] His model advocated a perfect dichotomy between the two groups: elected officials defined policy objectives while public agencies and administrators performed purely technical and professional functions. Policy makers did not interfere in administration, and administrators did not get involved in policy making (see Figure 1.1 (a)).

In Figure 1.1 (a) the sphere of public policy is divided in two parts: one makes policies, and one administers or implements them. In this strict hierarchy, elected officials make public policies, and administrators remain fully accountable to their political bosses while translating adopted policies into action. The horizontal line bisecting the circle defines the domains of policy makers and administrators and illustrates the strict hierarchical relationship between them. Introduced in the

Figure 1.1   Four Models of Policy Making

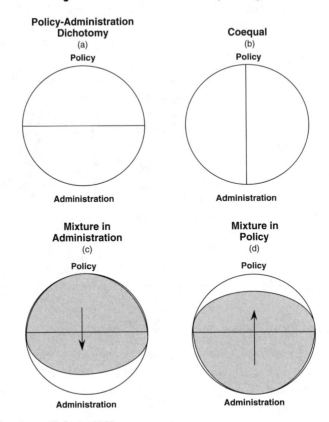

Source: Based on James H. Svara, 1995.

1930s, this **policy-administration dichotomy model** withstood strong attacks from various academic quarters to become, until the mid-1960s, the dominant model in the field.

This model primarily emphasizes democratic control over a burgeoning bureaucracy. Insulated from the corrupting influences of the political spoils system, in which elected officials ignore the merits of job applicants and offer administrative posts to their loyal supporters, administrators work toward achieving a greater degree of neutrality, professionalism, and efficiency.

In 1968, during a tumultuous period in American history, a group of young academics founded the "New Public Administration," a school of policy analysis. Like most young men and women of that time, they were deeply affected by the riots, the assassinations of prominent political leaders, and the ongoing war in Vietnam, all of which fostered in them a strong distrust of elected officials. These scholars distanced themselves from the policy-administration dichotomy model, which seemed to them to prescribe a machine-like devotion by administrators to the policies of elected officials.[3] They also questioned the loyalty of administrators to their political bosses. The scholars advocated a nonhierarchical, coequal arrangement in which administrators were loyal not to the hierarchy but to their ethical principles—their belief in the equality of policy makers and administrators and their commitment to protecting the rights of the powerless.[4] Radical in their approach, they urged administrators to become activists by developing a direct link with the people. The young academics admitted that such direct contact might sometimes conflict with the policies of elected representatives. Figure 1.1 (b) illustrates the **coequal model:** a vertical line divides the policy-administration sphere into two equal domains.

The sixties produced the New Public Administration, which questioned the authority of the political leaders. Another group of scholars went in the opposite direction. They developed models in which elected officials questioned the role of administrators in policy making. The **mixture-in-administration model** (see Figure 1.1 (c)) observes that elected officials prevent nonelected administrators from gaining too much authority in a democracy by encroaching on the domains of administrators.

At the national level, elected officials encroach on administrative domains when different parties control the White House and the legislative branch. Congress routinely called Clinton administration officials to testify about their operations, and lawmakers often tried to tie their hands by asserting legislative prerogatives, ordering inquiries, or passing oversight legislation that severely curtailed the administration's authority. Congressional hearings in the late 1990s on the excesses of the Internal Revenue Service severely reduced the agency's auditing capabilities. In 1993, when the FBI and the Justice Department inquired into events leading to the incineration of eighty-nine Christian fundamentalists in Waco, Texas, some lawmakers cited the investigation as evidence of the "uncontrolled bureaucracy."

In contrast to the mixture-in-administration model, the **mixture-in-policy model** (see Figure 1.1 (d)) describes the increasing role of bureaucracy in public policy making.[5] Three developments fostered this rapid encroachment by nonelected policy analysts and executives, particularly in local governments. First, as the nation grew more populous and urban, the demand for public services increased more than proportionately. New demands for public policies on crime control, education, health care, infrastructure, drug abuse, poverty, and environmental protection challenged city governments, which typically were ill equipped to deal with such a wide variety of issues. Second, the Great Depression and Keynesian economics, which prescribed an involved government, changed people's attitudes. People started expecting action on such issues as raising children's test scores in public schools and reducing gun violence. They also began to demand such action from government. As a result, public administrators and elected officials faced new rules of engagement. Finally, rapid advances in technology required that government regulate and promote activities that the Founding Fathers could never have imagined.

Economic Rationality, Quantitative Analyses, and Human Behavior

From the beginning, the founders of policy analysis as a distinct field of inquiry—defined by Robert Lynd in the 1930s and 1940s and by Harold Lasswell in the 1940s and 1950s—sought to improve government by making better use of knowledge from the social sciences.[6] Over the next half-century, numerous scholars established the academic credentials of policy analysis.[7] Today, the U.S. branch of this vast field comprises scholars; many private think tanks, such as the Brookings Institution and the RAND Corporation; and government agencies, such as the General Accounting Office, the Office of Management and Budget, the Congressional Budget Office, and the Congressional Research Service. A number of excellent trade journals and a growing list of books contribute to the policy debate. Although the field has evolved, several issues remain unresolved.

One of the deepest chasms in the discipline involves the place of quantitative techniques.[8] On one side of the debate are the economists. With their seemingly **deterministic** methods, they resolve every problem with logical arguments that lead to a unique solution, the best or **optimal** choice. Those who use these techniques—many of which are included in this book—make an assumption about human behavior and then build a model that, given a set of assumptions, provides a solution. For example, it is a common economic assumption that we tend to consume less if the price of an item goes up. Based on this basic assumption about human nature, economists argue for stiffer sentences for criminals, to raise the cost of participation in illegal activities. Stronger penalties, they say, deter "rational" criminals from wrongdoing as the cost of crime increases relative to the benefits.[9] But whether such a link exists between crime and punishment remains an open question. Economists also use quantitative methods when debating public policy on teen smoking. In April 1997 two articles on the subject appeared within three weeks of each other in the *New York Times*. The first article reported that antitobacco groups were pushing for a significant tax hike, which would boost the cost of a pack of cigarettes by one dollar. They argued that the price increase would discourage teen smokers from lighting up.[10] Casting doubt on this conclusion, the second article highlighted a nationwide survey indicating that teens were, in fact, smoking more than they had before. Although antismoking campaigns and price hikes had reduced the popularity of smoking among adults, they had had the opposite effect among teens.[11] Why do many criminals and teens confound the assumptions of economic analysis? If we follow strict economic arguments, we conclude that criminals and smoking teens are "irrational." The reason why economists may fail to explain seemingly aberrant behavior is that they define human rationality narrowly, considering only certain benefits and costs.

Sociologists tell us that kids often join street gangs to satisfy their need to belong to a group. To many kids, defying the law is an expression of solidarity and drawing a stiff sentence a badge of honor.[12] Similarly, smoking may satisfy teens' desire for independence. Having spent millions of dollars on antismoking campaigns to inform the public about the dangers of smoking, antitobacco groups may have increased the allure of lighting up for teens anxious to establish their own identities.[13]

In defense of their methods, economists argue that narrow assumptions are necessary to develop a **model,** which presents a limited version of reality. Similar to a model car, which merely depicts an actual vehicle, a policy model is but an impression of the real world. We build models because the reality is far too complex for us to comprehend. When we predict that a price hike will reduce demand for an item, we build a **behavioral model,** one that helps us to explain complex behavior. However, in building a model, we disregard what we consider the minor details, focusing instead on those that will explain a particular behavior. Any behavioral model must take a reductionistic view of human nature. Such narrow assumptions often draw criticism, particularly from analysts who do not use explicit behavioral models. In a famous essay economist Milton Friedman unabashedly defended the restrictive assumptions of economic analyses:

> Truly important and significant hypotheses will be found to have assumptions that are wildly inaccurate, descriptive representations of reality, and, in general, the more significant the theory, the more unrealistic the assumption.[14]

Friedman went on to claim that the true test of a theory lies not in the realism of its assumptions but in its ability to predict the future. A model with narrow assumptions is effective, he said, if it predicts the future with a reasonable degree of accuracy.

Another reason why policy analysts use logical tools (including mathematics, an extension of logic) is that they have created a body of knowledge. When you have proven a set of arguments, you need not go back and prove them again. Economists have determined that the principles of microeconomics are logically sound. When you develop a model based on those principles, you need not prove them each time you conduct an analysis. In many other, less quantitative disciplines, you do not start with accepted premises, the building blocks of analysis. In those fields, you take nothing for granted and must start from the beginning every time you attempt an analysis. In economics, on the other hand, once you have assumed that, above all, human beings maximize their self-utility, you can deduce many useful concepts, such as **marginal analysis, opportunity cost,** and **externality** (see chapter 2). This feature of economic analysis, one of its principal attractions, may account for much of its domination of other branches of the social sciences, including policy analysis. Some authors have suggested that the primary advantage of economic models is that they create "knowledge creep."[15] That is, as we build our arguments using solid methods, we expand our knowledge. While discussing the merits of a proposed project, we can debate the hidden opportunity costs without having to redefine the terms or the nature of our arguments. At the same time, logical lapses can easily be detected when we agree on the principles on which our arguments are based.

One drawback of mathematical reasoning is that it often gives the impression of macho objectivity. Many top policy makers have presumed incorrectly that such reasoning is superior to other, more "subjective" tools. On August 12, 1965, President Lyndon B. Johnson issued an executive order requiring every agency to institute what he called a "revolutionary" new system. In May 1966 all departments and most agencies of the federal government began submitting their rough spending plans to the Budget Bureau (now the Office of Management and Budget) through a new Planning-Programming Budgeting System (PPBS).[16] Using a **systems approach,** the PPBS allowed policy makers to see the federal budget as a system of identifiable and interrelated institutions and activities.[17] In contrast, the traditional, **incremental approach** considered each department's budget request individually in light of its allocation from the previous year. For example, if the Department of Defense submitted a budget request under the incremental approach, policy makers focused on how much the department had received last year and asked whether the department could keep up with inflation and other relevant demands. Then, after complex political bargaining, legislators allocated the money. However, what was lost in this process was the question as to whether any of the programs were worth continuing. In contrast, the PPBS, through a series of rigorous steps—such as defining the overall goal, finding alternative plans for achieving the goal, developing productivity indicators, and using a decision model such as cost-benefit analysis—determined the budgets not only of the Department of Defense but also of every office in the federal government, ignoring how much an office had received in previous years. In this way, its proponents claimed that the PPBS eliminated "politics" from the budget process and allocated resources to programs according to their relative efficiency. It funded the most productive programs while curtailing or even eliminating those that were inefficient. In his statement introducing the PPBS, President Johnson promised that the "[PPBS] will improve our ability to control our programs and our budgets rather than having them control us." This new system, bristling with the tools of the objective decision sciences, came to be known as the **rational model** of decision making. Pinning the term "rational" on one method made all other tools seem, at least implicitly, "irrational." Two decades later President Ronald Reagan issued an executive order directing that lawmakers analyze the costs and benefits of every federal regulation before recommending it for adoption.[18]

Despite the enthusiasm of two presidents (who, curiously, held opposite political views) and many others in the policy field, the PPBS failed to meet Johnson's expectations. Decision makers, doubting their ability to "control the programs and budgets," were instead controlled by them. In this confusion, political scientist Aaron Wildavsky emphatically stated, "*No one knows how to do program budgeting (PPBS).*"[19] Moreover, Wildavsky claimed that a "rational" method of budgeting is unknowable and warned that we should not even try to implement such a system. In sum, he argued that "rational" models deny a fundamental principle of democratic government: the political rationality by which elected representatives balance the numerous and often contradictory concerns of their various constituents. In a democracy politics is not about efficiency; rather, it is about bargains and compromises among competing interests. Wildavsky dismissed the PPBS because of its single-minded pursuit of economic efficiency—measured in terms of maximum output (benefits) relative to input (costs). Running the government with the efficiency of a private business, he said, was "downright undemocratic and un-American."

While Wildavsky questioned the criteria by which government programs should be evaluated, scholars Charles Lindblom and David Cohen pushed to the extreme the argument denouncing quantitative techniques and scoffed at the idea of using statistics to conduct "professional social inquiry." Instead of quantitative methods, Lindblom and Cohen urged policy makers to use "ordinary knowledge" when making decisions.[20] Lindblom declared forcefully, "For all the effort and for all its presumed usefulness, I cannot identify a single social science finding or idea that is undeniably indispensable in any social task or effort. Not even one." [21]

I would argue that Lindblom overstates his case and too quickly throws out all quantitative techniques. Peter DeLeon notes that policy analysis has made significant contributions to many government programs, such as those created by the 1988 Family Support Act and the 1990 Clean Air Act.[22] Besides these highly publicized cases, it is obvious that policy makers—from the chair of the Federal Reserve to the directors of financial management divisions in state and local governments—are influenced by economic analyses conducted in house or outside their agencies. They use analytical techniques when projecting revenues and costs, when evaluating the overall desirability of a project, and when submitting an environmental impact statement, which is required for all public projects. They may not always use the most sophisticated techniques of analysis, but they do use systematic, logical thinking, which takes them far beyond the reaches of "ordinary knowledge," far beyond the realm of unstructured, subjective assessment.

However, we should note that quantitative techniques, by themselves, cannot solve all of our problems. The wise men of antiquity told us that although it is important to know what we do know, it is even more important to know what we do not know. Before we discuss the techniques of analysis, we must first describe their limits. These limits arise because

1. we cannot prove or disprove our hypotheses with the precision of laboratory experiments;
2. our techniques may offer a limited view of reality;
3. our predilections, prejudices, and biases may cloud our judgment;
4. we cannot eliminate uncertainty;
5. we cannot define social values.

First, for the most part, hypotheses posed in the natural sciences can be proved or disproved by controlled experiments. If I hypothesize that two hydrogen molecules combined with one oxygen molecule produce water, I can prove my assumption conclusively in a controlled laboratory experiment. This result can then be replicated. However, if a president up for reelection claims that his economic policies caused the national prosperity, we have no way of proving the claim (see chapter 4).

Second, our techniques are based on a fragmented model of reality. Therefore, they will always be open to criticism by those who do not agree with the model we have selected. Further, the conclusion we get by using one technique may contradict the result we get by using another. Our conclusions also may vary when we rearrange the data (see chapter 7).

Third, our biases affect our judgments. How objective is our perception of reality? Do we view the same incident similarly? Of course not. When we observe, we receive information through filters of culture, religion, and personal life experience. In social sciences our observations (and the data we gather) admit biases of many kinds. If our data are biased, we do not get an objective result, regardless of how sophisticated our analytical techniques may be (see chapter 6 and discussion of imperfect data in chapter 11).

Fourth, mathematical models often fail us because they yield uncertain results. Other than death and taxes, nothing in this world is guaranteed (see chapter 13). Yet, by presenting a seemingly infallible, deterministic façade, quantitative models often raise our expectations. Mathematician John Casti reminds us of the futility of our attempts to completely penetrate the shroud of uncertainty.[23] As analysts we must be willing to admit the limits of the deterministic system. Just as we recognize the inadequacies of Newtonian physics, which tried to explain the chaotic world of quantum mechanics, we must view quantitative techniques in a realistic light and recognize their true powers. At the end of one highly mathematical textbook on macroeconomics, a discipline that is useful in analyzing public policy, the author concludes the chapter "Policy Making under Uncertainty" with this startling admission:

> Economic analysis has a long way to go until we can specify models with as little residual uncertainty as the ones posited in this chapter, and unfortunately economic analysis has little to say about the appropriate conduct of policy when there is uncertainty as to the correct model of the economy. Therefore, the actual practical usefulness of the analyses of this chapter may be quite limited.[24]

If we wait for the residual uncertainty to disappear from public policy analysis, we may never see a cogent book on the subject. However, this quotation shows that economists acknowledge the limits of their models. Alice Rivlin, former president of the American Economic Association and former director of the Office of Management and Budget, took her colleagues to task in the early 1990s for relying too heavily on models: "Economists ... in their usual fashion, have been short on realism and long on theory and prescription."[25] Political scientist Elinor Ostrom took a kinder view of economists in a 1997 address to the American Political Science Association: "While incorrectly confused with a general theory of human behavior, complete rationality models will continue to be used productively by social scientists, including the author."[26] Echoing Ostrom's sentiment, another political economist asserted, "I therefore find assumptions about ... [economic rationality] to be neither always true nor always good, merely almost always useful."[27]

Finally, analytical techniques fail us because we cannot define social welfare, or what is best for the society, and disagree over the public policies that will achieve it. Few policies create only winners. For every policy, there are those who win and those who lose. When we build a new airport, the region as a whole may win through increased trade, commerce, and ease of transportation, but those with buildings near the flight path lose property value. Spending on education helps the young but takes money from the elderly and those who do not have school-age children. As we will see in chapter 4, developing a satisfactory framework in which to "size up" the winners' wins and the losers' losses may exceed our powers of analysis.

Taking a comfortable middle road, however, will not end the debate over the usefulness of quantitative techniques in public policy analysis. Without a controlled experiment, we cannot prove the effectiveness of our analytical techniques. Even with only "ordinary knowledge," without the aid of "scientific models," we can safely forecast that we will continue to debate this issue—and fill the pages of professional journals—for the foreseeable future.

In the meantime, we use quantitative techniques to analyze public policy. But we must do so with full knowledge of their strengths and weaknesses. I later argue that scientific methods and their claims to objectivity apply only to the relatively narrow process that begins once we have defined the problems, identified the alternatives, and specified the techniques of analysis. *We must make subjective judgments every step of the way, decisions that reflect the goals and principles of public policy analysis.* From observation to analysis we are guided by the most wonderfully complex computer in the world: our brains. The quality of our analysis will be judged in the end not by the sophistication of our technique but by the wisdom of our judgment.

Value Judgments

My arguments can be illustrated with the help of Figure 1.2. When faced with a policy question, researchers observe the real world, gather data, and form hypotheses. Because the real world is too large and complex to understand completely, we build a model that helps us prove or disprove our hypotheses. We test our hypotheses by analyzing the data or observed behavior. After drawing conclusions from the analyses, we evaluate our results against the real world.

Except when using a technique specific to a data set, we make subjective judgments in every stage of this analytical loop. Subjective elements enter our analysis when we gather data, develop a behavioral model, and choose a technique of analysis. On completing the analysis, we again make subjective decisions when interpreting the results and drawing conclusions.

Let us consider an example. Suppose the city manager of Des Moines, Iowa, wants to claim that she runs her city efficiently. To support her claim, she would like to know the ratio of the number of city employees to the number of city residents. She also wants to compare this efficiency ratio with those of other cities. At the outset, her task seems simple. However, when she tries to collect data, she quickly finds out that she must define the total number of city employees. Like any large organization, the city has full-time and part-time workers. Even after she

Figure 1.2 Process of Scientific Inquiry

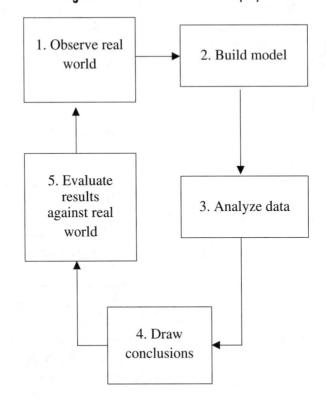

defines the number to her satisfaction, she must decide how to count those government functions that are contracted out to private corporations or other government agencies (many small towns contract out police and fire protection to the county government). Without a universally accepted way of counting, many areas of the analysis will remain subjective—matters over which even the most seasoned analysts might disagree.

After comparing the data collected for Des Moines and other cities, the manager may be asked about the validity of the comparison. Can Des Moines be compared with large metropolitan cities like New York or Los Angeles, or with small towns like Pittsfield, Massachusetts, or Great Falls, Montana? If not, which variables should the manager control to make a valid comparison? As you can see, to answer these questions, the manager must do more than follow a policy analysis "recipe." As she develops her model, she must make subjective decisions during every stage of the process.

After building a model, the manager chooses a technique for analyzing the data. If she selects statistical analysis, she may choose from a wide range of techniques. Having chosen a technique, she will rely strictly on logic to draw a conclusion. If she chooses regression analysis, for example, she will follow the objective rules of mathematics. However, *in the multistage process that links a problem to its analysis, only this small step will be totally objective.* Because not all the possible techniques of analysis will provide her with the same answer, her results will depend on the technique she chooses.

ETHICS AND PUBLIC POLICY ANALYSIS

When we think of scientists, we often think of scholars detached from their feelings, dissecting the facts in a sterile laboratory to find the "truth." Yet if we examine the relationship between scientists and the state, we discover a story far more complex than expected.[28] "Pure" science has not advanced along a straight line of interconnected innovations and discoveries and often has depended directly on the interest of the state. Government funding of certain projects, the result of policies made by top officials, has shaped the course of science all over the world. Scientists developed computer technology largely to help the government process large amounts of census data in the 1950s and to aid it in the space race with the Soviet Union in the 1960s and 1970s.[29] Therefore, it comes as no surprise that the question of "objectivity" in policy analysis is highly contested.

Public financing of professional sports facilities became a prominent issue during the late 1990s as many professional teams across the nation demanded new facilities built with public money.[30] Many articles and books analyzing the issue came to completely different conclusions. Some showed that public spending on new arenas is justified, while others disagreed. If the authors of the analyses used "scientific" and impartial methods, how could they have so many different views on the same subject?

The root of the problem becomes visible when we understand that analysts see the issue from various perspectives. Some are loyal to "professional integrity." Others conduct their analyses from the perspective of their clients or their ideology. Returning to the public financing of ballparks, an academic or analyst who has little vested interest in the issue and works for a nonpartisan agency, such as the Congressional Budget Office, may analyze the question using logic only and let logic draw its own conclusion. In contrast, a client advocate—an analyst employed by the Chamber of Commerce or the team owners—may come to a different conclusion. Finally, an advocate representing a certain issue or ideological position, such as a libertarian opposed to any government involvement in stadium financing or an activist worried about the environmental impact of a new sports facility, may draw still different conclusions.

These differences may follow from different methods, honest disagreements, or intentionally deceptive techniques. As shown throughout the book and particularly in chapter 7, the conclusions analysts make depend on the methods they use. To show the relative attractiveness of the proposed ballpark, analysts would forecast future revenues and costs. Because there is no single, universally accepted way of forecasting, their results could vary widely with their forecasting techniques.

Another reason that analysts arrive at different conclusions, honest disagreement, may arise as they represent the diverse interests of their clients. A ballpark may benefit a city but harm a neighborhood. It may aid one sports club but have an adverse impact on another. It may help the business downtown while draining the suburbs. Even when analysts share the same perspective, their results may vary because they often assign different weights to the costs and benefits. Without knowing that analysts value costs and benefits differently, you may believe that truth is an analyst's only client. Having learned how analysts work, however, you may decide that there is no absolute truth.[31]

The question of perspective becomes critical when we consider analyses done for a client with a stake in the outcome. In such cases, analysts may subordinate methodological integrity to the interests of the client. If they use deceptive techniques, these techniques may account for the variety of their conclusions. An analyst, like an attorney representing a client, may define her job simply as presenting the best case for her employer. She may exploit every ambiguous piece of evidence to build the strongest possible defense for her client's position.

Analysts working for a client will proceed differently from those representing an issue or ideology. Some national think tanks are generally associated with certain issue positions. The Hoover Institution and the Heritage Foundation usually espouse a conservative ideology, whereas the Urban Institute commonly takes liberal stands. The analysts employed by such organizations see themselves as issue advocates whose primary loyalty rests with an ideology.

Value Neutrality: Fact or Fiction?

The German playwright Bertolt Brecht once said that "art is not a mirror, it is a hammer. It does not reflect, it shapes." In other words, we should see art not as a neutral agent benignly reflecting society but as a vehicle of change. In a dynamic society, we are surrounded by ideologies and belief systems. Some of the more dominant ideologies in the United States include welfare liberalism, utilitarianism, religious conservatism, and a conservatism that seeks to maintain the institutional status quo.[32] John Dewey, the pragmatic philosopher and proponent of welfare liberalism, believed that policy analysis should help government proactively redress social grievances. His ideas helped lay the philosophical foundation for an activist government that would level the playing field for all citizens. Unlike welfare liberals, adherents of utilitarianism use the concepts and methods of economics to pursue governmental efficiency, their primary goal. Religious conservatives promote a world view based on their religious beliefs. Finally, some policy analysts seek to maintain the stability of society's institutions.

Suppose you are evaluating the school voucher system, in which the government pays each child a partial tuition credit to attend the school of her choice (see "A Case in Point"). When you try to define the desired outcome of the voucher system, you find that the term "objective analysis" has several meanings, depending on your ideology. If you are a welfare liberal, you ask whether the system helps poor and disadvantaged students to escape from failing public schools. You may point out that although the test scores of those who have stayed in school have increased, the dropout rate of poor and physically and emotionally challenged students has also increased. In that case, you would call the program a failure. In

A CASE IN POINT

Disputing the Data: School Vouchers[*]

In September 2000 Mathematical Policy Research (MPR) of Princeton, New Jersey, an educational research company, found that between 1997 and 1999, black children using school vouchers raised their percentile rankings on standardized math and reading tests an average of 6.3 percent. The study analyzed the test scores of fourteen hundred poor students, who were given vouchers worth $1,700 a year to attend private schools. Paul Peterson, a professor at Harvard University and a fellow at Stanford University's Hoover Institution, led the study. An enthusiastic supporter of the voucher system, Peterson claimed that the results proved his position: black children who switched to private school were significantly better off than those who remained in public school. His conclusion attracted intense interest in a nation caught up in a close presidential election race. Peterson's claims generated no fewer than thirty-six newspaper editorials across the country.

However, lest the publicity lead to misinterpretation of the study, MPR issued a statement calling the findings "premature" and cautioned against jumping to the conclusion that blacks did better in private schools than in public schools. David Mayers of MPR said, "If you ask the question, 'When I offered students vouchers, did I make a difference in their test scores,' right now you come away saying, 'no, there's no impact.'"

The evidence showed gains in test scores among black students. However, the level of improvement varied from city to city. Children in Washington scored twice as high, on average, as those in New York and one-third higher than those in Dayton.

Peterson, however, stood by his interpretation of the study, saying, "An average is an average." The average showed that the test scores of black children who enrolled in private school went up by a statistically significant 6.3 percent.

MPR also stood by its conclusions, noting that this gain was extremely uneven. Without knowing the reasons for the divergent results, said MPR, we should not use the study findings to justify the school voucher program.

Note

[*]Based on "Study Questions School Voucher Data," *New York Times*, September 15, 2000.

Discussion Points

1. How did ideology and perception affect the interpretation of the study results?
2. Can this dispute be resolved with objective analytical tools?

contrast, if you are a utilitarian, your primary objective is to make government spending more efficient. One way to measure spending efficiency is to analyze students' test scores. You may find that because of the new system, test scores have gone up and costs to the government have gone down. If your primary concern is promoting moral values, as defined by your faith, you may use another yardstick (for example, teenage pregnancy rate) to draw a different conclusion. Finally, if you support public education, you may think that the voucher system threatens a venerable, time-tested institution, as shown by the system's adverse effect on teachers' morale and turnover rate.

As you can see, in a world of ideologies, it is impossible to be perfectly value-neutral when conducting public policy analysis. We must accept the existence of norms, values, and ideologies without allowing them to stop us from using systematic analyses. As long as we recognize these external constraints, we can accommodate them in our scientific reasoning. Although the analytical techniques discussed in this book can help us make public policy conclusions, they cannot take the place of the conclusions themselves.

Value Conflict

Policy analysis does not permit us to evaluate a program with the dispassionate detachment of a laboratory investigator. We conduct policy analysis in the context of conflicting social, ethical, and political values. It is natural for us to encounter such conflict. Although you might conclude from our discussion that all values are relative, noting correctly that they are shaped by our personal preferences and beliefs, consider that all people share strong core values, which form the basis of a universal code of ethics. The U.S. Constitution guarantees our fundamental rights. The Helsinki Agreement, recognizing cultural, religious, and ideological differences, elevates certain human rights to a near-absolute level while acknowledging that we live in a world of varied perceptions, norms, and values.[33]

The values of analysts occasionally conflict with those of their clients. Let us say that you work as an analyst in the financial management division of your city and have been asked to write a report on the city's program serving the homeless. If you and your boss have different values, you may have an honest disagreement on the best way of analyzing the program. However, your value differences may go beyond honest disagreement if they involve universal values. For example, your boss might ask you to write a deceptive report based on data or methods you know to be biased or incorrect, or she might tell you to misrepresent data. In such cases, obeying your boss would put you in direct conflict with the core values of professional ethics. Chapter 7 discusses the fine line that separates differences in interpretation from deliberate deception. If asked to act in ways that conflict with your values, you may have to make hard decisions about your relationship with your boss or your institution.

As the profile of policy analysis has risen in recent years, so has the volume of literature covering the hard issues of professional ethics. Echoing their colleague Mark Lilla,[34] social scientists David Weimer and Aidan Vining suggest that the profession of policy analysis should work toward a new standard of conduct that "explicitly recognize[s] our obligations to protect the basic rights of others, to support our democratic processes as expressed in our constitutions, and to promote analytical and personal integrity."[35] As an analyst attempting a high-wire act, balancing conflicting values, you can do no better than observe this standard.

Key Words

Behavioral model (p. 7)
Coequal model (p. 5)
Deterministic (p. 6)
Externality (p. 7)
Incremental approach (p. 8)
Marginal analysis (p. 7)
Mixture-in-administration model (p. 5)
Mixture-in-policy model (p. 5)

Model (p. 6)
Opportunity cost (p. 7)
Optimal (p. 6)
Policy-administration dichotomy
 model (p. 4)
Rational model (p. 8)
Systems approach (p. 8)

Exercises

1. Write an essay on the role of a policy analyst in a public agency. Discuss the various balancing acts that this analyst must perform.
2. There is a continuing debate on the use of statistical and operations research techniques in the public policy–making process. What are the strengths and weaknesses of these techniques?
3. Should policy analysts be dispassionate scientists, or should they express their deeply held values? Consider an important public policy issue that your community is currently debating. How would you analyze the issue? Do you think that your analysis will be influenced by your values, your ideology, or the organization you work for? If so, should your analysis be considered "objective"?

Notes

1. For a delightful discussion, see Peter DeLeon, "Reinventing the Policy Sciences: Three Steps Back to the Future," *Policy Sciences* 27 (1994): 77–95. Also see Herbert Goldhamer, *The Advisor* (New York: American Elsevier, 1978), and Arnold Meltsner, *Rules for Rulers: The Politics of Advice* (Philadelphia: Temple University Press, 1990).
2. Woodrow Wilson, "The Study of Administration," *Political Science Quarterly* 2 (1887): 197–222.
3. These papers eventually were published in Frank Marini, ed., *Toward A New Public Administration* (San Francisco: Chandler, 1971).
4. Lewis C. Mainzer, *Public Bureaucracy* (Glenview, Ill.: Scott, Foresman, 1973).
5. James H. Svara, "Dichotomy and Duality: Reconceptualizing the Relationship between Policy and Administration in Council-Manager Cities," in *Ideal and Practice in Council-Manager Government*, ed. H. George Fredrickson (Washington, D.C.: International City-County Management Association, 1995), 3–19.
6. See, for example, Robert S. Lynd, *Knowledge for What? The Place of Social Science in the American Culture* (Princeton: Princeton University Press, 1939); Harold Lasswell, *Power and Personality* (New York: Norton, 1949); and Daniel Lerner and Harold Lasswell, eds., *The Policy Sciences* (Palo Alto, Calif.: Stanford University Press, 1951).
7. Frank Fischer, *Evaluating Public Policy* (Chicago: Nelson-Hall Publishers, 1995), chap. 1.
8. See, for example, DeLeon, "Reinventing the Policy Sciences." Also see William Ascher, "The Evolution of the Policy Sciences," *Journal of Policy Analysis and Management* 5 (1986): 365–389; and Douglas Torgerson, "Between Knowledge and Politics: Three Faces of Policy Analysis," *Policy Science* 19 (1986): 33–60.

9. Gary Becker and William M. Landes, eds., *Essays in Economics of Crime and Punishment* (New York: National Bureau of Economic Research, Columbia University Press, 1974).

10. David C. Johnston, "Anti-Tobacco Groups Push for Higher Cigarette Taxes," *New York Times,* April 3, 1997.

11. Barnaby J. Feder, "Surge in Teen-Age Smoking Left an Industry Vulnerable," *New York Times,* April 20, 1997.

12. C. Ronald Huff, ed., *Gangs in America,* 2d ed. (Thousand Oaks, Calif.: Sage Publications, 1996).

13. For dated but still relevant statistical data, see National Cancer Institute, *Cigarette Smoking among Teen-agers and Young Women* (Bethesda, Md.: U.S. Dept. of Health, Education, and Welfare; Public Health Service; National Institutes of Health; National Cancer Institute, 1976). Also see Yankelovich, Skelly, and White, Inc., *Cigarette Smoking among Teen-agers and Young Women* (Bethesda, Md.: National Cancer Institute, 1977).

14. Milton Friedman, *On the Methodology of Positive Economics* (Chicago: University of Chicago Press, 1953), 3.

15. Carl H. Weiss, *Social Sciences and Political Decision Making* (New York: Columbia University Press, 1980).

16. See, for example, Virginia Held, "PPBS Comes to Washington," in *Planning-Programming Budgeting: A Systems Approach to Management,* ed. Freemont J. Lyden and Ernest G. Miller (Chicago: Markham Publishing, 1968), 11–26.

17. For one of the earliest explanations of "systems theory" in politics, see David Easton, "An Approach to the Analysis of Political Systems," *World Politics* 9 (1957): 383–400.

18. For a discussion of President Reagan's executive order and the use of quantitative techniques, see William Ascher, "The Evolution of Policy Sciences," *Journal of Policy Analysis and Management* 5 (1986): 365–389; and Peter DeLeon, *Advise and Consent: The Development of Policy Sciences* (New York: Russell Sage Foundation, 1988). Also see Douglas Torgerson, "Between Knowledge and Politics: Three Faces of Policy Analysis," *Policy Science* 19 (1986): 33–60.

19. Aaron Wildavsky, *The Politics of Budgeting,* 3d ed. (Boston: Little, Brown, 1979), 197. Emphasis is Wildavsky's.

20. Charles Lindblom and David K. Cohen, *Usable Knowledge* (New Haven: Yale University Press, 1979).

21. Charles Lindblom, *Inquiry and Change* (New Haven: Yale University Press, 1990), 131.

22. DeLeon, "Reinventing the Policy Sciences," 78.

23. John Casti, *Searching for Certainty: What Scientists Can Know About the Future* (New York: Morrow, 1990).

24. Stephen McCafferty, *Macroeconomic Theory* (New York: Harper and Row, 1990), 360–361.

25. Alice M. Rivlin, "A New Vision of American Federalism," *Public Administration Review* 52 (1992): 321.

26. Elinor Ostrom, "A Behavioral Approach to the Rational Choice Theory of Collective Action: Presidential Address, American Political Science Association, 1997," *American Political Science Review* 92, no. 1 (1998): 21.

27. Mark I. Lichbach, *The Rebel's Dilemma* (Ann Arbor: University of Michigan Press, 1995), 344.

28. Chandra Mukerji, *A Fragile Power: Scientists and the State* (Princeton: Princeton University Press, 1989).

29. See, for example, Martin Campbell-Kelly and William Aspray, *Computer: A History of the Information Machine* (New York: Basic Books, 1996).

30. See, for example, Mandy Rafool, *Playing the Stadium Game: Financing Professional Sports Facilities in the 1990s* (Denver: National Conference of State Legislatures, 1997).

31. For an interesting discussion, see E. S. Quade, *Analysis for Public Decisions* (New York: American Elsevier, 1975), 273–275.

32. See, for example, Robert A. Heineman, William T. Bluhm, Steven A. Peterson, and Edward N. Kearny, *The World of the Policy Analyst: Rationality, Values, and Politics,* 2d ed. (Chatham, N.J.: Chatham House, 1997), 36–40.

33. For a discussion of human rights issues, see Dipak K. Gupta, Albert J. Jongman, and Alex P. Schmid, "Creating a Composite Index for Assessing Country Performance in the Field of Human Rights," *Human Rights Quarterly* 16 (1994): 131–162.

34. Mark T. Lilla, "Ethos, Ethics, and Public Policy," *Public Interest* 63 (1981): 3–17.

35. David L. Weimer and Aidan R. Vining, *Policy Analysis: Concepts and Practice,* 3d ed. (Upper Saddle River, N.J.: Prentice Hall, 1998), 57.

CHAPTER

2

GOVERNMENT
AND THE MARKET

The city of Boston and its surrounding region faced a housing crisis in the 1990s.[1] As the region experienced a nearly decade-long economic boom,
jobs were created and new housing developments sprang up everywhere. However, housing was priced far beyond the reach of low-income residents. According
to a government study, only eleven communities in the greater Boston area set
aside more than 8 percent of their housing for low-income families. Ninety-three
communities failed to do even that much. After months of pressuring reluctant
suburban politicians, Mayor Thomas Menino submitted legislation to the city
council to penalize neighboring cities if they did not set aside at least a tenth of
their housing in the affordable price range. If they did not meet this goal, and
made no effort to meet it, the legislation recommended that the state would with-
hold housing funds.

As you read this account about Boston, you may wonder why government
interferes in a free-market system. If some of its citizens cannot afford to live in a
particular city, is it the proper role of the government to force the city to create
housing for them? If so, on what basis should it intervene?

History tells us that governments, through kings, priests, and community leaders, have always dictated the lives of citizens. In fact, until recently, the grip of the

king and the church was almost total. Protests against such domination started in Europe. In 1776, while the first shots of rebellion were being heard in the colonial states, a revolution of a different sort was taking place on the Atlantic's other shore. An ex-customs official named Adam Smith published *The Wealth of Nations: An Inquiry into the Nature and the Causes of the Wealth of Nations*.[2] Smith wrote his book to repudiate the then-popular theory of **mercantilism,** which argued that a nation becomes prosperous when it maintains a trade surplus by maximizing exports and minimizing imports. To limit imports, mercantilism erected trade barriers. In contrast, Smith argued that the wealth of a nation increases when all restrictions to the free functioning of the market are removed. He reasoned that individuals, when free of outside restrictions, pursue their self-interest, allowing the nation to prosper.

Adam Smith's arguments regarding the efficient working of a market are shown in Figure 2.1.[3] The curve DD depicts the demand for a certain commodity, while the SS curve traces its supply. The point of **equilibrium** is reached where the curves intersect. This point is called equilibrium (a term borrowed from mechanics) for two reasons:

1. When the market rests at that point, no internal force will cause it to move away from equilibrium.
2. If the market departs from this point, the push and pull of demand and supply will bring it back to equilibrium (point E).

If a producer asks for a price higher than is warranted by the market (Po), the demand for the product will dwindle and, ultimately, the seller will have to lower the price. Similarly, if one producer makes an abnormally high profit by selling a new product, soon other suppliers will come in and flood the market with copycat products. A situation of oversupply will occur, pushing the price down from Po to Pe. The opposite scenario will take place if the market price is below the equilibrium point. Consumers will attempt to purchase more goods while the suppliers cut down on production. This situation of excess demand drives the market price from Pu to Pe.

This diagram—perhaps the most well-known illustration in the social sciences—forms the foundation of the entire field of economics. As you can see, if there is any outside intervention, the market is corrupted; it becomes inefficient because it cannot reach the point of equilibrium. When supply is arbitrarily restricted, buyers pay a higher price than they should be paying. This situation leads to unemployment and other market inefficiencies. On the other hand, when supply is increased beyond the point of equilibrium, buyers consume more than they should, leading to abusive overuse and waste.

You may note the normative implications of this discussion, which are apparent from our use of the imperative "should." The government *should* stay away from the marketplace so that prices reflect the "true" forces of demand and supply. When the government does not interfere, the **invisible hand** of market forces clears the market and allocates resources among the four factors of production—

Figure 2.1   The Foundation of Economic Reasoning: Market Equilibrium

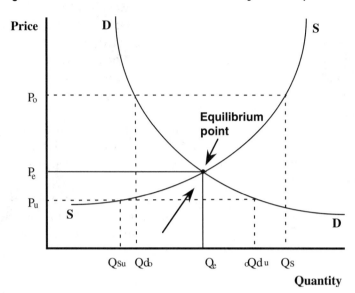

Note: The demand curve, DD, is downward sloping because as the price of a commodity goes down, its demand increases. In contrast, the supply curve, SS, slopes downward. When prices go up, supply increases in response to a greater expectation of profit. The point of intersection of the two curves is called the equilibrium point.

land, labor, capital, and organization—in the fairest way. Landowners get the rent they deserve, and laborers get the wages they merit. Moreover, market forces allocate the most appropriate amount of interest to the owners of capital and the right level of profits to the entrepreneurs. When anyone is paid more than he or she deserves, the market wipes out the excess profit through free competition.

THE FUNDAMENTAL CONTRIBUTIONS OF ECONOMIC ANALYSES

The success of an academic discipline can ultimately be gauged by the extent to which its core doctrines permeate our daily lives, social values, and accepted norms. By that measure, the intellectual revolution sparked more than two hundred years ago by the bored Scottish tutor of a nobleman's son is unparalleled in social science. In his analysis of a nation's prosperity, Smith placed the individual at the forefront of the economic system. Over the next two hundred years, following the publication of *Wealth of Nations,* economics grew in many diverse directions. If we were to point out the most fundamental contributions of economics as an analytical tool, we might mention the interrelated concepts of **economic rationality, marginal analysis** and **opportunity costs.** These concepts are so integral to systematic analysis that it is virtually impossible to engage in a meaningful academic discourse about public policy without taking them into account.

Economic Rationality

Can we predict what anyone will decide to do at any given time? So many factors influence the decision process that it is nearly impossible to understand, much less predict, human behavior. Yet as policy analysts, we must have some predictive capabilities. If we recommend a tax incentive for a national retail chain to locate in our city, we must have a reason for our proposal. That is, we must have some understanding of the behavior of a corporate decision maker vis-á-vis a tax incentive plan. The decision maker is guided by an innumerable number of factors, from profit motive (low costs, high revenues) to emotional factors (love or dislike of the city, desire to maintain a corporate image, and so on). We cannot predict behavior unless we use a model that reduces all of these factors to a small, manageable number. Economists use the so-called **rational actor model**, which assumes that human beings are guided only by the prospect of individual profit. Smith emphatically argued that each person is the best judge of his or her own interest and that everyone tends to choose the course of action that yields the maximum net gain (benefit minus cost). In fact, to Smith, the idea of equating human rationality with self-interest was so obvious that he thought only a fool would contest it:

> It always is and must be the interest of the great body of the people to buy whatever they want of those who sell it cheapest. The proposition is so very manifest, that it seems ridiculous to take any pain to prove it.[4]

Economists have found this reductionist assumption to be useful for analyzing behavior, as have many political scientists and sociologists from the **public choice** school of thought.[5] Self-utility maximization is so germane to economic reasoning that some have argued that it is synonymous with human rationality. Most of the techniques included in this text explicitly or implicitly rely on this rather restrictive assumption about human nature. Needless to say, such a blanket assumption invites a great deal of criticism.

Marginal Analysis

In the economic literature the term "marginal" means "additional." Although the word is used in classrooms as well as boardrooms, policy makers often make serious mistakes when they confuse "marginal" with "average." Let me explain marginal utility by giving you an example. Suppose you are thirsty and you come upon a stand selling cold drinks. You are so thirsty that you are willing to pay $2.00 for the first drink. However, the drink is too small to quench your thirst, so you want a second one. Because you are already somewhat satisfied, you are willing to spend up to $1.75 for it. After quaffing the second drink, you are still thirsty. You are willing to pay $1.00 for a third and $0.50 for a fourth. We plot your willingness to pay in Figure 2.2. Remember, these numbers reflect only your psychological willingness

Figure 2.2   Marginal Utility and Consumer Surplus

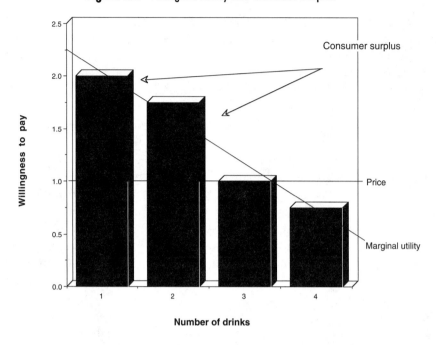

to pay and not the actual prices for the marginal, or additional, drinks. They represent the marginal utility you receive from the drinks.

The important question becomes, at what point would you stop buying drinks? Let us say the price of a drink is $1.00. You will stop after you have consumed three drinks. You will not stop before then because you are getting a bargain with each drink, and each provides you with more utility than it costs you. However, the price of the fourth drink is below your marginal utility. The first rule of consumption efficiency is to *stop consuming at the point where the marginal utility of the good is exactly equal to its **marginal cost.*** Your marginal cost (the cost of an additional drink) is fixed at $1.00. In a **perfectly competitive market,** you are a **price taker.** That is, because the market is too large for you to manipulate, you cannot influence the market price with your purchase. The additional utility you derive from three drinks, the amount above your market price ($1.00), is your **consumer surplus.** It is the difference between the market price and the total utility. For the first drink, the consumer surplus is $1.00 ($2.00 – $1.00), for the second drink, it is $0.75 ($1.75 – $1.00), and for the third drink, there is no consumer surplus ($1.00 – $1.00). The full implications of this concept are discussed in chapter 14.

So, as a consumer you know when to stop buying. What about the producer? A producer produces to the point where her **marginal revenue** equals the price. Suppose I am the owner of that drink stand and I am deciding how many gallons of drinks to produce. As I sell each drink, I make a certain amount of revenue. I keep buying the ingredients until I reach the point where the marginal cost (of buying, transporting, storing, and serving) is equal to the marginal revenue from the product. Because I am a small producer and cannot influence the prices in the market, I am—like the customer—a price taker. Therefore, *I will stop producing when my marginal revenue is equal to the marginal cost.* Together, the two dictums about consumption and production constitute the iron laws of microeconomics. They give us both the point at which a consumer would stop buying and the one at which a producer would set limits for production.

MARGINAL VS. AVERAGE: CAUSE FOR POLICY CONFUSION.   Although marginal costs and benefits are basic concepts of microeconomics, they are often misunderstood. Two examples, one drawn from the private sector and the other from a public policy debate, can help us understand the confusion.

The next time you board an airplane, look around the aircraft. Although each passenger will travel the same distance, the fare for each person will vary widely. Some passengers have paid full fair for, say, buying the ticket after the minimum number of stipulated days or for not spending a Saturday night at their destination. There are those who bought tickets at a discount due to their age (senior citizens or children), time of purchase, length of stay, or special arrangements with travel agencies. Besides these passengers, there may be students on board with cut-rate standby fairs or those who are flying for free on a "frequent flyer" arrangement. Does this wide variation surprise you? Does the airline lose money for selling certain tickets at a discount, since each discounted ticket brings down the **average price** per ticket?

The surprising answer is that the airline makes money even when it sells tickets at a significant discount (awarding free tickets to frequent flyers may fall under the separate category of giving incentives or promoting passenger loyalty). This is because most of the costs of flying an airplane are fixed. The salaries of the crews and the ground staff must be paid regardless of the number of passengers on board. The port authorities must be paid for landing rights at the airport. The costs of maintenance will not vary significantly with changes in the *additional* number of passengers. Therefore, the marginal cost of carrying an additional passenger is negligible. After those paying full price have covered maintenance costs, any revenue received from a senior citizen or a standby passenger will result in positive marginal revenue for the airline. If decision makers look only at the average fare—which goes down with every discounted ticket—they will surely miss the opportunity to increase the company's profit by carefully instituting discounted prices.

IMMIGRATION CONTROVERSY IN CALIFORNIA.   When it comes to the public sector, the confusion about average and marginal costs can lead to serious policy mistakes. Take, for example, the controversy over the cost of illegal immigration in California. During the mid-1990s, the state was caught up in a divisive debate over the cost of educating the children of illegal immigrants. A referendum was passed barring these children from public education. During the debate the proponents of the ban estimated the costs by taking the *average cost* per child (the entire state education budget divided by the number of students) and multiplying it by the number of children of illegal immigrants enrolled in California's public schools. In contrast, those who opposed the measure pointed out that much of the education budget is fixed. They argued that if we want to calculate the true cost of educating these children, we must look at the *marginal cost.* It is interesting to note that the two sides were arguing past one another without realizing the sources of the two widely varying figures.

Opportunity Costs

To understand opportunity costs, let us go back to the case of affordable housing in the Boston area. The state of Massachusetts set aside $400 million in housing aid as an incentive for cities to supply affordable housing to low-income families.[6] The mayor's plan also called for using some of the state's surplus funds to supplement this Housing Trust Fund. Of course, it is a noble idea to encourage cities to build houses for low-income people. But the money spent on affordable housing projects could have been put to other uses, such as making the streets safer, providing children with a better education, or assisting the elderly and the homeless. When we spend money for a project, other deserving projects remain unfunded or underfunded.

This argument is normal in most public debates. Accountants understand only the monetary cost, or the price to be paid in the market. However, other costs should also be considered, costs that often are unrelated to market prices. They include the costs of alternate projects. *What must you give up to get the project you are buying?* The answer to this question allows you to determine the opportunity cost of an activity.

Let us take a look at the cost of higher education. How much are you paying for your college degree? If you were a full-time student, you would calculate your expenses for tuition, room and board, supplies, transportation, and so on. In addition, you must factor in another cost. You gave up a job you otherwise would have had, had you not attended college. We must add the monetary costs and the estimated forgone income. It is impossible to overlook opportunity cost in public policy decisions because no resource is infinitely abundant and without alternate uses. Space, clean air, and ocean water all have alternate uses and opportunity costs associated with their exploitation. Harvesting an old-growth forest in the Pacific Northwest clashes with saving the endangered spotted owls. The sudden popularity of fishing for orange roughy off the Australian coast has deprived giant squid of their primary food source. A proposed ballpark vies for public money with other city needs, such as library facilities, garbage collection services, and programs to care for the downtown homeless population. When it comes to public policy analysis, economics—as a powerful analytical tool—teaches us to look beyond the market value of a resource to its opportunity cost.

MARKET FAILURE: WHY GOVERNMENT INTERFERES IN A FREE MARKET

A society based on free market principles and requiring no government intervention—except to maintain external and internal security and a fair judicial system—

sounds good in theory. Upon close scrutiny, however, the society that self corrects and attains equilibrium loses some of its appeal. Economist John Maynard Keynes aptly quipped that "in the long run, we are all dead." That is, if the market does not attain equilibrium in a reasonable time, then it is of little comfort to us.[7] When we realize that a perfectly competitive market depends on some of the most restrictive assumptions and truncated views of reality, it is apparent that the market will not always self-correct. A free market is based on four drastic assumptions:

1. There are numerous buyers and sellers.
2. There is perfect exit from and entry into the market.
3. There is perfect flow of information.
4. There is no externality, or no one is affected by the activities of any other person.

A perfectly competitive market is shattered when any of these four conditions is violated. Let us examine these conditions in more detail.

Lack of Competition

The competitive market that emerged from Adam Smith's analyses was rooted in the early days of the industrial revolution, when there were no significant monopoly forces in the market. When there are numerous buyers and sellers, no single individual or firm can single-handedly influence the outcome of the market. Each participant in the market is a price taker, as opposed to being a monopolistic **price maker.** Every buyer and seller must adjust his or her respective demand and supply in view of prevailing market prices. Landowners, laborers, moneylenders, and business entrepreneurs earn according to their respective merit. If anyone makes more than that, the excess profit will bring in other competitors, thereby eliminating any profit over what is warranted by merit.

Market conditions have changed significantly since the eighteenth century. Today the market is often plagued by monopoly power. The federal government's recent antitrust case against Microsoft is an example. The government argued that by bundling its Windows software with its Internet Explorer Web browser, Microsoft made it hard for consumers to use another browser such as Netscape. In its price-making capacity, a monopolist sets a price that guarantees a profit over what it would have earned if there was competition. The court decided that in a competitive market, Microsoft would have charged $29 for Windows '98, but because it was a monopolist, it could charge $49, nearly double the competitive amount.[8]

A market can sustain a higher price only when the supply is restricted; to hold a high price, a monopolist must reduce the total supply in the market. In a monopolistic market, society loses because of the restricted supply. In addition, a monopolist can choke off innovations because it has little financial incentive to make improvements for a captive group of buyers.

A monopolist does more than simply restrict its output to raise the prices of its products. Some economists have argued that because a monopolist has little incentive to lower costs to achieve maximum efficiency, it often operates at a less-than-optimal level of efficiency. Harvey Leibenstein coined the term **x-inefficiency** to describe such a situation.[9] In the late 1980s the Defense Department found itself in a public relations controversy when someone pointed out that it was purchasing items such as toilet seats and screwdrivers at exorbitant prices from its monopolistic suppliers. In summer 2000 the **oligopolistic** (with a few large producers) oil industry was accused of price gouging. In response, President Bill Clinton, as a stopgap measure, decided to release some of the strategic oil reserves held by the government for such an emergency.[10]

Barriers to Entry and Exit

The concept of ease of entry into the market has three aspects. The first is **factor mobility.** Take, for example, unemployment. In a perfectly competitive market, it does not exist. This is because an unemployed person is one who is able and willing to accept a job at the going wage.[11] If I want to become a guard in the National Basketball Association but lack the necessary talent and physical skills, I cannot be classified as unemployed because I am willing to play the position. Similarly, if I decline to take a job at the going rate, I am not considered unemployed because I am able to work. If wages are too high, the demand for labor goes down and exerts a downward pressure on the wage rate. In contrast, if wages are too low, firms hire more people until the market wage rate becomes equal to the market-clearing equilibrium rate. This typically has been the conservative argument in the United States against minimum wage restrictions. If there is unemployment it is because the government has set a minimum wage.

The second aspect of ease of entry relates to what is known as **indivisibility.** The biggest impediment to entry is the size of the required investment. For instance, in the early part of the twentieth century, a profusion of car manufacturers opened for business. Because the technology was not that complex, many prospective producers entered the market. However, as the technology advanced, and as Henry Ford radically altered manufacturing through his innovation of assembly line production, it became increasingly difficult for new manufacturers to spring up with new automobile designs. Now a huge investment was required to compete with the established car manufacturers. This impediment to market entry created an oligopoly in the automobile industry.

The third aspect of ease of entry is known as **rent seeking.** When the market is restricted, any source of unusual profit attracts those who can exploit product scarcity and make a fast buck. Restrictions can creep in from a variety of sources, both public and private. In the public sector, restrictions on factor mobility result from government regulations. When there is a huge demand for a particular good but the government imposes a limit on its availability, the resulting excess demand causes its price to increase and revenues to climb. This increased revenue becomes excess profit for some. For those regulating the product, it can become a bribe.

For those in the private sector, it provides a select group of business owners with the opportunity to make a monopoly profit. In the 1990s California's milk producers successfully lobbied state politicians to set wholesale milk prices at an artificially high level and to impose restrictions on imports from neighboring states.[12] In October 1999 the California Department of Food and Agriculture increased the wholesale price by 33 percent, one of the biggest increases in state history. The hike allowed California dairy farmers to earn forty-two cents for every gallon of milk they sold to processors. As a result Californians spent about $650 million more a year for milk than they would have in a free marketplace.[13] This situation can best be explained with a diagram.

The shaded area in Figure 2.3 represents rent seeking. Consider another example, drug trafficking in the United States. Without any government restrictions, the market price of an illicit substance would find its equilibrium, at which point the supply would satisfy all those who are willing to consume it at the going rate. However, when the government imposes sanctions, the supply is immediately restricted. This restriction increases its price and acts as a windfall to the drug smugglers—or as a bribe to corrupt law enforcement agents. Going back to our example of milk prices in California, the shaded area in the figure is the total rent. In the case of the California dairy industry, the rent was estimated to be around $650 million a year. In many developing countries, government corruption can be traced to officials' penchant for imposing too many restrictions on the economy.

Rent seeking, therefore, leads to market inefficiency, and can take many forms. Suppose your state awards a contract to a firm to build highways, at a profit

Figure 2.3   Rent Seeking

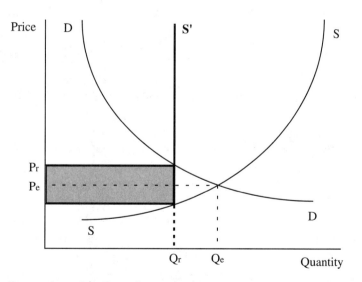

Note: The diagram shows the effects of an artificial restriction on supply. The curves DD and SS show the demand and supply of a commodity which, without any restriction, would reach its point of market clearing equilibrium at price Pe and quantity Qe. However, because the government has restricted the supply to SS, this action creates an artificial quantity decrease to Qr and a price increase to Pr. The shaded area shows the possibility for rent seeking or corruption.

deemed higher than normal by the firm's competitors. Say the normal profit for a similar project is $10 million, but firm A is going to receive $15 million. This situation may prompt firm A's competitor, firm B, to allocate up to $5 million to fight the decision in the court. If the decision is reversed in favor of firm B, and the firm spends only $3 million in legal costs, then it makes a windfall of $2 million over what it would have earned in a competitive market. In the meantime, the project is delayed, and waste and inefficiency are introduced in the market.

Restricted Flow of Information

We are told that the secret formula of Coca-Cola is kept in a vault in Atlanta. In a perfectly competitive market, it would be anathema to have such a secret. However, contrary to the ideal constructs of a perfectly competitive market, a producer can often benefit from secrets. If the recipe for the fizzy drink had not been a secret and had been as available as the formula for hot dogs, another company might have posed stiff competition when the drink was introduced. But the secret kept competition at bay. In its early days, as the drink became wildly popular, other firms could not break into its newly created niche market. Later, with clever advertising and distribution, the company established its influence over the soft drink industry.

Another impediment to the free market is asymmetry of information. If I am going to sell you my car, I am likely to know much more about it than you do. Because of this asymmetry, I can ask for a higher price than the car is worth, particularly when I am not interested in your repeat business.[14] The government must step in and help the competitive market through tort legislation and laws on full disclosure. The "lemon law" protecting customers from dishonest used car dealers is a case in point.

Externalities and Social Costs

Markets are efficient at producing goods that consumers want at a price they are willing to pay. This efficient process of allocating resources works well as long as an exchange between a buyer and a seller affects only those two parties. Unfortunately, their transaction often affects other parties. When it does, it creates an **externality.** The costs or benefits of individual externalities add up to what are known as **social costs** or **social benefits.** Externalities occur when the decisions of an economic actor (an individual, a firm, or a government unit) have an impact on another actor's well-being without the affected party's consent or compensation. If the impact is favorable, it is called a **positive externality**. If it is adverse, it is called a **negative externality** (see "A Case in Point: Trading Pollution").

Suppose your town wants to attract a large retail outlet. The outlet is interested but would like a significant tax break. How can you justify using public money to help a privately owned company? Supporters of the proposal will point out the positive externalities: creation of new jobs, ability to attract other small businesses, and the influx of additional customers for bars and restaurants. These businesses will need employees, so even more jobs will be created. All of these activities will generate tax revenues for your town. They are examples of social

A CASE IN POINT

Trading Pollution: The Clean Air Act of 1990

Ronald Coase of the University of Chicago, who won the Nobel Prize in economics in 1991, had a novel idea. He argued that if people were allowed to market their property rights, many problems resulting from negative externalities could be solved.[1] Take the case of environmental pollution.[2] Factories emit pollutants—sources of negative externalities—as by-products of their operations. However, some factories are more efficient than others and produce fewer pollutants. Regulating environmental pollution has a high opportunity cost because it causes production shutdowns, loss of income, and unemployment. If there are too many restrictions, the government imposes undue burdens on society, but if the laws are too lax, the social costs of the products far outweigh their market costs.

Guided by Coase's arguments, government experts determine the amount of pollution that can safely be tolerated, then give each polluting plant a permit to pollute up to its quota. If some plants pollute below their quota, they can sell their "rights to pollute" to plants that cannot meet the regulatory standard. Through trading pollution rights, the social costs can be brought in line with the market costs.

The Clean Air Act of 1990 introduced what is now known as *emissions trading*, by which the government sets pollution quotas and the efficient firms sell their unused pollution rights to the inefficient ones. In response to pressure to reduce the emission of so-called greenhouse gases, BP-Amoco's Western Gas business unit installed thousands of new valves that shunt fluids from the firm's network of wells. The old valves emitted whiffs of methane, a potent greenhouse gas; the new valves do not. Today, Western Gas sells its unused pollution rights to other subsidiaries of Amoco at a profit.[3]

Notes

1. For an excellent discussion of the theoretical issues, see Neil Bruce, *Public Finance and the American Economy,* 2d ed. (Boston: Addison-Wesley, 2001), 99–115.
2. A. Denny Ellerman, *Markets For Clean Air: The U.S. Acid Rain Program* (Cambridge: Cambridge University Press, 2000).
3. John Carey, "A Free-Market Cure for Global Warming," *Business Week,* May 15, 2000, 167–169.

Discussion Points

1. How can we bring social costs close to market costs through government action?
2. Do you think trading emissions offers a viable solution to the global warming problem?
3. Can you think of other negative externalities that could be treated with Coase's prescription?

benefits. Opponents of the project, on the other hand, will note the negative externalities, such as traffic congestion, an increase in crime, and the possible degradation of both the environment and the overall quality of life. These are the social costs of the retail outlet locating in your town.

The actor who generates positive externalities cannot redeem any of them. Similarly, those hit by negative externalities cannot recoup their losses through the market process. The **private,** or **market, cost** reflects the price of a good, the price we pay in stores. However, another cost may be associated with the consumption of this good. When I buy a pack of cigarettes, I pay the private, or market, cost. However, cigarette smoking is associated with a host of ailments that cost the states huge amounts of money to care for patients suffering from these illnesses. When society (or the government, as the agent of society) pays for their care, that cost should be added to the product's market price. When it is not, the cost of the negative externality of smoking causes the social price to exceed the market price. The market is unable to take corrective action on its own, so the government steps in with a tax to set the market price equal to the social cost. In the same way, when the government imposes taxes on a polluting firm, it bridges the gap between the market price and the social cost of the firm's product. In either case, the tax may be shifted to customers. The tax will reduce the demand for the good, thereby lowering the cost of consuming a socially harmful product.

Rising Service Costs: The Appearance of Market Failure

Another curious matter makes the functioning of the free market somewhat complicated. The cost of providing services—from education to health care, from personal services, such as plumbing, to car repair—is increasing much faster than are general commodity prices in the economy.[15] This phenomenon, although not directly related to market failure, calls for government intervention. As a society, we are bewildered by rising health care costs and appalled at the cost of higher education—especially at public universities. We wonder why the costs of government service delivery, at all levels of government, keep increasing, far outstripping the inflation rate. Moreover, as prices rise, the quality of many of these services seems to fall.

Although market failure and government intervention are responsible for some price increases, the major causes of such increases are rooted in simple economics, not "price gouging," **moral hazard** (the possibility that people who are insured will take less care to avoid loss than those who are not), or other kinds of market failure. Price increases also have very little to do with inefficiency in the government sector, though comparisons of government with the private manufacturing sector may suggest otherwise. Consider the cost of computing. With dizzying advances in computer technology, the cost of information processing is falling at an exponential rate. Technology is moving so fast that by the time this book is published, my one-year-old computer will have become obsolete. Then I will want a slicker, faster, and more advanced machine. As we take advantage of computer-assisted design and manufacturing, worker productivity continues to shoot up at an astronomical rate. However, most service delivery by the government and public health providers remains impervious to technological advances. Even in our technology-saturated society, a postman still has to deliver mail one house at a time, garbage must be picked up from the front of each house, doctors must spend time with individual patients, and teachers must observe class-size restrictions. As a result, cost escalation is typical of many labor-intensive services, such as restaurant businesses, retail stores, and automobile repair shops.

GOVERNMENT AS A PARTNER

Adam Smith saw the market as inherently self-correcting. If only we let the market run its course, he said, most of our miseries would be solved—if not immediately, certainly in the long run. Yet his critics pointed out that not all markets are self-correcting. The problems of market failure became painfully clear in 1929, when, following the stock market crash, the Great Depression set in. Keynes argued that the free market, if left on its own, would not be able to extricate itself from the quagmire of high unemployment (recession or depression) or high prices (inflation). For the economy to reach full employment with stable prices, it would require active government intervention.

Under the guidance of Keynes, the role of the government in the domestic and international economies became firmly rooted. Building on his work, Keynes's intellectual descendants determined that the government has four major roles: **allocation, distribution, stabilization,** and **growth.** First, because the market cannot allocate public goods, government must step in. Public goods are goods that must be shared with others in the community. While sharing these goods with others, the marginal utility we receive from them does not go down. Take, for example, the case of military protection against external threats. We share the protection of our armed forces with everyone else in the country. However, if we hear that a number of babies were born the night before, we do not get concerned about crowding under the defense umbrella. The definition of public goods will be apparent if we compare them with goods of personal consumption. If you have an apple, you are not obliged to share it with anyone else; if you do, your marginal utility from the apple will decline because you will get a smaller piece than you would have if you had the apple to yourself. The infrastructure, clean air, public education, health care, social welfare, and military protection are all examples of public goods. The problem with public goods is that the market fails to supply them; therefore, the government must do so.

Second, because the market inherently favors the rich and powerful, the government must help those who are caught in an endless cycle of poverty. In this way it plays a redistributive role. Finally, with active government intervention through stabilization policies, the market will not be exposed to wild swings of inflation and recession and will be safeguarded against the extremes of business cycles. Because the market is a poor allocator of resources between current consumption and future investment, an activist government—through its policies of support for research and development in science, technology, and education—can ensure future prosperity for the nation.

GOVERNMENT FAILURE

In many ways the 1960s were magical, particularly for the United States. An awestruck nation watched astronaut Neil Armstrong take a "giant leap for mankind" to become the first person to step on the moon. The space race was over, and the United States had beaten the Soviet Union to the moon. The United States was indisputably on top in terms of military might and advancement in science and technology. However, in the midst of this exuberance, the nation faced widespread, endemic problems, from poverty and racism to political assassinations and street riots. A bewildered nation asked, "If we can send men to the moon, why can't we solve our earthly problems?" President Lyndon Johnson unveiled his Great Society program as a way to solve some of these vexing social problems. In the area of public budgeting, Johnson introduced the Planning-Programming Budgeting System (PPBS), a process of allocating money through analytical means (see p. 8). In the area of planning, physical planning based on technology was in vogue. In the realm of public policy, "systems analysis" was used to dissect every social problem into neat analytical components.

Unfortunately, the government failed to deliver. The Great Society program did not eliminate poverty, [16] PPBS was a dismal failure, physical planning that emphasized building new public housing and freeways was unable to cure urban blight, and systems analysis grappled unsuccessfully with social problems. It was indeed easier to remove technological hurdles to landing on the moon than to find solutions to the age-old problems of human society. If in an imperfect world the market often fails to deliver, so does the government. There are ten reasons for this failure, each of which will be discussed briefly:

1. Inability to define social welfare
2. Limits of democracy and the paradox of voting
3. Inability to define the marginal benefits and costs of public goods
4. Political constraints
5. Cultural constraints
6. Institutional constraints
7. Legal constraints
8. Knowledge constraints
9. Analytical constraints
10. Timing of policies

Inability to Define Social Welfare

Recall the lofty list of inalienable rights in the Declaration of Independence. The sentence beginning "We hold these truths to be self-evident" boldly assumed that "we" included everybody in the new nation. Yet history has shown repeatedly that not everybody in the nation has held the fundamental rights guaranteed by the declaration, rights deemed universal regardless of race, religion, sex, or national origin.

Similarly, we frequently hear phrases such as "the welfare of society" or "the good of the people" in political rhetoric or social discourse. Yet in a secular, pluralistic political culture, a thoughtful reader of public policy analysis recognizes the fragility of such confident phrases. We can think of no policy that is a boon to every individual in society. Instead, we are apt to find cases in which there are winners and losers, victors and vanquished, benefits and costs (see chapter 14).

Limits of Democracy and the Paradox of Voting

If we cannot define "social welfare," then we can assume that people will articulate their wishes through the electoral process. Let us say that a rural county has recently experienced a spate of devastating forest fires. It is now trying to decide how many fire engines to buy—one, two, or three. The county population is divided over the issue. Three public opinion groups have emerged: those in a small minority who are most threatened by the possibility of another fire next summer (group A), those who are more concerned about the solvency of the county than about the prospect of another fire (group B), and those who are taking a centrist position (group C).

As you can see in Table 2.1, if a referendum were held and each group were allowed to vote for its first choice, we would observe no conclusive outcome. Although the moderate group is numerically the strongest, it does not command the majority of the votes. However, if each group were to vote on two alternatives, we would discern a conclusive majority preference. When the choice is between two fire engines or three, the two-engine option receives 80 percent of the votes (groups B and C prefer two to three). When groups must decide between one engine or two, two still wins (garnering 65 percent of the votes) because those who are most concerned about another forest fire would rather have two engines than one. In this case, a social consensus will be reached, and the outcome will reflect the will of the majority.

However, the situation gets more complicated if group A changes its preference ranking. Suppose group members are so frightened by the prospect of living without adequate fire protection that they vote for only one fire engine if they cannot have three. Perhaps in protest they move to another county.

Suppose that group A, the smallest and most intense, finds the compromise position of two fire engines just as unacceptable as that of only one (see Table 2.2).

Table 2.1 Preferences on Decision to Purchase Fire Engines

Group	Strength (percentage of votes)	First choice	Second choice	Third choice
Those most threatened by the prospect of fire (A)	20	3	2	1
Fiscal conservatives (B)	35	1	2	3
Moderates (C)	45	2	3	1

Table 2.2 Preferences on Decision to Purchase Fire Engines: Strategy Change by Group A

Group	Strength (percentage of votes)	Number of fire engines		
		First choice	Second choice	Third choice
Those most threatened by the prospect of fire (A)	20	3	1	2
Fiscal conservatives (B)	35	1	2	3
Moderates (C)	45	2	3	1

In that case, group members have made the strategic decision to rearrange their preference pattern. Now they do not prefer two to one, even though two is closer to their desired position of three. You can see that there will be no unique outcome of this election. The outcome will depend on who controls the agenda:

Choice between 1 and 2	1 wins with	55 percent of the votes
Choice between 3 and 1	3 wins with	65 percent of the votes
Outcome	3 wins	

Choice between 3 and 2	2 wins with	80 percent of the votes
Choice between 1 and 2	1 wins with	55 percent of the votes
Outcome	2 wins	

As a result of this new strategic position, group A has effectively eliminated the middle position. If it can control the agenda, it can win the election with only 20 percent of the vote! This is the paradox of voting. Its broad implications are obvious: *even with the fairest voting rules, the outcome of an election may not reflect the true preferences of the community.*

Inability to Define the Marginal Benefits and Costs of Public Goods

If we are at a loss defining "social welfare," we are similarly confounded defining the marginal utility from an additional dose of public expenditure. When President Ronald Reagan took office, during the height of the cold war with the Soviet Union, he declared that he wanted a 700-ship navy. Nearly a decade later, Bill Clinton, presiding over the lone superpower, opted for a navy of fewer than 400 ships, nearly half the number requested by Reagan. Why those numbers? Why not 701 ships or 420 ships? Would you, as a voter, sleep more soundly if you knew that one more navy destroyer than before were guarding your shores? These questions reveal the difficulty of calculating the marginal utility of a government purchase.

Political Constraints

In his first meeting with President Franklin D. Roosevelt, Keynes did not seem practical to the savvy politician. In Keynes's mind the policy implications of his economic strategy—expand government spending, even beyond revenues, during times of recession and reduce expenditures and government size during periods of inflation—did not affect the soundness of his theory. But as Keynes, Roosevelt, and the rest of the nation soon learned, it is much easier to raise the levels of expenditure than to reduce them. Every time policy makers create a government program, the program creates its own constituents. As a result, even when its utility is in question, closing it down often becomes nearly impossible.

Cultural Constraints

Like political constraints, the cultural context influences the public policy process. To be adopted and successfully implemented, public policies must conform to the cultural norms of the community. This cultural context perplexes us when we travel across the nation or to another country. A visitor to India might wonder why cows are allowed to roam freely through the already overcrowded city streets. In the same way, outsiders in America might ask about the cultural attachment of ordinary Americans to guns in the face of gun-related violence. They might also question those who oppose international abortion and birth control initiatives, even as United Nations' population control programs in poor, lesser-developed countries buckle under unsustainable population growth. Without cultural acceptance, even a perfectly reasoned public policy may not be considered appropriate for a community.

Institutional Constraints

Any public policy must depend on bureaucratic institutions for its formulation and implementation. An organization, like any other entity—collective or individual—develops its own cultural ethos, goals, and mythology. As a result, policies promoted by the social services division of a city can come into direct conflict with the mandates of its law enforcement branch. These conflicts, often seen as "turf battles," can render a policy ineffective. The Commerce Department promotes international trade. Therefore, it seeks to maximize the export of American goods. Yet its goals may collide with those of the State Department, which manages the country's foreign policy. For political reasons the State Department may bar U.S. companies from selling their wares, such as weapons and high-speed computers, to other countries.

Legal Constraints

Public policies must be formulated and implemented within a nation's legal framework. Generally speaking, laws from six sources govern our daily lives in the United States: constitutional laws, laws made by legislatures, executive orders, interpretations of laws by the judicial branch, agency rules, and public referenda. In our democratic system of checks and balances, laws passed by legislatures, executive orders, referenda, and agency rules can all be declared null and void by the courts. In certain cases the legislative branch fights the executive branch for control of the national agenda. Congress passed the War Powers Resolution of 1973 to curtail the president's ability to send U.S. troops into combat in other countries. A hugely popular referendum may face court challenges that block its implementation.

Knowledge Constraints

Any public policy is constrained ultimately by our present knowledge. As we learn more about the world around us, we realize the failings of our past policies. Take the problems of malaria abatement in many countries around the world. Malaria was once the top killer in the world's tropical regions. As scientists learned that the disease spread through mosquitoes, they sparked a huge international effort to kill the pesky insects in their place of breeding—swampy areas with stagnant water. Thanks to the massive spraying of the insecticide DDT, many lesser-developed countries declared victory over malaria's scourge. Yet within a decade people started noticing the chemical's devastating effects on the fragile ecology of marshland, which is essential to the survival of many species of flora and fauna. Again, policies had to be developed to eradicate not the disease but the effects of past policy. As these devastated habitats were restored, the disease came back, often with a vengeance.

Analytical Constraints

Analytical techniques tapped for public policy analysis, either at the formulation stage or the implementation stage, use numbers. Numbers have a magical quality. They give the impression of being totally objective. As we will see, however, there are many opportunities for subjectivity to creep into our analysis. When we learn statistical methods or the various techniques of operations research, they exude the impartiality of scientific reasoning. Yet when we dig deeper, we discover that *objectivity relates solely to deriving the conclusion once the problem has been formed.* In each stage of formulating the problem, we may confront not just confusion but also pressure to make quick decisions, which are often rendered for the convenience of the analyst or to suit the particular quantitative technique chosen for the analysis. These analytical constraints may creep into the analysis from a number of sources discussed throughout the book.

Timing of Policies

Biases or inefficiencies may arise due to the timing of policy measures. Consider a business cycle that moves the economy through a series of booms and busts. Critics of government's anticyclical policies point out that several steps must be taken before a policy is implemented and its effects felt. If the government decides to enact countermeasures to keep the economy at an even keel, it must first recognize that the economy is going into a recession. As we note in chapter 3, though, forecasting is sometimes like looking in a rearview mirror while driving a car. We consult past data to gauge where we should be going. But the data have been collected from the quarter before. We encounter a **recognition gap,** which requires that we study trends to understand its causes. Because it takes time to analyze a trend, unless we are studying a rapidly escalating situation, policies can become delayed. A time gap often occurs as analysts come up with appropriate policies. This gap is called a **prescription lag.** After a policy has been recommended, the appropriate legal body must consider it for adoption, causing an **adoption lag.** Finally, an **implementation lag** results when adopted policies are translated into action. In the meantime, if the economy has made a turn on its own, the "lagged" policies may backfire and choke off a natural recovery. This policy failure then creates a new problem.

LIMITING GOVERNMENT INTERVENTION: JOINT PARTNERSHIP IN A MIXED ECONOMY

When the market fails to reach the equilibrium point—its point of greatest efficiency—governments must step in to make the necessary corrections. The reverse is also true. When governments fail, because of inefficiency or corruption, the market forces of unencumbered demand and supply must be brought in to remedy the situation. The reintroduction of market forces can either **stimulate** or **simulate** the market. Market stimulation takes place when the barriers of entry into the market are removed, whereas simulation requires the government to provide public goods through exclusionary pricing.

Stimulating the Market

Market stimulation is achieved when the government **deregulates, legalizes,** or **privatizes.** As we have seen, government intervenes in the market through regulations when it deems such actions to be beneficial to society. One of the most regulated sectors in U.S. economic history is the banking industry. The specter of failing banks during the Great Depression motivated many to seek a solution. Through their lending commercial banks create an economy's money supply.[17] As the backbone of the monetary structure, banks can function only when people trust the system. It is essential that when people deposit money in a bank they are not worried about its safety. When we open a checking account, the Federal Deposit Insurance Corporation requires the banks to pay a small premium to buy insurance against a possible bank failure. If the bank fails, then each of the checking accounts, up to a maximum of $100,000, will be fully insured. When bank insurance was originally proposed, President Roosevelt was deeply suspicious of it. He feared that because customers could not lose a penny, bankers would be irresponsible with deposited money. The so-called supply-side economists successfully advocated deregulation of the market, which erased many of the restrictions that had prevented banks from engaging in highly speculative activities, such as selling risky commercial stocks or investing in commercial real estate. A decade after deregulation, the savings and loan crisis engulfed the nation. Many critics blamed the free-wheeling practices of unregulated banks and sought to reregulate the sector.[18]

Another area that is heavily regulated by the government is electricity. Regulations have caused inefficiency, prompting the U.S. government to deregulate the industry. Although advocates of deregulation often tout its virtues, evidence indicates that it has had mixed results. In North Carolina the deregulation of electricity did not reduce consumers' rates.[19] In fact, in the late 1990s, largely because of deregulation, electricity rates in fifty-one cities jumped 25–30 percent. In winter 2001 the deregulation of electricity brought California perilously close to an economic disaster. Not surprisingly, a recent study found that deregulation of the airlines industry failed to increase efficiency as had been predicted.[20] It is extremely difficult to establish unequivocally a causal relationship between deregulation and market failure. Therefore, the debate on deregulation's merits is likely to go on.

Legalization brings a previously illegal act into the realm of taxable, legal activities. The Supreme Court's judgment in *Roe v. Wade* legalized abortion for American women. This action drastically reduced the number of unsafe abortions. As the Court's opinion in *Roe* demonstrated, the decision to legalize an activity may not always be based strictly on economic grounds and must consider a host of moral and religious issues.

Privatization turns previously government-operated services over to the private sector. The conservatism prevailing in the nation following the election of President Ronald Reagan spurred a huge demand for privatization of government services. Although the initial enthusiasm waned with time, privatization continued to advance at all levels of government.[21] Despite the common assumption that privatization is a quick way out for cash-strapped governments, it also has been used by solvent governments to acquire superior management talent and specialized expertise. However, despite the growing interest in privatization, fierce political opposition, particularly from labor unions, continues to make outsourcing a hard sell. Proponents of privatization say that competition from private firms can often raise productivity in government-provided service areas. In the municipal waste disposal industry, evidence suggests that parallel providers have helped both private and public sector firms become "better, faster, smarter, and more cost-effective." Residents of cities and counties across the United States have been the primary beneficiaries of this competition.[22]

Simulating the Market

When it is not possible to stimulate a market through privatization, federal, state, and local governments reduce the inefficiencies of government control by simulating the market—that is, by charging prices for the products and services once offered for free. Charging fees for government services has become critical for cash-starved cities in many parts of the country. This has been particularly true in California, where in 1978 the voters organized a "tax revolt" and passed a sweeping referendum—known as Proposition 13—that reduced their property taxes. This proposition also significantly reduced the government's ability to impose new taxes. Because the voters said no to the government's request for finances but did not at the same time curtail their demand for services, the only answer to the problem was to charge user fees. With government as the service provider, users pay for the services they demand, simulating the market process.

Apart from allowing financially strapped cities to provide the services their citizens demand, simulating the market through user fees offers several other advantages. First, prices act as a signal for demand. Because it is impossible to quantify the demand for public goods, if a local government charges a fee for its services, then each consumer can bring his or her demand for public goods in line with their cost. Returning to our example of voting for fire engines, we may satisfy all three groups by charging them different rates for different levels of fire protection. The group that wants the most fire protection can pay for extra fire engines dedicated to their community, while the rest are charged the regular rate. This situation is known as **consumption efficiency,** in which an economic actor's marginal utility matches the marginal cost. Because nothing dispels enthusiasm more than a small entry fee, user fees often can curb the abuse of a publicly provided service.[23]

Along with consumption efficiency, the simulation of market may also introduce **production efficiency** by forcing government units to bring their marginal revenues in line with marginal costs. In fact, sending price signals through user fees may help even the private market correct itself. In the market the social cost of a product often becomes significantly higher than its market cost. Suppose the authorities of the indoor sports arena in your town want to host a pop music festival lasting several days. Although it may be profitable, this concert may impose extra costs on the surrounding areas in terms of higher street cleaning expenses and more traffic, pollution, and crime. Each business may have to hire extra help to clean up or protect its property during the festival. In addition, the city may have to pay police officers overtime to direct traffic and keep the festival orderly. As you might expect, festival organizers pass on their costs to the rest of the community. Therefore, if the city charges the organizers a fee for the privilege of holding such an event, an amount that compensates the affected parties, no one will be economically harmed, yet many (promoters, stadium authorities, musicians, and fans) will benefit from the festival. This strategy is effective for many nonprofit organizations, such as charitable, religious, and educational institutions, which are exempt from property taxes. By imposing user fees, they can bring their private costs in line with those of society.

The decision to charge for publicly provided services must be considered very carefully. Some services provide benefits not only to those who use them but also to the rest of the community. As a society we have decided that when children in grades K–12 are educated, the benefits are not restricted to them but spill over to the rest of the society. Therefore, it is not always prudent to emulate the market and charge tuition fees. Charging a fee may have an adverse effect on the poor. If a city wants to impose a fee for using public facilities such as basketball courts and baseball fields, the fee may have an adverse effect on the children of a poor neighborhood. In contrast, if the city wants to raise the fee for using public golf courses, such effects may not be felt.

A CASE IN POINT

The Internet: A Taxing Proposition

If there is one issue that unites the Republican party, it is taxation. Unlike Democrats, who tend to trust government activism in the market, Republicans want to minimize the role of government and reduce taxes—with one possible exception: the Internet. The question of whether to tax goods sold over the Internet divides Republican governors from their colleagues in Congress.* Sales taxes are the main source of tax revenue for many state governments. Yet consumers can often avoid paying sales taxes when purchasing online. In October 1998 Congress passed the Internet Tax Freedom Act, which declared a three-year moratorium on the "multiple and discriminatory" taxes imposed by various state and local governments. The act prohibits states from taxing Internet access or levying sales tax on merchandise sold over the Internet.

The problem is, when you buy a product in a real, as opposed to a virtual, store, you are charged sales tax. In its freedom from the tax, Internet commerce is similar to the old-fashioned mail-order business. In decisions concerning the mail-order industry, the Supreme Court has ruled repeatedly that states cannot compel businesses of other states to act as tax collectors.

For obvious reasons Republican governors do not like the congressional mandate. They are waging a war to impose a uniform tax code that will compel e-businesses to collect state sales taxes. The governors cite the hardships endured by local mom-and-pop stores, which have to collect the tax. The national retail chains, such as Wal-Mart, J. C. Penney, and Radio Shack, have used their impressive lobbying power to oppose the tax. The e-commerce lobby claims that a tax would stifle innovation as well as destroy the "greatest job-creating machine America has ever known." The resolution of this issue will profoundly affect how America shops.

Note

*For a comprehensive discussion of the issues involved, see Ramesh Ponnuru, "The Tax Man Cometh," *National Review,* January 2000, 44–46. See also Howard Gleckman, "The Great Tax Debate: Should the States Get a Slice of Every E-Commerce Dollar or Should Cyber-Sales be Free of Any Tax Burden?" *Business Week,* March 27, 2000, 228–236.

Discussion Points

1. Should state governments be allowed to collect sales taxes from an out-of-state e-business retailer?
2. What should be the government's role in controlling and taxing the Internet?

Even in the face of overuse or high social cost, charging a fee may not be technically feasible, or the cost of collection may be too high. Let us suppose that your city's traffic department wants to reduce congestion during peak traffic hours. It may make sense to charge motorists a fee for using the highways during those hours.[24] However, it may not be possible to collect those fees without creating an even bigger traffic jam. In such cases simulating the market is not a viable option.

Besides being technically unworkable, imposing fees for services that previously were provided free of charge may not be politically feasible (see "A Case in Point: The Internet"). If services are free, consumers view them as having no cost. Toward the end of the nineteenth century, San Diego faced a small tax revolt of its own. The city, like most other cities in the nation, was collecting fees for picking up garbage. When it became known that the city was selling this garbage to nearby hog farms, irate citizens passed a referendum to eliminate garbage collection fees. More than a hundred years later, the city has grown substantially and the pig farms have long left the vicinity. Yet it remains politically infeasible to reinstate a collection charge, one of the most common municipal fees in the United States.

Key Words

Adoption lag (p. 39)
Allocation (p. 33)
Average price (p. 25)
Consumer surplus (p. 24)
Consumption efficiency (p. 41)
Deregulate (p. 39)
Distribution (p. 33)
Economic rationality (p. 22)
Equilibrium (p. 21)
Externality (p. 30)
Factor mobility (p. 28)
Growth (p. 33)
Implementation lag (p. 39)
Indivisibility (p. 28)
Invisible hand (p. 21)
Legalize (p. 39)
Marginal analysis (p. 22)
Marginal cost (p. 24)
Marginal revenue (p. 24)
Mercantilism (p. 21)
Moral hazard (p. 32)

Negative externality (p. 30)
Oligopolistic (p. 28)
Opportunity costs (p. 22)
Perfectly competitive market (p. 24)
Positive externality (p. 30)
Prescription lag (p. 39)
Price maker (p. 27)
Price taker (p. 24)
Private, or market, cost (p. 32)
Privatize (p. 39)
Production efficiency (p. 41)
Public choice (p. 23)
Rational actor model (p. 23)
Recognition gap (p. 39)
Rent seeking (p. 28)
Simulating the market (p. 39)
Social benefits (p. 30)
Social costs (p. 30)
Stabilization (p. 33)
Stimulating the market (p. 39)
X-inefficiency (p. 28)

Exercises

1. Your city wants to contract out fire prevention services to a private firm. Argue for and against such a move.
2. Write an essay on the uses and limits of economic analyses, incorporating an appropriate example from your local or state government.

3. Write an essay on the deregulation of utility prices. When do you think deregulation works and when does it not?

Notes

1. Stephanie Ebbert, "Menino Bill Would Boost Low-Income Housing," *Boston Globe,* November 30, 2000, B7.
2. The instant success of the book—it went through five editions during Smith's lifetime—made the author famous, but his work failed to have significant influence on British public policy of the time. For a discussion of Adam Smith's contribution to modern economics, see David D. Raphael, *Adam Smith* (Oxford: Oxford University Press, 1985).
3. Adam Smith did not draw the famous demand and supply curves. Developing the geometry of his theory took about one hundred more years and a combined effort on both sides of the English Channel. For a detailed discussion, see Mark Blaug, *Economics Theory in Retrospect* (Homewood, Ill.: Richard D. Irwin, 1968), 38–67.
4. Adam Smith, *The Wealth of Nations* (New York: Modern Library, Random House, 1937), 461. Originally published in 1776.
5. See, for example, Elinor Ostrom, "A Behavioral Approach to the Rational Choice Theory of Collective Action: Presidential Address, American Political Science Association, 1997," *American Political Science Review* 92: 1–22.
6. Ebbert, "Menino Bill."
7. Since publication of Keynes's *General Theory* in 1936, Keynesian theory has defended itself against many challenges that have diminished his impact. It also has seen a strong resurgence of his ideas. For the best discussion, see Paul Krugman, *Peddling Prosperity: Economic Sense and Nonsense in the Age of Diminished Expectations* (New York: W. W. Norton, 1994).
8. Joel Brinkley, "The Verdict: Microsoft Is a Monopoly," *New York Times,* November 7, 2000.
9. Harvey Leibenstein, *Beyond Economic Man* (Cambridge: Harvard University Press, 1976). See also Roger S. Franz, *X-Efficiency: Theory, Evidence and Application* (Boston: Kluwer Academic Press, 1988).
10. Kate Gillespie and Clement M. Henry, eds., *Oil in the New World Order* (Gainesville: University Press of Florida, 1995).
11. There is no single, worldwide definition of unemployment. The official U.S. definition carries many restrictions, and the definitions of other nations vary significantly.
12. California's Department of Food and Agriculture increased the wholesale price of milk by 33 percent, one of the biggest increases in state history.
13. The Department of Food and Agriculture defended its action by arguing that it was only trying to ensure the survival of California's dairy farmers. Although this rhetoric evokes the image of small family farmers getting up with the sunrise every morning to milk their herds, in fact, dairy farming is a huge, $3.6 billion industry. The average farmer is a corporation with 602 cows and annual sales of $1.6 million.
14. A large literature on information asymmetry and the cost of information started with the publication of George Ackerlof's "The Market for Lemons," *Quarterly Journal of Economics* 84, no. 3 (1970): 488–500.
15. This concept of productivity lag was first presented by William J. Baumol, "Macroeconomics of Unbalanced Growth: The Anatomy of the Urban Crisis," *American Economic Review* (June 1967): 415–426.

16. Although the poverty rate did decline during periods of economic expansion, poverty was merely cut in half between 1959 and 1972.

17. The total money supply in the economy is referred to as M1, which consists of the currency in circulation (minted money) plus the amount held in checking accounts by private citizens and financial institutions. Commercial banks create money when a depositor opens a checking account. Knowing that the customer may withdraw all of her money the next day, the bank keeps a portion of it in reserve and lends out the rest. If she deposits $100, the bank may decide to keep 10 percent in reserve and lend $90 to another depositor seeking a loan. When the loan is approved, the bank opens an account showing $90 in the borrower's account. Again, the bank can keep 10 percent ($9) in reserve and lend $81 to the next borrower. In this way banks create "new money" valued at several times the amount originally deposited.

18. See, for example, Alan Gart, *Regulation, Deregulation, Regulation: The Future of the Banking, Insurance, and Securities Industries* (New York: Wiley, 1994).

19. Buster Kantrow, "Electricity Deregulation Runs into Static in N.C.," *Wall Street Journal*, July 26, 2000, S1.

20. Zinan Liu and E.L. Lynk, "Evidence on Market Structure of the Deregulated U.S. Airline Industry," *Applied Economics* 31 (1999): 1083–1092.

21. *USA Today*, "Privatization on the Rise Despite Surpluses," August 1999, 10.

22. Christie Clark, "How Privatization Helped Raise the Bar in the Solid Waste Field," *The American City and County* 113 (February 1998): 52–60.

23. Although this statement is made somewhat in jest, there is strong evidence that people are willing to pay for a public resource if doing so improves service. Kelly McCollum found in a survey of three thousand students in the California State University System that about 65 percent of the students would be willing to pay higher-than-usual student fees for better on-campus computing resources. Of those students who were willing to pay, more than 71 percent stated that they would spend an extra $10 per month for better on-campus computing, while 15 percent were ready to pay more than $20 per month. See "65% of California State U. Students Back a Technology Fee, Survey Finds," *The Chronicle of Higher Education*, September 17, 1999, A36.

24. In some parts of the country transportation departments have experimented with issuing permits for single motorists to use the carpool or High Occupancy Vehicle (HOV) lanes. These permits are often expensive because they must pay for highway patrol officers to enforce HOV restrictions.

CHAPTER

3

THE POLICY PROCESS

Something interesting is happening on the street corners of my city, though I did not notice it while driving through my neighborhood. I approached a yellow light, and instead of coming to a stop at the signal, I made a quick turn a split second after the light had turned red. Three weeks later, I received an envelope from the Department of Motor Vehicles. Inside were a picture of my license plate and a clear shot of this author looking intense while making an illegal turn in a hurry. The pictures came with a hefty fine and an invitation to spend a weekend at traffic school. On my next trip to that same intersection, I noticed the little birdhouse-type structure at the corner, its shiny camera lens sticking out, busily snapping away at delinquents. Within a few months I observed that most of the city's intersections, and many in neighboring towns, had been outfitted with these Orwellian devices. In June 2000 the cameras operated in forty-one U.S. cities.[1]

These devices clearly were installed at the direction of public policies. Students of policy analysis might ask, who placed the cameras on the policy agenda? How did policy makers decide to install them? How are city officials implementing the policies? How effective are the devices at preventing traffic violations? As the cameras become part of our daily lives, we may ask whether they raise constitutional issues. If so, how might this concern change future policies for catching red light runners? Finally, if policy makers find the cameras ineffective, how do they go about eliminating them? We may answer all of these questions by examining the **policy cycle,** or **policy formation,** the process through which policy is formed (see Figure 3.1). [2]

Before examining each stage of the cycle, we must remember an important caveat: the process is not as neatly segmented as the figure suggests. Rather, it is much more complex, resembling a seamless quilt in which all phases of the cycle are woven together.

AGENDA SETTING

The policy cycle starts when the government pays serious attention to an issue. If you look around, you notice that thousands of areas cry out for corrective action. However, not everything that needs the government's attention gets it. You may notice a particularly dangerous intersection in your neighborhood. When you turn into the intersection, your view is blocked by a large tree. You are concerned and so are some of your neighbors. Yet years go by and no one takes action. Or you may worry about the so-called greenhouse gases that reportedly cause global warming. You may wonder why political leaders do not pay more attention to a problem with such enormous consequences for our future.[3] You may also ask why some issues suddenly crop up, dominate the agenda, and surprise everyone, including those who study such matters for a living.[4]

Policy scientists identify two kinds of agendas: those that government institutions act on, known as **institutional,** or **governmental, agendas,** and those on which they delay action, called **systemic,** or **noninstitutional, agendas.**[5] Systemic agendas "percolate" in society, waiting to be elevated to the active agenda. A systemic agenda "consists of all issues that are commonly perceived by members of

Figure 3.1   The Policy Cycle

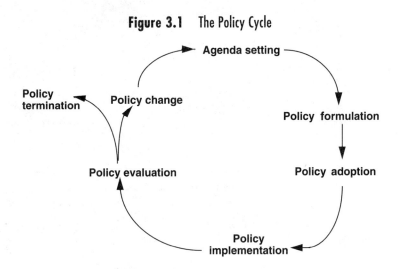

the political community as meriting public attention and involving matters within the legitimate jurisdiction of existing governmental authorities."[6] In contrast, an institutional agenda consists of those problems on which "legislators or public officials feel obliged to take appropriate measures."[7] Sometimes an agenda remains the focus of intense public debate but still never makes it onto the institutional agenda. At other times an agenda surprisingly and suddenly moves to the active list. Take, for example, the issue of teen smoking. Despite the fact that for years many prominent healthcare professionals had documented tobacco's ill effects and highly addictive qualities, the issue failed to reach the institutional agenda. However, circumstances changed in the late 1990s, when some states sued tobacco companies, the Food and Drug Administration issued stronger tobacco regulations, and the media covered the issue more widely—Congress responded by passing measures that sought to reduce underage tobacco use by prohibiting certain types of cigarette advertisements and reforming retail distribution practices.

As shown in Figure 3.2, the White House and Congress initiate official or institutional agendas at the federal level. The courts also set institutional agendas through their decisions and legal opinions. Because of the system of checks and balances, all three branches of government must cooperate to adopt an institutional agenda. All legislation must be passed by both houses of Congress. If a bill conflicts with the Constitution, the judiciary must step in. Just as government actors often pull institutional agendas from the vast pool of systemic agendas, they may at any time toss back an institutional agenda into the pool.

How does an issue reach the active agenda, and who ushers the issue through the policy cycle? Those who hold demand-side theories of agenda setting believe

Figure 3.2   Agenda Setting in the Federal Government

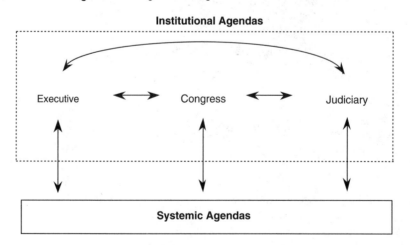

Source: Adapted from Roy B. Flamming, B. Dan Wood, and John Bohte, "Attention to Issues in a System of Separated Powers: The Macrodynamics of American Policy Agendas," *Journal of Politics* 61, no. 1 (1999): 76–108.

that policy makers determine institutional agendas in response to widespread popular demand. This view is known as the **pluralist model.** In contrast, those who support the **elitist model,** a supply-side view, believe that the power to set the agenda resides at the top of the political and economic hierarchies.

The Pluralist Model

The pluralist model is based on theories of American democracy developed in the 1950s and 1960s.[8] In this somewhat romanticized view of the American power structure, power rests with citizen activist groups. The model makes no permanent distinction between the elite and the masses, though a hierarchy may exist in which the elite control some institutional agendas. Any issue can reach the institutional agenda, and its success in doing so depends on the abilities of citizen activist groups (see Figure 3.3).

In the early 1970s Roger Cobb and his associates explained how an inactive agenda becomes active in the pluralist model.[9] To attain institutional status, an issue must possess the following characteristics: specificity, social significance, temporal relevance, simplicity, and categorical precedence.

SPECIFICITY.   This characteristic describes how broadly an issue has been defined. When advocates of an issue define it in a way that attracts wide public support, it is more likely to be picked up by the political elite. When a castaway Cuban boy named Elian Gonzales requested asylum from the United States, his supporters portrayed his cause as a fight between freedom and communism. Similarly, pro-tobacco forces depicted the debate over underage tobacco use as a battle for an individual's right to choose. In both cases, advocates improved the chances that their issues would reach the institutional agenda. By framing them in a wide context, they attracted far greater public support than they would have if they had

Figure 3.3   The Pluralist Model of Agenda Setting

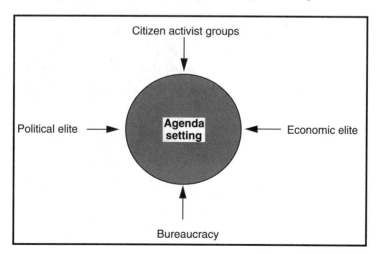

construed the issues narrowly—as one child's request for asylum or as a single industry's campaign to advertise its products as it wishes.

SOCIAL SIGNIFICANCE. When advocates frame a complex issue in a way that makes sense to constituents, the issue attains a level of social significance. This simplification makes it easier for a political leader to champion the cause and for others to lend support. Similarly, when setting an agenda for the courts, especially the Supreme Court, advocates give their issue social clout by defining its broad constitutional implications. The question of whether grandparents should retain visitation rights when their son or daughter gets divorced might be resolved by a family court, unless advocates couch their argument in terms of the parent's right to decide for his or her children. Such an argument could elevate the issue to the high court.

TEMPORAL RELEVANCE. This term refers to whether an agenda has only short-term relevance or deep and enduring implications. Supporters of Elian Gonzales claimed that they fought not only for Elian but also for Cuba's future generations, to liberate them from dictator Fidel Castro. Proponents of a ban on teen smoking asserted their intention to save today's children from future addiction, illness, and death.

SIMPLICITY. An issue improves its chance of being embraced by the political elite if it can be easily understood. Supporters of Elian Gonzales asked this simple question: Should Elian be reunited with his father, or should he settle in America to fulfill his mother's last wish? When advocates frame issues in a straightforward manner, they can communicate them easily to the general public. In contrast, when they convey complex scientific information—about global warming, for example—their arguments are likely to languish in the arena of public debate unless they can be summarized in terms of costs and benefits.

CATEGORICAL PRECEDENCE. Finally, lawmakers are more likely to champion an issue that is a matter of routine legislative action—or has categorical precedence—than one that is unique and far from routine. Issues such as environmental protection or global warming tend to face greater resistance in Congress than, say, a specific military procurement measure.

In his later work Cobb extended the pluralist model of agenda setting. In his original model, he had noted that agendas reach the institutional level when driven by public demand, as voiced through community leaders or the media. In his revised model Cobb observed that agendas also flow to institutions when initiated by political leaders, who rally widespread public support. Moreover, some agenda setting goes on beyond public view in the corridors of the legislative and executive branches.[10]

The Elitist Model

While some scholars ask *how* policy concerns reach the agenda, others ask *who* sets the agenda. Proponents of the hierarchical, or elitist, theory of agenda setting focus on the structure of decision making. They note that power is concentrated in the hands of a few. Political elites wield authority over a multitude lacking ready access to the corridors of power. The power structure resembles a pyramid, with power flowing from top to bottom (see Figure 3.4).[11]

Scholars favoring the elitist, pyramidal model adopt one of two views of agenda setting. The first view, described by decision scientists James March and Johan Olsen, points out that elites focus on issues in three ways.[12] First, they select issues randomly from a wide universe of possibilities. If you are a freshman representative in the House, you can focus on an infinite number of issues. You can pick up issues here or there—perhaps military appropriations now, the environment next, and possibly welfare down the road. Second, elites choose issues in which they specialize. If you are on the Defense Appropriations Subcommittee, you tend to pay attention to the issues in your area of expertise. You focus on defense spending while ignoring or setting aside other issues. Third, when selecting issues, elites observe hierarchies. A hierarchy governs the work of the Appropriations Committee. When the committee considers an issue, your staff reviews it first. As the member of Congress, you deal only with those issues that your staff has vetted. Because you are a junior member, your area of attention differs from that of the chair of the subcommittee. Within an organization, participants focus their attention in a hierarchical way. Therefore, the process of agenda setting is inevitably hierarchical.

The second view of elitist agenda setting, advanced by political scientists Thomas Dye and Harmon Ziegler, argues somewhat cynically that society's elites select issues that serve their own interests.[13] Separated from the masses, who are by and large apathetic, elites such as lawmakers, corporate representatives, and other interest groups exercise overarching influence on the institutional agenda.[14] Only when issues become important to elected officials or bureaucrats are they placed on the government agenda. Political and bureaucratic elites give priority not to the most salient issues but to those that best serve their own interests.[15]

Another model of agenda setting, one closely linked to the elitist model, is the subgovernmental model (see Figure 3.5).[16] The model describes an iron triangle,

Figure 3.4   The Elitist Model of Agenda Setting

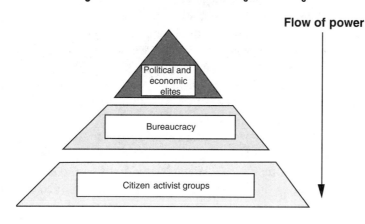

Figure 3.5 The Subgovernmental Model of Agenda Setting

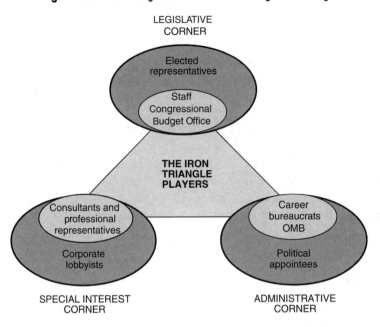

LEGISLATIVE CORNER

Elected representatives

Staff Congressional Budget Office

THE IRON TRIANGLE PLAYERS

Consultants and professional representatives

Corporate lobbyists

Career bureaucrats OMB

Political appointees

SPECIAL INTEREST CORNER

ADMINISTRATIVE CORNER

with political elites (Congress) at the apex and, at the base, those who dominate agenda setting—administrative elites (the bureaucracy) and special interests, along with their staffs and other experts. This rigid model assumes a stable coalition of players in the policy-making process. Some scholars have proposed a model slightly different from this one, in which the coalitions are flexible and open to outsiders. Outside players such as think tanks, academics, and journalists often make significant contributions to policy processes.[17] By publishing an insightful book or article, or by broadcasting a penetrating investigative report, these players can join a loose, informal coalition with policy advocates and community activists.[18]

John Kingdon presents another model of agenda setting, one that combines features of the pluralist, elitist, and subgovernmental models.[19] According to the **garbage can model,** when making decisions we act like a magician reaching inside a black hat and pulling out a rabbit. That is, we make choices in seemingly chaotic fashion, in a policy-making environment of "organized anarchy." We do not seek the absolute best decision. If we were to do so, we might spend our entire lives looking for it. Even if we did find the absolute best choice, the cost of the search might outweigh the benefits. Instead of searching, we choose the option that **satisfices**—that is, the one that is satisfactory and sufficiently good.[20] According to Kingdon, we make decisions using "imperfect rationality" (satisficing behavior), incomplete preferences (preferences that cannot be placed in strict order), and fluid participation (participation without structure or hierarchy). We make decisions in a mixed environment—one characterized both by the structure of the cozy iron triangle and by the randomness of the pluralistic model, in which we participate in give-and-take based on the mobilization of groups. Recent studies present evidence of this garbage can, or semichaotic, model of agenda setting but give greater weight than does Kingdon to the model's elitist, top-down features.

The distinguishing characteristics of the pluralist and elitist models, which present contrasting views of American politics, are listed in Table 3.1.

Impact of Sensational Events

Our discussion of how an agenda attains institutional status would not be complete if we did not mention the effects of sensational events on policy making. In his exhaustive work, Thomas Birkland analyzed the impact of hurricanes, earthquakes, and oil spills on agenda setting.[21] He found that we are easily moved by pictures of human suffering; incensed, we sometimes demand immediate action.

Exposed daily to television footage of children starving in Somalia, innocent victims caught in a vicious sectarian war, the nation demanded justice. A reluctant president George Bush responded by directing U.S. peacekeeping forces to lead a 1991 relief effort. Similarly, the public outcry over shootings at U.S. schools, covered widely by the nightly news shows, put enormous pressure on politicians to enact new gun control legislation (see "A Case in Point"). However, sometimes it takes more than pictures of disaster to force an issue from the systemic to the institutional agenda. Birkland argues that an agenda can be activated by a focus event that spurs a community to organize and demand legislation. The most effective community is a coherent group of professionals, experts, and activists—policy entrepreneurs—who mobilize and initiate a plan of action.

Table 3.1 Comparison of Pluralist and Elitist Models of Agenda Setting

	Pluralist model	Elitist model
Power	Based on size of group and its access to resources	Concentrated in the hands of a few
Centers of power	Multiple	Few
Values	Shared by masses and elites	Basic consensus among elites; values of elites differ from those of masses
Social mobility	High; elites permit input from masses and confer when making a decision	Low; masses exert minimal influence over elites
Influence	Individuals can influence elites	Individuals cannot sway elites; elites are highly insulated from apathetic masses
Outcome	Depends on many compromises among competing groups	Depends on elites directing policy from top to bottom, serving their own interests

A CASE IN POINT

The Pluralist Model of Agenda Setting: Making Schools Safe

Although policy makers have debated school safety for years, they gave it special attention in April 1999, when a series of highly sensational shootings brought the issue to
the institutional level and the American public demanded action. School officials
responded by starting a controversial program to identify potential killers.

The worst nightmare of every parent came true in April 1999, when TV news programs showed terrified students streaming out of the Columbine High School campus
in Littleton, Colorado. Responding to the bloodshed caused by two troubled teenagers,
the federal Bureau of Alcohol, Tobacco, and Firearms (ATF), along with school boards
all over the country, moved aggressively to combat school violence. Many schools
installed expensive metal detectors at school entrances while the ATF worked with a
threat-assessment company to help school administrators identify troubled students
who might be on the verge of committing a violent act. The program, known as
MOSAIC—2000, tested students in twenty schools as part of a national pilot study.*

One of the schools included in the study was Reynoldsburg High School, in a suburb
of Columbus, Ohio. MOSAIC identified potentially violent Reynoldsburg students by
rating them on a scale of one to ten. It asked students 150 questions crafted by two
hundred experts in law enforcement, psychiatry, and other related areas. Administrators conducted the program in grades one through twelve, focusing primarily on high
schools. They assessed students by evaluating questionnaires filled out by parents,
friends, school counselors, and the students themselves.

Needless to say, MOSAIC provoked controversy. School administrators, parents, and
the Reynoldsburg school board favored the program. So did Ohio's attorney general.
However, the Ohio chapter of the American Civil Liberties Union (ACLU) expressed
concern. The ACLU believed the program breached students' civil rights, including
their right of confidentiality. The group called MOSAIC a "technological Band-Aid" that
fed on parents' fear.

Many schools can afford MOSAIC, which costs about $10,000. The main problem
with the program is that it may not be effective in identifying potentially violent students. In Columbine violence was perpetrated by otherwise good students with access
to guns, students who unexpectedly snapped because they felt victimized by bullies
and the school system. When such students are involved, is MOSAIC just as helpless as
its administrators in identifying the potential assailants?

Note

*Francis X. Clines, "Schools Await High-tech Help for Evaluating Who's a Threat,"
New York Times, October 24, 1999.

Discussion Points

1. How did school safety reach the institutional agenda?
2. How did the Reynoldsburg school board respond to public concern?

Evaluating Costs and Benefits

Although the process by which policy makers give a systemic agenda official status is complex, we can develop a simple model that explains which agendas are likely to make the official list. We begin by evaluating systemic agendas in terms of their relative costs and benefits. If the benefits and costs are **diffuse,** they fall on a large number of people who do not belong to a well-defined group. Most environmental projects provide diffuse benefits—they help almost everyone in the community by fostering a clean environment. On the other hand, if the benefits and costs are **specific,** they affect a single group, which alone bears the project's favorable or harmful outcome. Hunting licenses, for example, benefit only those who enjoy hunting (see Table 3.2).

The easiest projects for lawmakers to accept are those that benefit a specific group of people while distributing the cost over a large, diffuse population. Included in this category are most of the so-called pork barrel projects that help a few specific segments of a legislator's constituency. Because the burden of these programs falls on faceless taxpayers, most of the projects go unopposed. However, when the benefits of an issue are diffuse but the costs are specific, political leaders find it extremely difficult to allocate resources, even when encouraged to do so by widespread popular support. An example of an issue in this category is gun control. Polls consistently indicate that a solid majority of Americans supports a measure that would make it hard for people to own certain types of guns. However, lawmakers have trouble passing such legislation because it promises only diffuse benefits, lacks a single powerful group of constituents to fight in its behalf, and faces strong opposition from the small but powerful gun lobby. In the third category, in which both the benefits and costs are diffuse, the most likely outcome is inaction. For example, almost everyone agrees that we need educational reform, particularly at the elementary school level. But lawmakers struggle to pinpoint winners and losers because both groups come from the citizens at large. It is hardly surprising that for all their rhetoric, legislators pass few measures in this category. The final category comprises measures with clear winners and losers. These bills address the most controversial redistribution issues. Examples of such measures include bills that support or oppose a new airport, pit environmentalists against the timber industry in the Pacific Northwest, or redress past injustice through programs such as affirmative action.

Table 3.2 Outcomes for Diffuse and Specific Costs and Benefits

Costs (losers)	Benefits (winners)	
	Diffuse	Specific
Diffuse	Inaction	Likely acceptance
Specific	Likely rejection	Conflict

Having explored agenda setting in terms of benefits and costs, we are prepared to briefly discuss the two ways people commonly assess the benefits and costs of a policy. Those who favor a narrow view hold that when considering costs and benefits, people strive only to maximize their own short-term self-interest. If the potential benefits for a group are diffuse, the group is likely to lose because no one in the group will be willing to bear the cost of a policy that will benefit the entire group, whether or not the other members share the costs. Mancur Olson called this situation the **free rider** problem, asserting that "rational" people do not want to participate in a collective action when they get something for nothing. Olson pointed out that as the group size increases, the problem becomes more pronounced.[22] In contrast, those who advocate the broad view contend that people are motivated not just by short-term self-interest but also by commitment,[23] group utility,[24] and ideology.[25] Supporters of this theory assert that if people defined benefits and costs as narrowly as the self-interest camp says they do, they would never embrace the most challenging causes—from improving the environment to supporting national liberation movements. Because environmental policies benefit many of us, we find it almost impossible to answer the question, why should I give my time to support these issues? Indeed, we cannot answer this important question if we assume that people follow only their narrowly defined self-interest. However, if we accept the premise that people often look beyond their own selfish needs and are inspired to contribute benefits to a larger community, we can explain a wide variety of altruistic behavior. For example, we contribute to public broadcasting stations even though we know that our radio or television reception does not depend on our contributions. Many people join volunteer organizations and make charitable contributions anonymously. When group members define an issue's benefits and costs as "specific" to them, they may fight to keep it in front of the political elite and get it onto the institutional agenda. By taking this approach, volunteers for Mothers Against Drunk Driving spurred passage of many local laws that got tough on drunk driving.

POLICY FORMULATION

Once an agenda attains institutional status, specific policies must be formulated. Legislators outline the course of action that the policy will follow. This plan can then be enacted into law. To determine the plan, lawmakers specify objectives, identify policy alternatives, and adopt the one alternative that gives the best results. Although analysts may participate in each stage of the policy cycle, their involvement is most critical in the phases of policy formulation, implementation, and evaluation.

Suppose we want to achieve a completely drug-free society—a desirable objective, though highly improbable. If we set an impossible goal, our policies, no matter how effective, will fail. Therefore, we start with the goal of reducing illegal drug use by 10 percent in the next five years.

How do we achieve this policy goal? We attack the problem by trying to curtail either the demand for drugs or their supply. We may choose to adopt one or more of the policy solutions outlined below. These policies may be enacted through legislation, executive orders, ordinances, or judicial decisions.[26]

Policies tend to provide either **positive** or **negative incentives.** Many drug users want to quit but cannot do so because of the high cost of treatment. To provide a positive incentive for quitting, the government may open rehabilitation centers for treating users free of charge. As a further inducement, the government may protect the privacy of those receiving treatment. On the flip side, negative inducements include stiffer penalties for drug possession and mandatory sentencing guidelines for repeat offenders. The government also may empower law enforcement agents to confiscate property gained through drug trafficking.

Another option available to us is to modify behavior by changing the **rules.** We might pass laws to make detection easier or to authorize locker searches. Students' fear of getting caught would raise the cost of using illicit drugs and might discourage them from bringing drugs to school. Moreover, we might decide to alter behavior with educational campaigns. We could distribute **factual information** on the physiological and psychological impact of drug abuse. Such information might take the form of advertisements, leaflets, or curricula on drug abuse, such as the Drug Abuse Resistance Education (D.A.R.E.) program.[27] Through D.A.R.E., school-age children receive information in language they can easily understand and in publications with catchy designs that grab their attention. We could also pass laws to give people **rights** that protect them from injuries or injustice related to drug enforcement and sentencing. Finally, we might accomplish the aims of our institutional agenda by shifting **power** over the agenda to a specific agency. In one of the most controversial antidrug proposals, the federal government considered engaging the airforce to intercept low-flying airplanes crossing the U.S.-Mexico border. It also authorized the navy and Coast Guard to seize high-speed boats and ships dropping off drugs.

Explaining Behavior

Before we formulate policy and do everything necessary to achieve our policy goals—offer incentives, change the rules, distribute factual information, give people rights, or transfer power—we first must determine if our proposed solution will be effective. To make this determination, we develop a **behavioral model,** making certain assumptions about human nature.

If we educate potential users about the ill effects of drug use on their bodies and minds, will we significantly affect their behavior? If so, why? The answer to this question will help us develop a fuller understanding of why people become addicted in the first place, and this information will shape the policies we propose. We might want to know where our target population is most likely to get its information. That way, if we conduct an advertising campaign, we will know from our behavioral model what the ad should say and what kind of ad to run.

To check our behavioral model we can use statistical techniques, testing our hypotheses with existing, **secondary data** or with data collected by the researcher, known as **primary data** (see discussion of statistical techniques in chapters 5 and 7; see also information on data gathering in chapter 6).

Forecasting Effects

We can use our behavioral model to make a forecast. Scientific forecasting is not fortune telling. The primary distinction between the two is that although fortune telling makes a prediction about a single unique event, answering a question with a definitive yes or no, scientific forecasting takes place in the context of probability. When a scientist forecasts a 99 percent probability and the event does not take place, the forecast may still be valid. Embedded in the forecast is a small but definite 1 percent chance of the event's not taking place. What the scientist intends to say with the forecast is that if the same conditions prevail over many tries, the event will occur 99 percent of the time. In forecasting we can never develop a model that fully eliminates uncertainty.[28]

Scientists base their forecasts on explicit or implicit assumptions about people's behavior, assumptions that they test by using **control variables.** Similarly, policy makers manipulate control variables to achieve their stated goal(s). If we assume that a rational human being is more inclined to abstain from drugs if given enough information about their harmful effects, such information becomes our control variable, or the factor designed to induce certain behavior. Forecasting is often like looking in the rearview mirror while driving a car. If we want to understand the future, we must study the past. We make most forecasts using past data. If the road behind is the same as the one ahead, we are in a good position to forecast our future. However, when the road changes, curving and zigzagging, our forecasts lose their accuracy (see discussion of forecasting techniques in chapters 8–11).

After setting goals and identifying alternatives, we pick out the best possible option. We make our choice using **cost-benefit** or **cost effectiveness** analysis (see chapter 14).

Conflict, Inaction, and Nondecision

We define public policy as what the government decides to do and not to do. The government can make as loud a statement by refusing to get involved as by taking action. Many agendas, from poverty to nuclear weapons, swirl around in society, are debated on college campuses, discussed in community halls, and written about on the editorial pages. However, the vast majority of them do not make it to the institutional agenda. The government and the power elite may actively prevent some of the agendas from ever reaching the institutional stage, either by force or through deliberate neglect. Government officials in the South did not make a concerted effort to address black poverty and discrimination until civil rights legislation compelled them to take action. Authorities frequently used brute force to block attempts to discuss the relevant issues.[29]

The government, however, does not need brute force to keep certain agendas from reaching institutional status. Most often, it blocks consideration of agendas unpopular with the elite simply through benign neglect. Why does it prevent some agendas from achieving institutional status? Evidence suggests two reasons for such failures (see Table 3.2). First, some issues provoke huge conflicts in society, especially when these issues identify specific winners and losers. If passions run high on both sides, political leaders often try to sidestep the issues. The primary goal of politics is managing conflict. No organized society can survive without suppressing certain disagreements that can develop into huge conflicts. Take, for instance, the issue of gun control. Suppose the governor of your state fervently believes that banning weapons is the only way of reducing violence. If the governor's party controls the legislature, the governor may feel free to take a radical stance on the issue. However, if others in the state passionately defend their right to own guns, the clash between the two viewpoints may lead to open conflict. Facing this ominous prospect, the political elite of both parties may refrain from pushing the agenda forward.[30]

In addition, if both the winners and the losers are diffuse, policy makers have no incentive to elevate an agenda from the nebulous systemic zone to the institutional stage. Many issues with merit never achieve institutional status. Thus, despite their scientific relevance, numerous environmental issues of global proportion remain unaddressed.

On the other hand, sometimes an issue that has been neglected for years all of a sudden commands the attention of the general public and the power elite. Adapting the arguments of social scientist Anthony Downs, we can show how an issue goes through an "attention cycle." As it proceeds through the cycle, it either fades from the public agenda or pushes toward institutional acceptance (see Figure 3.6).[31] At the systemic, pre-policy level, an agenda remains dormant. If a sudden discovery—such as news about the spread of the AIDS virus, the existence of an ozone hole over the Antarctic, or the alleged security leaks at the Los Alamos National Laboratory—mobilizes influential members of the policy community, they may issue an enthusiastic call for action. However, if they perceive an unacceptably high cost, the agenda may lose public interest and drop into "a twilight calm of lesser attention and spasmodic recurrences of interest." Downs suggests that such agendas have three things in common: they affect numerical minorities (for example, the poor, the homeless, and so on), they advocate social arrangements providing benefits (high-speed rail transport or new subway systems) to a majority or a powerful minority, and they no longer captivate the public with exciting ideas (the space program's lunar landing missions—routine flights to the moon did not sustain initial public fascination).

If influential policy makers find the costs to be reasonable, a sudden discovery may motivate them to transform a longstanding agenda into an accepted public policy. In the late 1990s advances in DNA technology brought the death penalty to the forefront of public awareness. A shocked public learned that the new technology had proven the innocence of a number of inmates slated to face the death penalty. In 1999 Illinois governor George Ryan, a Republican, suspended executions until he could be sure that only the guilty would be put to death.[32] In the Senate Patrick Leahy, D-Vt., and Gordon Smith, R-Ore., jointly proposed that defendants be guaranteed competent lawyers and provided with DNA testing that might prove their innocence. Some states, including California, made similar proposals.

Figure 3.6   Decision and Nondecision in Policy Formulation

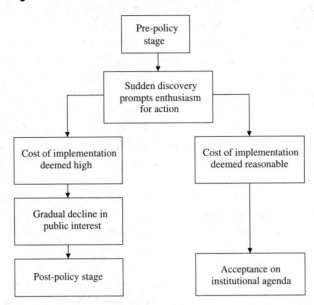

Several religious leaders and anti–death penalty advocates called for a moratorium on capital punishment. Once nearly forgotten, the movement questioning the appropriateness of the death penalty vaulted to public consciousness. Foes of capital punishment drew strength from a steadily declining crime rate during the past decade. The decline made the public willing to accept shorter sentences. Because policy makers saw as reasonable the cost of making DNA testing mandatory and abandoning the death penalty, the policies quickly gained the government's attention.

POLICY ADOPTION

Policy adoption comes at the end of the formulation process. Once the policy analyses are complete, they are sent to the official decision-making bodies, which enact legislation or issue an executive order. In the long cycle of policy formation, the adoption stage is for the most part well defined—if not at the beginning, then certainly at the end of the stage, when the legislature takes a vote or the chief executive issues a formal executive order. Typically the analyst's job ends with policy formulation, when decision makers review the alternatives and the analyses of their respective impact.

In a policy analyst's ideal world, her recommendations will be seriously discussed, and policy makers will pick from the alternatives she has identified. However, in the real world, lawmakers and the chief executive may be guided by a welter of conflicting concerns, of which her recommendation is but one. As the formal decision stage approaches, the outcome may reflect a long history of bargaining and deal making based on the decision makers' values, their constituents' concerns, their party affiliation, public opinion, and pressure from special interest groups.[33]

When we look at how decision-making bodies work, we may become cynical about the motives of elected officials. In opinion polls the American public repeatedly expresses its skepticism about Congress's ability to lead the country.[34] The question is, when deciding policy issues, do elected representatives vote only their self-interest (defined as the interest of their constituents and their political action committee), or are they also guided by "ideology"? In an interesting study, researchers Joseph Kalt and Mark Zupan followed legislation through the adoption stage of the policy cycle.[35] They evaluated the voting records of U.S. legislators debating the Surface Mining Control and Reclamation Act (SMCRA), which resulted from a protracted political struggle. Congress passed two versions of the act, in 1974 and 1975. President Gerald Ford vetoed them on both occasions. President Jimmy Carter finally signed the SMCRA into law in 1977. The act required that stripmined land be restored to its premining state. It also established an Abandoned Mine Reclamation Fund and clarified previously undefined rights to water and land in stripmining areas.

The self-interest theory says that lawmakers vote only the economic interests of their constituents, with a view toward winning reelection. However, the survey indicated that self-interest, as measured by the importance of mining in a lawmaker's state or district, does a poor job on its own of explaining voting records. The theory was a better predictor of voting behavior when researchers considered not only self-interest but also ideology, as measured by the League of Conservative Voters, an ideological watchdog. The survey indicated that when voting on legislation, U.S. senators and representatives are guided by both self-interest and ideology. Several other studies found similar results.[36]

POLICY IMPLEMENTATION

After a public policy has been adopted, it must be implemented. Adopted policies, particularly legislative acts, almost never specify exactly what is to be done. If a city council passes an ordinance prohibiting skateboarding on public sidewalks, it rarely tells administrators how to implement the measure. Administrators have numerous options. To understand the complexity of their choices, consider the following facts. Because it is impossible to patrol every street corner at all times, the city police department must decide where and when to enforce the new law. Police must decide whether to monitor only those streets with high volumes of pedestrian traffic or to patrol both these areas and those where young people are active, such as parks, schools, and beaches. They also must decide whether to patrol on foot, on bicycles, or in cruisers, which are fast but inefficient in crowded streets. Even after making these decisions, administrators must figure out what fraction of the police department's resources should be devoted to enforcing this new law. In some areas, the new mandate might come with a specific allocation of money, but that is not always the case. Because the police department might prompt legal challenges when enforcing the new law, officers must try to strike a balance between the rights of individuals and the demands of cities.

During the last fifty years, scholars have devoted a great deal of energy to understanding the major players and coalitions in agenda setting and policy formulation. But what happens after the laws have been passed? Do the formal and informal coalitions developed in the previous stages of the policy cycle disappear in the implementation stage? Or does the power coalition that brought about policy change remain active in overseeing implementation? If the power coalition continues to shape implementation, does the structure of the original coalition remain the same, or does it change?

In a series of studies conducted primarily in the 1990s, policy analysts made a number of useful observations about the implementation stage.[37] Figure 3.7 illustrates their findings.

As shown in the figure, institutional agendas are set and policies formulated by a loose coalition that may include several formal as well as informal players, who cluster around a set of "core values." According to Paul Sabatier and Hank Jenkins-Smith, these core values are the glue that holds together a disparate coalition.[38] This belief system is highly resilient and often resists changes, particularly by members of the advocacy groups in the broad coalition. Without any strong external shocks, these coalitions tend to remain stable throughout the implementation process. However, when economic conditions change, new information comes to light, or unexpected events—such as legal challenges or technical glitches—occur, the composition of these coalitions may alter significantly. Brian Ellison studied the Animas–La Plata River project in Colorado, near the New Mexico border.[39]

Figure 3.7   Impact of External Shocks on Policy Coalitions

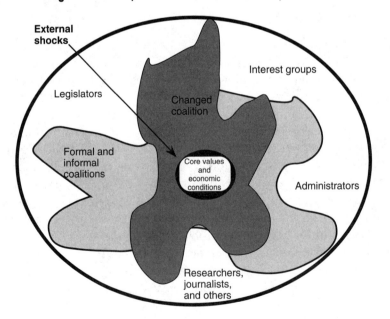

Originally seen as a water project, it enjoyed the support of a pro–water development coalition. However, when a government study questioned the financial feasibility of the project and noted that it could jeopardize the river's endangered squawfish population, these external shocks changed the configuration of the coalition of Indian tribes, environmentalists, and probusiness groups, thereby altering the project several times during implementation.

POLICY EVALUATION

If there is one area over which policy analysts exercise primary responsibility in the policy cycle, it is the evaluation phase. Analysts inquire about the possible impact of an adopted policy. Does the policy meet the greater needs of society and is it achieving its goals? The first question is broader than the second. We hope that the goals of society and those of the policy are compatible, but they sometimes conflict with each other. Suppose your state government has initiated a new education policy to boost school performance. It has allocated funds to prepare students for national standardized achievement tests. If at the end of a certain period the average test score has improved, we may conclude that the program has achieved its goals and that the money has been well spent. However, a broader question arises if we look at the total impact of the program, particularly on children from traditionally disadvantaged and non-English-speaking families. Suppose that while average test score have improved, the program's curriculum changes have devastated less-prepared students, increasing dropout rates. In addition, suppose that legislators funded this program at the expense of another project, a state-funded special initiative for children with learning disabilities. We might find that the opportunity cost of such a program exceeds the benefits. When we evaluate the policy on its stated goals, we get a much more positive picture than when we analyze its overall impact on society.

We may evaluate the impact of a policy on several levels. For example, we may examine **policy output**.[40] Returning to our example of traffic cameras on street corners, we note that in June 2000 traffic officials in San Diego, California, cited four thousand drivers per month for violations, fining them $271 per ticket.[41] Lockheed Martin IMS, the local manufacturer of the cameras, received $70 of each ticket. Therefore, we estimate that the policy output equals the city's net revenue per ticket ($271 − $70 = $201). At this rate, the city expects to make annual collections of about $9.65 million (4,000 × $201 × 12).[42]

We also measure the effect of public policy by conducting a **performance evaluation**—that is, by gauging the policy's impact on target groups. Our target group includes drivers that typically run red lights, causing accidents. However, performance evaluation does more than measure how many people in the target group are affected by a program; it also evaluates the program's total effectiveness. Analysts measure the performance of the cameras by looking at the accident data and conducting research to see if the devices reduced the total number of accidents.

In addition, policy analysts may want to evaluate the impact of a policy from an even broader perspective than the one afforded by performance evaluation. In that case, they look at **policy outcomes.** The effects of a policy may not be confined to the target group or even to the immediate program objectives. Instead, they may spill over into other areas of social behavior and social conditions. Because of the traffic devices, motorists may drive carefully not only where cameras are located but also everywhere else they drive, making areas beyond the monitored intersections safer for both pedestrians and drivers.

Finally, analysts measure policy impacts by evaluating **feedback.** A number of motorists complained that the cameras were unsafe. The drivers argued that if they were to stop suddenly to avoid a hefty fine, they might cause an accident. They also argued that at night the blinding flashes from the camera caused confusion, which led to accidents.[43] This kind of feedback helps analysts change policies to better fit objectives.

POLICY CHANGE

Analysts traditionally have reviewed policies up to the stage of evaluation and stopped there. However, the policy cycle continues beyond policy implementation, as adopted policies encounter the real world problems of interest group pressure, client complaints, legal challenges, and changing financial conditions. Facing these scenarios, policies evolve and go through numerous changes until some of them finally are terminated.

If we follow the life of any single public policy, we find that it is constantly shaped and reshaped by at least seven factors:

1. Incremental changes in the dynamics of society smooth out the rough edges of implementation.
2. New statutes contradict or invalidate parts of the existing policy.
3. Lawsuits or questions of constitutionality challenge the policy in court.
4. New technology alters the feasibility of the policy.
5. New discoveries or revelations change public support for a program.
6. Political and economic circumstances change, imposing different conditions on an existing policy.
7. Elections cause a major ideological shift that changes the policy.

In other words, as the world around us changes, so do all major policies.

If we look at the death penalty, we see how society's attitudes have changed over the years. A strict "eye for an eye" attitude of swift justice has given way to a more reasoned approach, one that considers carefully the social effects of such a policy. The history of the death penalty goes back to the earliest period of recorded penal codes. The Code of Hammurabi (1790–1750 B.C.) recommended the death penalty for twenty-five different crimes.[44] In the seventh century B.C., Draco the Athenian lawgiver, from whom we get the term "draconian," prescribed death for every kind of offense. Brought to the new world by European colonists, the death penalty was liberally administered for high crimes against the state as well as for petty theft. The issue occasionally provoked controversy. Supported by the Quakers and inspired by the writings of European intellectuals such as Voltaire, Montesquieu, and Bentham, a movement to abolish the death penalty gained ground in the United States. As governor of Virginia, Thomas Jefferson authorized a complete revision of that state's laws and recommended capital punishment only for treason and murder. After a stormy debate, the legislature defeated the bill by one vote. Nearly one hundred years later, in 1897, the U.S. Congress passed a bill reducing the number of federal capital offenses. The next landmark legal action on the death penalty occurred in 1972, when the Supreme Court, reviewing three separate cases, struck down the death penalty in several states and set the standard for capital punishment. Under this guideline, the Court would consider a death sentence "cruel and unusual punishment" if it (1) was too severe for the crime, (2) was arbitrary (that is, not uniform–applied to some but not to others in similar situations), (3) offended society's sense of justice, or (4) was less effective than another punishment.[45] However, during the next seventeen years, the pendulum of the Court's position on the issue swung back hard and fast. In a series of challenges, the Court upheld capital punishment in a number of state cases.[46] When opening old cases in the 1990s, several state courts started admitting DNA evidence. The death penalty remains an important election issue in the new century.[47]

Policy scientists note four patterns of policy change:

1. **Linear,** when one policy is replaced by another
2. **Consolidated,** when programs with similar goals are combined
3. **Split,** when an agency enforcing a certain policy grows too large to administer the policy effectively. The agency is broken into smaller components, and each of them receives part of the original policy.
4. **Nonlinear,** when social conditions change or technological advances generate new information, prompting drastic or major policy changes

POLICY TERMINATION

John Maynard Keynes, the father of modern macroeconomics, walked into the Oval Office to meet President Franklin Roosevelt. He brought with him a policy to counter wild swings in the business cycle. Keynes recommended that Roosevelt increase government spending during times of recession and reduce spending during periods of inflation or rapid economic growth.

More than sixty years later, after watching the government accumulate six trillion dollars of public debt, some policy scientists charge that the famous economist ignored political realities. They note that government spending has been elastic in only one direction: upward. Government officials have found it easier to increase spending or propose a new public policy than to terminate one after its initiation. As Gary Brewer and Peter DeLeon point out, the cavalry did not gallop into the sunset with the introduction of mechanized regiments; March of Dimes did not stop marching after the invention of the polio vaccine.[48]

Scholars define policy termination as "the deliberate conclusion or cessation of specific public sector functions, programs, policies, or organizations."[49] They have identified four types of termination—functional, organizational, policy, and program.[50]

- **Functional termination** is sweeping. If the government decided to abandon its education responsibilities, that decision would fall in this category. This termination would cause the complete privatization of education, with the private sector managing the entire field.
- When the government does not want to end its involvement in a field but does wish to withdraw support for an agency, it engages in **organizational termination.** Although nobody expects the government to drop its education duties entirely, many conservatives in U.S. politics have urged the federal government to end its involvement in the field by eliminating the Department of Education.
- **Policy termination** takes place when lawmakers abandon a specific policy to address changing social needs. In the American South legislators discarded discriminatory Jim Crow laws to respond to changes in the post–civil rights era.
- **Program termination** occurs when the government ends a specific program. The Reagan administration cut the Federal Revenue Sharing program as part of its policy to reduce the role of the federal bureaucracy in the financial affairs of state and local governments.

Why is policy termination a problem for government? Lawmakers adopt a specific public policy to address a specific human problem. They rarely solve a problem completely. Therefore, the policy lingers. It goes through many changes, but the essential goals of the policy remain intact. When legislators terminate a program, they must contend with the losers. Lawmakers' failure to distribute the losses effectively causes many of these programs to continue. This is particularly true when the costs of termination fall on a small, specific group (employees working at a military base, for example, and those who depend on the business generated by the base). It is equally true when the benefits remain diffuse (savings for U.S. taxpayers). A cynical observer would argue that every government program creates its own constituencies. These entrenched interests prevent political leaders from taking the hard step of terminating a policy, program, or agency. Many military bases were established in the United States to fight Native Americans during the early days of the nation's settlement. Yet most of those bases remain in use even a century after their original purpose was fulfilled. Anytime lawmakers try to close a military base, the agencies near the base lobby Congress to keep it open.[51] This pattern repeats itself when political leaders debate whether to end other government programs. As a result, few programs are ever completely terminated.

Key Words

Behavioral model (p. 57)	Elitist model (p. 49)
Consolidated policy change (p. 65)	Factual information (p. 57)
Control variables (p. 58)	Feedback (p. 64)
Cost-benefit analysis (p. 58)	Free rider (p. 56)
Cost effectiveness analysis (p. 58)	Functional termination (p. 66)
Diffuse (p. 55)	Garbage can model (p. 52)

Institutional, or governmental, agendas
   (p. 47)
Linear policy change (p. 65)
Negative incentives (p. 57)
Nonlinear policy change (p. 65)
Organizational termination (p. 66)
Performance evaluation (p. 63)
Pluralist model (p. 49)
Policy cycle (p. 47)
Policy formation (p. 47)
Policy outcomes (p. 64)
Policy output (p. 63)
Policy termination (p. 66)

Positive incentives (p. 57)
Power (p. 57)
Primary data (p. 57)
Program termination (p. 66)
Rights (p. 57)
Rules (p. 57)
Satisficing (p. 52)
Secondary data (p. 57)
Specific (p. 55)
Split policy change (p. 65)
Systemic, or noninstitutional, agendas
   (p. 47)

Exercises

1. Every newly elected president goes to the White House promising to overhaul the welfare system. Yet in the end, many research and policy debates produce only marginal changes in the system. In an essay explain why it is difficult to make radical changes in public policies.
2. What is the importance of interest group coalitions in public policy formation? Take an important policy that has recently been adopted and determine whether the coalition supporting it has been stable or whether it has changed over time.
3. Write an essay on the role of quantitative analysis—and those who use it—in public policy formation. Given the political nature of the process, should we look to economic analyses and statistical techniques for answers?

Notes

1. Jenifer Hanrahan, "Motorists Taking San Diego's Red-light Cameras to Court," *San Diego Union Tribune,* May 7, 2000, B1.
2. James E. Anderson, *Public Policymaking: An Introduction* (Boston: Houghton Mifflin, 1990), 78.
3. See, for example, Nick Maybey et al., *Argument in the Greenhouse: The International Economics of Controlling Global Warming* (New York: Routledge, 1997).
4. James P. Lester and Joseph Stewart, *Public Policy: An Evolutionary Approach,* 2d ed. (Belmont, Calif.: Wadsworth, 2000), 65–86.
5. Roger W. Cobb and Charles D. Elder, *Participation in American Politics: The Dynamics of Agenda-Building,* 2d ed. (Baltimore: Johns Hopkins University Press, 1983).
6. Ibid., 85.
7. Anderson, *Public Policymaking,* 83.
8. David B. Truman, *The Governmental Process* (New York: Knopf, 1951). See also Robert Dahl, *Who Governs?* (New Haven: Yale University Press, 1961).
9. Roger W. Cobb and Charles D. Elder, "The Politics of Agenda Building," *Journal of Politics* 33, no. 4 (1971): 892–915; Cobb and Elder, *Participation in American Politics;* Roger W. Cobb, Jennie-Keith Ross, and Marc H. Ross, "Agenda Building as a Comparative Political Process," *American Political Science Review* 70 (1976): 126–138.
10. Cobb, Ross, and Ross, "Agenda Building."

11. Thomas R. Dye and Harmon Ziegler, *The Irony of Democracy* (Monterey, Calif.: Brooks/Cole, 1981). See also Thomas R. Dye, *Understanding Public Policy*, 9th ed. (Englewood Cliffs, N.J.: Prentice Hall, 1998).

12. James G. March and Johan P. Olsen, *Ambiguity and Choice in Organizations* (Bergen, Norway: Universitetforlaget, 1976).

13. Dye and Ziegler, *Irony of Democracy*.

14. James E. Anderson, *Public Policymaking* (New York: Praeger, 1975).

15. Barbara Nelson, *Making an Issue of Child Abuse* (Chicago: University of Chicago Press, 1984).

16. Douglas Carter, *Power in Washington* (New York: Random House, 1965). See also J. L. Freeman, *The Political Process*, rev. ed. (New York: Random House, 1965).

17. For an excellent, detailed discussion of how conservative think tanks have shaped public policy, see Trudy Lieberman, *Slanting the Story: The Forces That Shape the News* (New York: New Press, 2000).

18. See, for example, H. Heclo, "Issue Networks and the Executive Establishment," in *The New American Political System*, ed. A. King (Washington, D.C.: American Enterprise Institute, 1978), 87–124. See also Paul A. Sabatier and Hank C. Jenkins-Smith, eds., *Policy Change and Learning* (Boulder, Colo.: Westview, 1993), 105–128.

19. John W. Kingdon, *Agendas, Alternatives, and Public Policies* (Boston: Little, Brown, 1984).

20. The term "satisficing" was coined by Herbert Simon. See, for example, his *Administrative Behavior: A Study of Decision-Making Processes in Administrative Organization* (New York: The Free Press, 1945).

21. Thomas A. Birkland, *After Disaster: Agenda Setting, Public Policy, and Focusing Events* (Washington, D.C.: Georgetown University Press, 1997).

22. Mancur Olson, *The Logic of Collective Action: Public Goods and the Theory of Groups* (Cambridge: Harvard University Press, 1965).

23. Amartya K. Sen, "Rational Fools: A Critique of the Behavioral Foundations of Economic Theory," in *Beyond Self-interest*, ed. Jane Mansfield (Chicago: University of Chicago Press, 1990), 25–43.

24. Howard Margolis, *Selflessness, Altruism and Rationality* (Cambridge: Cambridge University Press, 1982).

25. Dipak K. Gupta, *Path to Collective Madness* (New York: Praeger, 2001).

26. Deborah A. Stone, *Policy Paradox and Political Reason* (Glenview, Ill.: Scott, Foresman, 1988).

27. For an example of factual information designed to change behavior, see the D.A.R.E. Web site, http://www.dare-america.com/index_3.htm.

28. For an exciting discussion on forecasting, see John Casti, *Searching for Certainty: What Scientists Can Know About the Future* (New York: Morrow, 1990).

29. See, for example, Peter Bachrach and Morton S. Baratz, *Power and Poverty* (New York: Oxford University Press, 1970).

30. E. E. Schattschneider, *The Semi-Sovereign People* (New York: Oxford University Press, 1960).

31. Anthony Downs, "Up and Down with Ecology: The Issue-Attention Cycle," *Public Interest* 32 (summer 1972): 38–50.

32. Richard Cohen, "We Can Never Be Really Certain of Eliminating Mistakes in Capital Cases," *Washington Post,* April 20, 2000.

33. For an excellent discussion, see James E. Anderson, *Public Policymaking: An Introduction*, 3d ed. (Boston: Houghton Mifflin, 1990).

34. In a continuing national survey, the Gallup organization found in May 2000 that 39 percent of the public approves and 52 percent disapproves of the job Congress is doing. See the Gallup Web site, http://www.gallup.com/poll/indicators/indpublic _cong.asp.

35. Joseph P. Kalt and Mark A. Zupan, "Capture and Ideology in the Economic Theory of Politics," *American Economic Review* 74: 279–300.

36. E. J. Mitchell, "The Basis of Congressional Energy Policy," *Texas Law Review* 57 (1979): 591–630; J. B. Kau and P. H. Rubin, "Self-Interest, Ideology and Logrolling in Congressional Voting," *Journal of Law and Economics* 22 (1979): 365–384; and Joseph P. Kalt, *The Economics and Politics of Oil Price Regulation* (Cambridge: Cambridge University Press, 1981).

37. D. Mazmanian and Paul A. Sabatier, *Implementation and Public Policy* (Lanham, Md.: University Press of America, 1989); Paul A. Sabatier and Hank C. Jenkins-Smith, eds., *Policy Change and Learning* (Boulder, Colo.: Westview, 1993), 105–128; Hank C. Jenkins-Smith and Paul A. Sabatier, "Evaluating the Advocacy Coalition Framework," *Journal of Public Policy* 14 (1994): 175–203; Hank C. Jenkins-Smith, G. K. St. Claire, and B. Woods, "Explaining Change in Policy Subsystems: Analysis of Coalition Stability and Defection over Time," *American Journal of Political Science* 35 (1991): 851–880.

38. Paul A. Sabatier and Hank C. Jenkins-Smith, "The Advocacy Coalition Framework: An Assessment" (paper presented at the Department of Political Science, University of Amsterdam, February 1997), 7–8.

39. Brian A. Ellison, "The Advocacy Coalition Framework and Implementation of the Endangered Species Act: A Case Study in Western Water Politics," *Policy Studies Journal* 26, no. 1 (1998): 11–29.

40. Melvin J. Dubnick and Barbara A. Bardes, *Thinking About Public Policy* (New York: Wiley, 1983), 203.

41. In this example I measure output in dollars. However, we need not gauge public policy outputs in monetary terms. For example, we can measure the output of a drug education policy by the size of the target audience reached.

42. Jenifer Hanrahan, "Motorists Taking San Diego's Red-light Cameras to Court," *San Diego Union Tribune,* May 7, 2000, B1.

43. Ibid.

44. Michael H. Reggio, "History of the Death Penalty," in *Society's Final Solution: A History and Discussion of the Death Penalty,* ed. Laura E. Randa (Lanham, Md.: University Press of America, 1997), 1–11.

45. Ibid., 10.

46. *Gregg v. Georgia,* 428 U.S. 153 (1976); *Thompson v. Oklahoma,* 487 U.S. 815 (1988); *Penry v. Lynaugh,* 492 U.S. 302 (1989).

47. William Glaberson, "Fierce Campaigns Signal a New Era for State Courts," *New York Times,* June 5, 2000.

48. Gary D. Brewer and Peter DeLeon, *The Foundations of Public Policy* (Homewood, Ill.: Dorsey Press, 1983), 386.

49. Ibid., 385.

50. Lester and Stewart Jr., *Public Policy,* 156–157.

51. Louis Jacobson, "City, State Lobbyists Work to Head Off Base Closings," *Planning* 65 (Aug. 26–27, 1999): 26.

CRITICAL THINKING
AND RESEARCH DESIGN

In fall 2000 the Green Bay Packers felt restless. They wanted to renovate their stadium, Lambeau Field. Of the thirty-two teams in the National Football League (NFL) in the 1990s, ten built new stadiums, six had new facilities on the way, and eight extensively renovated their sports arenas.[1] The demand for new stadiums was not restricted to NFL teams. Most professional baseball, basketball, and hockey teams clamored for their own new or improved stadiums. Because the price tag of these projects often exceeded $100 million, team owners asked for public financing.[2]

Professional sports has come a long way since May 15, 1862, when William Cammeyer enclosed the ballpark on Union Grounds in Brooklyn, New York, to keep out the nonpaying spectators. Today, professional sports—a multibillion-dollar enterprise—seeks partnerships with cities all over the country.[3] Suppose the professional sports team in your city requests public financing of a new facility. You have been hired by the city to conduct an analysis. How do you proceed?

When French mathematician and philosopher René Descartes boldly claimed, "I think; therefore, I am," he placed thinking at the core of human existence. His notion of thinking forever changed how we view our place in the universe. We ask questions and do not accept propositions on faith alone. Faced with any problem, we can either make a decision on impulse or take the time to think critically before proceeding.[4]

In the course of a day, decision makers in public organizations are bombarded with questions: what are the present and future needs of our clients? Should we invest in that project? Of three possible projects, which one is best? When can we expect to finish this project? How many people will be on welfare five years from now? How much, how many, when, which one? As the questions pile up, decision makers can make up their minds by drawing on personal experiences or by acting on a hunch. If they are really desperate, they may call on their policy analysts or go outside the organization and hire a consultant to provide them with the answers. If these individuals want to make sense out of a jumble of seemingly meaningless numbers—or if they want to use a report submitted by a consultant or an in-house analyst—they will need a deep appreciation for the abilities and limits of the various tools of statistics and operations research.

FIVE STEPS OF OBJECTIVE ANALYSIS

The strength of modern social science is its ability to translate vague philosophical discourse into rigorous objective analysis. The *New Webster Dictionary* defines "objectivism" as a "doctrine which postulates that reality exists independent of mind," an outlook free of prejudice, feeling, or subjectivity. This outlook, also known as **objective professionalism,** has shaped the twentieth-century development of Western social science in general and that of policy analysis in particular. Objective professionalism is rooted in inductive logic—the practice of inferring a general conclusion from premises that can be verified empirically, through observation or experience. In contrast, medieval reasoning depended to a large extent on deductive logic, by which conclusions were drawn from premises whose validity was never questioned. Despite empirical evidence supporting Galileo's discovery that the earth revolved around the sun, the scientific authorities of his day could not accept his conclusion. They rejected his finding because it contradicted the established, church-sanctioned view, which was based purely on faith. Similarly, when Andreas Vesalius accurately described the human anatomy, the scientific community refused to consider the obvious evidence, believing the ancient Roman physician Galen's description to be infallible.

With the birth of scientific reasoning, the authorities gradually accepted empirical verification as the best way to conduct scientific inquiry. In fact, today, empirical verification is the hallmark of objective, scientific reasoning.[5] However, this principle runs counter to human nature, for we humans think subjectively, unscientifically. To gather information, we observe the world through filters of culture, upbringing, knowledge, values, ideologies, tastes, and personal interests. If our perceptions are subjective, how can we claim to be objective in our analysis? If we cannot, are we destined to drift around forever in a sea of subjectivity, without the anchor of objective reasoning?

Despite our subjective perceptions, we possess a lifeline to objective reasoning. This reasoning is shaped by our communal existence in a scientific society, which has developed a framework of objective analysis. Our paradigm of scientific reasoning has helped us identify the following five-step process for analyzing a complex problem:

1. Define the fundamental issue and lay out the goals of the analysis.
2. Identify the alternate courses of action.
3. Forecast the consequences of the alternatives.
4. Compare and evaluate systematically all possible outcomes.
5. Choose the most preferred alternative.

We must begin our objective analysis by clearly defining our investigation's content and goals. In other words, we must make sure that we know *what the fundamental issue is* and *what we want to establish by this analysis*. We do the same thing when buying a new car. To narrow our choices among the many cars available—both new and used—we must first establish our objective. We ask ourselves, For whom are we buying this car, and what needs will it serve? If we will use the car primarily to commute from home to the office, our options will exclude those automobiles that do not meet our needs, such as vehicles designed for taking a family on vacation or for projecting an image of success. As you can see, defining goals makes your work easier by narrowing down the virtually infinite number of possibilities.

Returning to our example of stadium financing, we must begin our analysis by defining the goal of our study. For whom are we conducting the analysis? Although the proposed ballpark may benefit the city and downtown businesses (including the team owners), it may harm some of the other neighborhoods in the city, or it may draw resources from regional or other local governments, such as the county or a neighboring city. The project may be good for the city's sports fans but bad for those who had hoped for a new library. It may favor one professional sports team (say, football) at the expense of another (say, baseball). Before starting our analysis, we must determine the purpose of our study.

Having defined our objective, we move to the second step of problem analysis, *identifying the alternate courses of action*. Our choice of alternatives will be guided by two factors: *consistency* and *feasibility*. Our alternatives should be consistent with our goal. If our goal is to buy a car for family outings, adding a small, two-seat sports car to our list of alternatives will be inconsistent with our goal. If we seek economic feasibility, choosing a Rolls Royce as an alternative will serve no purpose. Similarly, while considering the proposed new stadium, we will want to identify the alternatives. Our first choice may be between doing the project and doing nothing. Next, we might consider building in several locations, ever mindful that we can choose not to do the project if none of the other alternatives meets our goals.

We proceed to the third step in objective public policy analysis, *forecasting the consequences of the alternatives*. During public debates, the supporters of a new stadium will note the benefits of sports to the community—from creating jobs to reducing youth crime—in the loftiest terms. As an analyst, you must make an exhaustive list of these possible benefits.[6] You may note the following reasons for providing subsidies to a private enterprise, such as a professional sports team:

INCREASE IN TAX REVENUE.   Cities prosper when more people and businesses move in. As more people work, live, and spend their income in the city, they generate revenues for the city in the form of income taxes, sales taxes, license fees, other fees, and even fines. Building a new stadium may mean that more people will work for the club, more fans will flock to the games, and more businesses will flourish because of the increased economic activity.

POSITIVE EXTERNALITIES.   Many local governments value a major league sports team because it elevates their city to the "major leagues." "If the Jacksonville Jaguars aren't well known in other parts of the country, they will be—soon," announced the lead story in a Jacksonville newspaper on the eve of an American Football Conference (AFC) championship game against the Tennessee Titans.[7] "Basically, this game will be a three-hour commercial for the city and the team," said Mike May, director of communications for the Sporting Goods Manufacturers Association. Suddenly a second-tier city in Florida was talking about worldwide exposure. Some stadium proponents even suggested that the civic pride generated by a better sports facility would reduce crime among area youth.[8] The project's supporters also predicted increased business for the local service sector. Between the AFC championship game and the Jaguars' matchup against the Miami Dolphins the previous week, city officials estimated that more than fifty thousand visitors had traveled to Jacksonville and spent $1 million in the city, with $800,000 going to local hotels.

In addition to considering these benefits of the stadium project, you must evaluate the stadium's costs. Publicly financing a privately owned sports club could have the following negative effects:

"BLACKMAIL" POTENTIAL.   A professional team creates a strong constituency of fans. As a result, teams demand new stadiums or expensive repairs to existing facilities. If their demands are not met, they threaten to leave their city. In December 1982, after a highly public five-month battle leading to an agreement between the Raiders and the city of Los Angeles, the city controller announced that the Los Angeles Coliseum was on the verge of bankruptcy. The controller estimated that because of the deal extracted from the city, the Coliseum would run a deficit of $4 million in the third year of its lease.[9] Two years after the Raiders' agreement with the city, at least thirteen of the forty-two cities with professional franchises were asked to provide their teams with tax incentives, to improve their sports facilities, or to risk losing their teams.[10]

WEALTH TRANSFER.   When a city provides a team with subsidies, it transfers wealth from city taxpayers to wealthy athletes and multimillionaire club owners. Because the tax burden falls only on city residents, out-of-town fans receive, in effect, subsidized tickets.

NEGATIVE EXTERNALITIES.   Building a new stadium, or renovating an existing one, often displaces residents or small businesses from surrounding areas. For many of them, the cost of relocating far exceeds what the city is willing to give as compensation.

In the fourth step of objective policy analysis, we conduct a systematic *valuation of all possible outcomes*. At this stage, we place monetary values not only on the outcomes that are readily measurable in monetary terms but also on the intangible aspects of positive and negative externalities. Unfortunately, such valuations often lead to heated controversies.[11] In 1998, when San Diego was debating the merits of Proposition C, which would have authorized public funding of the Padres' new ballpark, the city hall projected that it would need an investment of $275 million. However, the city's consultant, Deloitte and Touche, sidestepping the fact that the project could not sustain itself from its own revenues, estimated that the project would generate $1.8 million annually in net revenues.[12]

Finally, after conducting a thorough analysis, we *choose the most preferred alternative*, in light of the goal of the project and based on some *decision criteria*. These decision criteria can take several forms. When the costs of the alternatives are the same, the criterion should be to maximize the total benefits. On the other hand, when the benefits are the same, we should choose the alternative that costs the least. When both costs and benefits vary, we try to maximize the net benefit (the difference between benefits and costs).

In real life our criteria for thinking critically about a project can become complex, particularly when we include uncertainty in our thinking. When faced with uncertainty, decision makers may not choose the alternative with the highest expected net benefit. If you are an extra-cautious person (in technical terms, a **risk averter**), you may choose the certainty of low earnings over the lure of more attractive but uncertain returns. On the other hand, if you are a **risk taker,** you may aggressively pursue high returns, regardless of the risk. Your ability or willingness to take risk plays a significant role in the real world—especially in a democratic, pluralistic society—because you will find that many of the steps in policy analysis do not provide certain, definitive answers. To deal with uncertain outcomes, we must follow a number of specific strategies (see chapter 13).

SETTING GOALS

Defining the goals of a project may be the most difficult step in policy analysis, because they are set not by analysts but by elected officials or higher-level government officials. Quite often public policy goals are not well formed even in the minds of those who make the ultimate decisions. In inviting a professional team to a city, the mayor and other elected officials may be thinking only about the immediate benefit of creating a broader image of the city. An analyst, then, should point out the other goals that the city ought to consider.

The project may pursue multiple goals, some of which may be vague or ill defined, while others may be contradictory. A city may build a stadium to attract a new sports franchise, which will enhance the image of the city.[13] If the city builds in a blighted area, the project may have an urban renewal objective. At times these

goals may be complementary, while at others they may be contradictory. A stadium may help rebuild the neighborhood around it, but if it creates congestion
and traffic problems by clogging up the surrounding highways, it may ultimately
harm the city's image.

In any case, when you set multiple goals, you should conduct your analysis
with respect to each of them. You may present your finding in a table (see Table
4.1) so that decision makers can honestly debate the project's merits.

The primary goal of any public policy is maximizing social welfare. But we have
yet to find a way to define "social welfare" to everyone's satisfaction. Terms like
"the people" or "the nation" are staples of political rhetoric. Politicians of all
shades, from democrats to demagogues, take liberty with these terms. The president sets national agendas and boldly declares what the nation needs. The opposing party claims to know what "the people" really want. The question of who is "the
nation" or who are "the people" has occupied some of the best minds in our intellectual history. French revolutionary philosopher Jean-Jacques Rousseau, the
most celebrated proponent of "general will," assumed its existence as a self-
evident truth. As political theorist George Sabine points out,

> The general will … presented a unique fact about a community, namely,
> that it has a collective good which is not the same thing as the private
> interests of its members. In some sense it lives its own life, fulfills its own
> destiny, and suffers its own fate. In accordance with the analogy of an
> organism, which Rousseau had developed at some length in the article on
> political economy, it may be said to have a will of its own, the "general will
> (*volenté générale*)." [14]

The problem with accepting the existence of an overarching social objective is
that it often conflicts with individual freedom and individual rights. If you assume

Table 4.1   Multiple Goals: Building a New Stadium

Project goals	Expected benefits	Expected costs
Enhance the city's image	National and international exposure from having a major league sports franchise	Excessive traffic on already heavily used highways—city could be labeled overcrowded
Foster urban renewal	Extensive construction of new hotels, restaurants, and other business facilities	• Uprooting of existing businesses • Loss of identity of established communities • Relocation of low-income residents in other poor and already congested areas of the city
Generate tax revenue for the city	Increased city revenues through licenses; fees; and property, sales, and income taxes	• Tax subsidies for the sports franchise • Increased financial liabilities for the city, particularly if the team does not live up to expectations

the existence of a collective will or, in economic terms, a **social objective,** you implicitly assume its predominance over individual aspirations. If you believe that for the world's collective good the hunting of whales must stop, the interests of the whaling industry and the people dependent on it must be sacrificed for the greater good of the community. Similarly, public officials fund antipoverty programs by taxing the rich and the middle class. Building a freeway helps some groups (communities near the freeway, the trucking industry, motorists, the suburbs) while hurting others (communities bypassed by the freeway, the railroad industry, people and businesses displaced by the highway, the city center). Because hardly any public policies let everyone win and no one lose, to make wise policy choices, we must find a way of comparing the winners' gains with the losers' losses.

Utilitarians and the Pareto Principle

Toward the end of the eighteenth century, a group of British social thinkers called the **utilitarians** tried to define "social welfare." Jeremy Bentham, the best-known member of this group, argued for the maximization of total utility in society. The utilitarians, in effect, argued that the marginal utility of a dollar diminishes with a person's level of income. A wealthy person, they asserted, would probably pay less attention to the loss of a dollar than would a poor person. Extending this logic, you could argue that by taking, say, $1,000 from the wealthiest individual on earth and giving it to a starving person, you would reduce the rich person's marginal utility to an extent less than the increase to the poor person's. As a result, the redistribution of income would increase the total utility of society. By following this formula, we could keep taxing the rich to fund social programs for the poor until the two groups' marginal utilities (one negative and one positive) were equal. The problem with such a plan is that interpersonal utilities are not measurable. We cannot quantify personal feelings about utility. If we take from a miserly rich person and give to a happy-go-lucky poor person, the redistribution of income may not affect the total utility of society at all.

Following this logic—that calculations of interpersonal utilities cannot be made—Italian economist and sociologist Vilfredo Pareto argued that a society's welfare cannot be improved by a redistribution of income from the rich to the poor. The only way society can be considered better off is if one member gets more income (by stumbling on an oil well, for example) without taking anything away from the other members. This theory is known as the **Pareto principle** (see Figure 4.1).

Suppose our society is composed of two individuals, A and B. A commands twice as many resources as does B. If as a result of a new public project A makes an extra $10 and B makes nothing, we move along the vertical axis from the point of initial distribution between the two members. If the reverse takes place and B makes money while A makes nothing, we proceed along the horizontal axis from the initial position. Extending rules to mark A's and B's respective positions in the two scenarios, we call the shaded space bounded by these lines **Pareto superior,** the region where either A or B or both gain and neither loses. If a project takes us

Figure 4.1   The Pareto Principle

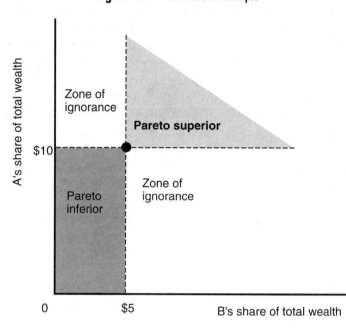

in this zone, we should immediately recognize it as desirable. In contrast, if a project causes either individual to lose with no one gaining, we should readily discard the project, because it will take us to a **Pareto inferior** position. Public projects that benefit one group at the expense of another fall in the **zone of ignorance** and cannot be justified in the name of aggregate social welfare. The implications of the Pareto principle are extremely conservative. First, it passes no judgment on the initial distribution of wealth, regardless of how unfair that distribution may be. Second, because it is almost inconceivable that a public policy would have no redistributive component, the Pareto principle is incompatible with any sort of government activism. According to Pareto, we would quickly reject any spending on public goods—national defense, health care, access to free education, or environmental protection—because they would have to be financed by tax revenue, the burden of which would fall mostly on the rich and the middle class.

The Kaldor-Hicks Compensation Principle

Two British economists, Nicholas Kaldor and John Hicks, developed a theory of policy analysis that sought to balance the needs of society and those of individuals. Kaldor and Hicks separately argued that society was better off when pursuing projects that generated sufficiently large gains for the winners, gains great enough so that the winners could compensate the losers for their losses and still remain better off.[15] Suppose a project causes A to gain $10 while costing B $7. A can pay B $7 as compensation, which leaves A with $3 of net gain. This arrangement does not violate the Pareto principle because one person's gain has taken nothing away from someone else. The question remains, how do we compensate the losers? In all democratic nations, if the losers can be clearly identified (as is the case when the government declares eminent domain to acquire land for building roads), the laws guarantee that the losers be paid adequate compensation. Yet in many cases the losses are spread over a large part of society, the losers cannot be identified, or their losses cannot be adequately measured. In such cases, Kaldor and Hicks argue that we should not worry about paying compensation. As long as we can demonstrate that the benefits outweigh the costs, we can proceed with the project with a clear conscience. Such a position ultimately rejects the Pareto principle in favor of a greater "social good" but fails to help those who have no recourse when denied adequate compensation for their losses. We can cite many examples of the most well-meaning public policies creating misery for a small group of individuals. Examples include much-needed highways that cut through the heart of a community and dams that, while producing electricity and irrigation, flood valuable land and ruin it for inhabitants.

The Rawlsian Challenge

In contrast to the Kaldor-Hicks principle, the theory of philosopher John Rawls offers different criteria for judging social welfare.[16] To deduce the fairest rule of distribution, Rawls proposes a method illustrated in the following scenario: suppose I have a pie that I am going to distribute to the class. I can cut the pie in unequal portions (with one person getting the largest share, while others literally get the crumbs), or I can divide the pie equally among the students. These portions will be distributed by a random drawing over which you have no control. Rawls calls this random drawing "the veil of ignorance." You must choose whether you want the pie to be cut equally or unequally. Rawls argues that if you follow the precept of rationality, you should opt for an equal distribution, minimizing your chances of maximum loss. Further, Rawls claims that because you cannot choose your parents, if asked how a society's wealth should be distributed, you must choose the option that protects the share of the most unfortunate group. According to the **Rawlsian criterion,** you should evaluate a distribution of income by the absolute level of well-being that it imparts to the community's least fortunate ones.

Suppose there are two communities, A and B, with the following sets of income distributions:

$$A = [\$10, \$25, \$8]$$

$$B = [\$200, \$150, \$5]$$

The figures in brackets show the wealth of the six members of the two communities. According to the Rawlsian criterion, you should prefer the distribution in A because the poorest member of A is better off than the poorest member of B. A drawback of the Rawlsian principle is that it throws its entire weight behind the well-being of the poor and disregards the welfare of others. We all know our relative positions in society, and if we are privileged members of community B, we are not likely to move to community A without serious prodding, a medicine that can be far worse than the ailment.

To return to our earlier discussion, when using the quantitative techniques discussed in this book, we must define a goal to be maximized. However, despite centuries of intensive searching, we have not yet found an adequate definition for the social welfare. Whenever we settle on one definition, we inevitably trample on individual aspirations. On the other hand, if we concern ourselves only with individual goals, we are left with anarchy. Our philosophical inadequacy and our inability to define social welfare leave a gaping hole in our understanding of project evaluation. We will return to this important problem several times in this book.

CHOOSING A METHOD OF ANALYSIS

Public policy analysts strive to link project goals (output) to investment (input). The purpose of policy analysis is threefold: to choose the methods or analytical processes that will identify a **causal link** between the dependent and independent variables, to **generalize** the results, and to establish the **control,** or the policy direction. We may illustrate this complex process by drawing an analogy from the game of pool. Suppose the object of our game is to send the eight ball to a pocket by striking the white cue ball with a cue (see Figure 4.2). Our **policy objective** is to shoot the eight ball (the **dependent variable**) into the pocket by hitting it with the cue ball (the **independent variable**). The cue ball is driven by the cue, which represents the **control variable,** or the strength of our action. To properly execute our shot, we must exert correct pressure in the right direction. If the eight ball goes in the pocket, we can claim to have a successful policy. If it does not, the policy will be considered a failure. If the eight ball hits other balls on the way and makes our position on the table extremely difficult, we call this position the **unintended consequence** of the policy. Let us assume that our goal in constructing a new stadium is to increase tax revenues for the city. Our policy objective is positive net tax revenue. The dependent variable is the revenue, which is influenced by the independent variable, the new stadium. The amount of investment toward the construction is the control variable. If the new stadium causes traffic gridlock and harms local businesses, we will regard these problems as the unintended consequences of the project.

Suppose we are concerned about the rising number of teen pregnancies in our state. We decide that our policy goal is to reduce the number by 15 percent in the next three years. If our analysis demonstrates a causal link between preventing pregnancy (the dependent variable) and disseminating information on reproduction through television advertising (the independent variable), we can estimate the amount of money (the policy, or control variable) that we will need to accomplish our goal. In this process, then, our first task is to establish the causal relationship between the dependent and independent variables through proper research design.

Figure 4.2   Methodology for Policy Analysis

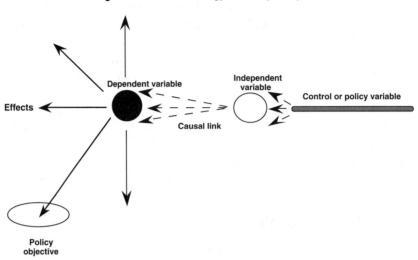

Research design, or the plan of inquiry, links the dependent variable with a set of independent variables. It can take a number of forms that vary in scientific rigor. Broadly speaking, we classify research designs under the headings "experimental" and "quasi-experimental." With **experimental designs,** we randomly assign the subjects of the inquiry across experimental groups and control stimuli, and we manipulate the independent variable as we like. Using a controlled experiment, we infer from the results about the strength of the causal link. We then generalize our inference to design appropriate policy to achieve a certain goal. In contrast, with **quasi-experimental research designs,** we do not use these criteria. The following examples will help to explain these terms.

Experimental Design

We find the classic experimental design in controlled group experiments, conducted primarily in the fields of medicine, the natural sciences, and experimental psychology. The most rigorous of all designs is the so-called Solomon Four-Group design (see Figure 4.3).[17] If we want to prove the effectiveness of a new drug, we randomly assign our subjects to two groups, A and B. We further divide each group into two more groups. We give the new drug to one subject from group A and one from group B, while others receive a placebo.

After administering the new drug, we monitor our patients' progress. If we find that the differences between the control groups $(a_1 - b_2)$ and $(b_1 - a_2)$ are significant, we can experimentally establish a causal link between the new drug and the disease.

In medical or biological experiments, researchers often exert such control over the subject population, drawing inferences and proving them with repeated experiments. New drugs come on the market, evidence mounts about various carcinogens, and clinical tests establish human behavioral patterns.

Figure 4.3   Solomon Four-Group Experimental Design

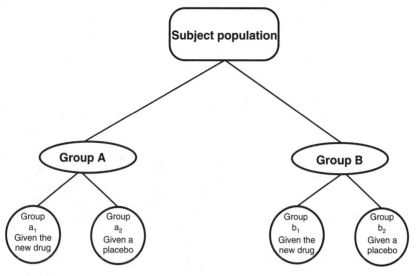

Although the Solomon Four-Group tests are the strongest in establishing a causal link between dependent and independent variables, conducting these elaborate tests can be extremely expensive, time-consuming, and, in many cases, particularly in the area of social sciences, virtually impossible. Therefore, we must frequently be satisfied with **post-test-only control group experimental design,** in which we simply observe the effects of experimental drugs on those who were exposed to them and on those who were not (see Figure 4.4).

In this less restricted research design, we randomly assign subjects to two, rather than four, groups: one exposed to the stimulus and one not. If we find the difference between the two groups to be statistically significant, we can establish the string of causality. Important to this research design is the random assignment of the subjects for the experiment. If we do not assign them in random order, we may allow systematic biases to creep into the experiment and contaminate the results. If we separate the groups by sex, for example, our results may be invalid if the division along gender lines introduces another independent variable along with the independent stimulus variable (in our example, the new drug). Unfortunately, however, even this less restricted research design is generally impossible to implement in the social sciences because it requires a laboratory setup, in which the subjects are randomly selected into two groups.

Quasi-Experimental Design

The problem with conducting research in the social sciences, of course, is that we can rarely control the real world. Experimental research designs require us to distribute subjects randomly, separate them into distinct groups, guard against time lapses that dilute the effect of the stimulus, and eliminate the influence of past

Figure 4.4 Post-test-only Control Group Design

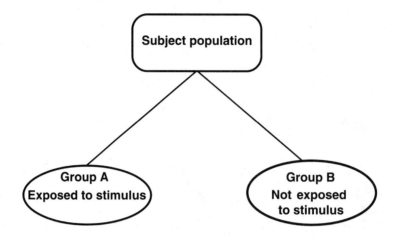

government policies. Therefore, in public policy research we must adopt quasi-experimental designs, in which we relax the rigors of experimental designs to meet the challenges of open society. These compromises create a number of problems for researchers.

If we want to use a strict scientific research design to test the hypothesis that the strength of family ties bears directly on a student's educational performance, we must be able to assign family stability to the subject group in a random fashion. But this clearly is not possible. Similarly, when the control variable is not amenable to change, we may have to make do with a comparison between groups that are not strictly similar. While trying to establish the relationship between family stability and educational achievement, we might find two groups, one with stability—perhaps measured by whether the parents are divorced or separated—and one without. As you can see, the marital status of the parents will not be the only difference between the two groups. The experiment will be affected by a variety of other intervening variables, such as the strength of the extended family, the status of religious and social community ties, and other factors.

A second problem with quasi-experimental research designs is that, in contrast to researchers in medicine, the natural sciences, and experimental psychology, those in the social sciences seldom seek to discern a stimulus-response reaction in the subject population. Instead, social scientists want primarily to understand the causal link between preexisting social or economic characteristics and revealed preferences, attitudes, values, and orientations.

Suppose we try to examine the impact of a school voucher system on a group of minority pupils. We give parents at a low-performing school the opportunity to send their children to the private school of their choice. After a year we compare the test scores of those who went to the private schools with those who remained in the public school. If we see a significant difference between the average test scores of the two groups of children, can we positively attribute the change to the voucher system? Not necessarily—at least not according to the strictest of the scientific criteria of experimental research design. We can argue that those parents who chose to send their children to private school may have introduced some self-selection bias into the experiment. That is, they may be more concerned about their children's education, and more involved in it, than are those who did not take advantage of the voucher system. Unlike medical research, social science experiments do not permit us to randomly assign students to private schools. As a result, we cannot completely rid ourselves of the effects of self-selection and other such biases.

Another important source of bias is the passage of time. The experimental design assumes an instantaneous response to a stimulus, a response that is free of time's influence. Suppose you are conducting research in microbiology and are interested in the impact of a certain chemical compound on the growth of a particular bacteria. If after applying the compound to the bacteria-coated dish you receive instantaneous feedback, you can clearly see the test results. If, on the other hand, you must observe the gradual growth of the culture over time, you will take precautions to protect the dish from exposure to the outside environment because you do not want the results to be contaminated by an external agent. However, in society no such protection from the outside elements can be provided.

This situation creates a number of intriguing problems. To continue our discussion of the voucher system, let us say that we decide to test the impact of the system on minority students by tracking those children who left the public school. If we can get data on their progress before and after the transfer, we can build a strong case for testing our hypothesis. Even under these circumstances, though, we may doubt the reliability of our data because of the possible contaminating effect of the passage of time. As children grow older, they go through many developmental stages. The critics of our experimental design may ask how much of our result may be attributed to the two school systems and how much to child development.

Take another example, national crime rates. A weary nation, jaded by sensational news stories, watched in disbelief as the crime rate declined steadily during the 1990s. President Bill Clinton claimed credit for the decrease by linking it to his recruitment of one hundred thousand new police officers. Matching his zeal, the Republicans declared that their get-tough policies caused this welcome trend. In fact, in every city or town where the rate declined, police chiefs and city fathers claimed victory for their own programs. Can we end the debate and prove through research what reduced the crime rate? Unfortunately we cannot. To be sure, some public policies were responsible but so were a number of broad social trends that had little or nothing to do with anticrime policies adopted at any level of government. This period saw unprecedented growth in the economy, with the lowest recorded level of unemployment in history. With more people working, fewer idle wrongdoers lived on the street. The nation was going through a major demographic shift. The children of baby boomers were passing through a crime-prone age group (between sixteen and twenty-five), but boomers had fewer children than their predecessors, causing the crime rate to decline nationwide.

So you see how difficult it is to establish a causal relationship in an open society. It is therefore not surprising that social scientists seldom resolve theoretical controversies, even when such disputes are part of accepted academic orthodoxy.

Then how do we discern a causal relationship between dependent and independent variables? First, we look at the strength of the correlation between the variables and, with the help of statistical tests, try to minimize the possibility of accepting a false hypothesis as true. Second, if external variables threaten to sway the results, we design the research plan carefully to remove their contaminating influence. The analyst addresses these two concerns by selecting the appropriate experimental design.

Quasi-experimental designs can take several forms: one-shot case studies, correlation analyses, cross-section analyses, or time series analyses. Analysts typically conduct **one-shot case studies** on unique events of history. Consider a state road made obsolete by recent highway construction. A close-knit small town that depended on the state route is economically devastated. If you want to study the town's plight, you may have to conduct a one-shot study. The problem with one-shot case studies is that they do not give us the advantage of a valid comparison, without which we often are unable to test our hypotheses. In these studies, the best we can do is to make sure that our arguments are logically consistent and supported by valid observations. Although one-shot studies may lack scientific rigor, they can shed important light on the problem in question.

Correlation analyses consider the degree of association between two variables. If we see that an increase or decrease in one variable is associated with an increase or decrease in another, we can hypothesize a correlation between the variables (see Table 4.2).

As you can see in the table, this hypothetical data set indicates that a correlation may exist between parents' marital status and children's academic achievement. We will discuss correlation analysis and hypothesis testing in chapter 5. Because researchers conduct correlation analyses by collecting comparable data for a number of cases, these analyses, unlike one-shot case studies, are amenable to statistical testing.

Analysts make **cross-section analyses** to compare the outcomes in a number of cases at a single point in time. We can compare the 2001 crime rates of similar-size cities and ask why variations occur from city to city. The strength of cross-section studies is that the data are not contaminated by the passage of time. Their primary weakness concerns our ability to select cases that are directly comparable with one another. If we compare the crime rate of Billings, Montana, with that of Atlanta, Georgia, the validity of our results might be questioned, because the two cities are quite different from one another. To avoid the proverbial comparison of "apples with oranges," we must take special care to eliminate the effects of external variables.

Table 4.2 Correlation Analysis: Marital Status vs. Student Achievement

	Student achievement	
Marital status	Percentage low	Percentage high
Parents divorced or separated	60	40
Parents together	30	70

Trend analyses study a single case over time. We may conduct research on the respective crime rates of Billings and Atlanta during a certain period. Much of econometric analysis involves trend, or time-series, analysis. We will discuss time-series analysis at length in chapters 10 and 11. Its strength is that it permits us to study the same case over a long period of time. The problem with time-series analysis is that time itself has an important impact on the case we are studying. If we are studying Atlanta's crime rate over the last twenty years, we may ask whether the city has changed culturally, demographically, or economically during that period. If these variables have changed over time, they may have altered Atlanta in a significant way.

CHOOSING THE RIGHT MODEL

Because we as social scientists are restricted to the quasi-experimental design to conduct our research, we must choose a model. As I explained in chapter 1, a model is an abstraction of reality, an impressionistic rendition of vast and complex behavioral relationships. What model should we use? Our fundamental problem is that we are trying to match two dissimilar worlds. We superimpose the world of quantitative techniques, based on objective, structured, scientific reasoning, on a largely unstructured, subjective world of public policy analysis. This incongruity raises two important issues: (1) A model is by definition a truncated version of reality. Can we trust it to shed light on real-world problems? (2) Models that seek to maximize social welfare assume agreement on the goal of society. How relevant are such models in a pluralistic, democratic society, in which policy goals may be diverse and multiple?

Analysts use abstract quantitative models to represent a complex reality. A model, by definition, *always* deviates from reality, and this deviation makes it suspect. As a model truncates reality by making assumptions, questions about its relevance become paramount. Because they use models extensively, often to reduce reality to unrecognizable forms, economists have been the objects of derision—and awe.[18] We should not reject a model just because it makes simple assumptions about the real world. Due to the world's complexity, we frequently need these restrictive assumptions to separate fundamental, global patterns from local, particular, or ephemeral effects. Assumptions help us define the domain where results are expected to hold. We can then expand the boundaries of this narrow domain by systematically removing some of the assumptions to make the results resemble reality more closely. Another important reason for building models is that they help us examine the internal consistency of our reasoning. If we build a model on the premise that education discourages illegal drug abuse, we can conduct statistical tests based on empirical evidence. Moreover, if we see that other variables are important in determining an individual's tendency toward drug abuse, we can take them into consideration. We can also drop a variable (for example, race or gender) if we see that it is not very useful to the explanation. Using this structured logic, models frequently explain behavior and reveal unsuspected relationships. They also eliminate the need for ad hoc reasoning and help us understand our mistakes when our predictions go awry.

Let us say that you want to forecast the number of students who might be using drugs on a college campus.[19] You base your forecast on a survey that shows how many freshman students used drugs last year and are continuing to do so. The survey also tells you how many nonusers have begun to use drugs since starting college. Guided by these findings, you assume that the ratios will persist throughout the college careers of the entering freshman class. You also suppose that no external factors will have a significant effect on the trend suggested by the ratios.

We easily find reasons to question the validity of these bold assumptions. For one thing, the study did not include entering transfer students, who may behave differently than the students surveyed. In addition, the forecast does not consider the effect of education or psychological maturity on the student population. Including these factors could alter your projections in important ways. In support of your forecasting model, you may argue that given your assumptions, you have identified the most likely trend. If you find reasons to believe that students' level of addiction goes down as they mature and become better educated, you can modify the model to allow for this change of relationship. Further, if you find at the end of four years that your projections were seriously flawed, you can go back to your original set of assumptions and try to correct the mistakes. The assumptions and structure of your model allow you to process feedback in a way that would have been impossible had you made your projections based solely on "gut feelings," intuition, or ad hoc reasoning.

DESIGNING POLICY RESEARCH

Our discussion confirms that there is no easy and elegant escape from the theoretical quagmire in which we find ourselves when we try to define social welfare. As professors Edith Stokey and Richard Zeckhauser eloquently put it,

> Philosophers and economists have tried for two centuries to devise unambiguous procedures for measuring and combining welfare of two or more individuals to provide a measure of total social welfare. Their quest has been as successful as the alchemists' attempt to transmute lead into gold. The occasional flickers of hope have all been extinguished; not only have no feasible procedures been developed, none are on the horizon.[20]

Confronted with limited insight into the question of how to define social welfare, Stokey and Zeckhauser offer pragmatic advice. They suggest that an analyst take a limited and practical view, seeking the best solution within a narrowly defined boundary instead of the one that optimizes outcomes globally, across boundaries.

Limiting the Number of Alternatives

In our stadium financing example, our alternatives are to build the arena or not to build it. Our decision to build may be complicated by the issue of location. For a project like this one, a number of sites are possible. Some may be attractive but also prohibitively expensive because of the land value. Others may offer all the desirable characteristics (adequate lot size, traffic flow, parking, and so on) but may be in an environmentally sensitive area. If you want to evaluate each possible location, you may find that the cost and time required for the study are excessive. In this case, you should eliminate those alternatives that clearly are inferior to the more feasible ones and those that obviously are not workable because of cost or other factors.

CONSIDER ONLY CHANGES IN SOCIAL WELFARE. Suppose you are analyzing a program to provide inner city youths with summer jobs. Rather than getting hopelessly entangled by the question of how to stop inner city poverty and by the larger problem of how to eliminate social injustice, you decide to evaluate the program incrementally, asking how much this program will change the youths' economic condition. In doing so, you limit the evaluation to a manageable framework by concentrating only on the marginal instead of the total change in social welfare.

USE INCOME AS A PROXY FOR WELFARE. "Money cannot buy happiness," goes the proverb, implying that the relationship between wealth and happiness (or utility) may not be a direct one. Yet in practice, we have no choice but to accept money as the measure of individual utility. In a situation in which one gains at the expense of another, we must be able to compare the gains and the losses in monetary terms. When we accept this proposition, we escape from the theoretical quicksand of utility measurement, only to land in another sort of trap—the confusion of imputing monetary values to gains and losses. Be assured, though, that our new trap is a practical problem with practical solutions rather than a theoretical problem with no solution at all.

Accepting or Rejecting a Project

To summarize, the utilitarian position does not provide us with workable criteria for analyzing public policy because we have no way of measuring interpersonal utility. The Pareto principle turns out to be equally unhelpful, because it builds barriers against government intervention. The Kaldor-Hicks proposal does not address the concerns of those who might lose as a result of a public project, while the Rawlsian criterion focuses only on the welfare of the poorest members of the community. Setting aside these unworkable theories, we suggest that you make your recommendations on the basis of the following criteria.

You should accept the project if

1. *The gains are much larger than the losses, the winners and losers are roughly equal in social stature, and the losses pose only a minor problem for the losing group.* Suppose you are evaluating a project to build an access road linking two major thoroughfares. The majority of inhabitants will benefit from the road; however, a small group of people living near the project is complaining

about increased traffic with all its accompanying problems. The commissioned environmental impact report detects no significant loss to the environment or to the community. In such a case, you may recommend the project over the objections of the adversely affected group on the basis of this first criterion.

2. *The benefits to society greatly exceed the cost to a specific group, or the cost of inaction is enormous.* The government's power of **eminent domain** entitles it to purchase, confiscate, or expropriate private properties for the greater public good as long as it provides property owners with adequate compensation. In the United States we usually associate eminent domain with the government's takeover of private lands to build highways. Other countries use similar powers to confiscate property or nationalize businesses. In any case, countries justify such actions by citing the overwhelming needs of society compared with the costs to a specific person or a small group.[21]

3. *The benefits of a proposed policy to the winners are greater than the costs to the losers, and the gains equalize some losses resulting from past discriminatory policies.* Many affirmative action plans and other projects to remedy racial inequality, such as forced school desegregation and busing, would fall in this category. In addition, if a group, community, or state has received special benefits in the past, as did California during the 1980s, when the state profited from increased defense expenditures, we may make a case for bypassing it when the time comes to allocate a second round of benefits. We also may argue for equalizing the beneficial effects of public investment and diverting the second-round benefits to communities that did not receive money the first time.

In contrast, a proposed project should be rejected if

1. *The net benefit is positive but the cost imposed on a specific group is significant.* Many of our laws enforcing the Endangered Species Act of 1973 are based squarely on this principle. Although a project may produce great benefits for the community, if it also may cause irreparable damage to a threatened species, the project will be rejected (see box).

2. *The effect of redistribution is highly desirable but the project does not pass the test of positive net social benefit.* We frequently encounter cases in which the cause is noble but the costs do not justify action. It is desirable to provide the most comprehensive health care to everybody in the country regardless of income, age, or level of care needed. Yet the costs of doing so are prohibitive. The high cost of health care has forced government agencies to come up with plans that prioritize health care needs.

These criteria are by no means perfect. However, given the practical needs of public agencies, the guidelines are probably the best we can come up with. When we support our analysis with generally accepted guidelines of fairness, we make our analysis more efficient and more acceptable to the vast majority of people.

A CASE IN POINT

Do You Give a Dam? The Fate of the Snail Darter

One of the most celebrated controversies in the battle to protect endangered species involved the snail darter, a three-inch-long member of the perch family. The rare fish's habitat was threatened in the mid-1970s by the construction of Tellico Dam on the Little Tennessee River.[1] After four years of construction, local landowners filed a lawsuit charging that the dam violated the Endangered Species Act (ESA), bringing the $100 million project to a halt.

This event divided the country. The United States was in a recession caused largely by a nagging energy crisis, and most studies showed that the benefits of the project exceeded the costs. The Tennessee Valley Authority (TVA) estimated the net benefits from the project to be around $11.51 million (approximately $33.5 million in 2000 constant dollars). Although the estimated net benefits later were revised to $3.66 million (about $10.65 million in 2000 dollars), the project's support among southern legislators was overwhelming.[2] Responding to their demands, Congress tried to bypass the ESA by exempting the Tellico project from the law. A highly reluctant president Jimmy Carter, aspiring to leave a legacy as an environmentalist, signed the exemption measure in 1979. The day after the president's action, the TVA's bulldozers started rolling. The project was quickly completed, destroying the snail darter's habitat.

Nearly a decade later, long after the dust had settled on the banks of the Little Tennessee River, policy analysts proved that the controversy had revolved around a dam that should not have been built and a species that did not require protection. They found the projected benefits to be even smaller than TVA's revised estimates. The project continued to run at a loss even before environmental impacts were factored into the calculation.[3] The fish thrived in the un-dammed parts of the river. On August 6, 1984, the Fish and Wildlife Service downgraded the status of the snail darter from "endangered" to "threatened."

Notes

1. Mark Van Putten and R. J. Smith, "At Issue: Has the Endangered Species Act Been a Success?" *The CQ Researcher,* September 15, 2000, 735.
2. Robert K. Davis, "Lessons in Politics and Economics from the Snail Darter," in *Environmental Resources and Applied Welfare Economics: Essays in Honor of John V. Krutilla,* ed. V. Kerry Smith (Washington, D.C.: Resources for the Future, 1988), 211–236.
3. John V. Krutilla and Anthony C. Fisher, *The Economics of Natural Environments: Studies in the Valuation of Commodity and Amenity Resources,* rev. ed. (Washington, D.C.: Resources for the Future, 1985).

Discussion Points

1. How was the project stopped and how was it revived? What criteria did policy makers on both sides of the argument use to evaluate the dam?
2. What lessons can we draw from this case study about the problems of critical thinking?

Ensuring the Process Is Fair

We will now explore issues of justice and fair play from the standpoint of procedural justice. The goal of procedural justice is not to alter the final outcome to achieve fairness but to ensure that the process by which resources are allocated is fair. We can promote the notion of fairness by using quantitative techniques to expose hidden assumptions and values.[22]

Lotteries are unfair because one ticket wins most of the money, while small amounts go to other winners. For the majority of players, the lottery yields nothing. Why do we not complain about the gross inequality? We do not protest because we know that the process of choosing the winner is fair. That is, we accept the final outcome because we believe that each person buying a ticket has an equal shot at winning the prize money. We know the process by which a winner is determined (because the drawings are often televised), and when purchasing the ticket we agree to play by the rules of the lottery. If these conditions were violated, we would be extremely dissatisfied with the outcome. When people go over the speed limit and get a ticket, they seldom complain about the ticket itself, focusing instead on the amount of the fine or the way they were treated by the police or the court system.

Political scientist Robert Lane points out that procedural justice has four important components. It must include dignity, relief from procedural pain, a uniform standard of justice, and justice itself.[23] The process must recognize, protect, and preserve the self-esteem of every individual. If you are stripped of your dignity, even the most equal distribution of wealth will seem oppressive, arbitrary, and capricious. Every individual should be assured swift disbursement of justice. If the process is cumbersome and time-consuming, justice cannot be served. The process also must guarantee resonance between the standards of justice followed by the judge and those recognized by the judged. If you are judged by a standard that is completely alien to you, you cannot accept the verdict as just. Finally, procedural justice must include some minimum guarantee of economic well-being.

MAKING QUICK DECISIONS

Throughout this book, we will discuss several important quantitative techniques for policy analysis. These techniques frequently require that we invest a great deal of time and money. It is, of course, a matter of common sense that we do not use elaborate analysis for everyday decisions but save it for the "important" ones. In practice, however, we rarely follow this conventional wisdom. We frequently base important decisions on quick analyses. Some of the most important economic decisions we make concern our choice of employment or the purchase of a home. We should make them with a great deal of care and cool calculation. Yet think of how often we make such significant decisions using intuition alone. In choosing between two homes, we may consider purchase prices, maintenance and commuting costs, and the prospect of future price increases, only to scuttle this information for something that appeals to us at an intuitive level—the "feel" of a neighborhood or a friendly neighbor next door. The memoirs of important politicians are full of examples of how they went against the best analytical advice on some of the most momentous decisions, basing these decisions on intuition alone.

In an important study Robert Behn and James Vaupel considered this aspect of decision making.[24] If you do not have the time or data necessary to conduct what they call a "researched analysis," you are apt to make decisions based on "rules of thumb," such as the mini-max strategy of minimizing the option with the least regret (or the least amount of potential loss). Behn and Vaupel suggest five steps for making quick decisions:

1. Think
2. Decompose
3. Simplify
4. Specify
5. Rethink

THINK.   In this stage of the process we frame the problem. We look squarely at the heart of a complex, multidimensional policy dilemma. To reduce a large problem to a manageable form, we often must use simple numbers—numbers that can convey the essence of a problem.

DECOMPOSE.   The essence of our analysis is decomposition: seeing the problem as a collection of various elements. If we can see a problem in its various parts, some complementary and some inconsistent, we have made significant progress. Bewildered students often cannot decide how to start their research projects. I ask them to write down the title of the paper. Once they have taken this step, I suggest that they prepare a detailed table of contents. Naming the project compels them to reduce the issue to its bare minimum. Preparing the table of contents forces them to decompose the problem.

SIMPLIFY.   With limited time, we must eliminate all but the most important components of the problem. By doing so we run less risk of exceeding our intellectual abilities or using intuition to make a decision.

SPECIFY.   Decision making is intuitive. No matter how convincing our analysis is, ultimately we must make a subjective judgment. We improve our subjective judgment when we make our problem statement specific. Try to be specific in your description of the process you are analyzing. Decision tree analysis may help you (see chapter 13). Specify the bare minimum branches of action (which Behn and Vaupel call "saplings") and a "do-nothing" option. A decision tree will force you to state what you mean when you use terms like "uncertainty," "risky," and "iffy." Describe your subjective assessment of the situation in numbers. If you think that your favorite team is going to win, quantify your prediction. After all, both 55 percent and 95 percent chances of winning can be described as "a great probability." By assigning a number you are specifying your level of confidence, which can then be compared with another person's assessment of the situation.

RETHINK.   Using the first four steps in the quick decision rule, you have arrived at a solution. Should you stick to it? Perhaps not. If you have time, rethink! Because all analysis ultimately is incomplete and is dependent on subjective judgments, you should take the opportunity to rethink your position if you have the time.

CHALLENGES TO CRITICAL THINKING: BIASES IN REASONING

Critical thinking requires that we conduct dispassionate, objective analyses of real life problems with uncertain outcomes. Yet our biases and preconceived notions prevent us from being completely objective in our analysis. To help us guard against biased results, we must know the most common pitfalls of critical thinking. Research in sociopsychology has shown that people rely on a few principles to simplify the complex task of assigning probability. Although these principles are useful in appraising an uncertain situation, they sometimes lead to systematic biases that cause severe errors in judgment.

These principles, which Amos Tversky and Daniel Kahneman call "heuristics," permit us to predict the probability of rain by looking at the sky or to judge distance by looking at the size of an object.[25] Because we associate dark clouds with a high probability of rain, we may overestimate the likelihood of showers during the fading daylight hours. Similarly, we gauge distances with the naked eye, knowing that nearby objects are larger and clearer. As a result, we often misjudge distances of very large objects, such as a mountain peak. Tversky and Kahneman reduced these heuristic principles for analytical thinking into three broad categories: **representativeness, availability,** and **adjustment and anchoring.** When asked to make a judgment about an object or event, we make decisions on the basis of representativeness, or how closely this object or event resembles others in our experience. We also make subjective judgments based on the availability of information. Finally, when our predictions differ from reality, we use new information to adjust and anchor our appraisal of the future.

Representativeness

At the root of all scientific discovery is association. If we draw a connection between the coat of a woolly caterpillar and the coming winter, or between a groundhog's shadow and the imminence of spring, we have in effect predicted the arrival of the seasons. Such associations have led scientists to make discoveries by causally linking events. At the same time, reasoning by association also has produced old folk tales and prejudices. When we cringe at the sight of rowdy youths in a subway but look favorably on individuals wearing business suits, we are making a judgment based on representativeness. Because we often base our associations on long-term observations, our predictions often turn out to be correct. However, unless we are careful, blind adherence to association can lead us to biased policy decisions.

1. *Guard against biases of irrelevant information.* Biases may result from our insensitivity to the probability of outcomes. In a psychological experiment

subjects were told that a group contained 70 percent farmers and 30 percent lawyers.[26] If we choose an individual at random from this group, the probability that we will select a farmer is 0.7. The subjects in this experiment used this prior probability to compute the odds of getting a farmer or a lawyer in a random pick. Subjects were given worthless information on a person from the group, such as

Dick is a thirty-year-old man. He is married with no children. A man of high ability and high motivation, he promises to be quite successful in his field. He is well liked by his colleagues.

After reading this passage, subjects were asked to estimate the probability that Dick is a farmer. Because the passage contains no information about Dick's profession, subjects should have stuck to the overall probability of 70 percent, the proportion of farmers in the group. Yet they ignored the prior probability and assigned a 50 percent likelihood of Dick's being from either group. In life we often are misled when confronted with useless information, which can trigger judgments based on representativeness. Despite conflicting prior information, we decide to ignore it.

2. *Pay attention to the sample size.* The second set of problems may arise from our insensitivity to sample size. Suppose I ask you the following question:

In your city you can have your baby delivered at one of two hospitals, one large and one small. The probability that you will have a boy is 50 percent, and the chance that you will have a girl is also 50 percent. If each hospital records the days in a year when the percentage of boy babies exceeds 60 percent of its births, which hospital can expect to have counted more such days at the end of the year?

You would be incorrect to choose the large hospital or to assume that both hospitals would have an equal number of days with 60 percent or more boy babies. This is because, as we will see later in the book, as the number of tries increases, the samples become less likely to stray from the average probability figure. Therefore, large hospitals, with more births, are less likely than small hospitals to record days with more than 60 percent boy births. If you made the wrong choice, take heart in the fact that many people make decisions based on faulty statistical reasoning—including the people whose profession is to teach statistics.

3. *Remember that chances do not self-correct—they merely dilute.* Suppose you are losing a game of cards. Do you tell yourself that because you have had a string of bad luck, your luck is due for a change? If so, you are making an erroneous inference about an independent probability distribution. As you may recall from our discussion of the independence of probability, if you receive four heads in a row in a coin toss, your chances of getting a tail do

not go up on the fifth try. Thinking that chances self-correct is a common mistake. But the anomalies of chances are not corrected over many tries; they are merely diluted. This idea is especially true for small samples. Remember that the smaller the sample, the less representative it will be of the larger population. Therefore, we place less faith in results based on small samples than in those drawn from large ones.

4. *If you do not have the relevant information, do not predict.* Suppose your department wants to complete a project in a tight time frame. You have been asked to recommend one out of numerous applications from a group of vendors. Because the vendors were not aware of the time constraint when they applied for the contract, their applications do not mention their ability to deliver on time. Instead, the applications contain the usual information: lists of projects the vendors have been involved in, the qualifications of the project team, and, of course, budget estimates.

What would you do in this situation? You might look into vendors' relative experience and qualifications and predict their ability to meet the accelerated deadline. If you did, you would be committing the error of judgment that Kahneman and Tversky[27] call the error of insensitivity to predictability. Because the available information tells you practically nothing about the vendors' ability to complete the job in a hurry, and because this ability depends on their present workload and capacity to devote key personnel to the project, you would need more information to make your selection. Without this information, you would be better off making no prediction at all.

5. *Beware of picking the "right" evidence.* The heuristics of representativeness require that we match an unfamiliar, observed event with a familiar one whose outcomes are known to us. Because an event has a number of characteristics, you must choose the most significant ones in determining this representativeness. Chances are good that you will choose evidence to suit your preconceived biases. This likelihood raises tough issues, especially if it involves your deeply held values and biases.[28]

6. *Do not ignore the regression toward the mean.* Suppose you are an avid but average golfer and you know your handicap. This morning you drive the ball well from the tee, and you nearly get a hole in one. However, you bogy the next hole, failing to put the ball in the cup from a close distance. You are disappointed, and you have every reason to be. But statistically speaking, you should not despair, because your performance shows simply that you cannot beat the mean. In other words, you are merely playing your average game. If you make one exceptional shot after another, then you are playing at a level much higher than your natural average. English scientist Sir Francis Galton noted more than one hundred years ago that outcomes tend to gravitate to the mean. He called this tendency the regression toward the mean.

Ignoring the regression toward the mean is another important source of error in subjective judgment. If you can find a long history of past performance, you will be much better off basing your prediction on the mean of that performance than on an optimistic or pessimistic extreme that reflects minor variations in external conditions.

7. *Consider the Allais paradox.* The precepts of objective reasoning state that when faced with an uncertain outcome, you should choose the option that maximizes your *expected returns.* We define expected return as the probability of winning multiplied by its reward. If I offer you $10 for calling a coin toss correctly, your expected return is $0.5 \times \$10 = \$5$. When facing two options, either the possibility of winning $10 in a coin toss or that of gaining $25 by rolling a die, you should stick with the coin, because the expected return of tossing the coin ($5) is greater than that of rolling the die ($1/6 \times \$25 = \$4.17$). Unless you are a real gambler (a risk lover), the laws of probability dictate that despite the chance of a larger reward with the die, you should choose the coin. In real life most of us fail to follow this principle, which is known as the Allais paradox, named after French mathematician Maurice Allais.[29]

Suppose you have been offered two options. The first option gives you a 100 percent chance (certainty) of winning $1 million; the second option gives you a 50 percent chance of winning $5 million. In experiments most people choose the first option in violation of the rules of expected returns ($1.0 \times \$1$ million $= \$1$ million, which is less than $0.5 \times \$5$ million $= \$2.5$ million). Why do people ignore the laws of probability? When we expect an outcome to occur with certainty or near certainty, we tend to focus less on the probability factor than we do when anticipating an uncertain result.

Consider two other options. In the first option you have a one in ten thousand chance of winning $1 million, and in the second, your chance of winning $20 million is one in a million. Which option do you choose? Most people choose the chance to win $20 million, despite the fact that expected returns are higher for the $1 million option. Again, contrary to the principles of statistical reasoning, when probabilities are small (one in ten thousand versus one in a million), people tend to focus more on the reward than on the odds of winning. Allais unearthed some important biases in human reasoning that often prove critical in the decision making of a public organization.

Availability of Information

We often estimate the probability of an event by observing the frequency of similar events. If your city is considering whether to build its own garbage recycling plant, you can appraise the probability that the plant will succeed by examining the available information on similar ventures. Tversky and Kahneman call this decision-making device *availability.* They assert that information on similar events yields valuable clues about future possibility. This information points toward a more certain outcome when similar examples are numerous than when they are scarce. As we gather information, the following biases may cloud our judgment: relative **retrievability, effectiveness of a search, biases of imaginability,** and **illusory correlation.**

BIASES OF RELATIVE RETRIEVABILITY.   Our memory works like a filing cabinet. If we know where to search, we can retrieve a stored item quickly. However, if we file it in the wrong place, we cannot retrieve it easily, even information that is quite important. One way to keep track of information is to associate an event with some recognizable pattern or some other event. We then retrieve the information we need by recalling this other pattern or event. For example, most people who were alive the day President John F. Kennedy was killed remember the day vividly. We may not recall something important that happened in the past three weeks, but we remember many details about an important national event that took place more than three decades ago. When we recall memorable events or those associated with other facts that made a strong impression on us, we are susceptible to biases in judgment. These biases may lead to biases of availability, causing us to give relatively unimportant factors more weight than they deserve. Our awareness of life-threatening diseases may be only cursory until we hear that a celebrity has a particular malady, or until we learn about the illness of a friend or relative. Then our awareness of that disease goes up, prompting fear and, often, hysteria. We may focus on the probability of getting that particular disease more than is warranted by our personal habits, lifestyle, or genetic history. We also may disregard another source of illness, one more plausible than that suggested by the condition of the celebrity or friend.

EFFECTIVENESS OF SEARCH.   Have you ever conducted a computer search for information through a library information retrieval system? Suppose you are looking for information on a certain subject (say, drug abuse in North Carolina). If you define your key words properly for this search, you will be rewarded with information on a number of highly relevant publications. However, if your choice of key words is too wide (simply "drugs"), you will be inundated with irrelevant information. On the other hand, if you define your key words too narrowly, you may miss a large number of important works on the subject. In our minds we use key words to retrieve information effectively. Our effectiveness depends very much on our ability to define the parameters of our search.

BIASES OF IMAGINABILITY.   If you are considering a risky venture, you would start your assessment by first listing both the difficulties and the advantages of the project. You would consider a full slate of possibilities before taking any action. Your options are limited only by your imagination. If you have difficulty estimating the relative risks and payoffs of a project, you may leave yourself open to biases. These sorts of biases seem to be most prevalent when a decision must be made about extraordinary events (such as when a disaster preparedness program must respond to catastrophic and unpredictable events like floods, tornadoes, earthquakes, or large-scale riots).

ILLUSORY CORRELATION AND ORGANIZATIONAL MYTHS.   People often make decisions based on long-held beliefs born out of illusory, or faulty, correlation. For example, do you believe that you have a "lucky" article of clothing that helps you during an uncertain situation? If so, you may be guilty of illusory correlation, which is described in Latin as *post hoc, ergo propter hoc,* or "after this, therefore because of this." In other words, you are taking past co-occurrences as signs of correlation. If you conclude that your decisive victory in a tennis match was due to the shirt you were wearing, then you are guilty of finding a causal link between the two events (wearing the shirt and winning the match) when, in fact, there is no connection.

The errors in judgment caused by illusory correlation are often deep rooted and cannot be easily corrected. We create myths based on such errors, myths that affect not only our individual decisions but also the decisions we make at the organizational level. We find in some of the taped conversations between President Richard Nixon and his aides during the Watergate crisis classic examples of organizational decisions made on the basis of a paranoid worldview. Time and again, Nixon and his staff made decisions rooted in a fortress mentality, ultimately contributing to the demise of his administration. In any organization the vision of the decision maker can be clouded by myths of illusory correlation created by a single key staff member or by collective myths produced by a number of people in an organization.

Biases of Adjustment and Anchoring

In estimating the uncertain outcome of a project, we are frequently influenced by the first estimate. In sociopsychology this tendency is known as anchoring. You can witness anchoring on a popular television game show, when a group of contestants is asked to judge the price of an item. You will notice that the first contestant's answer seems to have a great deal of influence on the answers of the rest of the contestants. Contestants appear to be calibrating their own answers by the previous answers. In real life we often arrive at a quantitative judgment by working from an initial number. This tendency can cause serious errors in assessing an event's probability.

In this section I have tried to show some of the major sources of cognitive bias that can produce errors in critical thinking. The list of sources is long but by no means exhaustive. Thanks to the prolific work of social psychologists, we are learning more about these natural biases. The most important conclusion that we can draw from this discussion is that these distortions of judgment are not necessarily caused by self-serving motivations such as wishful thinking, desire for reward, or fear of punishment. Instead, they are rooted in our thinking and the ways we process information. Proper knowledge of our cognitive biases may alert us to the pitfalls of objective analyses.

A FEW PARTING SUGGESTIONS

Quantitative models and numerical analyses are simply tools, aids to your natural analytical capabilities. Like all other tools, by themselves they are neither good nor bad—their ultimate value to you, your organization, and society at large depends on the way you use them. Along with knowing what you know, it is imperative to know what you do not know. Analysts should identify their zone of ignorance. By using an objective analysis, you can proceed up to a certain point, beyond which you must make judgments using personal, political, or social values. Quantitative techniques will take you to this point. To go further, you must seek help beyond the scope of these techniques. You must enter the arena of the decision makers and goal setters.

Another important contribution of quantitative techniques is that they force us to disclose our biases, hidden values, prejudices, and presuppositions. The light of quantification significantly illuminates the dark, hidden crevasses of subjective analysis. When we fully specify a problem in numerical terms, we can agree or disagree about the nature of the problem on level ground, without hyperbolic rhetoric masking our value judgments. When a policy based on an objective analysis fails, we can learn from its failure and recalibrate the policy by listening and responding to feedback.

As we have seen, the usefulness of objective techniques goes far beyond their substantive contribution to policy analysis. They also affect procedural justice in a public policy debate. Objective analysis not only provides policy makers with clearly defined evidence and a set of corresponding arguments but also gives them an intellectual framework for open discussion. Even when we find its conclusions unacceptable or infeasible, objective analysis shapes the structure, language, and issues of a policy debate.[30] The debate, focused on the ways of reaching the conclusion rather than on the conclusion itself, sets the stage for a broader understanding and an acceptance of the policy process. Once a policy has been adopted, its success depends on its economic viability, administrative feasibility, and, above all, political acceptability, as filtered through the legitimacy of the policy makers.

Key Words

Adjustment and anchoring (p. 92)
Availability (p. 92)
Biases of imaginability (p. 96)
Causal link (p. 79)
Control (p. 79)
Control variable (p. 79)
Correlation analyses (p. 84)
Cross-section analyses (p. 84)
Dependent variable (p. 79)
Effectiveness of a search (p. 96)
Eminent domain (p. 88)
Experimental research designs (p. 80)
Generalize (p. 79)
Illusory correlation (p. 96)
Independent variable (p. 79)
Objective professionalism (p. 71)
One-shot case studies (p. 84)
Pareto inferior (p. 77)

Pareto principle (p. 76)
Pareto superior (p. 76)
Policy objective (p. 79)
Post-test-only control group
   experimental design (p. 81)
Quasi-experimental research designs
   (p. 80)
Rawlsian criterion (p. 78)
Representativeness (p. 92)
Retrievability (p. 96)
Risk averter (p. 74)
Risk taker (p. 74)
Social objective (p. 76)
Trend analyses (p. 85)
Unintended consequence (p. 79)
Utilitarians (p. 76)
Zone of ignorance (p. 77)

Exercises

1. Your city is considering upgrading its sewage treatment plant, and you have been hired to make a recommendation. Think critically and discuss how you would approach the problem.
2. Write an essay on the pitfalls of objective analysis. How can you reduce their effect on your reasoning?
3. Suppose your local government is proposing the construction of a halfway house for nonviolent juvenile offenders in a city neighborhood. You have been hired to evaluate the project. Explain how you would begin your job and what problems you would face in arriving at an objective conclusion.

Notes

1. Christopher Clough, "Stadium Financing Is Usually a Public-Private Mix," *Green Bay News-Chronicle,* September 26, 2000.
2. Mandy Rafool, *Playing the Stadium Game: Financing Professional Sports Facilities in the 1990s* (Denver: National Conference of State Legislatures, 1997).
3. Dean V. Baim, *The Sports Stadium As a Municipal Investment* (Westport, Conn.: Greenwood Press, 1994). See also Joanna Cagan and Neil deMause, *Field of Schemes: How the Great Stadium Swindle Turns Public Money into Private Profit* (Monroe, Maine: Common Courage Press, 1998).
4. Anthony Flew lists the fundamental aspects of thinking as "find the motives. Watch your words. Look ahead. Figure it out. Look for causes. Don't be snowed. Be precise. Watch for sham. Sort facts from bunk. Reason with those who can reason. Don't set a plan in concrete. Take care without paranoia. Assert, deny, propose, refute." See Anthony Flew, *How to Think Straight: An Introduction to Critical Reasoning* (New York: Prometheus Books, 1998).
5. Karl R. Popper, *The Poverty of Historicism* (Boston: Beacon Press, 1960).
6. See, for example, Robert A. Baade and Richard F. Dye, "An Analysis of the Economic Rationale for Public Subsidization of Sports Stadiums," *The Annals of Regional Sciences* 22 (1988): 37–47.
7. Mya M. Borger, "Having a Ball: Sunday's AFC Championship Game a Financial Jagernaut for Team, City," *The Business Journal,* Jacksonville, Fla., January 24, 2000.
8. Baim, *Sports Stadium,* 5.
9. "Danger of Coliseum Going Broke Seen," *Los Angeles Times,* December 17, 1982, A2.
10. Arthur Johnson, "Municipal Administration and the Sports Franchise Relocation," *Public Administration Review* 6 (1983): 519–529.
11. We will discuss the problems of valuation later in the book. At this point, we will keep in mind that we are always assigning monetary values to intangible items, such as a human life, a person's reputation, and the pain and suffering claimed by a plaintiff in legal proceedings.
12. Phillip J. LaVelle, "Proposition C Is about a Lot More Than a Ballpark," *San Diego Union-Tribune,* October 20, 1998. Needless to say, this figure of $1.8 million in net benefits was used liberally by supporters of the project. The proposition passed by a wide margin, and by September 2000 the half-completed project already had run into financial problems.

13. In 1957 Norris Poulson, the mayor of Los Angeles, chided the opponents of his plan to bring the Brooklyn Dodgers to the city. He charged that they wanted to keep the city in the "bush league." See "LA Council Votes Dodgers Deal, 11-3," *Los Angeles Times,* September 17, 1957 (quoted in Baim, *Sports Stadium,* 5).

14. George H. Sabine, *A History of Political Theory,* 3d ed. (New York: Holt, Rinehart and Winston, 1961), 588–589.

15. Nicholas Kaldor, "Welfare Propositions of Economics and Interpersonal Comparison of Utility," *Economic Journal* 39, no. 195 (September 1939): 549–552. See also John R. Hicks, "The Foundations of Welfare Economics," *Economic Journal* 49, no. 6 (December 1939): 696–712.

16. John Rawls, *A Theory of Justice* (Cambridge: Harvard University Press, 1971).

17. For a detailed discussion of research design, see David Nachmias and Chava Nachmias, *Research Methods in the Social Sciences* (New York: St. Martin's Press, 1976). See also Carl V. Patton and David S. Sawicki, *Basic Methods of Policy Analysis & Planning* (Englewood Cliffs, N.J.: Prentice Hall, 1986).

18. You may have heard the story of an economist who is stranded with a group on a desolate island, with only a can of beans. The economist suggests, "Let us assume a can opener."

19. For information on how to use quantitative methods for this kind of forecasting, see the discussion of Markov's Chain in chapter 12.

20. Edith Stokey and Richard Zeckhauser, *A Primer for Policy Analysis* (New York: W. W. Norton, 1978), 276.

21. For a discussion of eminent domain, see Ralph C. Chandler and Jack Plano, *The Public Administration Dictionary,* 2d ed. (Santa Barbara, Calif.: ABC-CLIO, 1988), 62–63.

22. For a classic exposition of essentially the same arguments, see Allen Schick, "System Politics and Systems Budgeting," *Public Administration Review* 29 (March–April 1969): 139–150. The flip side of these views is that an agency might use quantitative techniques either to rationalize its preordained decisions or to conduct a public relations campaign to placate critics and ward off outside interference. A later study by Harvey Sapolsky claimed that, contrary to the highly touted success stories, PERT network analysis had nothing to do with the progress and problems of the navy's Polaris project. See Harvey Sapolsky, *The Polaris System Development: Bureaucratic and Pragmatic Success in Government* (Cambridge: Harvard University Press, 1972).

23. Robert Lane, "Procedural Justice: How One is Treated vs. What One Gets" (paper presented at the annual meeting of the International Society of Political Psychology, Amsterdam, 1986).

24. See Robert D. Behn and James W. Vaupel, *Quick Analysis for Busy Decision Makers* (New York: Basic Books, 1982).

25. Amos Tversky and Daniel Kahneman, *Science* 185 (September 1974): 1124–1131. Derived from the Greek word *heuriskein*—to find out—"heuristics" is defined by *The New Webster's Dictionary* as "teaching principles which allow students to make their own discoveries."

26. Ibid.

27. Ibid.

28. I would like to illustrate my point about self-selection bias by telling a story about two friends. One friend held an unshakable faith in astrology, while the other did not. All their lives they argued about the validity of astrology. One day, the believer

in astrology learned that he would have to make a long trip across the state by car. Having consulted all the relevant astrological signs, he chose the most auspicious day to start his journey, only to run into a serious accident within half a mile of his home. The poor man was taken to a nearby hospital, where his nonbelieving friend went to greet him with his best-rehearsed arguments against putting faith in such superstitious nonsense. Before the visitor could say anything, the injured man looked up from his hospital bed and asked, "You believe in astrology now, don't you? Can anybody survive such an accident without guidance from the stars? I am lucky to have consulted my chart before I started my trip. What do you think of astrology now?"

29. Maurice Allais, "Fondoments d'une théorie de choix comportant un risqueet critique des pustulates et axiomes de l'eloce Americane" ("The Foundations of a Positive Theory of Choice Involving Risk and a Criticism of the Postulates and the Axioms of the American School"), in *Expected Utility Hypothesis and the Allais Paradox: Contemporary Discussions of Decisions under Uncertainty with Allais' Rejoinder,* ed. Maurice Allais and Ole Hagen (Dordrecht, Holland: D. Reidel, 1952).

30. Giandomenico Majone, *Evidence, Argument and Persuasion in the Policy Process* (New Haven: Yale University Press, 1989). See also E. S. Quade, *Analysis for Public Decisions,* 3d ed. (New York: North-Holland, 1989).

CHAPTER

5

BASIC STATISTICS

NUMBERS AS STORYTELLERS

The footprints of history are preserved in recorded information. Properly collected and analyzed numbers can shed a great deal of light on the past. We know that we can numerically extend data collected from autopsies of Egyptian mummies to the general population of the time. But numbers can even reveal seemingly non-numerical aspects of human lives, such as feelings. For example, the authors Jeffrey Stonecash and Mack Mariani claim that income class has increasingly polarized American politics.[1] As evidence, they presented the data that I have plotted in Figure 5.1.

As shown in this graph, the lowest third of the white income group has increasingly identified with the Democratic Party, whereas the top third has been leaving that party. According to the authors, this growing gap in party identification demonstrates a picture of class polarization. Now, based on this scenario, you can develop many different stories about the current political condition in the United States and can draw conclusions about its future.

THE BUILDING BLOCKS OF QUANTITATIVE ANALYSIS

The present age is aptly called the Information Age. Every day sees a phenomenal amount of information collected. However, dealing with a large amount of statistical information poses a problem: The story behind the numbers is often hidden.

Figure 5.1 Affiliation to Democratic Party by Income Groups Among Whites, 1980–1996

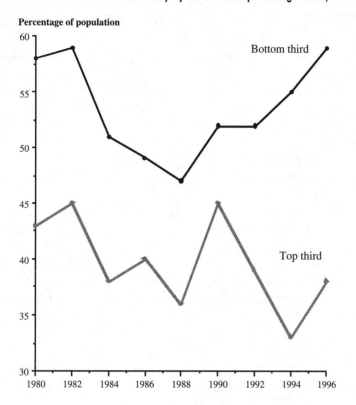

The task of quantitative analysis is to make sense out of this torrent of information. To do so the analyst or researcher discards the unnecessary information and arranges and rearranges the rest to create something new—a logically coherent set of arguments.

METHODS OF DESCRIPTIVE STATISTICS

There are many ways of looking at the world of information. We may look at the world as **ex post facto** and **ex ante facto**—that is, what has already taken place (ex post) and what will take place (ex ante). The basic tools for analyzing ex post data are the **measures of central tendency** and **dispersion;** and the tool for analyzing ex ante data is probability theory. Certainty is what has already taken place; uncertainty is what may follow.

Analysis of data expressed in numbers starts with the measures of central tendency and dispersion. Together these two are called descriptive statistics. The term "descriptive" obviously implies description—yet, from description one starts analysis; from the understanding of the past one looks for clues to forecast the future. Therefore, in this chapter we will start with the methods of descriptive statistics and correlation, and then in the following chapter we will introduce the theories of probability.

Measures of Central Tendency

The aim of descriptive statistics is to describe a situation or assess the prevailing condition with numbers. In our daily communications we can describe a situation verbally without the use of numbers. Anthropologists tell of primitive tribes whose abilities to express quantities with numbers are limited.[2] However, the power of description increases with the proper quantification of the situation. Thus, one may describe the day's temperature as "unusually hot," or one can express the temperature in measures of Fahrenheit or Celsius. The use of a recognizable index for measuring temperature immediately facilitates its understanding at the absolute level ("it is really hot today") as well as its comparative evaluation ("the highest recorded temperature in twenty years" or "it was hotter here today than it was in Phoenix").

A series of numbers do not readily convey a coherent picture. The purpose of descriptive statistics is to look for the number around which a series has a tendency to cluster, so that it can be seen as the representative of that series. The tendency of a numerical series to cluster around a number is called the "central tendency." By this measure, we offer the number that best represents the series. For example, consider Table 5.1, which presents the prices of five houses in a neighborhood. To convey a quick impression about this neighborhood, we can reproduce the entire table, which is rather cumbersome, or we may try to describe it by using a single number. Of the many measures of central tendency, three are most commonly used in the area of social sciences: the **mean, median,** and **mode.** The mean is the arithmetic average of a series and is expressed as

$$\mu \; = \; \frac{\sum\limits_{i=1}^{n}\left(x_i\right)}{n} \tag{5.1}$$

where x is a variable with n number of observations, and μ is the mean.

This is the formula for arithmetic average. Those of you who don't often look at a mathematical expression may recall that the Greek capital sigma (Σ) is used as a sign for summation. The term x with subscript i denotes that it is a **variable** (thus, in Table 5.1, it is the price of the houses, which varies with each house). The i refers to the specific observation, or in this case individual houses. If $i = 2$, then x_2 refers to the second observation in the series, which in this case is the price of the second

Table 5.1   Distribution of Housing Prices

Houses	Price
I	$65,000
II	$65,000
III	$150,000
IV	$230,000
V	$390,000

house, $65,000. The term n is a **constant** and measures the number of observations, which in this case is 5. The subscripts below and superscripts above the summation sign Σ read as, "the sum of variable X with observations (i) varying from 1 through 5." Therefore, in this case, we add up the values of our five observations to arrive at $900,000. Dividing it by 5, we get the average value of a neighborhood house as $180,000.

You may notice that I have expressed the mean with the Greek letter μ (pronounced *meu*). However, sometimes you will find the mean written as $\overline{X}$ (pronounced *X-bar*). It is important to note that it is a common tradition in statistics to denote the mean of a **population** (the entire group in question) as μ, and the mean of a **sample** (a small fraction of the population chosen by a researcher to observe) as $\overline{X}$. Unless I note otherwise, I am speaking of a population.

The arithmetic mean is the most commonly used measure of central tendency. You may notice that most quantitative techniques (many of which are discussed in this book) are built around the analytical anchor provided by the mean. This is because the implication of the mean is rather intuitive. Also, in mathematical statistics, the mean as the measure of central tendency has the highly desirable property of **asymptotic convergence**. Suppose I have an unbiased coin, which I flip, and every time I get a head, I note it. If the coin is not flawed, as I repeat my experiment a number of times, the ratio of the number of heads to the total number of tosses will come closer and closer to 0.5 as the number of tosses increases. This number (0.5) is the same as the theoretically derived ratio of **relative frequency**— the number of desired alternatives divided by the total number of alternatives. In this case we have just one desired alternative, a head, and two possible alternatives, a head and a tail. By using this rule we can calculate that the odds of getting a head are 1:2 = 0.5. Because a die has six sides, the possibility of getting either a 1 or a 6 with a throw of the die is 2:6 = 0.333. This neat mathematical property allows the mean to be used in statistical theorems.

However, extreme values in a series influence the mean, especially when the sample size is small. In our example of the unequal prices of a small number of houses in a neighborhood, the mean price of housing is $180,000, which is higher than two-thirds of the houses in our sample. The house priced at $390,000 has influenced the mean.

The **median** is the middle number in a series. In our example, the median price of a house in the neighborhood is $150,000. Because it is the middle number, it is impervious to the extremes in the series. However, determining the median requires the physical inspection of the series and thus cannot be calculated as easily as the mean. Also, it does not have the asymptotic property of un-biasedness that makes the mean such an attractive measure of central tendency in statistics and mathematics.

Finally, the **mode** is the most frequent number in a series. In this simple example, it happens to be $65,000.

Since the mean price of housing is $180,000, the median is $150,000, and the mode is $65,000, which number should represent the average price of houses in the neighborhood? Let us elaborate.

Consider, for example, Figure 5.2. The distribution is clearly symmetric. The choice of a measure of central tendency is not going to be controversial because, for this distribution, the mean, median, and mode will coincide.

Controversy will soon ensue if the distribution is not symmetric. In Figure 5.3, for example, all the numbers cluster close to each other, except for one, which is an extreme value. This unusually large number will unduly influence the mean. In this situation either the median or mode can be used to represent the series.

In Figure 5.4 one observation with a particular value predominates. Therefore, the modal value will best represent the series. The extreme value makes the mean an inappropriate measure. Similarly, because of the prevalence of one value, even the use of the median may be considered to be less than appropriate.

At the outset, presenting the day's temperature in your city on a local television station's weather map looks like a simple enough task. However, controversy would arise if the city recorded a high temperature at noon and the temperature then fell precipitously as a cold weather front moved in. The question would be to decide which measure to choose as representative of the day's temperature. Varied geographical areas with several small climate zones within the city would further complicate the problem. In this case, the weather station located in the coastal area may record a significantly different temperature from the one located inland.

The fundamental question is, Why do such problems arise? These kinds of controversies arise any time we try to describe a complex, multidimensional phenomenon with a one-dimensional measure. The more complex the situation, the more problematic its representation with just one set of numbers. The alternative is to describe a multidimensional phenomenon with several different sets of numbers. However, more than one number tends to numb one's senses. Representing a complex situation with just one number may have its disadvantages, but the alternative does not seem all that attractive either. The choice of the best measure of central tendency often calls for subjective judgment.

Figure 5.2 A Symmetric Distribution

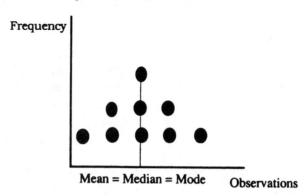

Note: The distribution of observations shows a clear tendency to cluster around the middle number. Therefore, since this series of numbers is evenly distributed, we may accept either of the three measures of central tendency as appropriate. Still, one should always calculate the mean when reporting the central tendency, unless there is a special reason not to do so.

Figure 5.3   Distribution with an Extreme Value

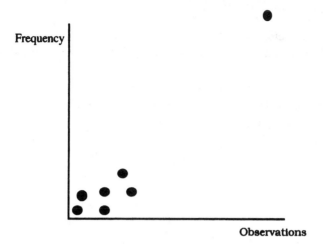

Note: When there is an extreme value, the total picture of a distribution becomes complex. In these cases, the use of any one measure of central tendency would be controversial, since one can always question the "representativeness" of the number.

WEIGHTED ESTIMATES.   If I ask you, "How long would it take you to go to the airport?" you might say, "If the traffic is *exceptionally* heavy, it can take fifty-five minutes; if it is *unusually* light, fifteen minutes; but *in general,* it takes me about twenty minutes." Not knowing the traffic conditions, we may estimate the travel time to the airport by averaging the three numbers. If we do that we come up with an estimate of thirty minutes. Notice that this time is far too pessimistic, because it is one and

Figure 5.4   Distribution with the Modal Value

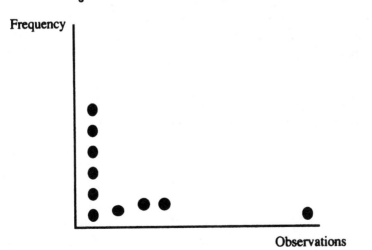

Note: This figure shows a hypothetical situation in which the use of the mode would be appropriate. Since there is an extreme value, the mean would be unduly influenced by it.

a half times the time it usually takes to drive to the airport. This average reflects the extreme nature of the most pessimistic assessment of the situation. In such cases, when you do not want to be influenced by the presence of extreme values, yet you do not want to disregard them, you may derive your estimate by giving **weights** to the observation. That is, you may give a weight of four to the average time. We can write the series as shown in Table 5.2.

From this data, we can calculate the weighted average as [(15 × 1) + (20 × 4) + (55 × 1)]/6 = 25. Notice that now we are not dividing the sum by the number of observations; instead, we are dividing the sum by the total of the weights. Also notice that this number (25) is a lot closer to the "most likely" number (20) than the unweighted average (30). By attributing weights, we have made the estimate a lot more realistic. In mathematical symbols, the calculation of weighted average is written as

$$\mu \;=\; \frac{\sum\left(f_i \times X_i\right)}{\sum f_i} \tag{5.1a}$$

where f_i represents the respective weights for the observations.

"GROUPED" DATA.   Similar logic is applicable when data are available in **groups**. The range of a group is called the **interval**. The data on housing prices for a neighborhood may be available only in groups. I have written the housing price data given in Table 5.1 in group form in Table 5.3.

By using the formula given by equation 5.1a, we can calculate the weighted mean as $3,700,000/25 = $148,000.

The median for interval data is calculated somewhat differently. To calculate the median, first inspect the data to locate the middle observation. As you can see from Table 5.3, there are twenty-five houses in the sample. Therefore, the mid-point is located on the thirteenth house. However, we don't know the exact price of the thirteenth house in the sample series. Hence, we assume that all the observations are evenly spaced within the range, which in this case is equal to $99,999. We can estimate the spacing of the prices by dividing the length of the range by the number of units within it. In other words, we assume that the difference between two successive houses is $99,999/17 = $5,882.3.

If we assume that within the range $100,000–$199,999 the seventeen houses are evenly spaced in price, the thirteenth house (the sixth one within the price range) will be priced at $100,000 + (5,882.3 × 6) = $135,293.8.

Table 5.2 Weighted Observations

Assessment	Time (in minutes)	Weight
Optimistic	15	1
Most likely	20	4
Pessimistic	55	1

Table 5.3 Grouped Data

Price range	Number of houses (f_i)	Midpoint of intervals (X_i)	Midpoint X number of houses [(f_i) × (X_i)]
$0–$99,999	5	$50,000	250,000
$100,000–$199,999	17	$150,000	2,550,000
$200,000–$400,000	3	$300,000	900,000
	$\Sigma f_i = 25$		$\Sigma f_i X_i = 3{,}700{,}000$

Therefore, *weighted averages are only approximations of the actual ungrouped data. So, whenever possible, use ungrouped data for the calculation of central tendency.*

Measures of Dispersion

A series is characterized not only by its central tendency, but also by how strong this central tendency is. That is, how closely does the series cluster around the measure of central tendency? In Figure 5.5 both of the series have the same mean, but obviously the first series (Figure 5.5 (a)) is more bunched together than the second (Figure 5.5 (b)).

The closer this clustering is, the more confident we can be of the representativeness of our measure of central tendency. To understand the measures of dispersion, let us compare our first neighborhood with a second neighborhood. We can measure the relative dispersion, or the "scatteredness," of a series by using **range**, **mean absolute deviation**, **variance**, or **standard deviation** (see Table 5.4).

Figure 5.5 The Effects of Different Dispersions

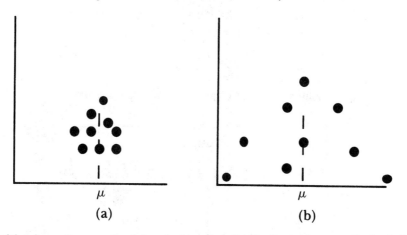

(a)   (b)

Note: If the observations are closely bunched together, the distribution has a smaller level of dispersion (a) compared with the one in which the observations are widely scattered (b).

Table 5.4 Relative Distribution of Housing Prices Between Two Neighborhoods

Houses	Neighborhood A	Neighborhood B
I	$65,000	$150,000
II	$65,000	$180,000
III	$150,000	$180,000
IV	$230,000	$190,000
V	$390,000	$200,000

The range simply measures the difference between the highest and the lowest values in a series. In Table 5.4, the houses located in neighborhood A have a range of $325,000, while the range for neighborhood B is $50,000.

The concept of range is also associated with what are known as the hinge and the midspread. One-quarter of the observations in the series lie below the **lower hinge,** and one-quarter lie above the **upper hinge.** The distance between the two hinges, containing half the observations around the median, is called the **midspread.** For example, the series of numbers 3, 17, 69, 85, 97, 117, 198, 211, 217, 300, 301 does not tell us very much about the nature of its distribution, but we may express it with the help of the range, the median, and hinges, as shown in Figure 5.6. This depiction sheds more light on the characteristic of the series. As you can see, in this series, 117 is the median value of the series of eleven numbers, the third and the ninth observations are the two hinges, and the difference between them is the midspread.

To measure how scattered or dispersed a distribution is, we need to find out the deviation from the mean, or the average distance between the individual observation within the series and the mean. However, if we add up the different distances from the mean, the positive numbers cancel out the negative numbers. Thus, we get the results shown in Table 5.5 if we subtract the mean value of the series ($180,000) from the various values of the housing prices of the two neighborhoods. From this table, it should be apparent that if we try to compare the deviation from the mean for the two series, the sum of column 3 ($X_i - \mu$) will give us 0, as will the sum of column 6 ($X_j - \mu$). Therefore, it is important to note that *the sum of deviations from the mean is always equal to 0.*

Figure 5.6 The Range, the Midspread, and Hinges

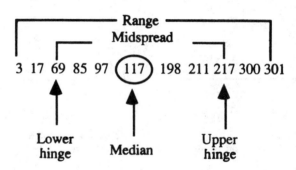

Table 5.5 Relative Distribution of Housing Prices: Deviation from the Mean (in dollars)

Houses	Neighborhood A (X)	$X_i - \mu$	$|X_i - \mu|$	Neighborhood B (X_j)	$X_j - \mu$	$|X_j - \mu|$
I	65,000	−115,000	115,000	150,000	−30,000	30,000
II	65,000	−115,000	115,000	180,0000	0	0
III	150,000	−30,0000	30,000	180,0000	0	0
IV	230,000	50,000	50,000	190,000	10,000	10,000
V	390,000	210,000	210,000	200,000	20,000	20,000
Total		0	520,000		0	60,000

We can avoid the problem of measuring dispersion from the mean by either disregarding the signs of the deviations or by squaring them (since the square of a negative number is positive). The first method of calculating the average dispersion of a series is called the **mean absolute deviation,** written as

$$\text{Mean Absolute Deviation} = \frac{\sum_{i=1}^{n}\left|X_i - \mu\right|}{n} \tag{5.2}$$

By using this formula, we can see in Table 5.5 that the mean absolute deviation for the first neighborhood is $104,000 = ($520,000/5), and for the second, $12,000 = ($60,000/5). According to the mean absolute deviation measure, the second neighborhood is nearly 8.7 times more homogeneous (less dispersed) in its distribution of housing prices than the first neighborhood.

However, the mean absolute deviation poses two problems. First, computationally it is cumbersome; second, it does not possess some of the most desirable mathematical properties. Therefore, we may try another way to eliminate the negative signs in the deviation from the mean—that is, by squaring the deviations. This process can be written as

$$\sigma^2 = \frac{\sum_{i=1}^{n}\left(x_i - \mu\right)^2}{n} \tag{5.3}$$

This is the measure of **variance,** expressed as σ^2. To calculate the variance of the two neighborhoods, we need to square the deviations from the mean (the third and the sixth columns in Table 5.5), add them up, and divide by 5. The problem with variance is that the numbers are often extremely large (see Table 5.6). In this case the calculated variances for the two neighborhoods are 14,790,000,000 (73,950,000,000/5) and 240,000,000 (1,200,000,000/5). We can reduce the size of the variance by taking its square root. The resulting number is called the **standard deviation** of the series. Owing to its several highly desirable mathematical properties, standard deviation (expressed by σ) is by far the most frequently used measure of dispersion. Standard deviation of a series is calculated by the following formula:

$$\sigma = \sqrt{\frac{\sum_{i=1}^{n}\left(X_i - \mu\right)^2}{n}} \tag{5.4}$$

Table 5.6 Calculation of Variance

Houses	Neighborhood A (squared deviation from the mean) $(X_i - \mu)^2$	Neighborhood B (squared deviation from the mean) $(X_j - \mu)^2$
I	13,225,000,000	900,000,000
II	13,225,000,000	0
III	900,000,000	0
IV	2,500,000,000	100,000,000
V	44,100,000,000	200,000,000
Total	73,950,000,000	1,200,000,000

By taking the square root of the variances of the two series, we calculated the standard deviations, which turned out to be $121,614.14 and $15,491.92. Obviously, these numbers are much more manageable than the variances. From these measures, we can see that the dispersion for the first neighborhood is more than seven times the dispersion for the second neighborhood.

When we are speaking in terms of population variance or standard deviation, we use the Greek alphabet σ^2 and σ. When we consider sample variance and sample standard deviation, we use the Roman (English) alphabet S and S^2. Therefore, you should note a rather important convention in statistical terminology: *When denoting population mean, variance, and standard deviations, we use the Greek alphabets μ, σ^2, σ. However, sample mean, variance, and standard deviations are written $\bar{X}$, S^2, and S.*

At this point, you should note another significant difference between the formula for calculating the population standard deviation σ and sample standard deviation (S). The sample standard deviation, which is only an estimate of the population standard deviation, has to be corrected for bias by dividing the sum of squares by $n - 1$, instead of n. This implies that as the size of the sample (n) increases, the subtraction of l will have less and less impact on the calculated value of standard deviation. I discuss the rationale of subtracting 1 from the number of observations, known as the **degrees of freedom**, in the following chapter. The formula for calculating **sample standard deviation** is given by

$$S = \sqrt{\frac{\sum_{i=1}^{n}\left(X_i - \bar{X}\right)^2}{n-1}} \qquad (5.4a)$$

DISPERSION OF DISTRIBUTIONS.   Suppose we want to know which of two distributions has more variations within it. Unfortunately, unlike the mean, we cannot readily use standard deviations to compare the relative dispersion of distributions. The problem with standard deviation is that it is an absolute measure. That is, it is influenced by the unit of measurement. Consider two sample distributions, I and II. You will notice that series II is series I $\times$ 5 (see Table 5.7).

Table 5.7 Comparing Dispersion of Two Distributions

Series I	Series II
0	0
1	5
2	10
3	15
4	20

The sample standard deviation (S) is calculated to be 1.58 for series I and 7.91 for II. Because series II is five times the value of series I, so are the values of the respective standard deviations. This can sometimes pose a practical problem. Suppose we want to compare the dispersion of housing prices of two diverse cities, Tijuana, Mexico, and San Diego, California. These two cities probably offer the greatest contrast in relative prosperity among neighboring cities around the world. When we try to compare the two, we face a problem: Because housing prices in San Diego are much higher than those in Tijuana, the dispersion in the San Diego real estate price will be magnified by the absolute difference in the price level. However, it is entirely possible that the disparity in housing prices is greater in Tijuana than in San Diego. To compare the relative dispersion between the two cities, we have to divide the standard deviation by the mean. This measure, known as the **coefficient of variation**, is then written as

$$\text{Coefficient of variation} = \frac{\sigma}{\mu} \tag{5.5}$$

Looking at the two neighborhoods in Table 5.4, we can calculate the coefficient of variation for them as

$$\text{Neighborhood A} = \frac{135{,}968.7}{180{,}000} = 0.755; \text{Neighborhood B} = \frac{18{,}708.3}{180{,}000} = 0.104$$

The calculated coefficients of variation show that the variance for the first neighborhood is more than seven times (7.26, to be precise) that of the second one. Incidentally, you may also notice that by using this measure, we conclude that despite the difference in scale, the distribution of values for series I and II has the same relative dispersion.

SKEWNESS AND SYMMETRY OF DISTRIBUTION. A question often asked about a series of numbers is, Where are the mean, median, and mode of the distribution? The positions of these three measures of central tendency can give decision makers extremely valuable clues about the distribution of the series. Take, for example, a series of numbers shown in Table 5.8.

The data from Table 5.8 have been plotted in Figure 5.7. The perfect bell-shaped distribution shown in this figure is called symmetric. For distributions like these, all three measures of central tendency—the mean, median, and mode—fall on the same point. If you calculate the mean for the distribution shown in Table 5.8, you

Table 5.8 Data Showing a Symmetric Distribution

Observation	Frequency
1	5
2	8
3	12
4	15
5	21
6	35
7	21
8	15
9	12
10	8
11	5

can see that it is approximately (with the appropriate rounding off for the decimal points) equal to 6. Also, since there are five numbers above and five numbers below, the median for the distribution is also 6. Finally, because the observation 6 has the highest frequency, it is also the modal point for the distribution.

However, this happy situation changes if the distribution is tilted to the right or to the left of the perfect bell shape. A tilted distribution is called a **skewed distribution**. A distribution tilted to the right is called a **positively skewed distribution;** one that tilts to the left is called a **negatively skewed distribution** (see Figure 5.8). Consider, for example, two new series along with the one given in Table 5.8. Data for three different series are presented in Table 5.9. The symmetric series is called

Figure 5.7 Example of a Symmetric Distribution

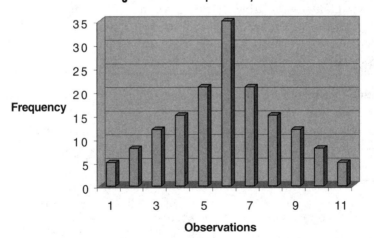

Table 5.9   Examples of Symmetric and Asymmetric Distributions

Observation	Frequency A	Frequency B	Frequency C
1	5	25	5
2	8	35	6
3	12	20	7
4	15	18	8
5	21	15	10
6	35	12	12
7	21	10	15
8	15	8	18
9	12	7	20
10	8	6	35
11	5	5	20

frequency A, and the two subsequent series are labeled frequencies B and C. If you plot these three series, you will see the curves shown in Figure 5.8.

Notice that the median for the three distributions remains the same. Because we have eleven observations, the sixth observation is the middle point for each of these distributions. The means for series B and C are 4.3 and 7.6, respectively. The

Figure 5.8   Comparison of Symmetric and Asymmetric Series

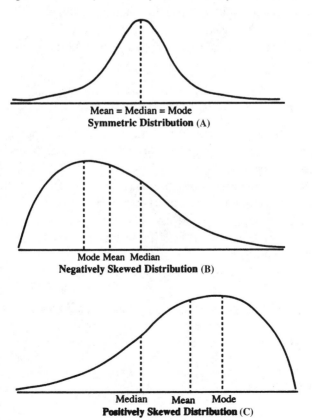

Mean = Median = Mode
Symmetric Distribution (A)

Mode Mean Median
Negatively Skewed Distribution (B)

Median   Mean   Mode
Positively Skewed Distribution (C)

mode for series B is 2, and for series C it is 10. Table 5.10 summarizes this information.

For a policy maker who needs to make a quick judgment about a data series, it is extremely important to remember that *for a negatively skewed distribution the mean is less than the median; and for a positively skewed distribution, the mean is greater than the median.* These two figures can give a rough picture for the distribution. In fact, you may notice that the greater the difference between the two, the greater the extent of skewness of distribution.

Which Measure of Central Tendency to Use

Previously I argued that the choice of a measure of central tendency depends on the subjective assessment of the person making a statement. However, there are a few rules of thumb.

1. In a symmetric distribution, all three measures are the same. Therefore, one could choose any one of the three.
2. In a highly skewed distribution, the median may be the most useful measure of central tendency.
3. An overwhelming preponderance of one number may indicate the use of mode.
4. Arithmetic mean should be used to calculate average, unless there is a special need to do otherwise.
5. If for any reason median or mode is used, this should be made clear to the reader.

A Quick Glance at the Distribution: The Stem-Leaf Method

A series of numbers often do not convey a coherent picture. For example, over a fifteen-week period local police officers arrested varying numbers of individuals on drug-related charges: 15, 23, 8, 31, 9, 45, 41, 18, 11, 3, 13, 25, 33, 40, 10, 102. Clearly, one cannot draw many conclusions from these numbers. Nevertheless, a policy analyst must frequently elicit quick conclusions about a distribution, such as housing prices in a neighborhood, ages of children in a detention center, or the time taken by various employees to complete a task. In such cases, the **stem-leaf method** offers a helping hand.

Table 5.10   Mean, Median, and Mode in Symmetric and Asymmetric Series

	Mean	*Median*	*Mode*
Symmetric distribution (A)	6.0	6.0	6.0
Negatively skewed distribution (B)	4.3	6.0	2
Positively skewed distribution (C)	7.6	6.0	10

Figure 5.9   Stem-Leaf Method and Histogram

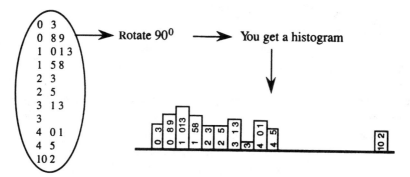

A stem-leaf method arranges a series of numbers by *stems* and *leafs*. For example, in the preceding series of numbers, the first digit of a number is the stem, and the second digit is the leaf. For the number 15, 1 is the stem and 5 is the leaf. For a single-digit number, such as 3, the stem is 0 and the leaf is 3. You may notice that you can get a histogram or a bar chart simply by rotating the stem-leaf diagram (see Figure 5.9).

The advantage of a stem-leaf method is that it contains a lot more information regarding the distribution. For instance, we can tell from Table 5.11 that although the data vary a good deal, the median value, 25, is much closer to the minimum, 3, than to the maximum, 102. Therefore, it is clearly a negatively skewed distribution. The output also indicates that the maximum value is an outlier, or a real exception to the rest of the values in the series. In many decision-making instances this method can provide some rather important insights.

Table 5.11   Stem-Leaf Analysis: Drug Arrests, $N = 16$

0 3	
0 89	
1 013	*Lower Hinge*
1 58	
2 3	
2 5	*Median Value*
3 13	
3	*Upper Hinge*
4 01	
4 5	
Outside value	
10 2	

Note: Minimum = 3.000; lower hinge = 10.500; median = 25.000; upper hinge = 36.500; maximum = 102.000.

CORRELATION COEFFICIENT: PEARSON'S *R*

You may often wonder if two sets of data are correlated. Throughout the ages, patient observers have gained scientific knowledge by discovering close associations between two phenomena. The ancient astronomers noted that the tides change with the change in the lunar cycle. In social science research, the *extent* and *nature* of association between two variables are often the subject of inquiry.

We may want to know if being a victim of child abuse is correlated with later criminal behavior. The nature of correlation between two variables is described as positive or negative. In Figure 5.10 the two variables, Yellow and Blue, are shown with Venn diagrams. If the two overlap, there is correlation. As the two move toward each other, the extent of correlation increases. The two circles correlate perfectly when they completely overlap and thus become indistinguishable from one another. If they do not correlate at all, they do not intersect.

If an increase in one variable corresponds to an increase in the other, there is a **positive correlation**. If the presence of childhood abuse is linked with higher levels of criminal behavior, we call it a positive correlation. In contrast, the presence of an abusive relationship linked to a child's lowered academic achievement is an example of a **negative correlation**. I have shown this in Figure 5.11.

We can numerically measure the extent and strength of correlation with the help of **Pearson's *r***, or simply the **correlation coefficient**. Suppose we have two sets of variables, *X* and *Y*. The correlation coefficient between them is measured by the formula

$$\text{Correlation coefficient} = \frac{\sum \left(X_i - \overline{X} \right)\left(Y_i - \overline{Y} \right)}{\sqrt{\sum \left(X_i - \overline{X} \right)^2 \sum \left(Y_i - \overline{Y} \right)^2}} \qquad (5.6)$$

The size of the coefficient indicates the extent of correlation. If it is equal to 1, there is a perfect correlation (or a complete overlap) between the two variables, and if it is equal to 0, the two variables are independent of each other (there is no overlap). The sign of the correlation coefficient shows the nature of their relationship. If the

Figure 5.10   The Extent of Correlation Between Two Variables

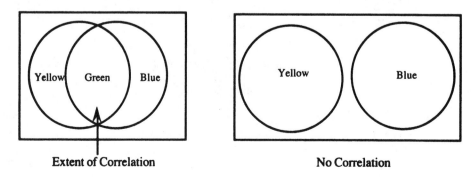

Extent of Correlation   No Correlation

Figure 5.11   The Nature of Correlation

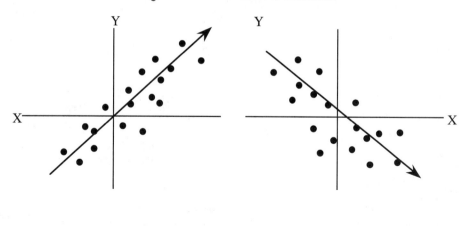

Positive correlation   Negative correlation

sign is positive, the relationship is positive and vice versa. Therefore, the correlation coefficient equals 1 when there is a perfect positive correlation, it equals –1 when there is a perfect negative correlation, and it equals 0 when there is no correlation at all.

Let us suppose the crime rate in your city has gone up in recent years. Of late, a few local newspaper articles have condemned this trend. Your police chief, however, contends that because the city is growing rapidly in size, the crime rate can be expected to rise as well. So, you want to know if there is a correlation between crime rate and population size. You have collected the data series shown in Table 5.12.

By using the formula in equation 5.6 you can calculate the correlation coefficient, which turns out to be 0.8655. The positive number corroborates your police chief's assertion regarding a strong correlation between crime rate and the population size of a city.

Table 5.12   Crime Rate and City Size

City	Population (000)	Crime rate (per 000 inhabitants)
A	50	1.5
B	57	1.7
C	65	1.6
D	68	2.9
E	88	2.0
F	92	3.1
G	96	2.5
H	100	3.5
I	120	3.8
J	125	3.7

Key Words

Asymptotic convergence (p. 105)	Mode (p. 104)
Central tendency (p. 103)	Negative correlation (p. 118)
Coefficient of variation (p. 113)	Negative skew (p. 114)
Constant (p. 105)	Population (p. 105)
Correlation coefficient (Pearson's *r*)	Positive correlation (p. 118)
(p. 118)	Positive skew (p. 114)
Degrees of freedom (p. 112)	Range (p. 109)
Dispersion (p. 103)	Relative frequency (p. 105)
Ex ante facto (p. 103)	Sample (p. 105)
Ex post facto (p. 103)	Sample standard deviation (p. 112)
Grouped data (p. 108)	Skewed distribution (p. 114)
Interval (p. 108)	Standard deviation (p. 111)
Lower hinge (p. 110)	Stem-leaf method (p. 116)
Mean (p. 104)	Upper hinge (p. 110)
Mean absolute deviation (p. 109)	Variable (p. 104)
Median (p. 104)	Variance (p. 109)
Midspread (p. 110)	Weight (p. 108)

Exercises

1. What is the implication of the name "descriptive statistics"? What are the measures of central tendency and dispersion? Explain the term "central tendency." Why do we face controversies regarding the appropriate choice of a measure of central tendency?

2. Consider the following series and choose the most appropriate measure of central tendency for each series. Explain your choices.

Series A	Series B	Series C	Series D
10	5	3	5
11	8	7	7
9	11	9	9
27	13	25	11
16	16	7	9
15	18	7	7
17	21	7	5

Suggestion: You may want to plot the data to determine the patterns.

3. What do we measure by the coefficient of variation? Give an example of its possible use in public sector decision making. Using this method, comment on the relative dispersions of the four series of data presented in the preceding table.

4. Which one of the measures of central tendency is most commonly used in mathematics and statistics? Why?

5. How is the correlation coefficient useful? Give an example of its possible use and abuse.

6. We often hear the argument that increased size of the government retards economic growth. The World Bank collects the most reliable cross-national data. Go to its Web site at http://www.odci.gov/cia/publications/factbook/index.html and

collect data on the size of government (budget revenue/GDP) for Japan, Australia, and New Zealand and for Western Europe and North America. Also gather data on rates of growth in regard to per capita income. Prepare a table, calculate the correlation coefficient between the two variables, and explain your finding.

Notes

1. Jeffrey M. Stonecash and Mack D. Mariani, "Republican Gains in the House in the 1994 Election: Class Polarization in American Politics," *Political Science Quarterly* 115 (2000): 93–113.
2. The people of the Nambiquara tribe of the Matto Grosso forest in Brazil, for example, lack any system of numbers. The closest they come to expressing equality between two sets of items is by using a verb that means "they are alike" (*Guinness Book of Records,* 1992, p. 269).

CHAPTER

6

PROBABILITY AND HYPOTHESIS TESTING

As the old adage goes, the only certainties in life are death and taxes. Even then, we cannot predict the exact time of our demise or foretell changes in the tax law. Therefore, we must venture into the world of uncertainty. The presence of uncertainty in public policy analysis means that decisions must be made *before* we know which one of many conceivable and perhaps even inconceivable outcomes will come to pass. While deciding on a possible outcome, we assign probability values, as we do when we assess the odds of winning the lottery, the chances of a rainstorm, or the behavior of the stock market.

The sources of probability measures are either objective (based on actual facts) or subjective (based on personal judgment). Let us discuss these two sources of probability.

OBJECTIVE PROBABILITY

The objective measure defines probability as the ratio of occurrence of a given event from a finite number of possible outcomes. Therefore, objective probability is also known as **relative** frequency. Say that 245 students with a certain range of grade point averages and SAT scores applied for admission to a public university and that 35 of them were selected. We can calculate the probability of a student being admitted as

$$p = \frac{35}{245} = 0.143 \tag{6.1}$$

In other words, the probability (p) of a student in that particular academic achievement category gaining admission is 14.3 percent. The formula for calculating objective probability by the measure of relative frequency can be written as

$$p = \frac{Observed\ frequency}{Total\ frequency} \tag{6.1a}$$

However, defining probability by observed frequency alone is problematical. If I ask you, for example, what the probability is of flipping heads in a coin toss, you will notice that it is impossible to use the above definition of probability because we cannot observe all the coin tosses and record their outcomes. In that case, we may define objective probability as

$$p = \frac{Target\ outcome}{Total\ number\ of\ possible\ outcomes} \tag{6.1b}$$

Suppose we toss a coin looking for one specific outcome, "heads," out of two possible outcomes. By using formula 6.1b we can calculate that the probability of flipping heads is $1/2 = 0.5$. Similarly, the probability of getting a "5" in the roll of a die is $1/6 = 0.17$.

We cannot keep on tossing a coin an infinite number of times to prove that the probability of flipping heads is $1/2$. Thus you must recognize that calculated probability in actual practice is only an approximation of the "true" probability. As the number of experiments becomes larger and larger, approximation poses less of a problem. Let us take a moment to explain this extremely important concept properly.

It is obvious that a weather forecast of a 50 percent chance of rain does not imply that it would rain half the day or that it would rain every half hour. In fact, it will either rain or it will not (even drizzle should count as rain). Interpreting such a forecast is the same as interpreting the outcome of a coin toss. Since by tossing a coin you will either win or lose, you should interpret the probability measure as if you were to toss the coin an unlimited number of times. You will see that as the number of tosses increases, the ratio of heads over the total number of attempts approaches 0.5 (see Figure 6.1). Suppose we are tossing a coin in groups of four. After each set of tosses we record the number and average it over the previous ones. Suppose in the first try, we flip heads one time and tails three times. This gives us a ratio of 1:3. Suppose in the next try, we flip heads twice and tails twice. By averaging the total number of tosses, the ratio of heads over tails is 3:4. If we continue to do this, we will see a curve similar to the one presented in Figure 6.1.

Figure 6.1   Probability and the Number of Tries

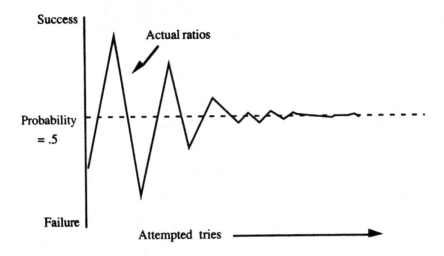

In the beginning, the fluctuations may be wide, but as the number of tries increases, the average approaches the "true" probability figure of 0.5.

This is the basis of objective probability. Embedded in this simple example of a coin toss are some of the most important assumptions and axioms that form the basic building blocks of statistical reasoning. A proper understanding must begin with the examination of these properties of objective probability. First, the events in a probability experiment (in this case, each toss) must be **independent**. Perhaps the most common cause of misinterpreting probability is the question of independence. Suppose you have placed a bet on a coin toss. You are calling heads, and you have called it correctly four times. On the fifth try, should you call heads again, or should you try to be smart by calling tails? Because the tosses are independent, what happened last time or any time before has no bearing whatsoever on what may happen this time.

The second assumption of objective probability is that the events are **mutually exclusive**, meaning they cannot take place simultaneously. For example, we cannot get both heads and tails in a single try. But it is entirely possible to have both rain and sunshine within a single day. Therefore, whereas the outcomes of a coin toss or the roll of a die are mutually exclusive, rain and sunshine are not, unless we define the outcome as "having rain any time during the day."

Finally, the probability measures are **asymptotic**. That is, the probability of getting a head with an unbiased coin is 0.5. However, that does not imply that we are going to get exactly two heads and two tails in four tries. It simply means that if we repeat the experiment many times, as the number of tosses increases the ratio will approach 0.5. Similarly, going back to our previous example, we must interpret the meteorological prediction as follows: If the weather conditions (temperature, barometric pressure, wind condition, humidity, and so forth) become the same as the condition we are having at this time, over a long period of time, this combination of conditions will produce rain half of the time.

Probability Distribution

When we assign probability to a series of independent and mutually exclusive events, we get a **probability distribution**. Let us suppose we want to find the probability of the size of a social worker's caseloads on a given day. We record the number of cases each day—say, for one hundred days. Then, by dividing each day's frequency by the total number of arrivals, we can construct the probability column of the arrival of the caseloads. This hypothetical data is presented in Table 6.1 and in Figure 6.2. By looking at the table, you can tell that the probability the social worker would handle just one case is 5 percent, two cases is 10 percent, and so on. The third column of the table shows the cumulative probability totals. Called a **cumulative probability distribution**, the numbers are the probability of having a value less than or equal to a specific value of x. The cumulative probability distribution data reveal that the probability of the social worker having four or fewer cases on a given day is 47 percent.

Knowledge of the mean and standard deviation of a probability distribution provides us with a good deal of information about the nature of the distribution. Most important, this information gives us some of the most powerful analytical tools in the field of applied statistics. Probability distributions can take on an infinite number of shapes. However, for analytical purposes, a perfectly symmetric distribution, known as the **normal distribution** (or in common parlance, bell curve), serves as the fundamental building block. Again, a symmetric distribution can also take on various shapes. In Figure 6.3 I have drawn three normal distributions with different means.

Symmetric distributions can also have the same mean and yet be different. In Figure 6.4 the three distributions, despite having the same mean, have their relative levels of dispersion, measured in terms of standard deviation, σ. Clearly, of the three normal distributions, the tall and skinny one has the lowest standard deviation, whereas the short and fat one has the largest dispersion. Because of these variations, a **standard normal distribution** is defined as the one whose mean is

Table 6.1   Probability and Cumulative Probability Distributions of Caseloads for a Social Worker on a Given Day

Number of cases (x)	Observed frequencies	Probability distribution	Cumulative probability distribution
1	5	0.05	0.05
2	10	0.10	0.15
3	15	0.15	0.30
4	17	0.17	0.47
5	20	0.20	0.67
6	15	0.15	0.82
7	8	0.08	0.90
8	7	0.07	0.97
9	3	0.03	1.00
Total	100	—	—

Figure 6.2   Plot of Probability Distribution

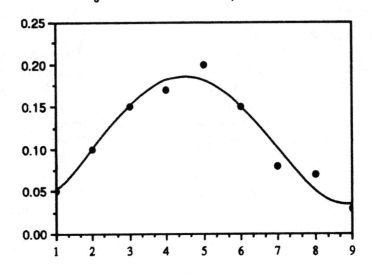

equal to 0 and standard deviation is equal to 1. This standard normal distribution serves as the "ideal type," or the benchmark against which the probabilities of an uncertain world are measured.

The beauty of a standard normal distribution is that the distribution is standardized, as the name suggests. That is, we are able to measure any segment of it with utmost precision. Because for a standard normal distribution the standard deviation is 1, any distance from the mean can therefore be measured in terms of the standard deviation. For example, from Figure 6.5, you can see that 68.26 percent of all the observations in the distribution will fall within $+1\sigma$ distance from the mean. Similarly, the area within the boundaries of $+2\sigma$ will capture 95.46 percent of the observations; 99.74 percent of the observations fall within $+3\sigma$, and nearly 100 percent are captured within the bounds of $+4\sigma$. The formula of the normal distribution enables statisticians to calculate any defined area under the curve.

Standard normal distribution is, of course, a theoretical concept. The **central limit theorem,** perhaps the most remarkable theorem in the field of mathematics and statistics, bridges the gap between the theory and its practical use.[1] This

Figure 6.3   Normal Distributions with Different Means

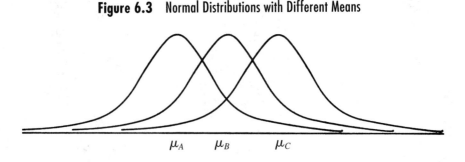

Figure 6.4   Normal Distributions with Various Levels of Dispersion

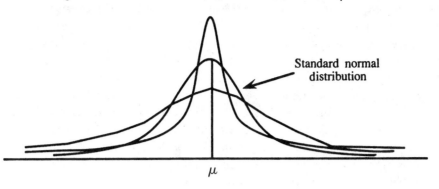

theorem is also often referred to as the **Law of Large Numbers**. An example will help you to understand the compelling nature of this theorem. We know that human beings come in all shapes and sizes. Therefore, if we plot the percentages of males in the United States falling in various groups of heights, we will see a distribution with a strong central tendency and relatively few observations on the extreme ends of the spectrum (extremely tall and extremely short). This plot will not show a perfectly symmetric distribution, but we can get a standard normal distribution if we follow a simple procedure. Suppose we already know the mean (μ) and the standard deviation (σ) for the height of the U.S. male population. We collect

Figure 6.5   Standard Normal Distribution

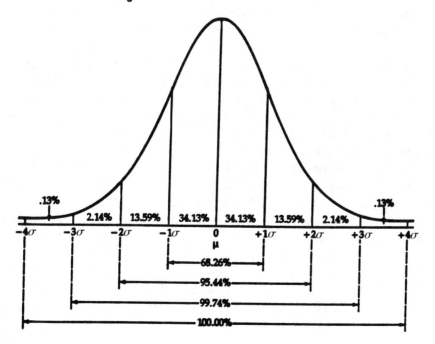

ten males at random, note their average (mean) height, and let them go. We then collect another group of men, note their average height, and let them go. If we perform this operation many times, we will get a series of numbers showing sample means, which we may call $\bar{X}_i$. The reason for the subscript i is that we are referring to a series of means and not just one single value of a mean.

The central limit theorem tells us that if we subtract the sample means from the population mean and then divide by the standard deviation, as we repeat the experiment we will obtain a standard normal distribution regardless of the shape of the original distribution. Suppose we know that the average height of an adult American male is 68 inches and the standard deviation is 2.0. Now we collect the average of three groups of ten men and see that their average height is 72, 73, and 65 inches. We then perform the following operations,

$$\frac{72-68}{2} = 2.0; \quad \frac{73-68}{2} = 2.5; \quad \frac{65-68}{2} = -1.5$$

As the number of samples increases, the series will have a mean of 0 and a standard deviation of 1. We can write this with the help of mathematical symbols as follows:

$$\frac{\bar{X}_i - \mu}{\sigma} \approx \left(0, 1\right) \quad \text{as } i \to \infty \tag{6.2}$$

We read the expression 6.2 as follows: *The series derived by subtracting the population mean from sample means, and divided by the population standard deviation, will be distributed with a mean of 0 and a standard deviation of 1.*[2] Another example will clarify the enormous practical implication of this property.

Several years ago, two neighboring countries in a bitter border dispute claimed the skeletal remains of some prehistoric settlers that had been found in the area. The discovery caused excitement because the racial identity of the ancient inhabitants could decide the current dispute. Thus, researchers took the average cranial measurement of the newly discovered skeletons. Thanks to previous anthropological studies, the average cranial measurement and the standard deviation of the present stock of occupiers of the land were known. It was decided to test the hypothesis that the people whose skeletons were discovered came from the same group of people as today's inhabitants.

However, in mathematics it is often impossible to prove the *existence* of a relationship. If we state that all A's are B, it would be impossible to check every A to prove the relationship. Instead, it is often simpler to nullify an opposite hypothesis in its negative form, such as "there are some A's that are not B." If we do not find any example of an A being a B in our sample, then as the size of the sample increases we become more and more confident in our assertion that there is no A that is B. In statistical terminology, this alternate hypothesis is called a **null hypothesis**. We call it "null" (defined by one dictionary as "none," "invalid," or "void") because while testing, the analyst is usually interested in the hypothesis being false.

Figure 6.5 can help explain the idea behind this test. If the cranial average of the skeletal remains is very close to that of the present group, then we can assume that they both belong to the same racial stock. However, if the average falls outside the 2σ measurement from the mean, then the probability distribution tells us that there is only about a 4 percent chance that these people belonged to the same racial group, because nearly 96 percent of all the observations (in this case, people of this particular race) will fall within this range. The process we just described is known as **hypothesis testing,** part of the fundamental construct of analytical reasoning.

Hypothesis Testing and Confidence Intervals

The theoretical framework derived by the central limit theorem can be used for testing the probability of a hypothesis or estimating a band within which we can reasonably expect to find the "true" value. Suppose the average drop-out rate in a school district is 15.5 percent, with a standard deviation of 1.05. Within the district, one particular school is being touted as exceptional in its achievement of a lower drop-out rate. Last year, this school showed only a 15.3 percent drop-out rate in a graduating class of 100. Is this truly exceptional or merely a result of chance factors? The basis of this question forms the core of hypothesis testing.

Hypothesis testing starts with a question. In the preceding example, the question is whether the drop-out rate of the school in question is significantly smaller than the average for the district. The second step in hypothesis testing is the formulation of a specific null hypothesis. Statistical convention generally expresses the research hypothesis as H_1 and the null hypothesis as H_0.

These two hypotheses can then be written as follows:

H_1: *The school's average is significantly lower than the district average.*
H_0: *The school is not exceptional, and the difference between its mean and the average of the school district can be explained by chance.*

Since it is extremely important to construct a null hypothesis correctly, I offer another example of setting up a research question and a null hypothesis. What to do with juvenile delinquents deeply concerns society. These youngsters should be punished for their offenses, yet sending them to prison might transform them into hardened criminals. Suppose we are attempting to find out if setting up military-style boot camps for first-time juvenile offenders has any bearing on their future criminal activities. We have collected data by tracking two groups of recently paroled offenders: those who were sent to the boot camps and those who were sent through the usual criminal justice system. We can form the two hypotheses as follows:

H_1: *Boot camps do reduce the probability of a juvenile's future conviction rate.*
H_0: *An individual's enrollment in a boot camp has no bearing on his or her future conviction rates.*

In the third step, we must determine the **level of significance** for rejecting the null hypothesis. That is, by using the standard normal distribution, we must determine the level of certainty we must seek for its rejection. This level can be set at

90 percent, 95 percent, or even 99 percent. The level of significance in statistical jargon is often denoted as α (alpha). Let us suppose, for testing our hypothesis, that we have set the α level at 90 percent. If we want to include 90 percent of the observations in a symmetric distribution, the remaining 10 percent must be divided equally between the two tails of the distribution. Therefore, in this case, when we want to know if the sample mean (the average for the particular school) is significantly *less* than the population average (the district average), we set the α value at half of 0.10, or at 0.05. This is called a **one-tailed test,** shown in Figure 6.6. The probability value corresponding to the predetermined level of α is also called the **critical value,** since it determines the threshold of rejecting the null hypothesis. If we set the critical value at the 95 percent level of probability, we want to be 95 percent certain that what we see in our sample result has only a 5 percent chance of being caused by chance alone. If the sample value falls below the critical value, we will not be able to reject the null hypothesis.

Z TEST.   Let us go back to our example of the school district. We know the mean and standard deviation for the district, so it is a simple matter to calculate how far the individual school's record is from the district average, measured by units of the district's standard deviation. We can then compare this number with a theoretical distribution for rejecting or not rejecting a null hypothesis. If the number of samples is large and we know the population mean and standard deviation, we can derive the value for a **Z distribution,** given by the formula

$$Z = \frac{\overline{X} - \mu}{\sigma / \sqrt{n}} \tag{6.3}$$

where n is the number of observations in the sample, which in this case is 100 (the number of graduating seniors).

$$Z = \frac{15.2 - 15.5}{1.05 / \sqrt{100}}$$

$$= \frac{-.3}{.105}$$

$$= -2.86$$

Our calculated **Z score** is –2.86, which means that the sample mean (mean of the school in question) is 2.86 times the standard deviation away from the population mean. The corresponding critical value of the Z distribution is given in Appendix A. The table in Appendix A gives the area under the right-hand side of the standard normal distribution, corresponding to the various calculated Z values. To determine the area of the normal distribution below our calculated Z value of 2.86, go down the first column and find 2.8. Then move to the right across the row to locate the number corresponding to column 0.06. The number corresponding to the row

Figure 6.6 One-Tailed Test

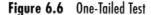

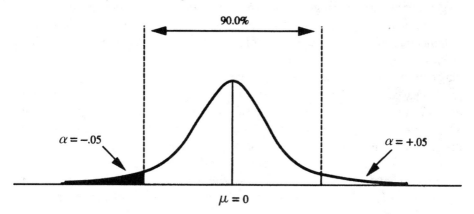

$$\mu = 0$$

2.8 and the column 0.06 is 0.4979, which is the area under the normal distribution below $Z = 2.86$.

Notice that this number relates only to the right-hand side of the distribution. Since it is a symmetric distribution, the other half contains 50 percent of the distribution. Therefore, by adding 0.5 to 0.4979, we get 0.9979, the cumulative value of the total area below the area of the Z value of 2.86. This implies that we can be 99.79 percent certain that the difference between the average district drop-out rate and the experience of the model school is not due to chance; this school is justified in its claim to have significantly reduced the drop-out rate.

Our calculated Z value has a negative sign. Because the Z distribution is symmetric, this sign is of no consequence. It simply points to the direction of the difference from the mean. After calculating the Z score, you can find the corresponding probability value. If it is greater than the standard level of significance that you have set (usually 0.05), you can reject the null hypothesis. If it is less, you cannot reject it. You may also set the critical level of the Z score value without setting the probability standard. If you set your critical value at 0.05, you can go down the Z table to find the approximate point where the area under the curve covers 95 percent of the distribution (Z score = 1.64). If your calculated Z score is greater than 1.64, you can reject the null hypothesis.

CONFIDENCE INTERVAL.   The results of the Z tables can also be used to develop what is commonly known as the **confidence interval**. Clearly, the "true" values of a population distribution are unknowable. For instance, if we want to know the average height of American females, we have to measure every female in the United States, which is an impossible task. Therefore, we will have to infer the average height from sample results. Sample results converge with the actual value when the sample size becomes extremely large. Unless we want to continue taking larger and larger samples, we would be safer to express the population value with a band or an interval. Without saying that the average is 5 feet, 6 inches, we will say that the average will lie between, say, 5 feet, 3 inches, and 5 feet, 8 inches. If we express this band as a probability (for example, "We are 95 percent certain that the average height falls within this range"), then we call it a confidence interval.

A confidence interval tells us the range within which we can expect the population mean to fall with a certain level of confidence or probability. When radio or television newscasters tell us poll results, they almost always include corresponding confidence intervals. We are told that "67 percent of people support the proposed legislation, which has an error margin of plus or minus three percentage points." In other words, we are being asked to hold with a high degree of confidence (usually at a 95 or 99 percent level) that the actual percentage of people in the general population who support this legislation fall within 70 and 64. To derive a confidence interval, we need to use a **two-tailed test** because we are not sure of the direction of deviation from the sample value. Therefore, consider the logic of a critical value for rejecting the null hypothesis on the basis of the Z score once again: Reject the null hypothesis if

$$Z = \frac{\overline{X} - \mu}{\sigma / \sqrt{n}} > Z_{.05}$$

or

$$Z = \frac{\overline{X} - \mu}{\sigma / \sqrt{n}} < -Z_{.05}$$

These two expressions tell us to reject the null hypothesis if the Z scores are greater than the stipulated value. Diagrammatically this means that if the Z scores fall outside the shaded area in Figure 6.7, reject the null hypothesis.

The two algebraic forms can be rewritten as, reject null hypothesis if

$$-Z_{.05} > \frac{\overline{X} - \mu}{\sigma / \sqrt{n}} > Z_{.05} \tag{6.4}$$

When we want to construct a confidence interval, we choose not to know a specific estimate for the population value μ. Instead, by manipulating equation 6.4, we can write

$$-Z_{.05} \times \frac{\sigma}{\sqrt{n}} > \overline{X} - \mu > +Z_{.05} \times \frac{\sigma}{\sqrt{n}} \tag{6.5}$$

which is again rewritten as

$$\mu - Z_{.05} \times \frac{\sigma}{\sqrt{n}} > \overline{X} > \mu + Z_{.05} \times \frac{\sigma}{\sqrt{n}} \tag{6.6}$$

Equation 6.6 gives us the confidence interval for our population (μ). In this equation, we set the value for the desired level of confidence, which in this case is 10 percent, or 5 percent on either side of the curve. By looking at the Z table, we can see that the value of $Z_{0.05}$ is approximately 1.65. We know that the population

Figure 6.7 Two-Tailed Test and Confidence Interval

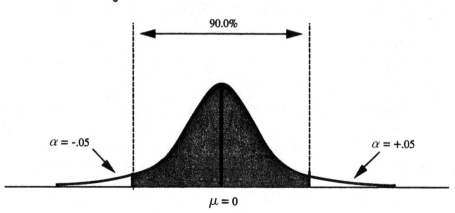

standard deviation (σ) equals 1.05, n equals 100, and the population mean μ equals 15.5. Therefore, the confidence interval for our population mean is calculated by inserting these numbers in equation 6.6:

$$15.5 - 1.65 \times \frac{1.05}{\sqrt{100}} > \overline{X} > 15.5 + 1.66 \times \frac{1.05}{\sqrt{100}}$$

or, $15.33 > \mu > 15.67$

In plain English, the results mean that we can expect 90 percent of all the schools in the district to exhibit a drop-out pattern that will vary between 15.33 and 15.67 percent. This information can be of great help to administrators in evaluating the performances of individual schools in the district. Those that exceed a drop-out rate of 15.67 percent are doing significantly poorly. Those that have drop-out rates of less than 15.33 percent are doing significantly better than the district at large.

T TEST.   The Z test assumes that we know the population standard deviation and that the number of observations in the sample is large (usually more than thirty). However, both of these assumptions are frequently violated in hypothesis testing. In such a case, the Z table becomes inappropriate. W. S. Gossett, writing under the pseudonym *Student,* devised another test for these kinds of problems, which has since been called the ***t* distribution.** The results of this distribution are presented in a t table (Appendix B). The formula for the use of t statistics is similar to that of Z, and with a large enough sample, the two will coincide. The formula for t distribution is given as

$$t = \frac{\overline{X} - \mu}{s / \sqrt{n - 1}} \tag{6.7}$$

Notice that this new statistic (t) differs from Z in that its denominator contains the sample standard deviation (s) instead of the population standard deviation

(σ), and we take the square root of the number of observations in the sample ($n-1$). The subtraction of 1 from n gives us the **degrees of freedom (df)**. One can easily explain the concept of degrees of freedom, but its use in statistics is not exactly intuitive. The term "degrees of freedom" refers to the number of free choices one can make in estimating a number. For example, let us say the sum of two numbers X and Y is equal to 10. There are, of course, infinite counts of two numbers that add up to 10. However, if I choose the value of one number (say, 27), there is only one number (–17) that will add up to 10. Therefore, in estimating the sum of two numbers we have the free choice of only one number ($2-1$). We call it the degree of freedom. By extending this logic, we can see that if twenty numbers add up to 10, we will have 19 degrees of freedom; after we have chosen 19 numbers, the twentieth number is automatically determined. Since we are attempting to estimate the population value with samples, we use $n-1$ degrees of freedom. Therefore, it is important to remember to subtract 1 from the number of observations for each set of samples. So, to calculate the t value, which is done on one set of samples, we use $n-1$ degrees of freedom. In the following section, we will compare two sets of samples. For that problem we will subtract 1 for each of the two sets of samples $n1$ and $n2$. Thus, the degrees of freedom for the t distribution will be equal to $(n1 + n2) - 2$.[3]

Let us go back to the example of the discovered remains of inhabitants of the disputed land. Suppose we found skulls of 17 adults, with an average circumference of 21.5 inches and a sample standard deviation of 1.4. The average for the present population is 23 inches. To test the null hypothesis that these ancient people belonged to the same race, we set up the t score as

$$t = \frac{21.5 - 23.0}{1.4 \ / \ \sqrt{17 - 1}}$$

$$= \frac{1.5}{1.4 \ / \ \sqrt{16}}$$

$$= 4.29$$

Let us suppose that we want to evaluate the null hypothesis at the 0.01 level (alternatively, the 99th percentile level), which as a one-tailed test is $\alpha = 0.005$. Now we can look up the t table. By going across the columns, pick out the 0.005 level. Then come down along the rows until this level is matched with 16 degrees of freedom (17 observations minus 1). This will give you the critical t value of 2.921. Our calculated t value is larger than the critical value, so we can reject the null hypothesis and conclude that it is highly unlikely that they belong to the same race of people. *It is important to note that in the empirical sciences, regardless of how large the Z or the t values are, we never establish the absolute "truth"; instead, we maintain that we can reject the null hypothesis.*

COMPARISON OF TWO DIFFERENT SERIES OF NUMBERS.   In the previous examples, we tested the hypothesis that *a particular sample was different from the population.* However, we may frequently need to test whether two samples are *significantly different from each other.* In the previous example, we discussed whether the remains of the ancient settlers belonged to the racial stock of the present population. In contrast, suppose we have found two sets of remains from two different time periods. We want to know whether these two groups of people came from the same stock. In such a case, we will test the null hypothesis that

$$\overline{X}_1 = \overline{X}_2$$

Since we are not making any assumption regarding the relative size of the difference between the two means (that is, if $\overline{X}_1 > \overline{X}_2$ or $\overline{X}_1 < \overline{X}_2$), we have to use a two-tailed test. If the number of samples (n_1 and n_2) is more than thirty for each series, we can use a Z statistic; otherwise we need to use a t statistic. To test the null hypothesis that the two means are equal, the difference between the two means is converted to a standard score by dividing it by the standard deviation. That is,

$$t = \frac{\overline{X}_1 - \overline{X}_2}{\sigma_{x_1 x_2}} \tag{6.8}$$

where $\overline{X}_1 - \overline{X}_2$ is the difference between the two means, and $\sigma x_1 x_2$ is the standard deviation of the sampling distribution of the difference between two means.

If the t statistic is applicable, its degree of freedom is given by ($n_1 + n_2 - 2$), where n_1 is the number of sample observations in series 1 and n_2 is the number of sample observations in series 2. Since we have the observations of the two series, we know their means. However, the question arises, What is the standard deviation of the distribution of the means? If there are reasons to believe that the standard deviations of the two sample series are, in fact, equal, the standard deviation of the combined series is calculated as

$$\sigma_{X_1 X_2} = \sqrt{\frac{n_1 S_1^2 + n_2 S_2^2}{n_1 + n_2 - 2}} \sqrt{\frac{n_1 + n_2}{n_1 n_2}} \tag{6.9}$$

If, however, there is no reason to believe that the two standard deviations are the same, then we should use the following formula:

$$\sigma_{X_1 X_2} = \sqrt{\frac{S_1^2}{n_1 - 1} + \frac{S_2^2}{n_2 - 1}} \tag{6.10}$$

Of course, the question arises, when should we assume that the standard deviations are the same and when should we not? The answer to this question may depend on your subjective assessment. However, the rule of thumb is that if the two means are coming from a similar population group, you may assume that the standard deviations are the same. For example, if you are comparing the average number of children per household in two suburbs of the same city that have similar socioeconomic and demographic characteristics, you may safely assume that their standard deviations are the same. However, if you are comparing the mean of an affluent suburb with that of a poor center city area, you may have to assume that the standard deviations are different.

Let us consider a numerical example. Suppose we have data of drug abuse per 1,000 high school students in two school districts with the characteristics shown in Table 6.2.

If we believe that the two standard deviations are equal, then by using equation 6.10, we can estimate the pooled standard deviation as

$$\sigma_{x_1 x_2} = \sqrt{\frac{28(5.75)^2 + 16(6.05)^2}{28 + 16 - 2}} \sqrt{\frac{28 + 16}{28 \times 16}} = .589$$

By substituting this estimated number in equation 6.8, we get

$$t = \frac{25.0 - 20.6}{.589} = \frac{4.4}{.589} = -7.47$$

Since t has 42 degrees of freedom $(28 + 16 - 2)$, the corresponding probability value for alpha $= 0.025$ is approximately equal to 2.02. Because our calculated t score, 7.47, falls outside the critical region of 2.02, we can reject the null hypothesis that the two means are equal. That is, drug abuse in District A is significantly lower than in District B.

If there is no reason to believe that the two standard deviations are the same, by using equation 6.8 we estimate the pooled standard deviation to be

$$\sigma_{x_1 x_2} = \sqrt{\frac{\left(5.75\right)^2}{28 - 1} + \frac{\left(6.05\right)^2}{16 - 1}} = 1.91$$

By plugging in 1.91 in equation 6.8, we get t value $= 4.4/1.91 = 2.30$. Again, this number is greater than 2.02, so we can reject the null hypothesis.

Although in this case both the calculations gave us a similar answer, it should not be assumed that the standard deviations in two series are equal.

DIFFERENCE OF PROPORTIONS TEST.   While doing a survey, you may face a situation in which you need to compare the proportions and percentages of the two sample populations. For instance, you are conducting a survey to find out the attitude of the citizens toward the police. Your survey indicates that 33 percent of the 320 whites polled agreed with the statement that "they do not have a great deal of trust" for the local police department, whereas 45 percent of the 267 minority

Table 6.2 Comparison of Means

	District A	District B
Mean	25.0 $(\overline{X}_1)$	20.6 $(\overline{X}_2)$
Standard deviations	5.75 (s_1)	6.05 (s_2)
Number of schools in the districts	28 (n_1)	16 (n_2)

respondents agreed with that assessment. In order to determine a policy of community relations for the police department, you want to know if the difference between the two communities is statistically significant. For this, you will have to use the following formula:

$$Z = \frac{\bar{p_1} - \bar{p_2}}{\sqrt{\left(\frac{n_1 \bar{p_1} + n_2 \bar{p_2}}{n_1 + n_2} \right) \left(1 - \frac{n_1 \bar{p_1} + n_2 \bar{p_2}}{n_1 + n_2} \right) \left(\frac{n_1 + n_2}{n_1 \times n_2} \right)}} \qquad (6.11)$$

where

$\bar{p_1}$ = proportion of first subgroup

$\bar{p_2}$ = proportion of second subgroup

n_1 = sample population of first subgroup

n_2 = sample population of second subgroup

For this example the values are as follows:

$\bar{p_1}$ = 0.38

$\bar{p_2}$ = 0.45

n_1 = 320

n_2 = 267

When we substitute these numbers in equation 6.11, we get $Z = 1.71$.

The Z table tells us that the critical value of the one-tailed test is 1.645. Our Z value exceeds the critical value, and thus we can conclude that the minority groups have less trust for the police department. Hence, any public policy for the community involvement must take into account this difference in perception.

The Chi-Squared Test

The preceding examples show that if we are confronted with a problem such as determining whether a subgroup is significantly different from the larger population, we can use the Z test (provided, of course, that we know the population mean and the standard deviation). If we do not know the population values but want to know if two different groups are "truly" different from each other, we can use the Student's t test. In contrast to these two common forms of hypothesis testing, we frequently encounter the situation in which we may be interested in finding out whether an observed phenomenon is significantly distinct from its expected behavior.

Suppose the Metropolitan Transit Authority (MTA), which employs 300 drivers, has the task of training new recruits and periodically retraining older operators. The MTA used to operate an in-house driver-training school. However, in a cost-cutting mood, it is experimenting with replacing trainers with a newly developed computer-based training method. By this method, trainees will sit in front of a computer terminal, go through each lesson, and at the end answer multiple choice questions. If they pass, they will move on to the next section and will ultimately pass the entire theoretical portion of their training program. Management finds this computer-based program attractive: It offers cost savings on salaries and benefits, and the training school can remain open twenty-four hours a day, thereby allowing the drivers to come at their own convenience and train themselves. As a consultant, your task is to determine whether the system is acceptable to the drivers of the MTA. You conducted a survey that asked the drivers whether they were

  a. Enthusiastic about learning through a computer.
  b. Indifferent between the computer and the training school.
  c. Upset about the change and would prefer the old training school.

Since fear of computers is likely to be related to an individual's gender, I decided to classify the trainees according to their sex and then look at the survey responses. I have presented the data in the form of a matrix, which is known as a **contingency table** (see Table 6.3). In this table, the numbers next to the word *observed* represent the actual number of responses corresponding to the attitude toward computer-assisted training, classified by the gender of the respondent.

Below each observed frequency of responses is an entry for the expected response. This expected response is based on the hypothesis that there is no age bias in the acceptance of computer-assisted training. Thus, the two figures are exactly the same proportion as the two classifying variables (sex and attitude toward computer). This expected number is derived by multiplying the column total (known as the *marginal*) with the row total for each sex and dividing by the total number of trainees (300). The expected value for the female trainees who like computers is calculated by

$$\text{Expected value} = \frac{\textit{Column marginal} \times \textit{Row marginal}}{\textit{Total frequency}} = \frac{135 \times 55}{300} = 24.75$$

The logic for this operation is that if preference for the computer does not depend on the gender of the respondent, then the females will prefer it in exactly the same proportion as all those who prefer the computer.

Table 6.3   Example of a Contingency Table

Sex of the trainees	Like computers	Indifferent	Do not like computers	Total
Females	Observed: 15	Observed: 10	Observed: 30	55
	Expected: 25	Expected: 13	Expected: 17	
Males	Observed: 120	Observed: 60	Observed: 65	245
	Expected: 110	Expected: 57	Expected: 78	
Total	Observed: 135	Observed: 70	Observed: 95	**300**

After we have determined the expected value for each cell, we can look into the difference between the actual and the expected values. Similar to the other probability distributions, the sum of the squared differences between actual and expected values is also distributed along a theoretical probability distribution, called χ^2, or **chi-squared**. This is written as

$$\chi^2 = \sum \frac{\left(f_o^i - f_e^i\right)^2}{f_e^i} \tag{6.12}$$

where f_o^i is the observed frequency of cell i, and f_e^i is its expected value.

Thus, we can write the formula as

$$\chi^2 = \frac{\left(Observed\ frequencies - Expected\ frequencies\right)^2}{Expected\ frequencies}$$

$$= \frac{(15 - 24.75)^2}{24.75} + \frac{(10 - 12.83)^2}{12.83} + \frac{(30 - 17.41)^2}{17.41}$$

$$+ \frac{(120 - 110.25)^2}{110.25} + \frac{(60 - 57.17)^2}{57.17} + \frac{(65 - 77.58)^2}{77.58}$$

$$= 16.60$$

Like the t distribution, the χ^2 distribution varies with the degrees of freedom. For the χ^2 distribution, the degrees of freedom are calculated by (the number of columns − 1) × (the number of rows − 1). Thus the degrees of freedom for our example are df = (column − 1) × (row − 1) = (3 − 1) × (2 − 1) = 2 × 1 = 2.

Now we can look up the chi-squared distribution given in Appendix E. As you can see, for 2 degrees of freedom, the critical value at the 0.05 level is 5.99. Since our calculated chi-squared value 16.60 is greater than this number, we can safely conclude that the results show a definite sex bias in the acceptance of computer-based training for the MTA bus drivers. You may notice that in this case we did not need to know anything at all about the mean and the standard deviations of either the sample or the general population. This is the strength of this test and why it belongs to a class called **nonparametric** tests. Also, you should note that whereas t and Z distributions compare the difference between only two values, the χ^2 distribution measures the significance of all the cells jointly. Therefore, it is called a **joint probability distribution**.

TESTING FOR CORRELATION: PEARSON'S R.   In Chapter 5 we discussed Pearson's r, or the correlation coefficient. As you know, the relation between two variables in the real world is seldom perfect. Therefore, by observing a less-than-perfect correlation, you may wonder if the calculated coefficient is statistically significant. One of the advantages of the correlation coefficient is that it can be used to test the hypothesis that two variables are correlated. To test this hypothesis, r has to be converted into a t statistic by using the following formula:

$$t = \frac{r\sqrt{n-2}}{\sqrt{1-r^2}} \quad\quad (6.13)$$

where n is the size of the sample.

For example, the correlation between X and Y has been found to be 0.65, with a sample of twenty-six observations. The correlation is less than perfect, so you can formulate the null hypothesis that there is no correlation between the two variables.

By using the preceding formula, you can calculate the t as

$$t = \frac{.65\sqrt{26-2}}{\sqrt{1-.4225}} = 4.18$$

Since there are twenty-six observations, the degrees of freedom for the t test are $26 - 1 = 25$. The critical value for t at a 5 percent level of confidence for 15 degrees of freedom is 2.060. Since our calculated t statistic is greater than this critical value, we can reject the null hypothesis.

THE RISKS IN HYPOTHESIS TESTING.   In testing hypotheses under uncertain conditions we run the risk of (1) rejecting the null hypothesis when it is, in fact, true, or (2) accepting a false hypothesis. A true hypothesis rejected as false incurs a **type I error,** whereas a false hypothesis accepted as true creates a **type II error.** The matrix shown in Table 6.4 best explains this dilemma.

Many public sector decisions affecting the health and welfare of citizens are based on the statistical reasonings of hypothesis testing. Therefore, the cost of an erroneous decision can be enormous. Suppose we are considering school funding based on the attendance record of pupils. A particular school shows a higher-than-average absentee rate, which puts it at risk for losing part of its revenue from the government. If we reject the hypothesis that the school is failing to provide a rewarding education system to keep students in class, and the hypothesis is indeed true, we will be wasting public funds on an inefficient (at least by this particular measure) institution. In contrast, if we accept the null hypothesis and find the school negligent of its duties, when in fact its attendance record is not worse than the other schools in the district, then we will be inflicting undue pain on a school.

Therefore, we try to minimize these two errors in determining the decision rules. Unfortunately, these two errors are inversely related. That is, when we want to reduce type I error, we create more of type II error. If we want to give the benefit of the doubt to the individual schools, we stand to encourage poor schools by

Table 6.4   Errors of Hypothesis Testing

Decision	Hypothesis is true	Hypothesis is false
Reject hypothesis	**Type I error**	Correct decision
Accept hypothesis	Correct decision	**Type II error**

failing to take punitive measures. In contrast, if we become extremely strict about attendance records in determining school funding, we inflict unnecessary punishment on some otherwise deserving schools.

In statistics, the type I error is the chosen level of significance, or the alpha. Therefore, when we choose the alpha level 0.05, we make sure that we will falsely reject a true hypothesis only 5 percent of the time. If we lower the significance level to 0.01, we reduce the chance of accepting a false hypothesis but increase the probability that we will inadvertently reject a true one.

The choice of the significance level depends on the type of problem under consideration and the consequences of rejecting a true hypothesis. The criterion for accepting a hypothesis is rather conservative, and given a choice, we would rather err on the side of the status quo than make a false move. An example may clarify the dilemma. In the early 1990s the Food and Drug Administration (FDA) came under fire from two different groups for two diametrically opposite reasons. On the one hand, the FDA was accused of taking too long to test and approve for sale experimental drugs for AIDS. On the other hand, the FDA was heavily criticized for approving silicone gels for breast implants too quickly, without proper testing. If we are dealing with a problem that requires utmost safety, we would be better off setting the level of significance as small as possible (say, at 0.001). However, it is a matter of common practice to set the confidence level at 95 percent (alpha equal to 0.05) for most research and policy analysis.

Steps Toward Hypothesis Testing
1. Check theories relating to the comparability of the variables for testing.
2. State the null hypothesis clearly, making sure of the opposite hypothesis.
3. Specify the significance level of α.
4. Specify whether to use a Z or a t test.
5. Compute the value of the test statistic.
6. Draw your conclusion regarding the rejection or nonrejection of the null hypothesis.

SUBJECTIVE PROBABILITY

Ron Potter and Chris Newman are members of the parole board. They are participating in a parole board hearing of Rob Muggs. The board must decide whether Rob is a safe enough risk to grant him parole. Ron and Chris have different views. Ron sees Rob as "high risk" for committing a serious crime, whereas Chris judges him to be a "low risk." Both Ron and Chris are assessing the probability that this convicted felon is going to be in trouble with the law in the near future. However, in this case, they cannot use the measures of objective probability because each individual parole applicant poses a unique case. Therefore, the decisions of Ron and Chris become prime examples of rendering judgment based on subjective assessment of probability.

In our everyday lives, all of us make subjective judgments about uncertain situations. We appraise the future by assigning chance factors or odds. Although in life it is often sufficient to state that "it is likely that the task will be completed within the next week," or "there is a good possibility that the shipment will not arrive on time," in professional work, these vague chance factors must often be expressed in numerical terms. It is more useful to know that an expert assigns a 30 percent chance of certain legislation passing congressional scrutiny, or an 80 percent probability of a survey's results being completed by next Thursday, than simply knowing the odds in qualitative terms ("small chance" or "highly probable"). This assignment of numerical value gives more precision to the statement and, as such, can be compared with the assessment of some other expert.

Long neglected by serious researchers, the issue of subjective probability is increasingly becoming a topic of serious scientific inquiry. To Frank Lad, "The logic of probability merely formalizes the coherent implications of specified beliefs about events when the beliefs are expressed in a graded scale from 0 (complete denial) to 1 (complete affirmation). . . . The 'scientific method' empowers the scientists with precisely the same inferential principles that it empowers the person on the street in the conduct of daily affairs, no more no less."[4] In fact, many studies in economics have found that subjective assessment of probability by experts can often rival the accuracy of those derived from sophisticated econometric models.[5]

Still, we may need to take a number of steps to ensure the accuracy of a subjective assessment. Returning to our example of the parole board, we may ask the following question: Is there a measure of overall accuracy so that we can compare the subjective assessment of one board member with another, or the judgment of one parole board with another? Statisticians offer a number of different measures of accuracy, but let us discuss the most commonly used measure, the **quadratic score**.[6] The quadratic score (Q) is given by the following formula: $Q = 1 - (p - A)^2$, where Q is the quadratic score of probability assessment, p is the assessed probability, and A is the actual outcome.

As you can see from this formula, if I assign 0 probability to an applicant and he stays out of trouble (actual outcome $= 0$), I have a perfect score of 1. However, if the parolee goes back to prison, my score becomes equal to 0.

Let us explain the method with the example of our parole board members Ron and Chris. They had categorized three successful parole applicants, Rob, Joe, and Phil, as "high risk" (probability of 0.8), medium risk (probability of 0.5), and low risk (probability of 0.2). After a year we saw that Rob and Phil had stayed out of prison (actual outcome is $= 0$), whereas Joe had committed a serious crime (actual outcome is $= 1$). Based on this information, we can construct the matrix shown in Table 6.5.

Table 6.5 Risk Assigned to Parolees

Parole board members	Parolees		
	Rob	Joe	Phil
Ron	High	High	Low
Chris	Medium	Low	Low

Table 6.6 Quadratic Score Matrix for Parolees

	Parolees			
Parole board members	Rob	Joe	Phil	Average score
Ron	0.36	0.36	0.96	0.56
Chris	0.75	0.96	0.96	0.89

Based on our method, we can calculate the accuracy score for the two board members with regard to Rob as follows:

$$\text{Ron's score on Rob: } Q = 1 - (.8 - 0)^2 = 0.36$$
$$\text{Chris's score on Rob: } Q = 1 - (.5 - 1)^2 = 0.75$$

This measure magnifies the error in judgment by squaring the difference between actual and predicted values. By following this method, we can score the board members on each of their judgments and average the score. From Table 6.6, we can see that Chris has been more accurate than Ron. You may notice that although in this case, we can claim that Chris has been a better forecaster than Ron, you may not say for sure if that is purely by chance. It is, of course, possible to establish statistical significance of the differences in performance; for that, however, we need many more observations. If we have a large enough sample size, we can use the techniques of hypothesis testing to find out statistical significance.

Finally, we should mention the shortcomings of subjective probability. The attribution of probability score by individual observers will always be open to question. We all assign probability values to uncertain events in our everyday lives. These attempted peeks into the future are based on our individual experience and expertise, and thus personal biases of judgment influence our assessments of probability. To understand subjective probability, we must know the sources of biases that may obscure our judgments. I have discussed the psychological obstacles to critical thinking in chapter 4. They are equally applicable to the assessment of subjective probability.

Key Words

Asymptotic probability (p. 124)
Central limit theorem (p. 126)
Chi-squared test (p. 139)
Confidence interval (p. 131)
Contingency table (p. 138)
Critical value (p. 130)
Cumulative probability distribution (p. 125)
Degrees of freedom (p. 134)
Hypothesis testing (p. 129)
Independent probability (p. 124)

Joint probability distribution (p. 139)
Law of Large Numbers (p. 127)
Level of significance (p. 129)
Mutually exclusive probability (p. 124)
Nonparametric tests (p. 139)
Normal distribution (p. 125)
Null hypothesis (p. 128)
Objective probability (p. 122)
One-tailed test (p. 130)
Probability distribution (p. 125)
Quadratic score (p. 142)

Exercises

1. What is an objective probability? What is a bias in objective probability?
2. What is a subjective probability? What are the main sources of biases that an individual faces in assessing subjective probability?
3. With an appropriate example, discuss the use of the central limit theorem as the foundation of statistical reasoning. Explain how it helps build a model of hypothesis testing.
4. The average SAT score for your state is 850, with a standard deviation of 65. The high school in your area has an average score of 980. Is this school an exception? Justify your answer.
5. From the information given in exercise 4, provide a confidence interval to develop a criterion for identifying schools with exceptionally good and unusually poor records.
6. Property tax is levied on the appraised market value of a property. However, it is often alleged that although the appraised values of the lower-priced houses are quite close to their market values (revealed when the properties are actually sold), the appraised values of the higher-priced houses are significantly lower than their market values. To investigate this allegation, the city of Masters conducted a study that found that for the forty lower-priced houses the ratio of assessed value/market value (A/M) was 0.89 with a standard deviation of 0.09. For a sample of forty high-priced homes this ratio was 0.65 with a standard deviation of 0.15.

    Do you agree that the poor homeowners in the city are carrying an unfair property tax burden?
7. The financial manager for the city of Masters is considering a switch from the existing money market fund to a new one. On the basis of the presented data series, do you believe that the difference between the two is significant enough to warrant a change?

Year	Existing	New
1	7.5	6.7
2	8.0	9.3
3	7.9	5.5
4	8.5	10.9
5	7.0	5.3
6	9.2	12.6
7	8.2	6.7
8	7.4	4.3
9	8.8	10.7
10	8.0	12.9

8. The city of Masters has been conducting a survey of police responses to emergency calls. A similar city has been chosen for comparison purposes. The following table shows the distribution of response time during a typical week. Is there any reason to believe that there is any significant difference in the record of the two cities?

Distribution of Police Response Time

Response time (minutes)	Masters	Other City
1–3	23	45
3–5	62	72
5–8	41	59
8–10	38	43
10–15	16	32
15–25	3	21
25–35	0	13
35–60	0	7

9. Let us continue with the example of Metropolitan Transit Authority's new computer-assisted driver-training program. Having examined the possible sex bias in the acceptance of the program, suppose you are trying to discover any possible age bias. Your survey resulted in the following table. By using chi-squared distribution, determine whether age imposes an additional barrier to the use of computers in the MTA.

Age of the trainees	Like computers	Indifferent	Do not Like computers	Total
18–25	30	25	10	65
26–45	65	30	60	155
46 and over	15	10	55	80
Total	110	65	125	300

10. Suppose we have observed ten individuals to establish the hypothesis that education has a strong correlation with income. Consider the following data, and test the hypothesis:

Education (years of schooling)	12	18	6	17	19	12	16	16	20	8
Income ($000)	25	35	22	56	85	20	45	48	65	20

11. The crime rate in your state is 4,455 per 100,000 population, with a standard deviation of 289. The city in which you live has a crime rate of 3,990 per 100,000 population. Your police chief is claiming credit for a low crime rate. Is your city an exception? Assume that the city and the state have the same standard deviation.

12. Your state is considering a program for reducing recidivism among its convicted felons. There is another state that instituted a similar program ten years ago. The following table provides us with information on the two states. Based on this data, what advice can you give to the policy makers?

Recidivism per One Thousand Convictions

Year	Your state	State with a running rehabilitation program
1	155	134
2	160	183
3	153	110
4	172	193
5	140	145
6	188	252
7	166	132
8	151	86
9	214	116
10	260	98

13. Your city has been conducting a survey of incidents of lead poisoning among children in the city's school districts. For the purpose of comparison, you have chosen your neighboring city. The following table shows the distribution of toxic incidents among various age groups of school-age children during a six-month period. Is there any reason to believe that there is any significant difference in the records of the two cities?

Distribution of Lead Poisoning Incidents

Age of children	Your city	Neighboring city
5–6	54	53
7–8	51	43
9–10	44	38
11–12	24	29
13–14	10	9
15–16	5	1
17–18	0	1

14. The public health officials in your city are considering using a new type of flu vaccine that is being touted as a better preventive. However, the new vaccine costs three times as much money per inoculation. On the basis of the following information, would you recommend the use of the new vaccine?

Comparison of Inoculation of Two Types of Vaccines

Year	Number of flu incidents in your city per 1,000 inoculated (with the old vaccine)	Number of flu incidents in a neighboring city per 1,000 inoculated (with the new vaccine)
1	150	142
2	155	164
3	142	110
4	157	112
5	120	128
6	174	210
7	157	142
8	133	99
9	135	143
10	156	155

15. Write an essay on subjective probability. Suppose you are attempting to determine the odds of your favorite football team winning the Super Bowl. What kinds of biases may cloud your judgment?

16. In 2001 a school district was experimenting with a new policy to reduce absenteeism in their schools. The following table presents the data from the ten schools for two years. The 2000 data does not include the new policy. By using the methods of hypothesis testing, tell us if the district has been successful. You will have to justify your methodology.

Comparison of Absenteeism

School	Rate of absenteeism in 2000	Regional average in 2001
1	4	9
2	3	5
3	4	6
4	5	4
5	3	9
6	9	9
7	2	7
	3	3

17. You are in charge of assessing the effectiveness of four parole board members. They assigned the levels of "high," "medium," and "low" with the corresponding subjective probability of 0.8, 0.5, and 0.2. You want to determine if their judgments were borne out by evidence after the parolee was out for a year. I have put (1) and (0) after the names of the parolees to indicate whether they were back in prison within a year. The number 1 indicates that the individual went back to prison and 0 indicates that he did not.

Parolees	Parole board members			
	Chris	Ron	Meg	Bob
A (0)	H	L	L	M
B (1)	H	M	L	M
C (0)	M	L	L	L
D (0)	H	L	L	M
E (1)	H	M	M	H
F (0)	H	H	L	M
G (1)	H	L	M	M
H (0)	M	L	L	L
I (0)	L	L	L	L
J (1)	H	H	L	L
K (0)	M	L	L	M
L (0)	H	M	L	L
M (0)	M	M	M	L
N (0)	H	H	L	L
O (1)	H	M	M	L
P (1)	H	L	L	M
Q (0)	M	M	L	L
R (0)	H	L	L	M

Parolees	Parole board members			
	Chris	Ron	Meg	Bob
S (1)	H	M	M	M
T (0)	L	L	L	M
U (0)	M	H	L	H
V (1)	H	L	M	M
W (0)	M	M	L	L
X (1)	H	M	M	L
Y (0)	H	M	L	L
Z (0)	M	L	L	M

Notes

1. For an excellent discussion of the central limit theorem and its implication in the field of statistics, see John Casti, *Five Golden Rules: Great Theories of 20th-Century Mathematics and Why They Matter* (New York: Wiley, 1996).
2. The fact that the mean of a normal distribution will be zero can be easily shown. Since the sample average $\bar{X}$ becomes equal to its true population value μ, with infinite sampling the sum of $(\bar{X}_i - \mu)$ becomes equal to zero.
3. For the mathematical explanation of degrees of freedom, see Robert S. Pindyck and Daniel L. Rubinfeld, *Econometric Models and Economic Forecasts*, 2d ed. (New York: McGraw-Hill, 1981), 42–43.
4. Frank Lad, *Operational Subjective Statistical Methods: A Mathematical, Philosophical, and Historical Introduction* (New York: Wiley, 1996), 13. Lad offers a comprehensive but demanding explanation of subjective probability.
5. See Harinder Singh, "Relative Evaluation of Subjective and Objective Measures of Expectations Formation," *Quarterly Review of Economics and Business* 30 (1990): 64–74.
6. J. Frank Yates, "Subjective Probability Accuracy Analysis," in *Subjective Probability*, ed. George Wright and Peter Ayton (New York: Wiley, 1994), 381–410.

7

SOURCES OF DATA

The first question facing an empirical researcher is, Where do I get the necessary information to prove my hypothesis or to answer my question? A recent survey sponsored by a major university library discovered that the vast majority of students do not know how to use library resources to obtain information for writing a report or a term paper. In chapter 1 we discussed the framework of an objective analysis, whereby the first rule is to define a project's goals or objectives. Similarly, before looking for data, you must define precisely the problem you want to investigate. If your task is to get information on the effectiveness of a particular public policy, you need to plan precisely how you are going to go about your task. Then you must collect the information, which may or may not be readily available. Information available in published form is called **secondary data** (that is, data collected by someone other than the researcher). Data that you must collect on your own is **primary data**. I have divided this chapter into two broad sections. The first section deals with the issues of measurement, and the second discusses primary and secondary sources of data.

WHAT ARE WE MEASURING?

We all like to quantify. We express the amount of rainfall, the speed of automobiles, even intelligence, in numbers. We collect numerical information on income, unemployment, crime, political violence, the extent of democratic values, and the level of authoritarian personality. As analysts, we aim to assign numbers to properties or attributes according to specific rules or measurements. Controversies, however, arise in regard to the accuracy of those measurements. Therefore, let us first discuss the various types of measurements and then concentrate on their relative merits as measuring units.

Types of Measurement

Phenomena to be measured can be assigned values according to nominal, ordinal, interval, or ratio scales. Of these measurements, the weakest form of assigning numerical value is the **nominal** scale. For example, while filling out census or other kinds of application forms, we are often asked to identify our ethnic background. Each ethnic group is assigned a number (1 through 5, say), numeral (I through V), or an alphabetic classification (A through E). Because these numbers and letters are not amenable to mathematical treatment, they do not give us any insight into their relative comparability, such as whether group B is closer to A in any attribute or physical quality than is group E. For nominal scales, assigning numbers is devoid of any intrinsic meaning.

Some phenomena are comparable, so we can arrange them according to some quality but cannot tell precisely the distances among them. We may rank-order presidential candidates according to their political philosophies, but we may not be able to tell that candidate A is 2.35 times more conservative than candidate B. This process of ranking is called an **ordinal** scale. It is important to note that because numbers for ordinal rankings do not carry any specific meaning, the direction of their assigned value does not make a difference. Thus, among five candidates the most conservative candidate may be assigned the value 1 or 5 without any consequence, as long as the ordering is in sequence. As you can see, ordinal rankings are stronger than nominal ones, since we can compare the relative position of the case in question (the "conservativeness" of the presidential candidates in this example).

Arrangement by **interval** scale offers us a greater amount of flexibility in comparing cases, both according to arrangement of ranking and the actual distance between any two cases. If the candidates are assigned a number in an interval scale, we can compare them by saying not only that A is more conservative than B but also that A is 2.35 times more conservative than B. Because of this desirable quality, the temptation to express orderings according to interval scale is strong. As a consequence a great deal of effort has been directed toward constructing interval scale measures for various kinds of social, political, and economic phenomena. Various conservative and liberal congressional watchdogs assign numbers to individual members of Congress according to their voting patterns. In other studies, countries have been given numerical values for their development potential, degree of democratization, and level of political violence.[1]

The interval scale, however, may not have a fixed and well-defined zero, at which point the quality we are measuring does not exist. In the progressive assignment of points (the higher the number, the higher the level of liberalism) to members of Congress, the senator with a score of zero must show no traces of liberal value whatsoever, an attribute rarely seen in human beings. In contrast, we may order various school districts by the percentage of minority enrollment, or airlines according to the ratio of delayed to total flight arrivals, and in each of these cases, the value of zero will have a specific meaning (a school district with no minority students or an airline that is always on time). This is called a **ratio** scale.

Accuracy of the Measuring Scales

When we try to quantify something, we need to know the accuracy of our measurements. If we want to measure a phenomenon that has a physical manifestation and only one dimension, our efforts are largely free of controversy. Measuring an individual's height or weight is done without any trouble, as long as we are measuring either height *or* weight. However, we are likely to run into a bit more trouble if we attempt to quantify the "largeness" of a person, a measure that must encompass both height *and* weight. Therefore, if we want to express a phenomenon that has no obvious physical manifestation, such as an individual's intelligence, attitude, or quality of life, or the regional inflation rate, national growth potential, or international political instability, we are treading in dangerous waters. Even measuring strictly physical, single-attribute phenomena can sometimes be controversial. James Gleick gives an interesting example in a popular book on mathematical theory of chaos.[2] In encyclopedias and other reference books, one frequently encounters various measures of national geography, such as the total square miles of land area or shoreline. Gleick points out that the measurement of jagged shoreline must vary with the size of the yardstick. When cartographers measure shorelines, they use an approximation. Consider Figure 7.1. When I use a large yardstick, I miss all the little edges. However, by using a smaller stick, I can try to be more precise. In so doing, the measurement of the shoreline will register an increase, as this more precise instrument would include areas that were not measured before. Unfortunately, this smaller stick would not give us a perfect measurement, as it would miss areas smaller than itself. Clearly, as we keep on reducing the size of the yardstick, we also increase the measurement of the total shoreline. In the end, when the yardstick becomes infinitesimally small, the measurement of the shoreline would also be recorded as infinitely long.

We live in an imperfect world. Therefore, along with everything else, we must live with the shortcomings of our indicators. The only recourse we have is to be aware of their inherent biases and problems and to interpret them with extreme

Figure 7.1   Measuring the English Shoreline

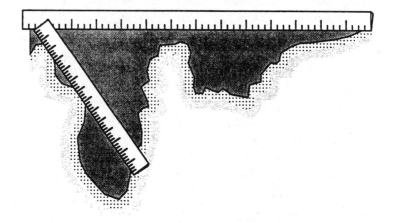

care. With these words of caution, we may examine the types of data and their sources.

PRIMARY DATA: CONDUCTING A SURVEY

Often, the kind of information you need is not available in archival records. In that case, you may need to collect information on your own. You can collect primary information through direct observation or through surveys. Traffic engineers routinely observe traffic patterns for more efficient and safer road design. They can send actual observers or use counters that automatically record the number of vehicles and their speed. Public health officials develop regional statistics by compiling data from local hospitals, and water management departments collect information through laboratory testing of water samples from local rivers, streams, and other sources of drinking water.

Public policy researchers, however, most frequently use surveys to collect primary data. For example, local governments often rely on opinion polls for needs assessments, prioritization of issues, or to shape a service delivery system. If county authorities want to improve elderly health care delivery in a community, they can commission a survey that assesses residents' needs through a series of specific or open-ended questions. A municipal service agency such as a rapid transit authority can design a survey for developing a more efficient mass transit system. A municipal government may also be interested in learning its constituents' views on a specific issue, such as a proposed ban on smoking in public places or the location of a proposed city library. The challenge for these and other surveys is how to collect unbiased information in a systematic way. Because it is often impossible to ask every member of a large group, we have to depend on surveys based on sampling theory. Sampling theory helps us determine the most cost-efficient way to derive unbiased information; or more simply, it helps us design a survey.

Designing a Survey

The starting point of any survey design is the question of **population**. The term "population" is defined as the entire target group from which the necessary information is to be extracted. Let us suppose that we want to determine whether the residents of a small town are willing to accept a proposed prison facility located on the outskirts of town. In such a case, we may define the population as all the city's adult residents. If we are trying to figure out the effects of a price hike on city buses, then the bus riders will form the survey's population.

In a perfect world, with no constraints on time and money, it is desirable to have a complete enumeration, or survey of each member of the population. However, in reality, we must confine our inquiry to a small group of representatives of the population, called the **sample population.** The single most important quality of the sample population is its *representativeness.* That is, how closely does this sample group represent the entire population? If it does not represent the population well, the sample population will give us biased (and therefore erroneous) information, as shown in Figure 7.2.

These biases are characterized as either **systematic** or **random**. Through proper understanding of sampling theory one can minimize systematic sampling errors, which result from inappropriate survey design. Random variations in the data are what cause random sampling errors, however. Such variations cannot be completely eliminated but can be managed through proper survey design. Let us discuss these in detail.

Systematic Errors in Sampling

Systematic errors result from biased sampling of the population. These biases have many sources. We identify some of the most common sources of systematic sampling biases below.

NONREPRESENTATIVE SAMPLE. A nonrepresentative sample group produces biased inferences about a population. During the 1936 presidential campaign, the now

Figure 7.2   Errors in Sampling

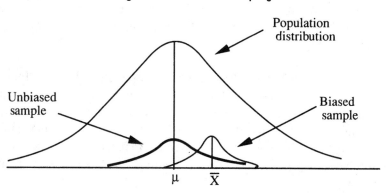

defunct *Literary Digest* conducted a telephone survey. Based on its sample of New York residents, the magazine predicted a comfortable margin of victory for Alf Landon against Franklin D. Roosevelt. However, when the actual poll results came out, FDR had won a decisive victory. Why was the survey wrong? The prediction was incorrect because it was based on a sample that did not properly represent the population. Telephones were still a novelty in 1936, restricted to the relatively affluent. The telephone was not the tool of universal communication that it is today. Therefore, a sample of telephone owners was an inappropriate representative for the rest of the population.

The designer of a survey should always guard against this kind of systematic bias. For example, if you pick names of individuals from the property tax roll for a survey to determine the mass transit needs of a low-income neighborhood, your sample may diverge from your intended group—the neighborhood residents. Because most residents rent, rather than own, their homes in a low-income neighborhood, the exclusion of the renter population will cause the poll results to deviate significantly from those of the target population. To avoid this error one must have an intimate knowledge of the population and the existence of biased "cells" or subgroups within it.

SELF-SELECTION BIAS WITHIN THE SAMPLE. Unfortunately, even correctly specifying the sample group will not always eliminate the problem of getting unbiased information. For example, suppose you carefully identified your sample group and administered a detailed questionnaire. When the results come in you find out that they are still biased. This may happen because of self-selection within the sample group, when those who choose to respond to a survey turn out to be different from the rest of the population. Thus, going back to my example of mass-transit needs in a low-income neighborhood, I may find that the respondents are disproportionately drawn from the English-speaking, better-educated, older, and nonminority population. In such a case, their opinion will obviously not reflect the entire neighborhood. This self-selection bias may not be restricted to individual respondents. The International City/County Management Association (ICMA) collects data on municipalities. However, its data sets are based on information voluntarily submitted by the municipalities. Such self-reporting can create a bias, because those local governments that are less affluent or are passing through hard economic times may not have the personnel or the inclination to fill out a detailed questionnaire. Thus, the data sets presented in the ICMA yearbooks carry an appropriate warning.

WHEN PEOPLE LIE. If you ask a sensitive question, people often do not tell the truth. People may lie about their beliefs regarding race relations, gender equality, homosexuality, or other matters of private attitude because they are afraid to be politically incorrect or are mindful of social sanctions for unpopular opinions. This is a particular problem for AIDS researchers. To make a proper assessment of a community's needs, they have to ask extremely sensitive questions regarding people's sexual habits. And unless they do so with the utmost care, their survey may produce biased results.

People are also typically reluctant to reveal their deeply held racial prejudices. As a result, time and again, forecasting of certain elections turns out to be incorrect. In the 1990 U.S. Senate election in Louisiana, the incumbent Democratic candidate was widely predicted to score an overwhelming victory over David Duke, a former grand wizard of the Ku Klux Klan whose platform rested on opposition to affirmative action. Pre-election polls projected that Duke would garner no more than 25 percent of the votes. Yet when the actual poll results were tabulated, he had managed to get 44 percent, including 60 percent of the white votes.[3] Even the exit polls turned out to be inaccurate, suggesting that many people would not admit to having voted for Duke. Similarly, on the eve of the 1989 mayoral election in New York, polls gave David Dinkins, a black candidate, a lead of 14 to 18 percent over Rudolph Giuliani (who is white). The exit polls predicted a 6 to 10 percent spread between the candidates. However, Dinkins actually won by a much smaller margin, a meager 2 percent.[4]

COLLECTION BIAS.   Natural obstacles to reporting may create biases. In several border states the issue of illegal immigration has been rather controversial. Because immigration has a tremendous impact on a region's economy, the Census Bureau would like a more accurate enumeration of the illegal immigrants in the area and more detailed knowledge of their socioeconomic attributes. However, for understandable reasons, illegal immigrants have been underreported.

Biases also result from the mode of collection. The *World Handbook of Political and Social Indicators* (1982), by Charles Taylor and Michael Jodice, makes a significant contribution to scholarly research by compiling international social and political data. Yet, as the authors readily admit, much of the political data are collected from the *New York Times* and a few other published reports. These newspapers are more likely to report on events that take place in Western nations than in some obscure country in Asia or Africa, so the data will contain systematic biases.

ERRORS DUE TO OBSERVATION.   In the early 1920s, the physicist Werner Heisenberg performed a series of famous experiments in an attempt to observe the position of subatomic particles. To ascertain the positions of these particles, they had to be charged with photon particles. But the very act of charging them caused them to change their original position in a random fashion, thereby making it impossible to know where they were before. These experiments gave birth to what is known as Heisenberg's uncertainty principle, which simply states that for certain cases no experimental design is available that would not create errors caused by the process of observation.

In an analogous way, social scientists often alter the behavior of the people they are observing. In other words, if we are told that we are being observed, our behavior may differ from that in our day-to-day lives. In a famous experiment conducted in the early 1970s, the psychologist Stanley Milgram demonstrated the power of authority figures in influencing individual behavior.[5] His subjects were told that they were taking part in a test to determine the effect of punishment on memory. They were asked to give electrical jolts to another "subject," a man in another room, whenever he made a mistake. In fact, the voice from the other room was that of an actor and was taped for the experiment. They were also told to increase the voltage each additional time he made a mistake. To the amazement of the experimenters, the subjects continued to increase the voltage despite desperate pleas from the unseen voice, simply because they were told to do so by the laboratory psychologist. Nearly 60 percent of the subjects increased the voltage to the fatal level. Although the findings of this sensational experiment paint an unflattering picture of human nature, it is extremely difficult to say whether such blind obedience could be replicated on all of us in an open society.[6]

One of the ways to avoid the errors resulting from observation is to collect data on what is known as **revealed preference.** That is, although people's actual preferences are not apparent to an outside observer, they are revealed through their past choices. If you ask people if they will go to the polls in an upcoming election, those who may not vote may attempt to hide their actual intent because of a reluctance to admit their failure to carry out their civic duty. For another example of how observation influences behavior, see "A Case in Point, Errors of Observation."

BIAS IN THE SURVEY INSTRUMENT.   Survey results can be biased if the instruments (the questions) are loaded with hidden values that elicit certain reactions from the respondents. During the early days of the former Soviet Union's dissolution, the government of President Mikhail Gorbachev objected to a referendum in a breakaway republic that asked, "Would you like to be free or be willing to be dominated by the forces of communist Russia?" Naturally, the election results were never in doubt. In public policy analysis, a faulty survey instrument can often distort the results. Thus, for example, when asked in a general context, most people are likely to show their preference for such public goods as a clean environment, abundant wildlife, or a safer and well-maintained infrastructure. However, these answers may not truly reflect public opinion because people are just as likely to change their minds when these same questions are asked with reference to how much the programs may cost them.

Further, calls for subjective judgment can create biases. Asking people to categorize something as "high," "low," "large," "small," and so forth, elicits the subjective nature of people's judgment, which may stand in the way of determining the "true" opinion of the public.

Random Sampling Errors

Random sampling errors occur because of unexplained variations around "true" population values. Because these variations are random (or are caused by factors that cannot be determined), they can fall in any direction around the true values.

A CASE IN POINT

Errors of Observation: The Hawthorne Experiment

The fact that observation can alter the behavior of those being observed can signifi-cantly reduce the validity of research findings. The most celebrated example of this is the so-called Hawthorne experiment. In 1932 a group of researchers reported the results of an experiment they had been conducting for the past five years at the Hawthorne plant of the Western Electric Company. They discovered, by accident, that people generally seem to work better and are more productive when their performance on the job receives the flattering attention of a group of university researchers.

The researchers, headed by Elton Mayo and F. J. Roelithsberger, were originally try-ing to find at what level the garment factory's illumination needed to be set to maxi-mize production.[1] They started with a very high degree of light and slowly reduced its intensity to see if it would influence productivity. The workers became aware of the fact that they were being observed. As the light got dimmer and dimmer, they took it as a matter of group pride to work even harder. Needless to say, their sensitivity to being observed spoiled the original intent of the research. However, the results of this exper-iment made scholars of organizational behavior aware of the strength of group identity as a motivating force in the workplace and started the so-called humanistic school of organizational behavior.

Note

1. For one of the most recent reviews of the implications of the Hawthorne Experi-ment, see J. H. Smith, "The Enduring Legacy of Elton Mayo," *Human Relations* 51 (1998): 221–250.

Discussion Points

1. Why should we be extra careful in designing our research, particularly when it comes to observing human behavior?
2. How can you maintain objectivity in observing human behavior or derive truthful answers through survey questions?

For example, if you throw stones at the middle of a target some will hit the bull's-eye, some will not. The stones will have a strong central tendency because you have aimed at the bull's eye. Therefore, however poor a marksman you are, the stones will form a more or less normal distribution (unless, of course, your arm gets tired and creates a bias as a result), which will look like a Mexican sombrero. Similarly, if the errors are randomly distributed around the mean in a three-dimensional situ-ation, they will form normal distributions in any direction around the mean (μ). I have attempted to depict this in Figure 7.3. As you can see, the true population value (of, say, the proportion of the population favoring handgun control) is μ.

Figure 7.3   Random Sampling Errors

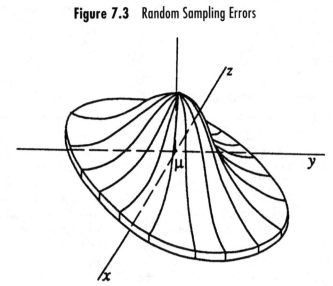

However, owing to the presence of random variations, the sample value may turn out to be different from this true value.

Because these variations are random, we cannot completely eliminate them. Instead, we try to increase the precision of the sample results by reducing the random error factor. How can we do this? Recalling the discussion of the Law of Large Numbers in chapter 6, we know that as the size of the sample increases, the domain of the error term shrinks. So when the number of samples approaches infinity or the sample size becomes the same as the entire population (in which case it is no longer a sample but a complete enumeration), the sample value becomes equal to the true population value. As already mentioned, however, costs often preclude a complete enumeration. Hence, we need to design a survey that is within our financial means yet provides us with a tolerably precise result, that is, one with a reasonably low error level. We will discuss this more at length when we tackle the question of sample size later in this chapter.

Armed with the knowledge of possible pitfalls, we may now discuss the process of designing a survey. This process essentially centers around four questions: (1) Who is chosen? (2) How many are chosen? (3) Which questions should be asked? and (4) What is the mode of polling?

Choosing the Sample Population

There are numerous methods of choosing a group of subjects, some of which are called **objective sampling** or **probability-based sampling,** in which the sample subjects are drawn according to a set of rules meant to maximize the probability of achieving an accurate account of the population. In contrast, one may use the **judgmental method of sampling,** in which one uses specialized knowledge about the population to get to the correct information.

Objective Sampling

- ***Random sampling.*** When we conduct random sampling, each element in the population has an equal chance of being picked. There are many ways of ensuring that the samples are drawn in a truly random fashion. For example, you may use computer-generated random numbers to pick the subjects. Or, in a large metropolitan city, you may go by the listings in the telephone book (say, by choosing the tenth person on each page). This method is most likely to give us the desired results when the population is relatively homogeneous. If we are interested in gathering information on social norms and mores, a random sample may be the most appropriate design, because each member of the society has an equal voice when determining individual attitudes.

- ***Stratified sampling.*** In contrast, when a population is divided into distinct subgroups, or *strata*, it may be better to identify each stratum of society and poll them separately. An example may clarify the situation. Suppose a school district is considering switching from the traditional academic calendar to year-round schooling. To assess the reaction to this proposed change, the school district wants to poll the residents of the district. Because the population is fragmented along the traditional lines of income and race—and because the district authorities want to be sensitive to the special needs of single parents—it is advantageous to poll each subgroup separately.

- ***Cluster sampling.*** When an extremely large population must be polled, a pollster may find it difficult (or too expensive) to include each member on the list of potential subjects from which the sample is to be drawn. Instead, the pollster may concentrate on a microcosm of the larger population. Let us suppose that we need to examine an aspect of urban America and we find it impossible to reach every city. We may argue, then, that a particular city (say, Buffalo, New York) can serve as the "typical city." Hence, we can poll the residents of Buffalo and draw conclusions about the rest of the urban areas of the United States. As you can see, the accuracy of this procedure depends on how representative of the population the cluster is.

Choosing the Size of the Sample

The development of theoretical statistics has given us some of the most powerful tools of quantitative decision making. One of these tools helps us determine sample size by linking the concepts of **confidence interval** and **sample error**. As discussed in chapter 6, confidence interval is calculated by using the following formula:

$$-Z_\alpha \times \frac{\sigma}{\sqrt{N}} > \overline{X} - \mu > +Z_\alpha \times \frac{\sigma}{\sqrt{N}} \tag{7.1}$$

where Z_α is the value from the Z table at the desired level of confidence, α,

σ is the population standard deviation,
N is the population size,

$\bar{X}$ is the sample mean, and

μ is the population mean.

This formula tells us that we can be confident at any desired level of α that the difference between the sample mean and the population mean will fall within a particular band. We can rewrite this formula as:

$$\left(\bar{X} - \mu\right) \pm Z_\alpha \times \frac{\sigma}{\sqrt{N}} \qquad (7.1a)$$

or

$$\mu = \bar{X} \pm \left(Z_\alpha \times \frac{\sigma}{\sqrt{N}}\right) \qquad (7.1b)$$

The problem with using this formula is that it uses the population standard deviation, which is unobservable. We can estimate the population standard deviation from the sample standard deviation by correcting the formula with the degrees of freedom:

$$\mu = \bar{X} \pm Z_\alpha \times \frac{s}{\sqrt{n-1}} \qquad (7.1c)$$

where s is the sample standard deviation and n is the size of the sample population.

Let us take an example. Suppose that from a sample of one hundred residents of a city we learn that 67 percent of them support a proposed referendum. We also know that the survey has a standard deviation of 0.15. To be safe, we want 95 percent accuracy. Therefore, we can look up the Z table for the value of $Z_{0.05}$, which turns out to be approximately 1.96. Using these numbers in equation 7.1, we can be 95 percent certain that the population mean, which we cannot observe, will fall within the range

$$\mu = \pm 1.96 \times \frac{0.15}{\sqrt{100-1}} \quad = \quad 0.67 \pm .0295$$

That is, we can be 95 percent sure that the opinion of the population will vary within the range of approximately 70 percent and 64 percent. In other words, the sample result contains a sample error of ±3 percent (by rounding off 0.0295).

As you can see, there is clearly a tradeoff between the need for accuracy and its cost. If you want a very low sample error, you will have to interview a lot more people, which increases the cost of the survey. For example, you need a high degree of accuracy to predict the outcome of a close election but may not demand such a high standard for other policy-related polls.

Choosing Effective Survey Instruments

Although choosing the size of the sample is mechanical, the real art (derived from experience and creativity) of conducting a survey lies in designing the questionnaire. Many concerns arise when developing a questionnaire; we may classify them in five broad categories:

- ***Be on a level with the respondents.*** Questionnaires must be developed with the respondent in mind. If you are developing a questionnaire for middle school children, would you ask questions with words that are beyond their vocabulary? Certainly not. And since you are asking youngsters, you would be careful about the way you phrase your questions. The same caution applies to questions put to adults. The question "Do you belong to the poor, middle, or wealthy class?" would draw a mixed reaction, because definitions of these class boundaries vary considerably. Instead, you can get a much more specific answer by asking, "Which of the following income groups do you belong to—less than $10,000; between $10,001 and $20,000; … ?"

- ***Choose the right format for answers.*** Questions in a survey can be either open ended or fixed. In an open-ended question, answers can be long and descriptive. To determine positions on handgun registration, questions may be phrased as, "What is your position on handgun control?" Alternatively, questions may be put within a fixed format, such as:

  "I believe all handguns within the State should be registered."
  __ Strongly Agree
  __ Agree
  __ Neither Agree nor Disagree
  __ Disagree
  __ Strongly Disagree
  __ No Opinion

Both types of questions have advantages and drawbacks. Open-ended questions draw out a full spectrum of responses without restricting respondents. However, the answers to these questions, by virtue of being unstructured, cannot be easily fitted into a specific coding system for quantitative analysis. A highly structured question, however, may miss an answer that many respondents might have chosen.

- ***Avoid words provoking emotion.*** If your goal is to develop an objective set of questions, you should avoid terms that evoke strong emotional reactions. For example, you are trying to determine public support for the U.S. government's food aid to drought-stricken parts of Africa. Consider three questions:

A. "Do you support U.S. aid to drought-stricken parts of Africa?"
B. "Do you support U.S. aid to the starving people of Africa?"
C. "In view of all the problems facing this country, do you support U.S. aid to Africa?"

Although, in general, few people are against food aid to a starving group of people, it is fairly obvious that the answers to these similar questions are likely to be quite different. However, to an unsuspecting audience, you can report the results of this survey as "people's opinion on U.S. aid to Africa" by picking the one that suits your purpose the best.

- *Choose the proper sequence of questions.* The sequence in which questions are put to respondents can be crucial. The questions can be asked in a random sequence, or they can be asked in a funnel or an inverted funnel sequence. If respondents are likely to be familiar with the broad issues, it is better to use a funnel-like sequence, starting with the most general question and then narrowing down to a more specific one. Suppose a school district is debating the distribution of literature on birth control devices to its high school students. Because most people hold some kind of opinion on the state of family values, you can start by asking respondents to assess the state of family values and then, within that context, ask their opinion about birth control. In contrast, most people are not well informed about the problem of the external trade deficit and may require some help in framing the issue. Therefore, in such a survey, you may do well by starting out with a set of specific questions, which can help them focus on the broader issue.

- *Choose the appropriate length of questionnaire.* Because conducting a survey is expensive and time consuming, there is a tendency to load questionnaires with as many questions as possible. This tendency is to be resisted, as most people lose interest in answering questions if they are too long or there are too many. This is particularly true for mail or telephone surveys. Greater latitude is often possible when interviewing face-to-face.

Choosing Polling Methods

Surveys are about asking questions. Determining the mode of questioning is an extremely important aspect of survey design. Much thought must be given to choosing an appropriate medium. Generally speaking, there are three methods of interview:

- *Face-to-face interviews.* The personal, face-to-face interview is the most expensive, although probably the most accurate, method of gathering information about a population. Face-to-face interviews are particularly appropriate when the questionnaire has many open-ended questions or is lengthy. Frequently this form of personal interview can put the subjects at ease with the interviewer. Yet this personal contact may have its drawbacks, as the interviewer and the interviewee may find each other less than acceptable, and as a result, the survey results may be skewed.

- *Telephone interviews.* Telephone surveys may be the least expensive type of survey to administer and are not likely to create systematic biases. They are most effective in conducting quick, rather than in-depth, surveys. However, people are often squeamish about opening up to a faceless voice over the telephone and tend to be guarded in their responses.

- *Mailed questionnaires.* Relatively inexpensive and free of the influences of individual interviewers, mailed questionnaires allow subjects to think over their responses and can also be used to elicit long answers to open-ended questions. Also, once the questionnaires are returned they can be processed and data can be recorded, tabulated, tested, and reported with relative ease. In many cases these surveys are recorded on paper and scanned by a computer, creating files for subsequent testing. However, mailed questionnaires often suffer from extremely low response rates. While for personal interviews response rates are typically around 95 percent, for mail surveys these numbers have been observed to be between 2 and 40 percent. The low response rate should warn us that unless we are careful, the results can exhibit a self-selection bias. In other words, as discussed earlier, if the rate of returns is extremely low, those who have taken the initiative to fill out the questionnaires and mail them may represent a special subset of the population.

QUANTIFICATION OF SURVEY DATA

Survey results are typically expressed in absolute numbers or in percentages and ratios. We are also told survey results in terms of means. Because it is difficult to report the results of open-ended questions in numbers, most surveys use fixed-format answers. As noted at the beginning of the chapter, certain questions are answered in numbers (income, age, years of education, and so on), others in nominal scales (sex, race, religion, and the like). Finally, data that relate to matters of attitudes and values cannot be readily translated into numbers. To express these variables in numbers, we use predetermined scales.

In the social sciences, **Likert scales** are the most commonly used. In a Likert scale respondents are asked to express their feelings on a continuum varying from highly positive to highly negative. On a five-point scale, the respondents will be asked whether they "strongly agree," "agree," "are undecided," "disagree," or "strongly disagree" with a particular statement. These answers can then be assigned weights either in ascending (1, 2, 3, 4, 5) or descending (5, 4, 3, 2, 1) order. Based on their answer, the respondents will be given points, which will indicate their individual stance on a particular issue, or the average of the responses can be calculated for determining the "average" attitude or feeling.

REPORTING OF SURVEY RESULTS

Surveys are conducted to gather information and to test a specific set of hypotheses. It is very important, then, to report the results of a survey properly. Most are reported with tables, graphs, and charts. I will discuss these techniques in chapter 8. However, because survey data can be misused and misinterpreted, you must spell out in detail the assumptions, sampling method, sample error, level of confidence, and often the questions themselves. In a typical example, the *Los Angeles Times,* when reporting the results of a nationwide opinion survey, informs readers how the poll was taken:

The *Times* poll interviewed 1,146 registered voters nationwide, by telephone, from August 12 to 14. Telephone numbers were chosen from a list of all exchanges in the country. Random-digit dialing techniques were used to ensure that both listed and nonlisted numbers had an opportunity to be surveyed. Results were weighted slightly to conform with census figures for sex, race, age, education, and household size. The margin of sampling error for the total sample is plus or minus three percentage points. For certain subgroups, the error margin is slightly higher. Poll results can also be affected by other factors, such as question wording and the order in which questions are presented.[7]

CONDUCTING FOCUS GROUPS

Focus groups are becoming increasingly popular as a tool for gauging public opinion regarding policy issues at all levels of government. For a focus group, a small representative group of the target population, usually numbering between eight and twelve, are assembled for in-depth discussions on a certain topic. Under the guidance of a trained interviewer, the group discusses structured questions relating to the central topic. Focus groups can shed light on complex areas of public policies and other important issues that may be missed by a survey, which can be too structured (see "A Case in Point, Focus Group for Growth Management Policies").

In conducting focus groups, which can be powerful tools of policy formulation, you must address a number of methodological and procedural questions. Unlike a survey, there is no set methodology for focus groups. Since they are small and the questions open ended, strict statistical techniques cannot be used for their verification. A great deal of advanced thinking and planning must compensate for methods that are less than rigorous. In light of the Palm Beach County example, I can make a few suggestions for developing successful focus groups:

1. ***Determine a clear-cut set of goals.*** For example, in Palm Beach County, it was decided to concentrate only on the respondents' views on the proposed public policy of dividing up the region into five distinct zones of growth.
2. ***Identify the critical characteristics of potential participants.*** In the Palm Beach County case, do the focus groups include "constituents," meaning a group drawn from the resident population, or is it their intention to understand the views of key interest groups (for example, the Chamber of Commerce, small business groups, the commuters, builders and developers, agricultural workers, the environmentalists, and so forth)?
3. ***Recruit skillful group leaders.*** You should note that it is extremely important to use skillful discussion leaders who can keep the focus of the group tightly on the issues at hand. Discussion leaders must balance the need for the participants to freely express their opinions on controversial issues with that of avoiding futile arguments.

A CASE IN POINT

Focus Group for Growth Management Policies

The problem of managing economic growth confronts many regions of the nation. Palm Beach County is one of the largest counties in Florida, comprising 2,223 square miles and 39 municipalities. The county is currently experiencing some of the fastest economic growth in the United States. Located between the ecologically sensitive Everglades, Lake Okeechobee, and the Atlantic Ocean, the county's population of one million is growing by an incredible 20 percent per year. In 1998 the Sierra Club ranked Palm Beach County as one of the most sprawl-threatened medium-size metropolitan areas in the nation. Therefore, the problem of managing runaway growth is paramount to the region's planners. However, this issue is quite complex, since it aims to reconcile often contradictory interests of the citizens.

In 1997 the county introduced a "Managed Growth Tier System," which divided it up into five distinct regions: urban-suburban, ex-urban, rural, agricultural reserve, and the Glade. Palm Beach County's plans were tested by more than twenty-two focus groups for a year and a half. These groups, representing various interest groups in the region, discussed the plans in order to fine-tune various proposals. At the end, when the growth management plan was approved, it received the American Planning Association's award for 2000.[1]

Note

1. Stuart Meck, "Growing Smart: Initiatives and Applications—Palm Beach County Managed Growth Program," *Planning,* April 2000, 3–5.

Discussion Points

1. When is it appropriate and when is it not to use focus groups in public policy analysis?
2. Why was Palm Beach County successful in using focus group findings?
3. Consider a particular issue in your community. Do you think you can recommend the use of focus groups to determine citizens' position on the issue? Why or why not?

4. *Analyze the discussion for summary and conclusion.* There is no set procedure for analyzing focus group discussions. They can sometimes be taped with the permission of the participants, or the discussion leader may take copious notes for analysis. The summary and conclusion must be presented in a clear and concise manner so they answer the decision makers' pertinent questions.

5. *Determine the number of focus groups.* Because focus groups are typically composed of eight to twelve people, you need to have a number of such groups to get a feel for the community's diverse views on public policy questions.

SECONDARY DATA

Opinion polls and focus groups are excellent tools for needs assessment or for prioritizing needs for a local government. However, most public policy research involves the use of secondary information, collected by someone other than the researcher. When you are confronted with an unfamiliar topic, you may be at a loss as to where to begin. Chances are there is a vast amount of information, but you must be able to conduct an effective search so you can find the information you need.

Let us take an example. Suppose you are a junior analyst, working for your city, which wants to address a great deal of abandoned or dilapidated housing in the downtown area. The city wants to provide an incentive to homeowners to make substantial improvements through a proposed property tax rebate program. Under this program, homeowners in the designated area will qualify for a property tax rebate for three years if they improve their properties. Your job is to research the project's effectiveness.

To fully understand the issues relating to your project, you must first find out what work has already been done on such issues. Your literature review will help you

- gain a fuller view of what other researchers have discovered through their investigations, as well as point to areas that still need to be addressed.
- identify causal linkages that may help explain your hypothesis.
- conceptualize and measure key concepts.
- identify data sources.

Thus, a literature review will quickly tell you about the experiences of other cities that have experimented with similar programs. These published books and articles will help you develop your own hypotheses and methods of formulating the analysis. Based on the literature, you may decide to try to find out if a tax rebate does in fact spur investment in housing renovation.

However, the decision to improve one's property is complex and depends on factors other than property taxes. It involves the calculation of, for example, the condition of the neighborhood (neighborhoods with higher property values would provide the investor with higher returns), levels of property tax rates, and current economic conditions. A review of the relevant literature will help you identify the factors that are important to a potential investor in property improvements.

Once you know these causal linkages, you can start thinking about how to define and operationalize (numerically measure) these variables. You can operationalize the economic condition of a neighborhood either by its average household income or the median property value. Although these two figures are closely linked, they do not convey an identical measure of the neighborhood's relative prosperity. A quick reading of the literature will provide you with a good idea of which measure other researchers have used and why.

After you have decided how to operationalize the relevant variables, you need to find data containing such information. For example, if you know that fifty cities have attempted tax rebate programs in the past, you may start searching for comparable data on those cities. Many sources can provide you with the information you seek (see this and following pages). Once you have gathered the relevant data, you may proceed with your analysis.

Searching for Information

Thanks to advances in technology, sources of secondary information are literally unlimited, and most college and university libraries offer their students online services. However, before you start searching—and perhaps get frustrated—you must develop a strategy. Not all the searches you attempt will deliver the right information. I have classified information sources into three broad categories (see Figure 7.4). You can conduct an internal search within a library for books and scholarly journals. During such a search, you can explore by using an author's name, a title, a subject, or words in the title. If you know the names of prominent authors in the field, or you know exact titles, you can easily find out if the library has sources you would find useful. If you do not have a good idea about the topic, it is always smart to start with a recognized textbook, because it provides you with a well-rounded introduction to the subject matter. You can also search by key words. For example, for our inquiry, I typed in "property tax" and found a number of useful books. Once you come across a relevant book or article, look at the list of references. These citations can lead you to other relevant works. This process of building a bibliography is called **pyramiding citations** because you can develop a substantial list from a small number of initial sources. However, you should note that library searches lead you to books and journal articles that you will now have to check out to see if they are useful to you.

Online Searches

An Internet search, in contrast, offers a great deal of information without your having to leave your desk. By "surfing the net," you quickly discover that a world of

Figure 7.4 Searching with the Computer

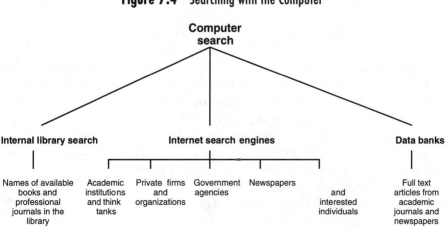

information awaits you in cyberspace. The problem, however, is how to focus your search to find pertinent information, and then once you find that information, how to determine its reliability. In this intimately interconnected information network, the first problem is to find a proper starting point.

Today, most people are familiar with general search engines or portals, such as Yahoo, Altavista, Infoseek, and Google. These search engines are excellent tools for locating institutions, government agencies, particular newspapers, and people. I went to Yahoo and typed in "property tax." I received a large number of "hits," which included, among others, tax consultants, the Internal Revenue Service, individuals trying to sell books on how to lower your property tax bill, lists of unclaimed properties, and Georgia's property tax forms. Therefore, if you are interested in reaching a certain government agency, a university, a certain newspaper, or a particular expert in the field, these search engines can be of great help.

Once you are at your destination, you can make an internal search for appropriate information. I went to "Brookings Institution," a leading think tank, and conducted a search. It quickly gave me a list of the institution's publications on property tax. You can also use these broad-based search engines to go to a specific newspaper and search its daily contents or archives. Suppose I came to know about a study in Kansas that examined a proposal to consolidate small school districts to save money and raise academic standards. I can go to one of the search engines and type in "Wichita, Kansas." My list of hits leads me to the city's newspapers, and I am able to search the contents and archives of the *Wichita Eagle*.[8] Nearly all major newspapers and magazines now offer online archives. Some of them, like the *New York Times* and the *Wall Street Journal*, charge money for archival copies of their articles, but many more do not. You can access *Time* and *Newsweek* magazines free and conduct an archival search. Similarly, you can now access major newspapers around the world through the Internet.

Today, all search engines depend on a keyword search for accessing the right information. As stated above, this type of search (often called a Boolean) allows you to create a word or words that best represent your area of inquiry. Some engines allow you to use the operators AND, OR, and NOT to create either a very broad or very narrow search. Usually these operators are found under the heading advanced search.

Say you are interested in looking for articles on school district consolidation. You began the search with the broad keyword "school financing." Because this is too broad a search, you get a large number of hits, most of which are of little or no interest to you. In that case, you can narrow the search by adding another keyword following the operator AND, which combines search terms so that each result must contain both terms, such as "school AND consolidation." If you are interested in further narrowing the search, you could add another word (say, "Midwest" or "Kansas") along with the two, separated by another AND. If you want to broaden your search, use the operator OR. The OR operator combines search terms so that each result contains at least one of the terms. For example, "school OR consolidation" will give you results that contain either term. Some advanced searches also allow you to use the operator NOT. This operator excludes the results that contain the term that follows NOT. For example, if you are interested in the consolidation of individual schools and not school districts, you may restrict your search to find results that contain the term "school" but not the term "district."

The results from a search often hide the information you need within a heap of unrelated, inaccurate, or incomplete materials and links. It is up to you, then, to determine whether or not the site is to be trusted, if the information is accurate, or if a more advanced search would produce better results. A search of the name "Einstein" gives me information on the life and work of the famous physicist, but it also produces sites for a garage, a laboratory auction house, and a chain of bagel stores. It is, therefore, important to remember that anyone with knowledge of Web design can put up a Web site. It is also important to remember that unlike a published book, postings on the Internet have no physical existence. Therefore, a site that looks interesting and useful to you may not be there tomorrow. Or, even if it is there, unlike a published book or an article, it may change significantly. This lack of permanence can cause problems when you include references to Web sites in your report.

So exactly how do you judge the reliability of a Web site's information? The answer to this question is less complicated than it may first appear. Because of the wide variation in the reliability of printed sources as well, you should not accept any kind of information without a critical review. You should always test the information's validity, accuracy, and authority. When getting information from the Web, see if the information follows a valid sequence of reasoning. Analysis based on critical reasoning differs from propaganda based on rhetoric only. However, even if a piece appears to be based on sound reasoning backed by empirical observations, you may question the validity of the data. If the data are not widely available, you may have to establish their accuracy through cross-referencing. That is, you may want to know if the data have been used in published work in a reputable scholarly journal, magazine, or newspaper. You are much safer in accepting the validity of the information if the source is a reputable organization, such as a university, a well-known independent research outfit, a well-regarded publishing house, or an official government entity. But even then you should be aware of the possible shortcomings of the information. The data may contain deliberate biases stemming from ideological positions or from vested interests. If I am looking for information on the effects of environmental pollution, I may have reason to be skeptical of data provided either by an environmental activist group like the Sierra Club or by an industry with a stake in the outcome of the public debate. In such a situation, you should look for corroboration by other independent sources.

If you are interested in articles published in scholarly journals, magazines, or newspapers, you can go to specialized databases. Databases are different from general search engines in that they cover only a specific pool of information. Some may cover a set number of professional journals. You can log on to such a database and look for articles published in these journals. Unlike Yahoo or Google, they will not go outside their limited area of information. However, some of these databases provide the advantage of your being able to download entire articles without having to go to a library. Searching by the key words "property tax" and "abatement" in the Pro Quest database, I found some excellent articles detailing the experiences of Syracuse, New York, and Dayton, Ohio, in regard to tax rebates for property improvements.[9]

For public policy analysts, perhaps the best sources of secondary data are U.S. government publications (see "A Case in Point, Politics and Government Statistics"). Government agencies in the United States are the most inveterate collectors of statistical information. Further, most government organizations are becoming part of this incredible information-sharing network. Although a multitude of extensive databases are available and new ones are being created, I mention a few important ones at this point.

- **EBSCOhost Academic Search Elite** provides access to a large number of journal articles from various academic disciplines. It covers more than twelve hundred periodicals starting around 1990.
- **Lexis/Nexis Academic Universe** allows you to retrieve full-text versions of national and international news articles. Its coverage generally starts from around the late 1980s.
- **ProQuest Research Library** is one of the most comprehensive sources of scholarly articles. Its core research module covers traditional academic journals and is supplemented by subject-specific modules, such as Arts, Education, Humanities, and International and Multicultural studies. Coverage begins in 1986.
- **PAIS International** (Public Affairs Information Service) is also one of the most comprehensive data sources, containing an index to journal articles. This database is particularly important to us because of its primary focus on public policy. Its coverage starts in 1972.
- **JSTOR** provides access to full-text scholarly journals in the humanities, sciences, and social sciences and some in natural sciences and population studies. This database provides full texts of published articles in the most prestigious scholarly journals in the fields of social science, demography, environmental sciences, and statistics.

Having gone through the relevant literature, you are now ready to collect numerical data on your topic. You should start with the *Annual Statistical Abstract of the United States,* the annual *Report of the President,* the *Handbook of Labor Statistics,* and the *Census Catalog and Guide.* Several excellent publications provide state and local government data: *Census of Governments, County and City Data Book, County Yearbook,* and *Municipal Yearbook* are a few of them.

There are also excellent sources for international data. However, international data are often not comparable, as different governments use different criteria for classifying information, which makes cross-national comparison problematic. Nevertheless, a number of large international agencies, such as the United Nations and the World Bank, compile information cross-nationally. For example, you may start with the *United Nations Statistical Yearbook, Yearbook of International Trade Statistics* and the *United Nations National Accounts Statistics.*

A CASE IN POINT

Politics and Government Statistics

When we use data from U.S. government publications, from census figures to the rate of inflation, we tend to take their objectivity for granted. Yet, like everything else the government does, its data collection is not completely free of political considerations. Alonso and Starr point out that "[o]fficial statistics do not merely hold a mirror to reality. They reflect presuppositions and theories about the nature of society.... [P]olitical judgments are implicit in the choice of what to measure, how to measure it, and how to present and interpret the results."[1] This political intrusion can cause serious public policy implications in the collection and interpretation of the data.

Stephen Feingold provides a vivid example of how politics affected the effort of the Centers for Disease Control (CDC) to collect data on acquired immune deficiency syndrome (AIDS).[2] The problem of defining the disease with precision complicates the collection of data. A relatively large number of people carry the human retrovirus known as HIV. Of those who do carry it, only a small portion actually develops AIDS-related complex (ARC), and a much smaller proportion of this group actually develops full-blown AIDS. The population groups with the highest incidence of AIDS are homosexual men, intravenous drug abusers (and their children), and hemophiliacs.

In the 1980s data on the spread of AIDS was based on an antiquated system of counting that used a much more stringent definition of the disease. Because of its political position that "the spread of AIDS was not a serious matter for most Americans," the administration of Ronald Reagan was reluctant to allocate money for a more complete survey.[3] Further complicating the matter was the conflict between the measurement issue and both the government's "war on drugs" and a general prejudice against homosexuals. When the CDC proposed an intensive national survey for an accurate count, Senator Jesse Helms (R-N.C.) argued that it was not intended to stop the spread of AIDS but to provide evidence that homosexuality was "just another normal lifestyle."

In the end, the survey was conducted in 1992, funded by private donations. When the results came out, much to the surprise of the scientific community, the threat of a rapid spread of the dreaded disease was found to be a lot less than expected.

Notes

1. William Alonso and Paul Starr, eds., *The Politics of Numbers* (New York: Russell Sage Foundation, 1987), 2.
2. Stephen E. Feingold, "Ethics, Objectivity, and Politics: Statistics in a Public Policy Perspective," in *Statistics and Public Policy*, ed. Bruce D. Spencer (Oxford: Clarendon Press, 1997), 62–83.
3. Ibid., 76.

Discussion Points

1. Discuss how politics can influence data gathering by even the most trusted government agencies.
2. As a policy analyst, how can you guard against biases in the information used in your analysis?

In addition to these vast amounts of economic, political, and social information, a huge array of data on attitudes and opinions is available. The Institute for Social Research at the University of Michigan collects and compiles data on many aspects of social, political, and psychological attitudes.

Finally, if your research project involves a particular government agency, the agency's annual budget reports can supply a great deal of information. The agency may collect for its own internal use a good deal of information that may not be available in a ready-to-use form. However, you may be able to make effective use of these pieces of information by arranging them in a proper way. Most of these sources are open to public use, although some of them sell more elaborate data sets through CD-ROM. If you are looking for national or local level data, you may consult the following resources:

- **Statistical Abstract of the United States** (http://www/.census.gov/statab /www/) provides a large number of national census data sets. It also contains most comprehensive data sets on state and local governments. For more detailed sets, you may have to purchase the CD-ROM.
- If you are interested in data on the consumer price index and information related to labor, you may log on to the **Bureau of Labor Statistics** (http://stats.bls.gov/).
- For international country data, one of the best sources is the Central Intelligence Agency's (CIA's) **Handbook of International Statistics.** You may access the handbook on the Web by connecting to http://www.odci.gov/cia/di /products/hies/.
- If your library subscribes, you may also access the online data bank of **STAT-USA.** This data bank allows you to access daily economic news, frequently requested statistical releases, the National Trade Data Bank (NTDB), the Economic Bulletin Board, and the Bureau of Economic Analysis.

Searching the Old-Fashioned Way

If your library does not allow you to search electronically, the traditional, time-honored places to start are the published versions of the *Public Affairs Information Service Bulletin* (PAIS), the *Social Science Citation Index,* or the ABC index of *Political Science and Government.* If you are specifically interested in urban issues, there are selective publications like the *Index to Current Urban Documents.* Many specialized indexes for various areas of the social sciences, public policy, and planning are available, as are subject-specific abstracts of important articles in the fields of business, economics, education, law, political science, public administration, public policy, sociology, urban and regional planning, and so on.

Finally, for a thorough literature survey, you may also build on other students' accepted work. This is an often-overlooked area of a literature search. Although most Ph.D. dissertations and master's theses are not formally published, upon their acceptance for degrees they become public documents. Because the students who wrote them have already spent a great deal of time developing a bibliography, access to relevant theses or dissertations can be extremely useful to you as a researcher, especially if you are not familiar with the topic. Accepted dissertations and theses are available online from *Dissertation Abstracts/Digital Dissertations,* a proprietary database to which many libraries across the nation subscribe.

When Data Are Not Available

Having gone through numerous data sources, you might feel frustrated. The specific information you are looking for does not seem to exist anywhere. It may be that your topic is too specific. Or it may be that for political or cultural reasons, such data have not been collected. You may not find time series data on the homeless population in your city because the subject is too specific and no agency is currently collecting the information. In some cases, the data for a few crucial years may be missing from an otherwise complete series. Or, suppose you are interested in estimating the possible effect of a new convention center on your city's economy. You will not find much information because the convention center has not been built yet. Suppose you are looking for data on smoking-related deaths on a cross-national basis. It may be that because of lack of awareness, such data have not been collected for many countries around the world.

In such cases, your job becomes tenuous. You may consider inferring the data. That is, if you can find a comparable city with a similar demographic, cultural, and economic background, you may draw a parallel. These kinds of inferences are often permissible when no data are available. However, if you must have a series prepared through inference or interpolation, you must make absolutely clear to the reader the nature of your data and the procedure by which they were obtained.

Key Words

Cluster sample (p. 159)
Confidence interval (p. 159)
Focus group (p. 164)
Interval scale (p. 150)
Judgmental method of sampling (p. 158)
Likert scales (p. 163)
Nominal scale (p. 150)
Objective sampling (p. 158)
Ordinal scale (p. 150)
Population and sample (p. 153)
Primary data (p. 149)

Probability-based sampling (p. 158)
Pyramiding citations (p. 167)
Random sample (p. 159)
Ratio scale (p. 151)
Revealed preference (p. 156)
Sample design (p. 160)
Sample error (p. 159)
Sampling biases (p. 153)
Secondary data (p.149)
Stratified sample (p. 159)

Exercises

1. What are primary and secondary data? Discuss the various scales of data. What are their relative strengths and weaknesses? What are their respective uses?
2. The city of Masters (population 150,000) wants to enlarge its airport to accommodate a growing need for a small commuter airline landing. The city wants to conduct a survey to assess public opinion on possible locations for the landing. Specif-

ically, the city wants to know who would support and who would oppose such an expansion effort in certain already identified sites. The survey must be completed within three months. Design a survey, specifying the sampling method (random, stratified, and so forth), number of people to be surveyed, questions to be asked, and the mode of interview.

3. Write a short essay on the biases of sampling. Collect information from the real world to elaborate your points.

4. Consider the following three scenarios and give your recommendation regarding which type of sampling method (random, stratified, or cluster) or focus group to use.

  a. The mass transit department in your city is considering a rate hike. Before it makes the final decision, it wants to learn more about the possible effects of such a hike on its customers.

  b. The professional football team of your city is threatening to move to a different city unless yours is willing to spend many millions of dollars to expand and renovate the existing stadium. The city council wants to know the opinion of its citizens.

  c. Your town is concerned about the scarcity of low-income housing. It is considering a new subsidy program that has been found to be effective in a different town of similar size. Your job is to design a survey to determine the effectiveness of the proposed program.

5. Suppose your town has received federal funding for educating the target population about sexually transmitted diseases. Your department has decided to conduct a survey. In an essay, discuss the problems you might face in obtaining a correct picture of the problem.

6. What are the advantages and disadvantages of conducting focus group research over a traditional survey design? Provide specific examples in which a survey would be more appropriate than a focus group and vice versa.

7. Consider an important issue facing your community. If you were to conduct a focus group, what steps would you take and what sorts of questions would you ask? Where would you meet?

8. Write a short essay on information gathering from the Internet. How would you ensure the credibility of the information?

9. Think of an appropriate focus group or survey design for your community. How would you estimate its cost?

10. Consider an important public policy issue. Prepare a bibliography and gather data through a Web search. If it is a controversial issue, such as gun control or abortion rights, rank the sites mentioned in your paper according to their reliability.

Notes

1. Professor Ted Gurr (*Polity II* database, Interuniversity Consortium) quantified the degree of "democratization" of countries. Among several others, Dipak K. Gupta developed indexes of political instability. See *Economics of Political Violence* (New York: Praeger, 1990).

2. James Gleick, *Chaos* (New York: Viking, 1987).

3. See P. Thomas, "The Persistent 'Gnat' that Louisiana Can't Get Out of Its Face," *Los Angeles Times,* October 14, 1990, M1.

4. See A. Rosenthal, "Broad Disparities in Votes and Polls Raising Questions," *New York Times,* November 9, 1989, A1, B14.

5. Stanley Milgram, *Obedience to Authority: An Experimental View* (New York: Harper & Row, 1974).

6. For a detailed discussion of human beings' proclivity to obedience to authority figures, see Dipak K. Gupta, *Path to Collective Madness: A Study in Social Order and Political Pathology* (New York: Greenwood Press, 2001).

7. *Los Angeles Times,* August 16, 1992, A6.

8. By following this method, I found the following article: Steve Painter, "Study: Merge Small Districts: Consultants Tell the State that Consolidation Will Help with School Funding," *Wichita Eagle,* January 11, 2001.

9. On Syracuse, see William P. Barrett, "Willis Carrier's Ghost," *Forbes,* May 29, 2000, and on Dayton, see Clifford A. Pearson, "Dayton Tackles Brownfields to Create Houses and Offices," *Architectural Record* 188 (June 2000).

CHAPTER

8

MAKING SENSE
OF NUMBERS

Much of a busy executive's workday involves making decisions. These days executives find themselves increasingly surrounded by information, often expressed in numbers. The spectacular advances in technology have made collecting and storing information inexpensive and data retrieval and the display of their analyses quite simple. A large series of numbers, however, tends to numb our senses and push us beyond our cognitive capabilities. Therefore, decision makers prefer seeing large sets of numbers in an understandable form.

The purpose of this chapter is to provide students and practicing analysts with a guide for rendering social, political, or economic phenomena in graphs or tables. It is important to be creative without being misleading or deceptive. I will take you through some familiar terrain and expose you to the advantages and pitfalls of the most commonly used and abused methods of presenting numerical arguments to decision makers.

Descriptive statistics and graphical techniques are useful in assessing social conditions, such as per capita income, rate of population growth, and crime rates. These techniques are often neglected in more sophisticated statistics and operations research textbooks because they seem too simplistic. However, an overwhelming number of decisions in both public and private organizations are made on the basis of simple decision rules: a brief assessment of relative desirability based on quick impressions rather than thorough research.

A PICTURE'S WORTH: THE GRAPHICAL METHODS OF ANALYSIS

Let us consider a hypothetical situation. Suppose the city manager of a medium-size city, Masters, Pennsylvania, would like to know how much the city depends on state and federal grants. The financial management division for the city gives the city manager breakdowns of the city's state and federal grants for 1990 through 1999. (see Table 8.1).

Current vs. Constant Dollars

The numbers in Table 8.1 indicate that state and federal funding for the city is growing every year. A better appreciation of the historical trend can be obtained by plotting the data. However, as you will soon discover, there is more than one way of drawing a picture.

Of course, the plotted information shown in Figure 8.1 is a great improvement over the table. The diagram clearly shows the generosity of the state and federal governments to the city. The dollar amount of the grants has increased steadily over the years, with the greatest increase coming during the early 1990s. However, the city manager is skeptical; this diagram does not take into account the rate of inflation for the period. Therefore, the price deflator (the consumer price index for the United States) was obtained for the period, and the yearly numbers were converted to constant dollars (see Table 8.2).

Time series data requires the conversion of current dollars into constant dollars because the value of money does not remain the same over time. The books that you purchased last year probably cost more today. Such increases make the value

Table 8.1 State and Federal Grants to Masters, Pennsylvania, in Current Dollars, 1990–1999

Year	State and federal grants in current $
1990	71,000
1991	75,000
1992	85,000
1993	89,000
1994	91,000
1995	91,500
1996	93,000
1997	95,000
1998	98,000
1999	102,000

Figure 8.1   State and Federal Grants to Masters, Pennsylvania, in Current Dollars

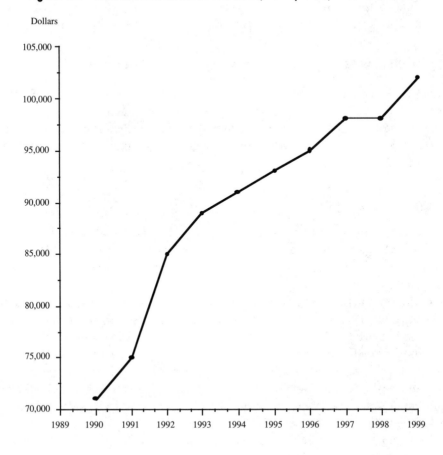

Table 8.2   State and Federal Grants to Masters, Pennsylvania,
in Current and Constant Dollars, 1990–1999

Year	State and federal grants in current $	Consumer price index number[a]	State and federal grants in constant $
1990	71,000	100	71,000
1991	75,000	110	68,182
1992	85,000	117	72,650
1993	89,000	122	72,951
1994	91,000	127	70,930
1995	91,500	129	67,883
1996	93,000	137	68,345
1997	95,000	139	68,534
1998	98,000	143	68,531
1999	102,000	147	68,388

[a] The consumer price index data are hypothetical.

of money decrease with the passage of time. Therefore, by using the actual dollars received by Masters from the state and the federal government, we paint a deceptive picture. The rate at which the dollar loses its value is measured by a price index number. In the United States the Bureau of Labor Statistics (BLS) collects data on price changes and other employment-related information.[1] Price changes are measured in terms of a base year, which is expressed as 100. For example, most of the current series in price indexes measured by the BLS hold the period 1982–1984 as 100.

A price index is calculated on the basis of what is known as **variable weight,** or **fixed weight.** The variable-weight price index states price change as a ratio of a set of goods and services in the current period and their costs in the base year. More precisely, it is written as:

$$\text{Variable-weight price index} = \frac{value\, of\; goods\, at\, current\text{-}year\, prices}{value\, of\, those\, goods\, at\, base\text{-}year\, prices}$$

The effects of price changes are, of course, not universal. If you do not like turnips, you are not affected if their prices go through the roof. However, if you practically live on turnips, your well-being will be affected. If you are making the same amount of money as last year, you are poorer this year than you were before. Your income in current dollars is called the **nominal income,** and the true value of your reduced income is called the **real income** (meaning, adjusted for price change). You may note that the variable-weight price index takes an overall picture and does not consider whether the price changes are going to affect any single segment of the population. As a result, the most commonly used variable-weight price index is called the **GDP deflator,** which is used to compare the GDP of the past year with that of the current year.

In contrast, the fixed-weight price index considers a typical basket of goods that a consumer would consume and tracks its prices over the years. The fixed-weight price index is used to measure the **consumer price index,** or the changes in prices that will affect a typical consumer. The BLS produces data series on the consumer price index for various regional centers (urban, rural, a specific city, and so forth) as well as GDP deflators. For example, suppose you have a job offer from two different cities. By comparing the price levels of the two, you can decide which one is offering you a higher salary in "real" dollars. In Table 8.3 I show the change of prices facing all urban consumers.

From this table you can see that between 1982–1984 and 1999, a dollar lost 66.6 percent of its value. That is, a dollar in 1999 was worth about 34 cents in 1982–1984.

You can also calculate the amount of inflation by changing the base. For example, if you want to use 1990 as the base year, you can recalculate the series by using the following formula:

$$\pi_{t+1} = \frac{P_{t+1} - P_t}{P_t} \times 100 \qquad (8.1)$$

Table 8.3   Consumer Price Index—All Urban Consumers, 1990–1999

Year	CPI (1982–1984 = 100)	CPI (1990 as the base year)	Rate of inflation
1990	130.7	100.00	—
1991	136.2	104.21	4.21
1992	140.3	107.34	7.34
1993	144.5	110.56	10.56
1994	148.2	113.39	13.39
1995	152.4	116.60	16.60
1996	156.9	120.05	20.05
1997	160.5	122.80	22.80
1998	163.0	124.71	24.71
1999	166.6	127.47	27.47

where π_{t+1} is the index of price change for the year $t+1$, P_t is the consumer price index for the year t, and P_{t+1} is the consumer price index for the year $t+1$. The results are shown in the table under the heading "Rate of inflation."

Looking again at the case of Masters, Pennsylvania, it is obvious from the calculation of constant dollar figures that the city is not doing as well with state and federal grants as was assumed. In fact, the inflationary forces in the early 1990s have eroded so much of the purchasing power that they caused an actual decline in the grant money in **real terms** (see Figure 8.2).

Figure 8.2   Comparison of State and Federal Grants, in Current and Constant Dollars

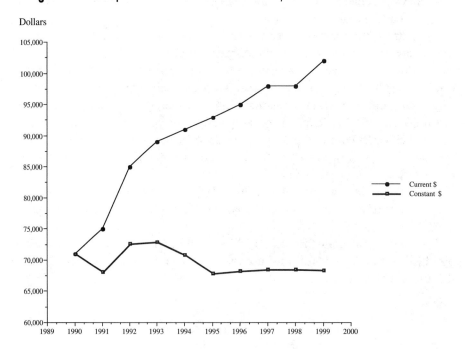

As you can clearly see, we can get radically different conclusions each time we transform the data. You can further transform the data by comparing it with other variables, such as population or the size of the city budget; the data may also be compared with a national or regional average, or the series can be looked at by its rate of increase. In each case, the data will tell us a different story. In a sense, the data are like a kaleidoscope, in which you can see a completely different picture by slightly changing the angle of the device. Let us consider some other ways of looking at the same information.

We can expand the data presented in Table 8.2 to include information on total city revenue during the period of study. If we express the dollar amount of grants received by the city as a percentage of its total revenue, we will be comforted by the fact that we have done well over the years (see Table 8.4). We can be further comforted if we look at the national trend of the ratio of state and federal government assistance to cities as a percentage of their total revenue. While external assistance to cities across the nation was going down in the 1990s, our city held its ground and was doing better than the national average during the latter part of the decade (see Figure 8.3).

Each of these transformations tells a slightly different story. Through them we get glimpses of different facets of the situation. Therefore, the question is not which one is telling the "true" story, but which one contains the most important message from the perspective of the inquirer.

Percentage Change

You may want to look at the information in yet another way. You may calculate the yearly percentage change in constant dollar grants to Masters. This information, presented in Table 8.5 and plotted in Figure 8.4, can be quite useful in discerning year-to-year changes in state and federal assistance to the city.

Table 8.4 State and Federal Grants to Masters, Pennsylvania, as Percentage of Revenue, 1990–1999

Year	State and federal grants in current $	Total government revenue in current $	State and federal grants as ratio of total government revenue	National average of grants as a percentage of local government revenue
1990	71,000	360,000	19.7	35.5
1991	75,000	369,000	20.3	32.3
1992	85,000	382,000	22.3	30.2
1993	89,000	385,000	23.1	26.8
1994	91,000	398,000	22.9	22.8
1995	91,500	410,000	22.3	21.5
1996	93,000	419,000	22.2	20.2
1997	95,000	425,000	22.4	20.3
1998	98,000	432,000	22.7	19.8
1999	102,000	444,000	23.0	19.5

Figure 8.3   Comparison of State and Federal Grants as a Percentage of Local Government Tax Revenue

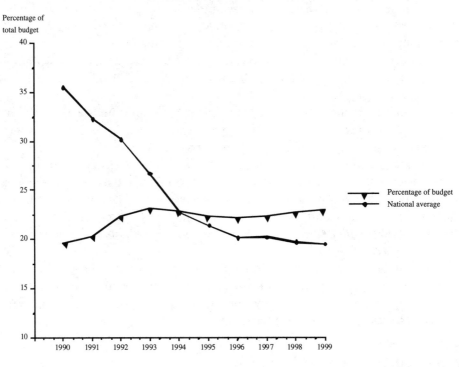

Creating an Index

Finally, it may be useful to look at the data with the help of an index. As noted earlier, an index is created when we take a particular figure as the **base** and then express the series in relation to this particular number. For example, if we take the

Table 8.5   Yearly Percentage Change in State and Federal Grants to Masters, Pennsylvania, 1990–1999

Year	State and federal grants in constant $	Yearly percentage change (1990 = 100)
1990	71,000	—
1991	68,182	-3.97
1992	72,650	6.55
1993	72,951	0.41
1994	70,930	-2.77
1995	67,883	-4.30
1996	68,345	0.68
1997	68,534	0.28
1998	68,531	0.00
1999	68,388	-0.21

Figure 8.4   Plot of Yearly Percentage Change in State and Federal Grants to Masters, Pennsylvania, in Constant Dollars

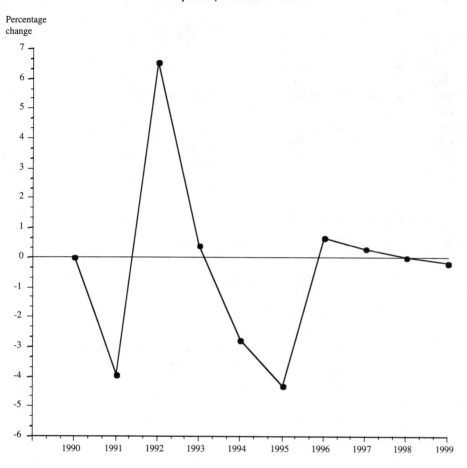

grants figure for 1990 as the base (expressed as 100), we can calculate the index by dividing each year's data by this number and then multiplying it by 100. That is,

$$\text{Index for } 1991 = \frac{1991}{1990} \times 100$$

or

$$\frac{68{,}182}{71{,}000} \times 100 = 96.03$$

The data presented in Table 8.6 are plotted in Figure 8.5. As you can see, each presentation of the same information tells a slightly different story. Therefore, how you present your case will depend on your need.

Table 8.6   Index of State and Federal Grants to Masters, Pennsylvania, 1990–1999

Year	State and federal grants in constant $	Index (1990 = 100)
1990	71,000	100.00
1991	68,182	96.03
1992	72,650	102.32
1993	72,951	102.75
1994	70,930	99.90
1995	67,883	95.61
1996	68,345	96.26
1997	68,534	96.53
1998	68,531	96.52
1999	68,388	96.32

Choosing the Type of Graph to Use

In the previous examples we used only line graphs. Today's managers use a variety of graphs, such as **scatter plots**, **bar graphs,** and **pie charts**. Each kind of graph presents the information in its own unique way. You should be familiar with each kind of graph and determine which kind of pictorial rendition gets your intended message across in the most effective way.

Figure 8.5   Plot of Yearly Percentage Change in State and Federal Grants to Masters, Pennsylvania, by Indexing

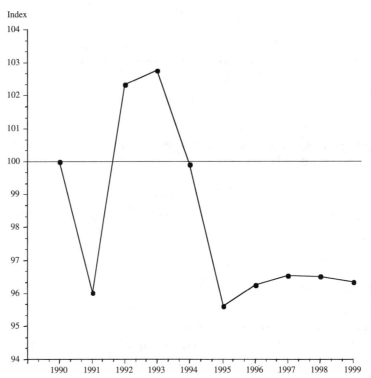

Specifically,

- Line graphs are used for time series data.
- If you have cross-section data, you should use a bar diagram or a scatter plot.
- If the data are in fractions of a total (or in percentages), use a pie chart.

During the now-famous presidential race of 2000, the two candidates, Republican George W. Bush and Democrat Al Gore, were running neck and neck. As the votes were tallied, Florida took on added prominence because the state's twenty-five electoral votes would determine the outcome of the election. Within the state of Florida, the voting of Palm Beach County residents generated an unexpected twist of irony. In the 1992 presidential election, Ross Perot, the candidate of the newly founded Reform Party, drew a respectable number of votes, which many thought gave the presidency to Bill Clinton. In 2000 the Reform Party candidate was Patrick Buchanan. In Palm Beach County, the election commission approved a "butterfly" ballot, a double-faced ballot on which the names of the candidates appeared side by side. The name Al Gore was opposite to that of Pat Buchanan, creating confusion among many Democratic voters. Many Gore supporters made a mistake and voted for Buchanan instead. When the votes were tabulated, Buchanan received 3,400 votes.

In Figure 8.6 I show the number of votes garnered by Buchanan in Florida's sixty-seven counties, before they were hand counted, as a scatter diagram. As you can see, the numbers clearly show an unmistakable spike for Mr. Buchanan.

Figure 8.6   Number of Votes Cast for Patrick Buchanan in the Florida Counties

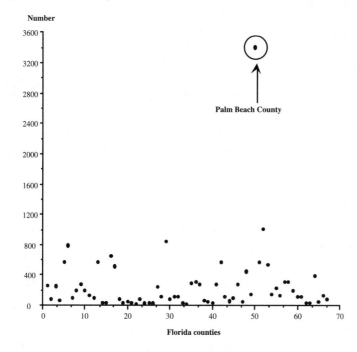

The scatter plot clearly identifies those Palm Beach Buchanan votes as an obvious outlier. However, in the social sciences, for every obvious solution, there is always a different angle. When we calculate the number of votes as a percentage of the total votes in each county, Palm Beach County's record does not appear so strange (see Figure 8.7). In fact, in terms of percentages, at least six small counties (Baker, Charlot, Indian River, Liberty, Suwannee, and Washington) polled higher than did Palm Beach.

Graphical Methods in Decision Making

Graphical presentations describe a situation by visual means. However, they should not be considered as passive tools of description; they can also be used as extremely powerful decision tools. Consider the following situation. The police department in Masters is trying to reach as many youngsters as possible to educate them about the perils of drug use. Last year the department spent considerable effort in arranging school appearances of officers and experts. It also advertised on local radio and television. Suppose last year the city spent $7,500 on school lectures, $13,000 on radio advertisements, and $20,000 on local television ads. A recent survey by the city shows that of the children who are aware of the

Figure 8.7 Percentage of Votes Cast for Patrick Buchanan in Florida Counties

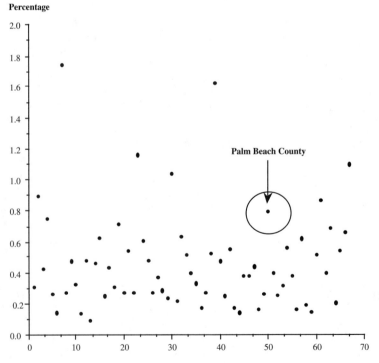

city's drug prevention effort, 35 percent became aware of the issue through face-to-face contact with officers, 15 percent through radio ads, and the remaining 50 percent through watching television. In the two pie charts of Figure 8.8 I show the expenditure for each method of contact.

The side-by-side placement of these two diagrams visually demonstrates that face-to-face contacts are the most cost-effective way to disseminate drug prevention information to school-age children. The same information could have been presented as simple percentages in a table. However, as is often the case, a picture is worth a thousand words. For another example of how diagrams may enhance presentation of data, see "A Case in Point: Racial Profiling."

TO TELL THE TRUTH AND NOTHING BUT THE TRUTH

Over the years, statistics have been characterized in less-than-flattering ways. One of British prime minister Benjamin Disraeli's famous quips is, "There are three kinds of lies: lies, damned lies, and statistics." We have come to accept expressions such as "statistical artifacts" or "cooked-up statistics." We must recognize that deception, misunderstood implication, or the existence of a bias in the process of collecting information can cause problems.

The deceptive use of numbers must be defined with respect to the intent of the user. Thus, an individual or organization that puts out information knowing full well that the data have no real-life validity is defrauding or deceiving the user. During times of national emergencies or war, government agencies routinely use data for propaganda purposes. A nation at war may exaggerate or downplay claims about its military or industrial strength, or its war casualties, depending on its strategy. China, in the course of suppressing the prodemocracy movement, under-reported the number of student casualties and released figures that were widely

Figure 8.8   Expenditure on Drug Prevention Program

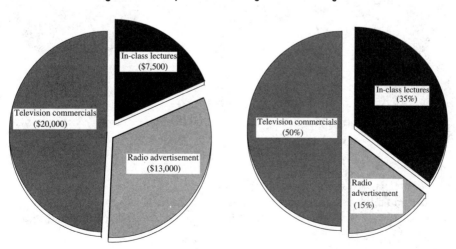

A CASE IN POINT

Racial Profiling

Many minority drivers have been protesting racial profiling. That is, police stop non-white motorists and search their vehicles at a disproportionate rate. This practice started the joke that these drivers are guilty of DWB—Driving While Black or Brown. The rising demands from San Diego's minority population prompted the city's police department to initiate a study. The study covered more than 90,000 instances of police stopping drivers between January and June of 2000. The *San Diego Union Tribune* published the data as pie charts (see charts below).[1]

The publication of this data created a big stir, particularly when they were presented visually in pie charts similar to the ones here. "We have known this [racial profiling] for a long time," said an African-American community leader. However, in support of police practices, San Diego's police chief, David Bejarano, pointed out that although Latinos make up only about 20 percent of the city's drivers, because San Diego is a border town, a large number of motorists come from Mexico. Further, he pointed out, the figures might be misleading because police are often deployed in areas close to the border and other high crime areas. Therefore, considering the entire city population does not allow for valid comparison. A more detailed study is required to control for the influence of these two external factors.

Comparison of Police Stopping by Race

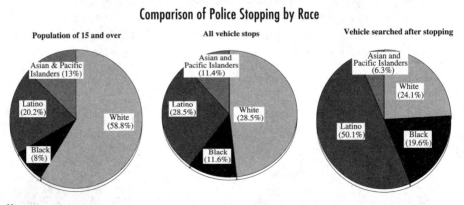

Note

1. Mark Arner and Joe Hughes, "Police Stops Blacks, Latinos More Often: Data from Profiling Report Echo Fears of S.D. Minorities," *San Diego Union Tribune*, September 29, 2000.

Discussion Points

1. How effective was the presentation of the data?
2. Can you think of a better way to present the information?
3. What are the points raised by Chief Bejarano? How would you respond to these points?

disputed by such knowledgeable people and agencies as Chinese student groups in the United States and Amnesty International. Similarly, the figures for North Vietnamese war casualties were routinely inflated by Pentagon officials during the Vietnam War.

Another source of contention frequently centers on the "true" implication of a statistic. We often use the per capita gross domestic product (GDP) as a measure of the relative economic development of nations. However, it is obvious that the word "development" used in a national context should imply more than a measure of a country's per capita GDP, because "development" implies a certain degree of progress and maturity in social, political, and economic institutions. Tiny oil-rich nations may have the highest per capita GDP, but one would be hard-pressed to characterize those countries as the most developed in the world.

Biases resulting from other factors may also cause a statistic to be misinterpreted. Valid questions have been raised about whether or not IQ tests measure relative levels of intelligence in children. For years, entrance to the U.S. Civil Service was based on the scores of a multiple-choice examination. However, it was eventually determined that such an examination was biased in favor of white, middle-class males. Therefore, the test score could not be accepted as the best measure of a candidate's suitability for a position.

Then there are data that, by their very nature, call for subjective judgment in the way they are defined and compiled. A good example is the consumer price index, discussed earlier in this chapter (see page 179). As mentioned earlier, a "typical" basket of goods and services that an "average" American consumes yearly is used to measure the rate of inflation. However, we know that each of us has a unique consumption pattern, based not only on our individual tastes but also on various factors such as age, income, race, and geographical location. If the price of skateboards goes up, senior citizens are less likely to be affected than are young people. Similarly, an increase in the cost of health care may not affect single young adults as much as the increase in the index would suggest. Whoever compiles this basket of goods thus faces two problems in making the index relevant to the majority of Americans. First, the compiler must discern what is "typical," in terms of what kinds of goods and services and at what level of consumption. Errors that severely distort the data creep in during the collection of information in many ways; not recognizing this means that the results of analyses may be meaningless, misleading, or even damaging.

You must be extremely wary of accepting data for analysis, and you cannot be too careful in looking at possible sources of biases and errors. At the same time, remember that it is impossible to find a perfect set of data in an otherwise imperfect world. Like the proverbial fastidious eater who dies of starvation, a researcher who is too cautious will know all the flaws of the data and its analyses without being able to draw any useful conclusions from them.

The rule of thumb, then, is to evaluate carefully the sources of bias in the data and be aware of the cost of doing an incorrect analysis. If you are conducting medical research for a new type of vaccine as an antidote for a disease, or calculating trajectories for the reentry of a space shuttle into the earth's atmosphere, the margin of acceptable error is rather low. However, mercifully, in the areas of social science or public policy research the demand for numerical accuracy may not be that critical. It is most important to be aware of and open about the shortcomings of the data and the possible sources of bias in the analysis and interpretation.

Interpretation and Deception

The last source of skepticism to keep in mind is that to most people, numbers portray a rigid, self-evident truth. In a cocktail party discussion, a friend claimed that homosexuality was purely biological, since every society seems to have homosexuals as 10 percent of its population. It is fairly obvious that this statement is the kind designed to end all discussions, as it purports to present a totally scientific, incontrovertible fact of life. To many people, numbers pose an immediate threat because of their appearance of "scientific" objectivity. However, closer scrutiny will reveal problems resulting from the various biases we have described; and a significant source of disagreement may be that any information (numerical or otherwise) about a complex social situation is bound to be open to interpretation.

In 1954 Darrell Huff wrote an extremely interesting, humorous book, *How to Lie with Statistics.* In it he systematically demonstrated many ways to distort information to suit the purpose of the investigator. In his tongue-in-cheek introduction he states, "This book is a sort of primer in ways to use statistics to deceive. It may seem altogether too much like a manual for swindlers. Perhaps I can justify it in the manner of the retired burglar whose published reminiscences amounted to a graduate course in how to pick a lock and muffle a footfall: The crooks already know these tricks; honest men must learn them in self-defense." [2]

Huff's highly acclaimed book advanced understanding of the various ways one can use descriptive statistics among generations of undergraduate students. However, in all honesty, we may pose the question differently. If the manipulation of data is always suspected of "distorting" the picture, then there must be a truly undistorted version of real life. In other words, are we to assume the universality of truth? Does it always require a statistician to obfuscate an otherwise obvious situation? A famous early-twentieth-century Japanese play, *Rashomon,* by Ryunosuke Akutagawa, brings home the point of relativity of perception. In the play a bandit rapes a young woman traveling with her Samurai husband. A number of different individuals witnessed this terrible act of violence. When they are brought to the trial (including her deceased husband, who speaks through a medium), the incident is found to have variations of interpretation. As the play shows, there may be honest differences of opinion in the way one looks at a situation, even when expressed in "cold, hard, objective numbers." We live in a complex world in which "truth" may have more dimensions than can be effectively captured by any one-dimensional measure. However, if we use multiple indexes to characterize a situation, our cognitive limitations stand in the way of formulating any definitive picture. Like everything else in life, quantification of social phenomena requires a trade-off between the confusion of a total picture and the clarity a limited view offers.

For example, consider our hypothetical city of Masters, Pennsylvania. The demographic composition of Masters is typical of the region, with a large number of working-class people, along with pockets of urban blight, characterized by persistent levels of high unemployment. However, a few areas of the city house extremely wealthy families. Let us focus on three individuals plying their trade in Masters: a real estate broker, a college professor, and a city planner. All three of these individuals want to present the "true" economic picture of this city with a single number—the average income of the city's people. However, these three have different objectives. The real estate broker wants to portray the city as a nice place to live and raise a family. Therefore, in talking to clients he mentions as "average" the mean income of the residents of the town. However, although small in number, the extremely wealthy households influence the mean. The prospective buyer gets a much rosier picture of the average affluence of the city than that espoused by the professor. The professor is conducting research in urban economics, for which he is using the figure of median income. The median, the middle income from the highest to the lowest, presents a less attractive picture of the economic well-being of the city because it is not affected by the presence of the wealthy sector of the community. However, even this number is far superior to the one used by the city planner. The city planner of Masters wants to respond to a request for a grant proposal from the state government to bring in money earmarked for the economically depressed areas. For this proposal, she uses the modal income of the town, which is the most frequently found income of the inhabitants.

Is it possible to pick out which of the three individuals, who use three different measures of average income owing to their different objectives, is engaged in an act of deception? I would argue that none of them can be accused of such an act unless some other kind of deception is present. When it comes to the definition of "average," most people intuitively use the arithmetic mean, median, and mode, in that order. Therefore, by convention, if one uses the term "average" for the mean, one can feel justified. The use of the median may require justification, and the use of the modal income would certainly require its mention in the report, to be ethically fair and aboveboard. However, the use of any of these measures cannot be called a deception. Therefore, we must conclude that without the intent of deception none of the figures can be characterized as a lie; there can be honest difference of opinion, even among those whose business it is to deal with numbers, as to which one of these three represents the most valid picture of the city.

Another source of bias, Huff claimed, comes from the deceptive use of pictorial information—graphs. Because a picture is often worth a thousand words, the desire to convey information by graphical means is rather strong. But in the process one might take advantage of certain trickery. Consider the example in Figure 8.9, where we have depicted nonwhite unemployment as a percentage ratio of white unemployment. In 1955 the unemployment rate within the nonwhite population was 62 percent higher than that within the white population.

Does this presentation of the information suit your needs, or do you want to portray more dramatically the plight of the minority population in the United

Figure 8.9   Ratio of Nonwhite to White Unemployment Rate

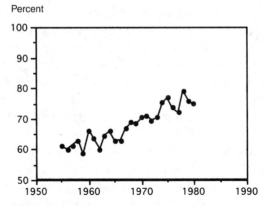

Source: U.S. Bureau of Labor Statistics.

States? If you do, you can s-t-r-e-t-c-h the graph for added visual effect showing the same information (Figure 8.10). Obviously, in this case the difference between nonwhite and white unemployment is portrayed in a much more striking fashion.

What if you contend that the situation for the minority population is really not that bad, or that the situation has not changed appreciably over the years? In that case, you can use another trick. You can increase the range of the vertical axis, which allows you to present the same information in a different light. Against a much wider range of possible ratios of unemployment, the ethnic difference in the relative measure of economic deprivation does indeed look small (Figure 8.11).

Figure 8.10   Ratio of Nonwhite to White Unemployment Rate (stretched graph)

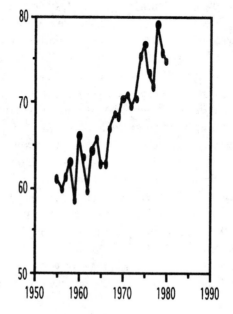

Figure 8.11   Ratio of Nonwhite to White Unemployment Rate (elongated vertical axis)

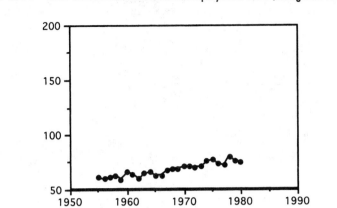

Yet another effective way of representing a series is to use selective years for comparison. For example, you may want to present the same information contained in the three graphs, but even more emphatically. You may want to show them in either of the following ways without "lying" with your statistics. The two graphs in Figure 8.12 show only three years—1960, 1970, and 1980. This restriction removes the distracting effects of yearly fluctuations and allows us to present long-term trends. Then, by simply manipulating the vertical axis, we have two radically different visual effects.

Now that I have shown you various ways of presenting the same information, which do you think represents the "true" picture? The answer is simple: We do not know which of these diagrams would be classified as a deceptive representation of the reality. However, Figures 8.11 and 8.12 (a) might be interpreted as edging toward questionable practices, since the vertical axes in those figures have wider ranges than is required by the data. But would you call that lying? In real life, truth, like beauty, lies in the eye of the beholder.

In the preceding examples, the difference between interpreting and deceiving might have been subtle, but consider the rendition of the same information in Figure 8.13. In this diagram, you are not only presenting facts but also trying to make

Figure 8.12   Ratio of Nonwhite to White Unemployment Rate (1960, 1970, and 1980)

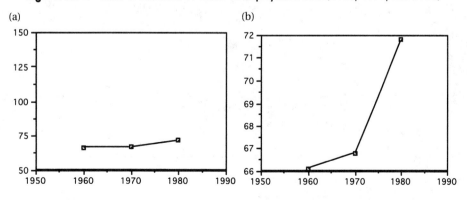

Figure 8.13 Ratio of Nonwhite to White Unemployment Rate (shortened vertical axis)

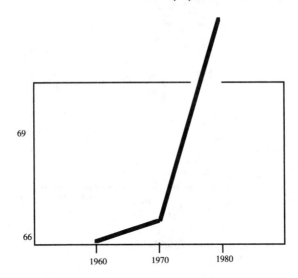

a rather loud statement with the obvious analogy of the ratio going through the ceiling.

Huff pointed out that, intended or unintended, deception may creep in more readily when one uses graphics instead of lines and bars, which are drawn according to scale. Consider a diagram showing the plight of African elephants (Figure 8.14). It is shocking to realize that in ten years the elephant population has diminished to one-third of its 1980 size. Although the numbers themselves speak volumes about the plight of the hapless pachyderms in Africa, the pictures in the figure are not drawn according to scale. We catch the relative size difference in the picture more readily than the difference in magnitude between the numbers, but we may not be able to catch that the 1980 drawing is much more than three times the size of the 1990 drawing. These kinds of disproportionate pictorial renditions are popular with those who present data at legislative hearings and in administrative decision-making sessions because the message is direct and dramatic. With

Figure 8.14 African Elephant Population, 1980–1990

1980   1990

computer graphics so easy to use, the possibility of some creative minds deceiving the unwary has never been greater.

The power of strong visual presentation is well recognized and well documented. A 1985 *Wall Street Journal* story documents how the use of such a tool helped Caspar Weinberger, then secretary of defense, to avert a cut in the Pentagon budget by David Stockman, director of the Office of Management and Budget.

> In staving off Mr. Stockman's assault on the planned buildup, Mr. Weinberger turned to a tactic for which he has since become famous, the chart and easel. The defense secretary's charts, presented in a meeting with President Ronald Reagan, showed large soldiers bearing large weapons, which were labeled "Reagan budget." They towered above small soldiers with small weapons labeled "OMB budget." President Reagan went along with the "Reagan budget." [3]

Tabular Presentation of Data

A long series of numbers pushes us to the limits of our cognitive capacities. For that reason, the value of an effective table as a means of communication cannot be overstated. Presenting data in useful tabular form is an art, which can be perfected only through practice.

The preparation of an effective table requires considerable thought and time (and therefore, money). First, have a clear idea of exactly what you want to communicate to the reader. Second, choose a title that parsimoniously describes the contents of the table. Third, consider various ways of presenting the raw data so that they make the point you want to make most effectively.

For a table to be useful, its purpose must be absolutely clear from its title. The title should be concise, but not so brief that it does not convey the true intent of your presentation. The numbers, taken together, must tell a coherent story. Consider, for example, Table 8.7. You may notice how much information has been packed into a concise table. You can find out from the table how much money the government spent on selected items in 1995. During that fiscal year, education accounted for 12.10 percent of all public spending, and local governments paid the bulk (68.24 percent) of education costs. The table also tells you that the federal government originated half (50.87 percent) of total government spending.

In my discussion of graphical presentation, I have shown you how to look at a data set from different perspectives. Similarly, before preparing a table, you may draw interesting conclusions by using absolute numbers, ratios, percentages, and so on.

THOSE NOT-SO-INNOCENT NUMBERS

It is relatively easy to define outright deception or lying by the measure of intent and the sheer fabrication of data, but the line between deception and differences in interpretation is murky. Often the intentions of presenters are not obvious; nor

Table 8.7 Spending by Function and Level of Government, 1995

Function	Spending by level of government (in million $)				Percentage of spending by level of government			
	Federal	State	Local	PS (percent)	Federal	State	Local	Total
Defense	327,231	—	—	9.60	100.00	—	—	100.00
Education	27,270	101,510	276,763	12.10	6.72	25.03	68.24	100.00
Highways	731	48,893	30,216	2.38	0.92	61.24	37.85	100.00
Welfare	57,246	160,421	32,669	7.47	22.87	64.08	13.05	100.00
Police	7,563	5,735	52,329	1.96	11.52	8.74	79.74	100.00
Health	26,517	49,487	56,460	3.95	20.02	37.36	42.63	100.00
Administration	19,416	24,781	35,237	2.37	24.44	31.20	44.36	100.00
Insurance	558,291	93,692	13,648	19.86	83.87	14.08	2.05	100.00
Other	680,857	402,563	262,046	39.93	50.60	29.92	19.48	100.00
Total	1,705,122	887,082	759,368	100.00	50.87	26.47	22.66	100.00

Source: U.S. Department of Commerce, Bureau of Census and Tax Foundation, Washington, D.C.

Notes: PS = percentage of total public spending. Some percentages may not add to one hundred because of rounding.

are we capable of detecting purposeful contamination of data. Because we tend to believe in the objectivity of numerical information more readily than in the subjectivity of qualitative statements, deceptive use of statistics can bring incredible misery to people.

In 1896 Frederick L. Hoffman, a nationally famous statistician for the Prudential Insurance Company of America, wrote a book titled, *Race Traits and Tendencies of the American Negro.*[4] Hoffman's thesis was that since their emancipation, African Americans (having left the protective care of their slave owners) had gone back to their "basic racial trait" of "immorality of character." Hoffman based his theory on a number of different statistics that he had collected. He noted that in 1890 there were 567 blacks in prison for rape, which constituted 47 percent of the prison population convicted on rape charges. Because this number was significantly greater than the proportion of the African-American population (about 10 percent at the time), according to Hoffman, rape and other sexual crimes were reflective of the "Negro racial trait." Hoffman thus concluded that "[a]ll the facts brought together in this work prove that the colored population is gradually parting with the virtues and the moderate degree of economic efficiency developed under the regime of slavery. All the facts prove that a low standard of sexual morality is the main and underlying cause of the low and anti-social condition of the race at the present time."[5]

Hoffman then connected the "Negro racial trait of immorality" to the high mortality rate among the black population. On the basis of this causal linkage, disregarding the fact that the census of 1890 showed a steady increase in the size of the black population, Hoffman predicted that African Americans were doomed to face a "gradual extinction of the race." The name of Hoffman's publisher, the American Economic Association, added a dose of respectability to this statistical study, which was widely used as a weapon in promoting white supremacy for decades to come. However, another important consequence of this and other internal statistical studies was that Prudential judged blacks to be bad actuarial risks and promptly started to cancel all black life insurance policies. Within four years, by the end of the century, most insurance companies got out of the business of insuring African Americans.[6] In a similar manner, statistics have been used over the years to perpetrate many kinds of heinous crimes, or their faulty uses have led to extremely inefficient public policies.[7]

STRUCTURE ABOVE A SWAMP

The discussions in this and the previous chapter may be confusing to you. On the one hand, I emphasize the relative nature of truth and, on the other, I advocate objective analysis. A quotation by Karl Popper, the eminent philosopher of science, may resolve this contradiction.

> The empirical basis of objective science has thus nothing "absolute" about it. Science does not rest upon rock-bottom. The bold structure of its theories rise, as it were, above a swamp. It is like a building erected on

piles. The piles are driven down from above into the swamp, but not down to any natural or "given" base; and when we cease our attempts to drive our piles into a deeper layer, it is not because we have reached firm ground. We simply stop when we are satisfied that they are firm enough to carry the structure, at least for the time being.[8]

Therefore, although we can empirically test "scientific laws" regarding society, we cannot know their truth. The ability to test hypotheses has lent social sciences and policy science a considerable degree of credibility. Hence, on this shifting ground of "truth," we want to achieve objective analyses by being systematic in our definition of goals, consistent about our method of analysis, and forthright about our implicit assumptions.

In psychology it is often held that the strength of one's character can also be the source of one's weakness. Similarly, the appeal of objective methods of policy analysis is the ability to present complex phenomena with simple, easy-to-understand numbers and figures. At the same time, the unquestioned acceptance of these statistical artifacts can lead to serious flaws. Therefore, we should know how to use with skill the extremely useful and powerful tools called statistics. This skill is honed with practice and by knowledge of the methods of manipulation.

Key Words

Bar graphs (p. 184)
Base (p.182)
Consumer price index (p. 179)
Fixed weight (p. 179)
GDP deflator (p. 179)
Nominal income (p. 179)

Pie charts (p. 184)
Real income (p. 179)
Real terms (p. 180)
Scatter plots (p. 184)
Variable weight (p. 179)

Exercises

1. Write an essay on truth and objectivity in quantitative analysis for public policy. Within this context, describe the relative advantages and disadvantages of the various measures of central tendency and dispersion. Provide appropriate examples.
2. Collect data on the growth rate of per capita GDP, rate of inflation, and unemployment from 1950 (consult *Economic Report of the President* and *Statistical Abstract of the United States*). First make the case that the nation has been better served by the Republican presidents, and then make the case for the Democrats based on the same set of data.
3. Consider the following table, which shows yearly data on percentages of the population living under poverty. Plot the data and derive as many different (and even contradictory) conclusions as you can from them.

Year	All	White	Black
1959	22.4	18.1	58.2
1960	22.2	17.8	56.4
1961	21.9	17.4	56.8

Year	All	White	Black
1962	21.0	16.4	56.1
1963	19.5	15.3	51.1
1964	19.0	14.9	49.8
1965	17.3	13.3	47.1
1966	14.7	11.3	39.7
1967	14.2	11.0	38.2
1968	12.8	10.0	32.8
1969	12.1	9.5	30.9
1970	12.6	9.9	31.6
1971	12.5	9.9	31.3
1972	11.9	9.0	32.4
1973	11.1	8.4	29.3
1974	11.2	8.6	29.7
1975	12.3	9.7	29.8
1976	11.8	9.1	29.5
1977	11.6	8.9	29.0
1978	11.4	8.7	29.4
1979	11.7	9.0	28.1
1980	13.0	10.2	29.9
1981	14.0	11.1	34.2
1982	15.0	12.0	35.6
1983	15.2	12.1	35.7
1984	14.4	11.5	33.8
1985	14.0	11.4	31.3
1986	13.6	11.0	31.1
1987	13.5	10.5	33.1
1988	11.6	8.8	29.1

4. Look at some of the recent news reports presented with quantitative data. See if you can derive a different conclusion from the same information.

Notes

1. You can access data collected by the Bureau of Labor Statistics by logging on to http://stats.bls.gov/blshome.htm.
2. Darrell Huff, *How to Lie with Statistics* (New York: W.W. Norton, 1954), 9.
3. Tim Corrigan, "Weinberger Finds His Well-Worn Strategies Always Succeed in Blunting Defense Budget Axe," *Wall Street Journal*, March 1, 1985.
4. Frederick L. Hoffman, *Race Traits and Tendencies of the American Negro*, quoted in Joel Williamson, *The Crucible of Race: Black-White Relations in the American South Since Emancipation* (New York: Oxford University Press, 1984), 329.
5. Ibid.
6. For a detailed discussion, see Williamson, *The Crucible of Race*.
7. For an excellent discussion of measuring people's abilities with numbers, see Stephen Jay Gould, *The Mismeasure of Man* (New York: Norton, 1981).
8. Karl Popper, *The Logic of Scientific Discovery* (New York: Harper and Row, 1959), 65.

CHAPTER

9

PROJECTION TECHNIQUES: WHEN HISTORY IS INADEQUATE

PROJECTION VERSUS CAUSAL PREDICTION

One of the most important of an organization's functions is planning for the future. How would you begin the process? It is not merely a cliché that it is impossible to predict the future without knowledge of the past. In history we look for **trends** and the **causal connections** that offer explanations for the events at hand. We may call the analysis of trends **projection**. In contrast, **prediction** is an inquiry into the causal relationship that binds the variable to be explained (the **dependent** variable) to a set of variables (the **independent** variables) that purport to explain it.

We call trend analysis "projection" because it contains an underlying hypothesis that whatever factor(s) set in motion a past pattern of change will continue to operate in the future, leading to the same rate of growth or the same pattern of behavior. This postulation, called the **assumption of continuity,** is the underlying premise of all forecasting methods. In using projection techniques we aim to find a past trend and project it into the future. Of course, forecasting on the basis of past trends raises the philosophical question of whether history really repeats itself. Without getting embroiled in this age-old controversy, we can safely point out that because progress in the realm of social sciences is mostly evolutionary and incremental, the study of any long socioeconomic series would point to the existence of some sort of trend pattern.

With causal analysis, in contrast, we hypothesize that the future development of the dependent variable is not related to its past trend (at least not to any significant extent), and, therefore, a past pattern cannot solely predict future behavior. Instead, it is determined by a complex causal linkage between the dependent variable and a set of independent variables.

An example may clarify the difference. If we want to know the extent of future health care needs, we can look at past trends and see that health care costs increased a certain percentage every year, and then forecast that in five years we will need a corresponding amount of money to meet health care needs. Or we may look at various explanatory factors, such as the percentage of children and elderly in the population, expenditures on preventive medicine, trends related to food and nutrition, education levels, or rate of growth of income. Then, by developing a model in which all these factors influence the outcome, we can attempt to forecast future health care costs (see Figure 9.1).

Both projection and prediction methods have their relative advantages and drawbacks. Projection methods often turn out to be easier to use for forecasting— particularly for short-term "policy prescription"—because these models require data points of a single series to calculate the trend. In contrast, causal models require a thorough understanding of the causal linkages between a dependent

Figure 9.1 Trend Projection Versus Causal Prediction

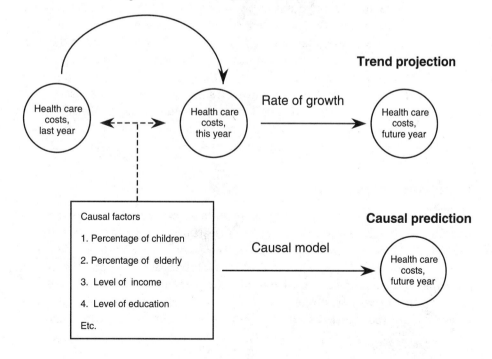

variable (outcome) and a set of independent variables (cause). These types of models are better suited for policy research and for longer-term forecasting. In general, when choosing an appropriate method of forecasting, you should consider the following points. You should choose a trend analysis in preference to a causal model if

- The past trend is linear and stable, which means not much has changed over time, at least in the short run.
- You do not have a good understanding of the causal factors explaining the dependent variable.
- You do not have a great deal of time and resources to conduct the appropriate research.

INADEQUACY OF HISTORY

If we want to forecast the future with the help of the past, we need a minimum amount of information from the past to provide us with any kind of meaningful insight into the future. Unfortunately, researchers and policy analysts often face the problem of inadequate past information. This inadequacy may result from (1) lack of history itself, (2) past lack of interest in collecting information, or (3) scattered past information whose compilation in a series would require too much time and money.

For example, if you are attempting to forecast population growth for a newly incorporated city, you do not have much of a history to fall back on. Or in an attempt to estimate the influx of tourists in a city, you may find out that such data exist for only the last two years or that no systematic effort to collect them has ever been made. Or you may discover that although various agencies have collected the data over a number of years, each one has done so independently without cooperating much with the others; as a result, the compilation of that data in one continuous series would require a great deal of resources. In such cases, you can still make a projection on the basis of one or two past data points, or none at all. For these kinds of cases, I discuss a number of techniques that can be classified under two broad headings: **single-factor projection** and the **judgmental method** of projection.

Single-Factor Projection

Suppose we are interested in projecting the number of cases of AIDS infection in our city, which was incorporated a couple of years ago. Our town has data on the number of AIDS victims for only the last two years. Last year, there were 150 reported cases, and the year before there were 138 cases. Therefore, the rate of AIDS infection in our area increased by nearly 9 percent last year. On the basis of this information, we may project the next year's infection rate by multiplying the number of this year's cases by 1.09. In symbolic terms, this can be written as

$$P_1 = \left(1 + r\right) \times P_0 \tag{9.1}$$

where P_1 is the future year's population

r is the rate of population growth

P_0 is the present year's population

Using this formula, we can predict that if the current population of AIDS victims is 150, then by one year later, this number will reach $150 \times (1.09) = 163$. Using the same logic, we can see that the year after, this number is going to increase by another 9 percent. Thus, if P_2 is the population for the second year, then it can be estimated by

$$P_2 = \left(1 + r\right) \times P_1 \tag{9.1a}$$

Since we know from equation 9.1 that P_1 is equal to $(1 + r) P_0$, we can substitute this expression for P_2 to obtain

$$P_2 = \left(1 + r\right) \times \left(1 + r\right) \times P_0$$

which means

$$P_2 = \left(1 + r\right)^2 \times P_0 \tag{9.2}$$

Therefore, it is obvious that if the population grows at a constant rate, to estimate the second year's population we must multiply the current year's population by a factor of one plus the rate of growth to the power *two*. If the population keeps growing at this constant rate, in three years we can expect the number to reach the current year's population multiplied by the factor of one plus the rate of growth to the power *three*. Therefore, by generalizing this logic, we can write the formula as

$$P_n = \left(1 + r\right)^n \times P_0 \tag{9.3}$$

where n is any year in the future.

Thus, if we want to estimate the number of people who might be infected with the deadly virus ten years from now, we set the number of years equal to ten in the preceding equation ($n = 10$). Thus, we write equation 9.2 as

$$P_{10} = \left(1 + .09\right)^{10} \times P_0 \tag{9.4}$$

Using this formula, we can estimate that ten years from now, *if the present rate of infection continues,* we can expect to see 355 people infected.[1] This is the formula of geometric growth, which is also used to calculate compound interest rates. The use of this formula can make the analyst's task easy because the size of any future population can be estimated simply by substituting the appropriate numbers in equation 9.3.

For policy analysis, it is often important to know not only the point estimate of the number of cases n years in the future but also the total number of cases for the entire time span. To estimate the total number of people infected with the AIDS virus during the next ten years, we can estimate the size of the afflicted population for each year by using equation 9.5 and then adding them up. Since this process is cumbersome and time consuming, we can estimate the sum of any geometric series using the following formula:

$$\sum_{N=1}^{K} P_n = \frac{\left(1+r\right)^{n+1} - 1}{r} \times P_0 \qquad (9.5)$$

Using this formula, we can estimate with a hand calculator the total number of patients needing treatment and public assistance to be nearly 2,634.[2] By multiplying this number by the current level of medical costs and public funding per patient, we can provide a rough-and-ready estimate of the total medical costs for these potential patients and the amount of money required in public assistance for the next ten years.

In the preceding example, we projected the future values of a variable on the basis of its past rate of growth. However, we can use many other factors as the basis of projections. For example, suppose a large parcel of vacant land is being considered for rezoning. The new zoning ordinance will allow residential housing, apartments, or commercial buildings. Analysts may use past information on land use patterns and their fiscal impact to project the future needs of the new community. By looking at the prices of the proposed residential units, planners can get a good idea about the economic capabilities of the newcomers. From the data of a larger city or a similar neighborhood, projections can be made for detailed demographic characteristics, such as the number of school-age children and elderly, commuting behavior, and recreational needs. If we expect 10,000 people to settle in the new neighborhood, by calculating the percentage for each demographic segment, we can project their numbers. These projections, in turn, would allow for the projection of future resource needs for schools, libraries, recreational facilities, roads, sewer systems, and other necessary infrastructure. These data can also be used for projecting traffic congestion or crime rates.

Fiscal Impact Analysis

Suppose your town is considering a large residential development project. Since the building of new homes will create increased demands for public services and infrastructure, you would like to prepare the town for such a change. The housing development will create demands for new schools, health care facilities, shopping areas, new roads, sewage systems, energy, pollution control, public transportation, and police and fire protection. At the same time, it will create new employment and generate local taxes such as those on property and sales. To plan for such extensive changes, you must forecast the impact of this new development. **fiscal impact analysis** (FIA) is particularly suited for these kinds of predictions.[3]

Let us explain this analysis with an example. A developer is planning to build 500 new single-family housing units, of which 40 percent have two bedrooms,

35 percent have three bedrooms, and the remaining 25 percent have four bedrooms. The houses are going to sell for $90,000, $110,000, and $150,000, respectively. The demographic profile of your town indicates that, on average, each two-bedroom house is expected to accommodate 2.354 occupants with 0.148 children. The figures for three- and four-bedroom units are 2.512 occupants with 0.614 children and 2.689 residents with 1.302 children. From this information, you can find the projected demographic profile for the newly developed community (see Table 9.1).

As you can see, by using similar logic we can generate a wide range of forecasts, from employment and income generation to the need for additional police, fire, and city employees. The question then becomes, how do you get the necessary numbers (the "multipliers") to estimate the future demand, revenues, and costs? There are several methods for getting these numbers.

- The **per capita multiplier method** is the most popular among all others for estimating the basis for future projection because it can be done quickly and relatively inexpensively. This method assumes that the resource utilization pattern of tomorrow will not be any different from today's. For example, to estimate the day-care needs of a new community, we can look at the city-wide estimate of the average number of children of appropriate age per household. Then, by multiplying that number by the number of new homes, we can calculate the expected number of children in the neighborhood. Since only a fraction of these children will require day-care facilities, we can consult other sources for information on the average day-care requirements of children from similar social and economic backgrounds. Moreover, by using this method, we can estimate such diverse aspects as the number of cars, pollutant emissions, and traffic congestion. If the current average occupant of a three-bedroom house owns 1.98 cars, this pattern will remain unchanged in the next two years when this hypothetical project is scheduled to be completed.
- The **case study method** involves interviewing municipal department heads, school administrators, and other experts in the field. The premise behind such a method is the assumption that these are the individuals who know

Table 9.1   Projected Demographic Profile of New Community

	No. of units		No. of residents		No. of children		Property tax revenue (at 1 percent of sales price)	
Two-bedroom units	(500 × 0.40)	200	(200 × 2.354)	471	(200 × 0.148)	30	(200 × $900)	$180,000
Three-bedroom units	(500 × 0.35)	175	(175 × 2.512)	440	(175 × 0.614)	107	(175 × $1,100)	$192,500
Four-bedroom units	(500 × 0.25)	125	(125 × 2.689)	336	(125 × 1.302)	163	(125 × $1,500)	$187,500
Total		500		1,247		300		$560,000

the conditions best. Therefore, without the analyst getting data on per capita resource consumption (as in the previous case), we can get the experts' assessment of the relevant multipliers.

• The **comparable city method** looks at an analogous project and can be used profitably as long as the two projects are similar in nature.

Problems of Single-Factor Analysis

The principal advantage of the methods discussed above is that they are relatively inexpensive and provide a quick estimate of the future course of events. As a result, these techniques remain the most commonly used in the area of public sector analysis. We frequently come across estimates derived by these methods in policy debates about crime rates, population growth, and the number of drug addicts. The problem with such estimates is the implicit assumption that whatever happened during the previous period will continue unchanged. However, in life, relationships hardly remain unaltered over time. If we project the rate of AIDS growth in the United States based on the last five years, we can see that there is already some empirical evidence to suggest that the virus's rate of growth may have slowed down, at least among some target groups, as a result of greater public awareness through education and media exposure. Therefore, the reality of the future may not turn out to be as dire as predicted by our method.

Figure 9.2 illustrates the predicaments of a single-factor projection. In Figure 9.2(a) the two black dots represent two known points in history. On the basis of this meager knowledge, we are predicting a linear trend shown by the arrow. However, an infinite number of nonlinear trends can be drawn through two points. In Figure 9.2(b) I have drawn two such nonlinear trends. If either of these is the actual trend, a projection based on a straight-line trend will cause serious errors. (To learn how San Diego County used single-factor projection to estimate the cost of illegal immigration, see "A Case in Point: Single-Factor Analysis.")

Figure 9.2   The Problems of Single-Factor Projection

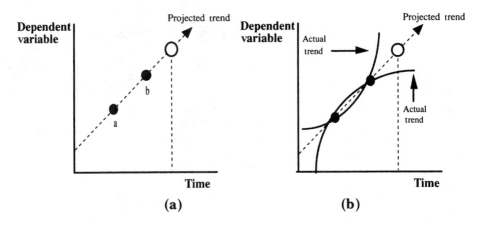

(a)   (b)

A CASE IN POINT

Single-Factor Analysis: The Fiscal Impact of Illegal Immigration in San Diego County

Because of the various problems associated with single-factor projections, they are always highly controversial. Yet when no reliable information is available, they can effectively serve as the starting points of policy debate and eventual policy formation. Since these techniques are extremely common in the public sector decision-making process, let me give you an example.[1]

Located on the border with Mexico, San Diego County faces the problem of large numbers of illegal immigrants, mostly from Mexico and other Central American countries. Nearly all of these people are extremely poor, so the county must bear a great deal of the costs of health care, education, and law enforcement. In 1992 the state of California commissioned a study to estimate the number of illegal immigrants in San Diego County. However, the researchers faced the problem that nobody had any information on the number of illegal aliens. Therefore, they used some simple but imaginative methods. They estimated the number of illegal aliens by the following procedure:

During the twelve-month period ended September 30, 1991, the Immigration and Naturalization Service (INS) apprehended 540,300 undocumented immigrants in San Diego County. It has been estimated by the San Diego Border Patrol that between 1 in 3 and 1 in 5 undocumented immigrants are actually apprehended. This implies that from 1,080,600 to 2,161,200 undocumented immigrants succeeded in entering San Diego County during the year.[2]

The researchers estimated the cost to the state and county governments for the care of the illegal immigrants by calculating their proportion to the total population served by health care services, the education system, social services, and the criminal justice system and then multiplying that number by the total expenditure. This was claimed to be the total cost to the state and local governments. Following a similar procedure, the researchers estimated the tax revenue contributions by the undocumented alien population of the region. The total net cost to the state and local governments was estimated to be $145,921,845.

Notes

1. This study generated a lively controversy on the cost of illegal immigration in the region. Without taking any side in the controversy, I am simply reporting the results as an example of single-factor projection when no other data are available.
2. Auditor General of California, *A Fiscal Impact Analysis of the Undocumented Immigrants Residing in San Diego County,* Report C-126, August 1992, 11.

Discussion Points

1. Why is the count of illegal immigrants problematic? How did this study use single-factor analysis to estimate the costs of illegal immigration to San Diego County?
2. Discuss the accuracy of the study's methodology. Can you suggest a better one instead?

JUDGMENTAL METHODS OF PROJECTION

Frequently in life we encounter situations in which forecasting cannot be performed in a structured way, either because of a lack of knowledge of the past or because the causal linkages are too complex to be quantified properly. In such cases forecasts must be based on special insights and intuition. Let us consider an example. The passage of a piece of legislation through the U.S. political process is a highly complex affair. After it works its way through a maze of committees, it must pass both chambers of Congress. After its passage, if the president signs it, it becomes law. Disagreement between the House and the Senate or a presidential veto can easily derail this process. However, it may be necessary to predict the future of a particular piece of legislation so that those with a stake in the matter can be prepared for a change in the course of action. Or consider the case of policy makers in the State Department who are waiting for a certain development to take place in a foreign country and want a reliable forecast of the situation. They must depend on forecasts based on the intuition or subjective judgment of experts. Out of this necessity, a good number of techniques have been developed to deal with these unstructured forecasting needs.

In the previous section, we attempted to estimate the spread of the AIDS virus with the help of only two data points. We also saw the problems posed by such simple techniques. For example, one must consider the effects of increased awareness of the virus and the development of curative and prophylactic drugs. With such a complex issue, it is entirely possible that no single individual possesses all the necessary information to draw a realistic conclusion. We must depend on judgmental methods of projection based on the collective wisdom of experts. In the following sections I discuss a few of these methods.

The Delphi Technique

The name **Delphi technique** was coined after the famous oracle in the Apollo temple in the ancient Greek city of Delphi, where the oracle (in fact, the priests hiding behind it) used to forecast the future of the devotees. The Delphi technique is an important subjective predictive tool that was developed in 1948 by researchers at the RAND Corporation and since the mid-1950s has seen wide use in many countries around the world. Like most of the other techniques in the field of operations research, the Delphi technique owes its origin to attempts to solve problems of military strategy systematically.[4]

The Delphi technique was developed to bring a systematic, unbiased reasoning process into subjective group forecasting. We may form a panel of experts and let them sit around a table and come to an agreement about what may take place in the future. However, decisions made by a group may suffer from several sources of biases. If there is a well-known authority in the panel, the lesser members may become intimidated. If the rest of the panel is dispassionate about an issue, they may be swayed by one individual with a strong personality who approaches the issue with a particularly strong opinion. Also (as I discuss in the final chapter) research shows that most people are victims of **groupthink.**[5] That is, most of us loathe being the odd person out with a different point of view from the rest of the group. As a result, more cogent points with differing points of view may never be raised in a group discussion.[6]

One way of solving this problem is to ask the experts to forecast independently. In this case, the problem of succumbing to a groupthink will be averted, but if the experts have conflicting conclusions, we will have no way of achieving a consensus. Therefore, the Delphi technique was developed to find a happy medium between preserving the individuality of opinion and a synthesis of ideas. It is based on five principles.

1. *Anonymity.* Individual anonymity is achieved through strict physical separation of panel members. In some cases, even the names of the members should be kept secret from each other.
2. *Iteration.* The judgments of the panel members are summarized and circulated so group members can modify their original positions. Each round of individual deliberation initiated by information on others' opinions is called an iteration. During the entire process, there may be two or three such iterations.
3. *Distribution of statistical summary.* The individual responses are tabulated and the measures of their central tendencies and dispersion are provided to the members. To eliminate the extremes, often the median value is presented for the measure of central tendency. As for dispersion, a range of measures is usually provided. The members may also receive detailed graphs and charts specifying the shapes of the distribution of response.
4. *Group consensus.* Finally, on the basis of this process of iteration and feedback, efforts are made to achieve a group consensus on the issue.

The Delphi technique was created primarily for forecasting technical information from a largely homogeneous group of experts. The overall homogeneity in value creates a strong central tendency for the distribution in the forecast values (like a bell-shaped curve). In such a situation, the mean value is a fair representation of the group's judgment on a particular issue. However, when it comes to forecasting a sociological phenomenon, such unimodality of distribution of opinion may not exist. Let us consider, for example, an emotionally charged issue: the future of race relations in the United States. A group of experts assembled to discuss the matter are likely to reflect diversely held value positions and strongly disagree. The group may not be able to form a consensus. In such cases, a slightly different method, called the **policy Delphi technique,** may be more appropriate.

The policy Delphi technique starts with the initial assumption that the experts are not homogeneous in their points of view. In fact, the panel members may not even be experts but instead be individuals who represent various interest groups. Therefore, for the policy Delphi technique, the original steps are modified to reflect the changed reality.

1. *Selective anonymity.* It is recognized that there will be subjectiveness in arguments based on interest or value positions. Therefore, the participants are frequently kept anonymous only during the initial stage of discussion. After everybody has a chance to state his or her view, the issue may be debated openly in the subsequent iterations.

2. *Informed multiple advocacy.* Unlike the original Delphi technique, this method directs that the panel members be chosen not for their expertise but for their special interest in or position of advocacy on the matter. The panel considering policy options on how to contain outbursts of racial or ethnic hostility may include conservative advocates of strict law and order, liberal advocates of social reform, and members of opposing ethnic groups.

3. *Multimodal response.* Since opinions are likely to reflect the multimodal distribution of opinion of such a panel, the statistical summary to be provided to the members for the subsequent iterations may not include an attempt to find the central tendency. Instead, the summary may simply provide, as accurately as possible, a picture of the multipolar distribution of opinion.

4. *Structured conflict.* The original Delphi technique depends on the convergence of views, but the policy Delphi is built around conflict. In a contentious world, it is often helpful to be able to define opposing points of view clearly. Therefore, policy Delphi does not always aim at resolution, and sometimes it shows a final unbridgeable gap between parties.

Both Delphi techniques seem deceptively simple. For their successful use, you must follow the same path of structured reasoning as we discussed in the critical thinking chapter (see chapter 4). The steps are outlined here.

Define the problem. The success of this process depends on the clear definition of an issue. For example, an agency faces a probable cut in funding. Before it assembles a panel, it must decide the perimeter of the issue: Should it attempt to forecast the amount of money available for the next fiscal year, or should it tackle the question of specific cuts corresponding to certain levels of funding? An ill-defined issue can easily cause confusion and cost the organization a great deal in wasted effort, time, money, and morale. The proper definition of the issue is even more critical for a policy Delphi because social issues are likely to be far more complex than a technical problem facing an organization.

Choose the right panel. Choosing the right panel is equally critical for the success of a Delphi technique. Hard thinking must precede the selection of the panel members. Often the individuals designing a Delphi may not have adequate knowledge of the important persons relevant to the issue. William Dunn suggests a practical solution to this problem.[7] Frequently, the planners are at least able to name the most influential figure in the debate. They may ask this individual to identify the person with whom he or she agrees most closely and another with whom he or she disagrees most vehemently.

By asking these individuals the same question, the planners are well on the way to selecting an entire panel that shows a full range of opinion.

Develop the first-round questionnaire. The success of Delphi depends on the type of questions that are put before the panel, and you, the analyst, must decide what the questions will be in the first and subsequent iterations. Although there are no hard and fast rules about developing these questionnaires, you must develop the questionnaire for the first round with an eye to the next. Suppose the purpose of the exercise is to obtain a forecast, say, of the number of AIDS victims in the next five years. Some very structured questions regarding the future spread of the disease can start off the discussion. Or the panel can discuss trends in people's attitudes, sexual practices, changing social mores, and the attitude of the administration toward a frank discussion of unsafe sexual and intravenous drug use practices among the target groups and the distribution of prophylactic devices. In this case, the first-round questionnaire can be relatively unstructured and contain a number of open-ended questions. If the questions are not open ended, then the answers should be quantified according to some scale.

Analyze first-round results. The results of the first round of questionnaires should be analyzed to determine the position of each panel member. These results should be tabulated, and for each question the measures of central tendency and dispersion should be calculated. The panel members should have these results available for subsequent rounds. For example, if the question was, "How much do you expect teenage sexual practices to change in view of an increase in awareness campaigns?" and the answers were rated on a five-point scale (5 being significantly changed, 0 being no change at all), the panel members should be given at least the mean, median, standard deviation, and the range of distribution of the answers. If you have the graphics capability, it may not be a bad idea to show panel members visually the distribution of their answers. This may be a particularly good idea if the members are not expert statisticians.

Develop questionnaires for the subsequent rounds. Comparison of the group results with the individual responses paves the way for further discussion in the Delphi process. If the answers indicate a significant responsiveness of teenage sexual behavior to a concerted ad campaign, a more detailed discussion on this topic can help develop forecasts (and future policies). Also, note that although panel members may not have stated their basic assumptions in the first round, they are allowed to do so in successive rounds. Policy Delphi usually involves three to five rounds, so members have ample opportunity to evaluate each other's arguments in greater detail. These rounds of discussion may cause the members to modify their positions.

Arrange the panel discussion. At the end of the process a group meeting can allow the panel members to see if a consensus finally emerges through an open, face-to-face discussion. These group discussions can be particularly fruitful since by now each member of the panel is thoroughly conversant with the positions, arguments, hypotheses, and logic of others in the panel.

Therefore, the group discussion can often take place in an atmosphere of mutual understanding, if not agreement.

Prepare the final report. The last step of a Delphi process is for the analyst to prepare the final report. It should describe the entire process. If an overall agreement appears, the report should mention it, but you should be careful not to ignore minority or extreme positions, if any. If there is no consensus, you must take care to document the diverse points of view and the extent of divergence of opinion. (For a report on how Long Beach State University used the Delphi process to revamp its public affairs program, see "A Case in Point: The Use of the Delphi Technique in Devising a Public Policy Curriculum.")

The Feasibility Assessment Technique

The **feasibility assessment technique** (FAT) is a commonly used judgmental method of projection. This method is particularly useful in forecasting the outcome of a contentious issue, fought by a number of interested parties. Therefore, FAT has found wide application in the forecasting of political, economic, military, and institutional outcomes of a conflict. It is a versatile technique and can be used at any phase of the policy-making process. It can be used for predicting which issues are going to come to the forefront, what the legislative outcome will be, or how a policy will be implemented.

For example, suppose we are trying to forecast the outcome of a bill for the funding of AIDS information to high school students before a state legislature. To forecast the outcome of this debate, we need to make a list of the interested parties who play an active role in determining the outcome of the bill. We can make a list of the major players as follows: the governor, the liberal lawmakers, the media, the conservative lawmakers, the public health groups, the conservative Christian church groups, and the gay activist groups. Let us assume that the governor is a moderate conservative who shows mild opposition to the bill. The liberal lawmakers strongly support the measure, and the conservative lawmakers are solidly opposed to it. The public health groups support the issue. Finally, the church groups are vehemently opposed to the public funding of explicit sexual education, and the gay activists are equally visceral in their support for the bill. In FAT terminology, the relative position of the "player" groups (those who exert some power and influence over the policy outcome) is called the "issue position."

An analyst (or a group of analysts) assesses the relative issue position by estimating the probability of support by each player group. This probability measure is assigned to each group, and it varies between $+1$ and -1. If a group is certain to support the issue, then its issue position will have a value of 1. If it is certain to oppose it, its issue position value is assessed as -1. If the group is likely to be indifferent, then its value will be 0. It is safe to assume the gay activist groups should be assigned a $+1$ value and the conservative church group should be given -1. Let us assume that the support of the public health groups is 0.9, the media 0.8, liberal lawmakers 0.6, the governor -0.1, and the conservative lawmakers -0.7. The

A CASE IN POINT

The Use of the Delphi Technique in Devising a Public Policy Curriculum

I have mentioned the use of the Delphi technique as a forecasting tool. You can extend this and all other techniques of numerical analysis in solving problems far beyond their principal use. For example, the members of the public administration department at Long Beach State University wanted to revise their public policy curriculum, which would fundamentally reorient the direction of the department's program.[1] However, public policy may be taught from many different angles, requiring a wide variety of analytical skills. Since the faculty members could not come to an agreement, they decided to use the Delphi technique to devise the new curriculum. For that, the faculty took the following steps:

1. *Identification of the problem.* The faculty first wanted to know "what practicing public managers, academics, students, and alumni thought MPA [master of public administration] graduates should know and be able to do, and second to rate or rank the relative importance of those knowledge and skill components." They also wanted to identify "which components should be taught in required courses and which in elective."[2]

2. *Identification of the monitor/team.* Three faculty members with the required skill and knowledge of the Delphi technique were selected to make up the research team.

3. *Identification of the sample.* The team identified the stakeholders (the students, alumni, faculty, and public managers), from whom they chose more than one hundred participants for the first round. The participants were required to have access to e-mail. This requirement was not seen as a bias in the study, since nearly 85 percent of the students worked for public agencies and had e-mail addresses. A high percentage of alumni, faculty, and public managers also had e-mail.

4. *Round 1.* The participants received two open-ended questions: What should MPA graduates know, and what skills should they have?

5. *Round 2.* The research team tabulated the responses under the headings "knowledge" and "skills" and sent them back to the participants with the request to add, delete, or otherwise modify the lists.

6. *Round 3.* The team compiled a complete list under "knowledge" and "skills" and sent it back to the participants, asking them to award weights from 0 to 10, with 10 being the most important to the MPA students.

7. *Round 4.* The team members tabulated the responses for mean and standard deviation and ranked them according to their relative importance. Finally, they sent the results back to the participants and asked them to assign "core" or "elective" to each of the categories of "knowledge" and "skills."

8. *Sharing of information.* The faculty shared the gathered information and from it devised seven required and five elective courses.

Here is the list of the ten most important topics in the "knowledge" and "skills" categories, ranked from most to least important:

Knowledge	Standard deviation	Mean
1. Economics, politics and markets, microeconomic theory	9.7	0.55
2. Administrative theory, theory of the state	9.5	0.70
3. Research methods	9.5	0.70
4. Policy analysis	9.0	1.40
5. Strategic and comprehensive planning	9.0	1.40
6. Statistics	9.0	1.40
7. Financial management, politics of financial management	9.0	1.40
8. Program evaluation	9.0	1.40
9. Budgeting	8.5	2.10
10. Intergovernmental relations	8.0	1.00

Skills	Standard deviation	Mean
1. Writing skills	9.4	0.55
2. Analytical skills and techniques	9.0	1.00
3. Policy analysis skills	8.6	1.34
4. Leadership skills	8.4	1.14
5. Oral presentation skills	8.4	3.50
6. Finance and budgeting skills	8.2	1.48
7. Political awareness and interaction	8.0	1.58
8. Interpersonal management/behavioral skills	8.0	1.87
9. Cultural competency/diversity management	7.8	1.30
10. Listening skills	7.8	2.95

Notes

1. Michelle A. Saint-Germain, John W. Ostrowski, and Martha J. Dede, "Oracle in the Ether: Using an E-mail Delphi to Revise an MPA Curriculum," *Journal of Public Affairs Education* 3 (2000): 161–172.
2. Ibid., 163.

Discussion Points

1. Discuss the relative importance of the top ten "knowledge" and "skill" requirements, particularly in light of their mean and standard deviation scores.
2. Can you think of other areas in which the Delphi technique can be profitably used?

---

relative positions are shown in Table 9.2. Note that we are assigning values based on our subjective assessments. In a class exercise, you can simply make your estimations. However, a great deal of serious thinking has gone into "mental modeling," by which an expert in the field can arrive at a subjective assessment. Analysts must conduct these subjective forecasting techniques with the utmost care because of the influence of a great number of possible biases. I have mentioned some of these biases at the end of this chapter.[8]

Looking at Figure 9.3, you might think that because more groups with passion appear to the left of the spectrum (right-hand side of the diagram), the issue is certain to be decided in favor of funding. Reality, however, is more complicated than

Table 9.2   Relative Issue Positions

Groups	Relative positions
Gay activist groups	+1.0
Public health groups	+0.9
Media	+0.8
Liberal lawmakers	+0.6
Governor	−0.1
Conservative lawmakers	−0.7
Conservative church groups	−1.0

that. To begin with, not every player has equal influence over the outcome of the debate. For the next step, we would want to measure the players' available resources on the issue. The resources within the disposal of each group would include prestige, legitimacy, money, time, administrative capabilities, and communication capabilities. The available resources are measured within the range of 1 (having a great deal of resources to bear) and 0 (having no resources whatsoever). We may hypothetically assign values to our lineup as shown in Table 9.3.

The potential influence of each player can now be calculated by multiplying the issue position of each group with its total available resources. Thus, we can derive Table 9.4.

The total potential of policy influences predicts a positive outcome for the measure. However, the potential does not often foretell the actual outcome. Every player faces a slate of issues it considers to be vital to its mission. The governor has many agendas, of which fighting the funding of the AIDS information project is one. Facing an issue, the players must decide on the relative importance of the issue in relation to their other obligations. In other words, this particular issue, like all others facing each group, must have the group's commitment to invest a percentage of its resources. This commitment is called the "ranking of resources." Let

Figure 9.3   Relative Issue Positions on Public Funding of AIDS Information

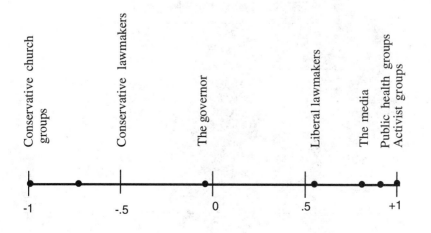

Table 9.3 The Availability of Resources

Groups	Resource availability
Governor	0.90
Liberal lawmakers	0.40
Conservative lawmakers	0.50
Media	0.80
Conservative church groups	0.30
Gay activist groups	0.10
Public health groups	0.05

us assume that the players have decided to allocate their total available resources as shown in Table 9.5.

In other words, the liberal lawmakers are willing to commit 15 percent of their resources, the gay activist groups are estimated to spend 80 percent of their resources, whereas the largely disinterested media are expected to commit no more than 2 percent in promoting this measure. The governor has decided to spend no more than 10 percent of his resources in fighting this measure, but the conservative lawmakers have made this issue a hallmark of their conservative agenda and are expected to spend 30 percent of their available resources. Similarly, the conservative church groups are expected to commit 90 percent of their resources to fight public funding of what they consider to be offensive. This commitment factor multiplied by the total potential determines the outcome. Thus, we may construct Table 9.6.

Table 9.6 gives us the total feasibility score; the opponents of the measure will have more support than will the proponents (–0.3840 as opposed to 0.1558). Therefore, despite popular support (more groups in favor), the measure will be defeated.

You may find the conclusion of this hypothetical study somewhat surprising, especially in view of the initial assessment based on Figure 9.3 and Table 9.4. In

Table 9.4 Potential for Policy Influence

Groups	Issue position (a)	Available resources (b)	Potential for policy influence (a) × (b)
Governor	–0.10	0.90	–0.09
Liberal lawmakers	0.60	0.40	0.24
Conservative lawmakers	–0.70	0.50	–0.35
Media	0.80	0.80	0.64
Conservative church groups	–1.00	0.30	–0.30
Gay activist groups	1.00	0.10	0.10
Public health groups	0.90	0.05	0.045
Total			+0.285

Table 9.5 The Ranking of Resources

Groups	Resource ranking
Governor	0.10
Liberal lawmakers	0.15
Conservative lawmakers	0.30
Media	0.02
Conservative church groups	0.90
Gay activist groups	0.80
Public health groups	0.60

fact, the ultimate outcome of any public policy depends on the relative issue position and the fraction of the total resources that the player groups are willing to invest to achieve a favorable outcome. You may notice that although the governor is the most resourceful person in this debate, his reluctance to invest a great deal of resources reduces him to the position of a minor player. In contrast, by combining their total resources and a stronger determination, the coalition between the conservative lawmakers and the church groups becomes a formidable force in stopping public funding. This technique explains very well many different social and political events. Consider, for example, the impact of the so-called Moral Majority, a coalition of right-wing religious groups and conservative politicians put together by the Reverend Jerry Falwell in the late 1970s and early 1980s. Although not supported by the majority of the American public, this group had a profound impact on the course of American politics that went far beyond its numerical strength.

Table 9.6 Calculated Policy Influence

Groups	Potential for policy influence (a)	Ranking of resources (b)	Feasibility score (a) × (b)
Opponents			
Governor	−0.09	0.10	−0.0090
Conservative lawmakers	−0.35	0.30	−0.1050
Conservative church groups	−0.30	0.90	−0.2700
Subtotal			−0.3840
Proponents			
Liberal lawmakers	0.240	0.15	0.0360
Media	0.640	0.02	0.0128
Gay activist groups	1.000	0.80	0.0800
Public health groups	0.045	0.60	0.0270
Subtotal			0.1558
Total			−0.2282

Steps of the Feasibility Assessment Technique

1. Identify the issue.
2. Identify the player groups.
3. Estimate the issue positions of the groups.
4. Estimate the available resources for each group.
5. Estimate the resource rank within each group.
6. Calculate the feasibility assessment index.

The Expected Utility Model

Some analysts have found a variation of the **expected utility model** to be a useful forecasting tool for predicting the outcomes of an incredible variety of social phenomena, from international relations to banking regulations. Bruce Bueno de Mesquita of the Hoover Institution at Stanford University and his associates are at the forefront of such predictive efforts.[9] Their methodology for forecasting is far too complex to be discussed in this book, but I can give you the basic idea behind these prediction methodologies.

Suppose we are forecasting the probability of a change in a certain government policy. By scanning the political landscape, we can pick out the major players in the game. They may then be classified as proponents of a change or opponents of a change. Let us assume that the government and its allies do not want any change and the opposition groups do. Those groups that are proposing a change are inviting a confrontation with those who prefer the status quo. Each group recognizes that just like investing in a risky project, the investment of resources to fight a rival has its own risks. A loss might cause an embarrassment and expose the group's vulnerability to its foes. In contrast, a win will bring highly desired spoils. Therefore, a group's strategic move in determining whether to confront its opponent and how much to invest in the process will reflect its expectations about the future. The following example can help show the relative positions of the proponents and the opponents of a policy change.

Suppose opposition groups propose a change in government policy (for example, in hand gun control, or increased funding for urban renewal, or conservation of open space), whereas the government and its supporters oppose such a change. The expected payoffs of the two groups can be shown with the help of a diagram. In Figure 9.4 the quadrants created by the intersection of the two straight lines have been subdivided into octants. These octants are marked with Roman numerals. The expected payoffs of the two groups are plotted on a Cartesian plane. In the northeastern quadrant—comprising octants I and II—each contestant expects to gain by confronting the other. If both contenders feel that they can win in a confrontation, the chances of open confrontation are extremely high. However, if the government's expectations of the outcome of a confrontation fall in octant I, along the point x, then the government expects to gain more than what the opposition parties would gain. Therefore, we can expect the government to take an aggressive posture and start a confrontation. In an authoritarian regime, this confrontation

Figure 9.4 Expected Payoff of the Government and Its Opposition

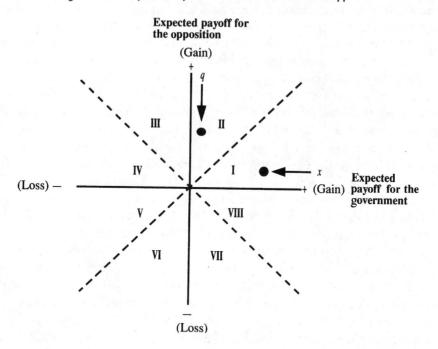

may take the form of cracking down on the opposition. In a democratic system, it may be a presidential veto.

In contrast, if the government's expectations of the outcome of a confrontation fall on a point such as q on octant II, then it would expect to win but its win would be less than that of its rival. As a result, if mutual expectation patterns fall in this region, we can expect a role reversal, wherein the opposition parties more aggressively seek confrontation with the government. However, since both parties expect to win, the chances of a confrontation are extremely high. In an international context, the disputes that fall within these two octants have escalated into war about 90 percent of the time.[10]

In the northwestern quadrant (octants III and IV), the opposition expects to win and the government expects to lose. In octant III, although the challenger expects to win, its gains will be smaller than the other's loss. Therefore, seeing the prospect of a relatively small loss, the government will sit down with the opposition and negotiate a compromise that gives the opposition an edge.

In octant IV, in contrast, the government is expected to suffer a heavier loss than what the opposition would gain. If the government's expectations match this kind of a pattern, we can expect it to accede to the demands of the opposition. In 1987, as a part of a wide-ranging budget compromise, President George Bush decided to go along with the Democrats in increasing taxes. At that time the president decided he had more to lose by opposing a compromise. In view of his earlier unequivocal campaign pledge of not increasing taxes ("Read my lips, no new taxes"), however, his action became a liability and came to haunt him later.

In the southwestern quadrant, both parties expect to lose. You may note that in octant V the government's losses are expected to be greater than the losses of the opposition. The situation is reversed in octant VI. Facing the prospect of a lose-lose situation, neither party shows much enthusiasm for a head-on confrontation.

Finally, the southeastern quadrant is the mirror image of the northwestern quadrant. That is, in this case, the government is expected to win in confrontation, and the opposition expects to lose. When the condition of octant VII prevails, the government perceives that it is making a legitimate demand on the opposition, and it has a good deal to gain from its position; but, more important, the opposition has a good deal more to lose. Situations such as these prove to come out peacefully because the opposition is effectively shut off with the prospect of a heavy loss. In the spring of 1984, President Ferdinand Marcos of the Philippines called for elections. President Marcos often used the results of highly corrupt elections to gain political legitimacy for his regime. The widespread disenchantment with his rule prompted many observers to predict organized opposition to Marcos or a call for the boycott of the elections and even violence. However, the leading opposition groups did not expect to defeat Marcos and expected to lose far more than the loss they could inflict on his regime by opposing him in the election. Based on their perception, Bueno de Mesquita correctly predicted no serious challenge to Marcos's presidency and a relatively uneventful election. I show the expected outcomes of confrontation in Figure 9.5.

Figure 9.5 Dynamics of the Policy Outcome

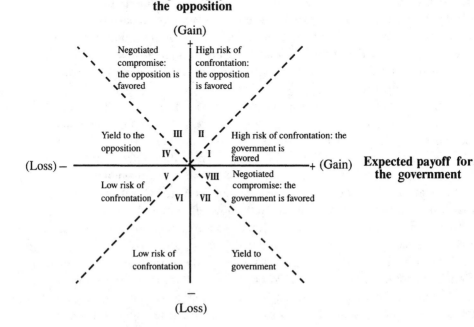

Expected payoff for the opposition

(Gain)

Negotiated compromise: the opposition is favored

High risk of confrontation: the opposition is favored

Yield to the opposition

III   II

IV   I

High risk of confrontation: the government is favored

(Loss) —

+ (Gain)   **Expected payoff for the government**

Low risk of confrontation

V   VIII

VI   VII

Negotiated compromise: the government is favored

Low risk of confrontation

Yield to government

(Loss)

Origin of the Numbers

The numbers in a FAT model or the estimation of the expectations of the two rivals in an expected utility model come from the judgment of those who are experts in the area. The expected utility model requires the identification of the major players and the estimation of their expectations. For these estimations, similar to those in the FAT model, you can use the expertise of those who have direct knowledge of these groups. Having ascertained the groups' positions, you may first plot them in their respective octants to see if a pattern emerges. These results will tell you whether you can expect a confrontation.

Although I gave you examples from international relations, a versatile technique such as the expected utility model can be used to forecast many different outcomes in contentious situations facing all levels of government. Let us suppose that during a police chase in your town, a police cruiser crashed into the car of an innocent citizen, injuring her. The risk management division of your local government is interested in settling the case. However, before offering a settlement amount, the risk manager wants to know if the injured party would want a lengthy and extremely expensive court case. The expected utility model can help you develop a scenario that will justly compensate the victim for her suffering and yet save a good deal of the city's tax dollars.

Shortcomings of the Judgmental Methods

Often in life, issues are so complex that it is extremely difficult to capture all their dimensions within the confines of structured techniques of analysis and forecasting. In addition, in real life you will encounter situations in which there is no history to depend on for predicting the future. In such cases, judgmental methods give us extremely useful alternatives. Time and again, the various subjective methods of prediction have proved their usefulness. However, the very sources of their strength in one situation become their liability in another.

Although the techniques of judgmental methods offer more flexibility than do the other, more rigorous statistical methods (discussed in the following chapters), they still must operate within some structure. In analyses of group interaction (say, between the government and the opposition), we assume that all groups are making their decisions at the same time yet independently. It stands to reason, however, that they are interdependent. Also, group interactions are part of a dynamic process in which groups communicate with each other, compromise, and form or break coalitions. Even the most flexible open-ended forecasting method cannot accommodate many of these complex behaviors.

However, the more serious problem with the judgmental methods is that because there is no systematic way of discussing the assumptions and arguments of the "experts," preconceived ideas, prejudices, unarticulated agendas, self-interest, or other psychological pitfalls and cognitive limitations frequently contaminate their judgments. Few experts (in and out of the government) predicted the war between the United States and Iraq. Even at the last minute, most were willing to dismiss the threats and counterthreats (for example, Saddam Hussein's apocalyptic "mother of all wars") as simple bravado, posturing, or face-saving gestures. When President George Bush ordered Iraq to get out of Kuwait or face war, he was not bluffing. And when Hussein, facing incredible odds, said his army would never leave Kuwait on its own accord, he meant it. Yet most experts saw the prospect of this strange war as so farfetched that they refused to believe the resolve of the two contenders almost until the first bullet was fired. Similarly, because of these psychological impediments, the Central Intelligence Agency was caught off guard by the sudden collapse of the Soviet Union. Having poked and prodded, studied and analyzed the Soviet system for decades, agency experts completely failed to understand the fundamental fragility of the system.

Key Words

Assumption of continuity (p. 200)
Case study method (p. 205)
Causal connections (p. 200)
Comparable city method (p. 206)
Delphi technique (p. 208)
Dependent variable (p. 200)
Expected utility model (p. 218)
Feasibility assessment technique
  (p. 212)
Fiscal impact analysis (p. 204)

Groupthink (p. 209)
Independent variable (p. 200)
Judgmental methods of projection
  (p. 202)
Per capita multiplier method (p. 205)
Policy Delphi technique (p. 209)
Prediction (p. 200)
Projection (p. 200)
Single-factor projection (p. 202)
Trends (p. 200)

Exercises

1. Consider the following facts in your community and explain how you would go about forecasting them for the next five years:
    a. The number of homeless
    b. The number of child abuse cases
    c. The number of school-age children
    d. The number of violent crimes
    Explain your data needs, point out the possible sources, and choose a projection model.
2. Suppose the indigent elderly population that depends on public assistance is growing at a rate of 4 percent per year in your county. At present there are 3,500 individuals in this category. How many such people would you expect to see three years from now? If it costs the county $2,300 per person for health care, estimate the total cost of indigent health care for your county.
3. Explain the problems of single-factor projections. Despite these problems, single-factor projection remains one of the most commonly used techniques of projection. Taking a real-life example, account for the wide-scale use of single-factor projection in public policy analysis.
4. Explain the process of the policy Delphi technique. What are its strengths and shortcomings?
5. The city of Masters, Pennsylvania, faces a controversial issue. The marshland adjacent to a prosperous neighborhood is not being used. A developer has submitted a

proposal to make it into a golf course. However, the marshland is the habitat for migratory birds. Hence, the project is opposed by powerful environmental groups. The conservative, probusiness council members support the project. This is a divisive issue, and the mayor has expressed her mild opposition to the project, whereas the liberal members of the city council are in vehement opposition. The table shows the relative position of the various parties, their available resources, and the ranking of resources. Predict the outcome of the debate.

Groups	Issue positions	Ranking of resources	Available resources
Mayor	−0.20	0.30	0.80
Developer	+1.00	0.90	0.30
Conservative city council members	0.85	0.60	0.40
Liberal city council members	−0.65	0.80	0.50
Environmental groups	−0.90	0.90	0.90
Chamber of commerce	+0.50	0.40	0.10

6. Take any current controversial issue facing your community, state, or the nation, such as gun control, abortion, or the amount of national defense funding. Then, working with others in a group project, predict the policy outcome using the feasibility assessment technique. How accurate do you think your predictions are? What are the major weaknesses of your predictions? Would you feel comfortable using these techniques in a real-life situation? Explain. (Suggestion: The size of the group is often crucial to the success of such a project. A group size of about five is the best. A larger group can be broken into several groups, each one attempting to forecast the same issue or different ones.)

7. Suppose you are going to forecast the outcome of an upcoming sporting event. As a group, discuss and write down the factors (quality of the players, past performances of the two teams, and so forth) that may help you in your prediction. Then, by using the judgmental method, develop a forecast. Compare your forecast with the actual outcome of the game.

Notes

1. Those of you who have hand calculators with a button that says [y^x] can be spared the task of having to multiply 1.09 ten times. The [y^x] key raises a number to the desired exponent. To calculate this number, you need to (a) enter 1.09; then (b) hit the [y^x] button followed by (c) the number 10; (d) press the [=] sign to obtain the value for the expression $(1 + 0.09)^{10}$. By multiplying this number to the initial number of cases (P_o), you can estimate the value of P_{10}.

2. To arrive at this number, we write equation 9.5 as follows:

$$\sum_{1}^{10} P_n = \frac{(1 + .09)^{10+1} - 1}{.09} \times 150$$

3. For a detailed discussion of FIA, see Robert W. Burchell and David Listokin, *The Fiscal Impact Handbook: Estimating Local Costs and Revenues of Land Development* (New Brunswick, N.J.: Rutgers University Press, 1978).

4. For a historical account of the development of the Delphi technique, see Harold Sackman, *Delphi Critique* (Lexington, Mass.: D. C. Heath, 1975). See also Juri Pill, "The Delphi Method: Substance, Contexts, a Critique, and an Annotated Bibliography," *Socio-Economic Planning Science* 5 (1971): 57–71. However, for an excellent discussion on Delphi and other techniques of subjective decision making, see William N. Dunn, *Public Policy Analysis: An Introduction* (Englewood Cliffs, N.J.: Prentice Hall, 1981).

5. The term "groupthink" was made popular by the psychologist Irving Janis. For a more detailed explanation and many more examples, see his *Groupthink: Psychological Studies of Policy Decisions and Fiascoes,* a revised and enlarged edition of *Victims of Groupthink,* 1972 (Boston: Houghton Mifflin, 1982).

6. People often choose not to express their "true preferences" in public because of peer pressure or the fear of social ostracism. If the need to be "politically correct" overwhelms the need to be truthful, your publicly held views will deviate from what you prefer or believe to be the truth. The price of this distortion of a citizen's preferences may be considerable, as public policies based on misconstrued views can lead to inefficiency or social conflict. For an interesting discussion of the need for anonymous discourse for the articulation of genuine preferences, see Timur Kuran, "Mitigating the Tyranny of Public Opinion: Anonymous Discourse and the Ethic of Sincerity," *Constitutional Political Economy* 4, no. 1 (1993).

7. Dunn, *Public Policy Analysis,* 198.

8. See, for example, Herbert Simon and Dorothea Simon, "Individual Differences in Solving Physics Problems," in *Children's Thinking,* ed. Robert S. Siegler (Englewood Cliffs, N.J.: Prentice Hall, 1986). See also David Klahr and Kenneth Kotovsky, eds., *Complex Information Processing: The Impact of Herbert A. Simon* (Hillsdale, N.J.: Erlbaum, 1989); Vadim D. Glezer, *Vision and Mind: Modeling Mental Functions* (Hillsdale, N.J.: Erlbaum, 1995).

9. See, for example, Bruce Bueno de Mesquita, David Newman, and Alvin Pabushka, *Forecasting Political Events: The Future of Hong Kong* (New Haven: Yale University Press, 1985).

10. Douglas Beck and Bruce Bueno de Mesquita, "Forecasting Policy Decisions: An Expected Utility Approach," in *Corporate Crisis Management,* ed. Steven Andriole (New York: Petrocelli, 1984).

CHAPTER

10

PROJECTION TECHNIQUES: ANALYSIS OF HISTORICAL DATA

Forecasting based on projection techniques requires an understanding of the basic pattern of behavior. Without a pattern, variations are totally erratic or random, in which case future behavior cannot be predicted. In the previous chapter we discussed using forecasting methods when faced with a paucity of past information. In such instances, when making projections, we must rely on one or two data points over time or on expert judgment. To make the most of what little historical data we have, we use projection techniques specially suited to situations of data scarcity, such as single-factor projection and judgmental methods of forecasting. However, we select different techniques when we have a long history of behavior to study. In this chapter we examine those techniques that lend themselves to discerning trends in series of data.

To understand the trend of a series (or the direction in which it is heading), we need to plot the data first. Sometimes, though, a scatter plot does not reveal a strong trend. Consider, for example, a hypothetical series of tourists visiting the Pennsylvania town, Masters, which has a strong tourist industry that attracts vacationers primarily during the skiing and summer seasons. Masters's chamber of commerce has collected data on the number of tourists quarterly (in three-month periods) for thirteen years, from 1988 to 2000. The data are plotted in Figure 10.1.

Figure 10.1   Number of Tourists in Masters, Pennsylvania

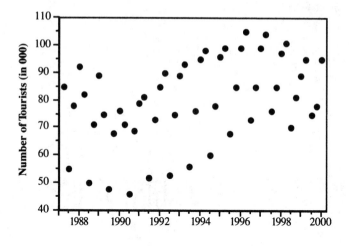

THE COMPONENTS OF A DATA SERIES

You may conclude that the scatter plot of the quarterly tourist population looks quite confusing and that you can determine little from it. Often, a series contains elements that obscure our vision. In general, a data series tends to head in a general direction, or contains an element of a trend. A series that grows over time is called a **positive trend,** whereas a series that declines is said to have a **negative trend.** Besides the trend, a data series may also reflect fluctuations resulting from the effects of seasonality. Further, a data series may exhibit effects of long-term economic cycles. As the economy expands and contracts during the course of a business cycle, it affects many kinds of economic and social activities. Finally, a series contains the effects of purely random fluctuations, which are caused by factors outside our consideration. Natural calamities (floods, earthquakes, devastating tornadoes, and the like), political events (riots, assassinations of important political persons, the election of a new chief executive or political party, and so forth), or institutional factors (such as changes in government regulations) can have an unpredictable effect on a series. The collapse of the Soviet Union had an extraordinarily important but unforeseen effect on the U.S. defense industry. Since these external factors cannot be factored into a model, their effects are called **random errors.** Therefore, time series data (data recorded over time) may contain the following:[1]

Data = Trend + Seasonality + Cyclical Effect + Random Error.

Let us examine these components in greater detail. Figure 10.2 depicts two **linear trend** patterns. Many aggregate social, economic, and demographic data (such as the per capita GDP of a country and population growth in the short term) show positive linear growth when plotted over time. However, as shown in Figure

Figure 10.2 Linear Trend Patterns

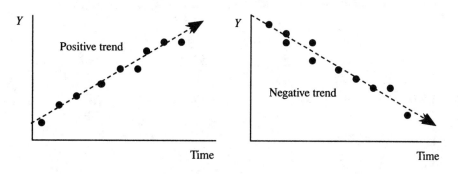

10.2, not all points of observations fall on the trend line. Since these deviations cannot be accounted for within the model, we assume that aberrations reflect the effects of the random error component.

In the case presented in Figure 10.1, the rate of growth does not seem to change over the delineated time period. This trend can be viewed as upward or downward. Despite little peaks and valleys for economic booms and recessions, the GDP per capita, measured in constant dollars, has shown an upward trend over the years in the United States. But during the 1980s, federal government assistance to state and local governments demonstrated a steady downward trend.

When data values fluctuate around a constant mean, a **horizontal trend** pattern develops. This is characteristic of a series in which there is no trend and the data seem to fluctuate in a random fashion. In technical terms, such a series is called a **stationary series.** In a stationary series, a trend line will go through the mean ($\overline{Y}$). Since there is no seasonality in the human reproductive process, for example, the daily number of births in New York City hospitals within a year will depict such a series. Figure 10.3 is an illustration of a horizontal pattern of fluctuation.

A **seasonal trend** is shown in Figure 10.4. The quarterly data plotted in the figure depict a trend of regular fluctuations of peaks and valleys during the course of a year. Home construction, unemployment, crime, and highway accidents often tend to show this kind of seasonal variability.

Figure 10.3 Horizontal, or No-Trend, Pattern

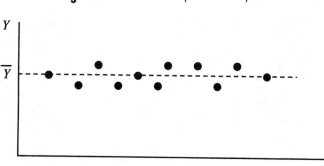

Figure 10.4   Seasonal Trend Pattern

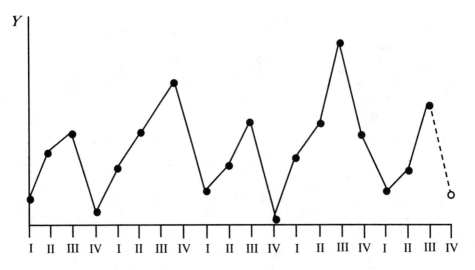

A **cyclical trend** exists when long-term economic fluctuations associated with the business cycle influence the data. Thus, during a period of slow economic growth, housing construction will go down. Most of the economic data tend to be sensitive to the business cycle and fluctuate according to the phase of the cycle. Figure 10.5 reflects the cyclical variability of a series.

Returning to our example of quarterly tourist data, we can plot the data again according to the effects of various elements in a series (see Figure 10.6). Now the patterns are quite clear. The series reflects an overall positive trend over time, although it shows strong seasonal fluctuations along with effects of the economic recession of the early 1990s, the rapid economic expansion of the mid-1990s, and the slowdown toward the end of the decade. Now that we have succeeded in showing definite patterns, our task of forecasting becomes a lot more manageable.

Figure 10.5   Effects of Economic Cycles

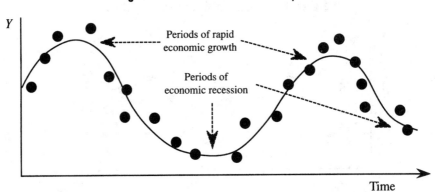

Figure 10.6 Discerning Trend Patterns in the Tourist Data from Masters, Pennsylvania

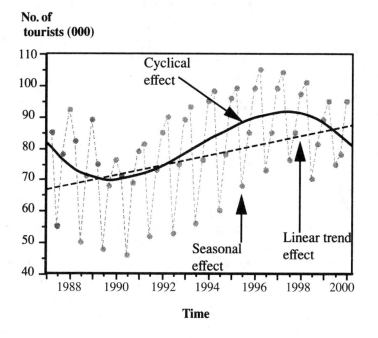

THE PATTERNS OF TIME TREND

Seasonal variations, the effects of a business cycle, and other external factors influence a data series. However, data may include a complex relationship with time that can cause it to change directions in many different ways. Figures 10.7 (a) and 10.7 (b) show patterns of **quadratic trends.** The reverse U-shaped pattern is typical of a situation in which the dependent variable shows a pattern of increase followed by a decline. Data on the percentage of Americans living under the official poverty line demonstrate this kind of quadratic structure during the period 1950 to 1990. The relation between agricultural production and the application of fertilizer is an example of a causal linkage in a quadratic trend. As one increases the use of fertilizers, the level of production tends to go up. However, after the point of saturation, these chemicals reach a toxic level and, consequently, begin to have a deleterious effect on production.

This U-shaped pattern is also typical of a per unit cost curve in a situation of increasing inefficiency as the scale of operation increases. Consider the operation of a county sheriff's department. If the sheriff's department operates on a very small scale, its cost of operation will be extremely high, because it will have to bear a large fixed cost for administration and other necessary operations. However, as the size of its operation increases (maybe because other small, incorporated cities start contracting their police work out to the sheriff's department), its per unit cost of operation (whichever way it is measured) will go down. But this downward trend cannot continue forever, and at a certain stage the increased size of the

Figure 10.7   Quadratic Trends

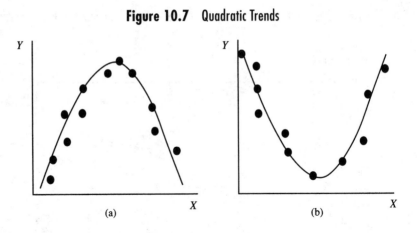

(a)   (b)

department is going to hamper its efficiency. Beyond this point (which in economics is regarded as the point of maximum efficiency), the unit cost of operation will start to increase. Therefore, by measuring the efficiency of an expanding organization over time, one may discern such a quadratic relationship.

A series may also depict an **exponential trend,** as shown in Figures 10.8 (a) and 10.8 (b). For example, viewed over time, population growth exhibits a negative exponential rate with income. That is, birth rates are highest among the underdeveloped nations in the world. However, this rate drops and then reaches a plateau when nations attain high levels of economic prosperity. This pattern is shown in Figure 10.8 (a). In contrast, data on life expectancy show a positive exponential pattern similar to Figure 10.8 (b). Advancements in medical technology have increased people's life expectancies at a fairly rapid rate. But as we approach a biological limit on how long we can survive, the rate of growth slows down considerably.

A series can also depict a rather complex pattern of growth. For example, a series can have a **logistic trend,** or an S-shaped trend, such as the one shown in Figure 10.9. This trend shows a changing pattern of growth. The rate of growth is

Figure 10.8   Exponential Trends

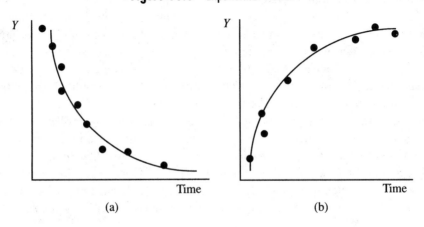

(a)   (b)

Figure 10.9   Logistic Trend

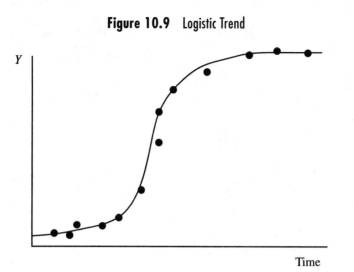

slow at the beginning of the series but changes during a transition period, at which time the rate of growth becomes quite rapid. After a certain point this rate slows as the series reaches a steady state or an upper asymptote (a ceiling). This behavior is considered typical of a learning situation. When we try to learn something new (say, a foreign language), at the beginning our progress is painfully slow. After we have mastered the basics, our ability to absorb material accelerates, only to reach a point of saturation when we attain the upper limits of learning.

A series is said to have demonstrated a **catastrophic trend** when there is a sharp discontinuity (see Figure 10.10). This kind of a precipitous rise or fall occurs as a result of a war or some other kind of national calamity. If one examines the growth of per capita GDP of the former Soviet Republics, the catastrophic impact of the dismemberment of the Soviet Union is apparent as their GDP plunges. The technique of catastrophic **trend analysis** is still in its infancy and, therefore, is not commonly used in social science research or public policy analysis.

ADJUSTMENT METHODS

Looking again at Figure 10.1, we would probably agree that the true nature of a trend can be lost in the seasonal fluctuations of a series. In such cases, you may want to examine the data by filtering out the effects of these fluctuations. Suppose you want to know if the unemployment rate went up in December. The unemployment data will show the natural effects of a seasonal fluctuation because many types of outdoor work, from construction to agriculture, either stop or slow down during the winter months. So in order to get a proper perspective you will have to seasonally adjust monthly or quarterly unemployment figures. You may have noticed that the statement "seasonally adjusted" always qualifies quotations of unemployment statistics. Similarly, the presence of a strong trend can muddle the pure effects of seasonal fluctuations. That is, a rapidly growing economy can

Figure 10.10   Catastrophic Trend

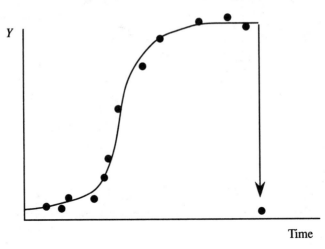

blunt the seasonal fluctuations in employment statistics. Unless this trend factor is eliminated, the effects of the seasons on the data may not be apparent. Perhaps the simplest way of eliminating the effects of seasonal fluctuations and trends is the method of seasonal and trend adjustment.

Let us return to Masters, our Pennsylvania resort town known for its winter and summer recreational facilities. The city's chamber of commerce is trying to understand the nature of tourist demand for its facilities. Consider the records of quarterly figures of tourist populations for the last three years (Table 10.1).

The data presented in Table 10.1 do not reveal a great deal of information regarding the nature of the town's tourist industry. Neither does their plot, shown in Figure 10.11. Indeed, we would be hard pressed to draw too many conclusions from the information we have at hand.

Seasonal Adjustment

The method of seasonal adjustment can lend a helping hand. The reason for this apparent confusion regarding the data is that two factors are at play: the seasonal effect and the trend effect. The presence of these two factors is obfuscating the picture presented by the raw data. Let us begin by suppressing the effects of seasonal variations to accentuate the effects of the trend. If you look at the data carefully,

Table 10.1   Tourist Population (in thousands)

Quarter	1998	1999	2000
I	45	46	49
II	35	36	38
III	42	44	45
IV	33	38	42

Figure 10.11   Plot of Number of Tourists per Quarter

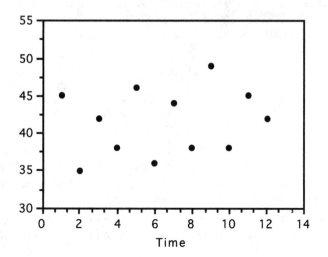

you will see that the first and the third quarters, which cover the peak skiing and summer seasons, tend to bring in more tourists. If there were no seasonal variation whatsoever, the quarterly totals would have been the same. Therefore, we can adjust for this variation by forcing each season to be the same (see Table 10.2).

The quarterly totals in the table were calculated by adding the number of tourists for each of the four quarters during the three-year period. During the first quarter 45,000 tourists visited the town in 1998, 46,000 in 1999, and 49,000 in 2000. Therefore, during the first quarters of these three years, the town had a total of 140,000 visitors. By dividing the quarterly total by three, we calculated the average quarterly figure for the study period. You may notice that during this period there was a total of 493,000 visitors, which calculates to about 41,100 tourists per quarter. This is the average number of tourists that we could expect if there were no seasonal effect. Therefore, we can calculate the **seasonal adjustment factor** by subtracting the grand average from each quarterly average. This is the adjustment factor, which, subtracted from each individual quarter, will give us a seasonally adjusted figure (see Table 10.3).

Table 10.2   The Calculation of Quarterly Adjustment Factors (in thousands)

Quarter	Quarterly totals (1998–2000)	Quarterly average	Quarterly adjustment factor (quarterly averages minus grand average)
I	140	46.7	+5.6
II	109	36.3	−4.8
III	131	43.7	+2.6
IV	113	37.7	−3.4
Total	493	41.1	

Table 10.3   Seasonally Adjusted Quarterly Tourist Population (in thousands)

	1998			1999			2000		
Quarter	No.	Adjustment factor	Adjusted no.	No.	Adjustment factor	Adjusted no.	No.	Adjustment factor	Adjusted no.
I	45	−5.6	39.4	46	−5.6	40.4	49	−5.6	43.4
II	35	+4.8	39.8	36	+4.8	40.8	38	+4.8	42.8
III	42	−2.6	39.4	44	−2.6	41.4	45	−2.6	42.4
IV	33	+3.4	36.4	38	+3.4	41.4	42	+3.4	45.4

Armed with this new series of numbers the chamber of commerce can plan more effectively for the future, knowing that at least for the last three years, there has been a definite upward trend in the number of visitors coming to town. By comparing Figure 10.11 with Figure 10.12, you can see how this process of seasonal adjustment has subdued the quarterly variations and has emphasized the trend pattern.

Trend Adjustment

The chamber of commerce may also want to understand the patterns of seasonal fluctuations without the distorting effects of a trend. Trends can be eliminated simply by adjusting the data for yearly variations. Again the logic is the same. If there were no trend pattern, there would be no variation across time. In this situation seasonal factors will be the sole cause of fluctuations. We can calculate the yearly totals for the three years and then subtract each year's total from the yearly average to get the yearly adjustment factors, or the **trend adjustment factors** (see Table 10.4). These yearly adjustment factors show the average change from the

Figure 10.12   Plot of Seasonally Adusted Quarterly Data

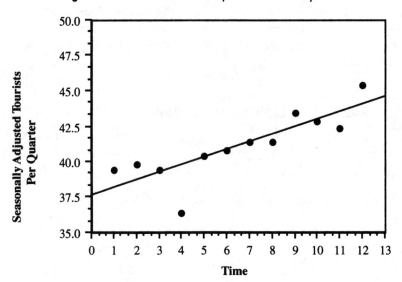

Table 10.4 The Calculation of Yearly Adjustment Factors (in thousands)

Year	Yearly total	Yearly average per quarter	Yearly adjustment factor (yearly average minus grand average)
1998	155	38.8	−2.3
1999	164	41.0	−0.1
2000	174	43.5	+2.4
Total	493	41.1	

mean. By adjusting the data for each quarter by this factor, we will be able to suppress the influence of the trend.

Now, by adjusting the yearly data, we can eliminate the effects of the trend factor and accentuate seasonal variations. This adjustment process can be seen in Table 10.5.

In Figure 10.13 the emphasis is on seasonal changes and the trend factor has been filtered out. This diagram will help the policy makers in Masters visualize the seasonality of the tourist trend and plan for the future. Although the methods of seasonal and trend adjustment are not methods of forecasting per se, they can shed a good deal of light on the behavior of a seemingly chaotic data series. As you can see in Figure 10.13, the trend-adjusted data show that the number of tourists visiting Masters in the first two quarters of the three years remained stable, but that the numbers went up steadily for the fourth quarter. This insight into the data can be a powerful planning and analysis tool for developing appropriate public policies to bring more tourists to the area during the off-season. Based on this analysis, the city may hire a public relations firm to publicize the city's attractiveness to potential visitors for the first half of the year.

SMOOTHING OUT THE FLUCTUATIONS

In the previous section, we discussed ways to smooth out seasonal fluctuations to reveal the underlying trend. However, when we want to consider a time span that is longer (say, a year or six months) or shorter (a week or a month, for example) than a season, or when fluctuations are more random than seasonal effects, we

Table 10.5 Trend Adjusted Quarterly Tourist Population (in thousands)

Quarter	1998			1999			2000		
	No.	Adjustment factor	Adjusted no.	No.	Adjustment factor	Adjusted no.	No.	Adjustment factor	Adjusted no.
I	45	+2.3	47.3	46	+0.1	46.1	49	−2.4	46.6
II	35	+2.3	37.3	36	+0.1	36.1	38	−2.4	35.6
III	42	+2.3	44.3	44	+0.1	44.1	45	−2.4	42.6
IV	33	+2.3	35.3	38	+0.1	38.1	42	−2.4	39.6

Figure 10.13   Plot of Trend-Adjusted Tourist Data

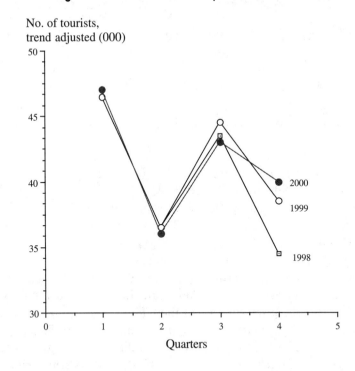

seek the help of a different method of smoothing. In these cases we use such techniques as **naive projection** or **moving average.**[2]

Let us return to the quarterly time series data on tourists visiting Masters during the thirteen-year period from 1988 to 2000 (see Table 10.6). I plotted this data series in Figure 10.1. As noted earlier in the chapter, the trend line is hidden behind fluctuations caused by seasonal variations and cyclical fluctuation. By examining this figure you can now clearly see a positive trend, the fluctuations caused by the four seasons, as well as the impact of a strong business cycle. Now we want to use this data series to forecast values for the next quarter. If we do not want to be restricted to the four quarterly figures, we will have to use one of the following methods of projection.

Projecting the Immediate Past: Naive Projection

If I were to ask you to predict your earnings for the coming year, your prediction would probably be based on what you earned this year. Prediction based on the last period's performance is often called the naive method of projection. In Table 10.6, the quarterly data is listed in the first column. In statistics this process is called **lagging.** If we lag a column by one period, we express it in terms of what happened in the immediately preceding period. Similarly, a three-period lag would present the series in terms of what happened three periods ago. When we write in algebraic symbols, we express periods in subscripts. For example, X_t

Table 10.6 Quarterly Series on Number of Tourists Visiting Masters, Pennsylvania

Year	Quarterly data	Lag (1 year)	Moving average (2 years)	Moving average (4 years)
1988.1	85	—	—	—
1988.2	55	85	—	—
1988.3	78	55	70.0	—
1988.4	92	78	66.5	—
1989.1	82	92	85.0	77.50
1989.2	50	82	87.0	76.75
1989.3	71	50	66.0	75.50
1989.4	89	71	60.5	73.75
1990.1	75	89	80.0	73.00
1990.2	48	75	82.0	71.25
1990.3	68	48	61.5	70.75
1990.4	76	68	58.0	70.00
1991.1	71	76	72.0	66.75
1991.2	46	71	73.5	65.75
1991.3	69	46	58.5	65.25
1991.4	79	69	57.5	65.50
1992.1	81	79	74.0	66.25
1992.2	52	81	80.0	68.75
1992.3	73	52	66.5	70.25
1992.4	85	73	62.5	71.25
1993.1	90	85	79.0	72.75
1993.2	53	90	87.5	75.00
1993.3	75	53	71.5	75.25
1993.4	89	75	64.0	75.75
1994.1	93	89	82.0	76.75
1994.2	56	93	91.0	77.50
1994.3	76	56	74.5	78.25
1994.4	95	76	66.0	78.50
1995.1	98	95	85.5	80.00
1995.2	60	98	96.5	81.25
1995.3	78	60	79.0	82.25
1995.4	96	78	69.0	82.75
1996.1	99	96	87.0	83.00
1996.2	68	99	97.5	83.25
1996.3	85	68	83.5	85.25
1996.4	99	85	76.5	87.00
1997.1	105	99	92.0	87.75
1997.2	73	105	102.0	89.25
1997.3	85	73	89.0	90.50
1997.4	99	85	79.0	90.50
1998.1	104	99	92.0	90.50
1998.2	76	104	101.5	90.25
1998.3	85	76	90.0	91.00
1998.4	97	85	80.5	91.00
1999.1	101	97	91.0	90.50
1999.2	70	101	99.0	89.75
1999.3	81	70	85.5	88.25
1999.4	89	81	75.5	87.25
2000.1	95	89	85.0	85.25
2000.2	75	95	92.0	83.75
2000.3	78	75	85.0	85.00
2000.4	95	78	76.5	84.25
2001.1 (forecast)	—	95	86.5	85.75

would mean the value of the variable X in period t, which in this case is the current year. Similarly, X_{t-1} would mean last period's value (or value lagged by one period), and X_{t-10} would be value lagged by ten periods.

Because an organization's decisions are almost always made on the basis of incremental reasoning (an argument like, "Last year, this program cost \$150,000; therefore, this year we expect it to cost ------"), forecasting on the basis of what happened last period is probably the most frequently used method. This method produces a reasonably good forecast if there is little trend, positive or negative, and there are few fluctuations. If you have steady salaried employment, your current year's earnings would serve as a good proxy for the next year's prediction. If your income tends to fluctuate, however, this method will not give you a very good forecast. For example, because seasonality causes ample variations, the lagged data presented in Table 10.6 act as a poor predictor for the following quarter.

Projecting by the Mean

Another method of projection is calculating the mean. For instance, consider a series:

$$X_1\ X_2\ X_3\ X_4\ \ldots\ldots\ X_{t-1}\ X_t$$

In this case we can make a prediction for the following period, X_{t+1}, simply by taking the mean of the series—that is, by calculating

$$\overline{X} = \frac{X_1 + X_2 + \ldots\ldots + X_{t-1} + X_t}{T} = \hat{X}_{t+1} \tag{10.1}$$

where t is the total number of observations and $\hat{X}_{t+1}$ = the projected value for the period $t+1$.

Therefore, the forecast of X_{t+1} is given by the mean of the series:

$$\hat{X}_{t+2} = \frac{X_1 + X_2 + \ldots\ldots + X_t + X_{t+1}}{T+1}$$

You might wonder when this simple method is appropriate for forecasting a series. This method is useful only if you have a stationary series with no observable trend (see Figure 10.3). In such cases, the mean of the series would give you the best possible forecast for future behavior. While predicting fluctuations in rainfall you may do best by taking the yearly average. The same may be true for predicting price movements for a specific period in the stock market.

Moving Average

When there is a clear trend, the variations within a series can be ironed out by what is known as the method of moving average. A moving average is calculated by averaging two or more consecutive values in the series and accepting the computed value to be the forecast for the next period, as shown in Table 10.6. By this method, we would predict for X_{t+1} as follows:

$$\hat{X}_{t+1} = \frac{X_t + X_{t-1}}{2} \tag{10.2}$$

Lagging the data by one period is called the moving average of order 1, or first-order moving average. As you can see in Table 10.6, while calculating the moving average of order 2, we lost information on the first two observations because these were used to calculate the forecast for the third period. We can increase the order by taking the average of a larger number of lagged data. If we want to calculate a fourth-order moving average, X_{t+1} will be computed as:

$$\hat{X}_{t+1} = \frac{X_t + X_{t-1} + X_{t-2} + X_{t-3}}{4} \tag{10.3}$$

If you have quarterly data that reflect a strong seasonal effect, a four-period moving average would essentially iron out the seasonal fluctuations. This has been shown in Figure 10.14. As the order of moving average increases, the top of the series loses more information, and the series shows a greater degree of smoothing out.

The moving average method requires you to decide on the number of periods to use to smooth the series. You can see from Figure 10.14 that if you want your newly created series to look like the original data, you should choose a smaller lag period. Hence, if a series has a clear trend with a relatively small degree of fluctuation, use a short (perhaps a two-period) lag. However, if the series contains a large

Figure 10.14   Adjusted and Unadjusted Data on Tourists Visiting Masters, Pennsylvania

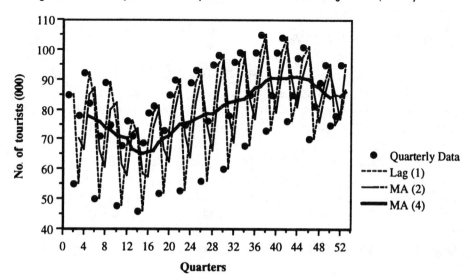

degree of seemingly random or seasonal variations, use a larger lag period. Although the choice is highly subjective and dependent on the needs of your client, for the series under discussion, given the high degree of seasonal variation, I would choose a longer lag, perhaps a four-period one.

When you do a trend analysis, it is imperative that you proceed in a systematic way. Here is a quick list of steps you can follow when conducting your analysis.

1. Specify the objective of your study.
2. Plot the data.
3. Look for a trend pattern.
4. If the series is monthly or quarterly, look for seasonal variability.
5. For a long yearly series, look for cyclical effects.
6. Correct for seasonality or trend, depending on the purpose of the study.
7. If there is no trend, use the mean for forecasting.

Choice of Projection Technique

In this chapter we have discussed several different projection techniques. As you can see, each method has its pros and cons. Note that you may receive a different forecasted value based on the technique you choose to use. Although there is no definitive roadmap for selecting the "best" method, I suggest following these steps:

1. Define the objective of projection.
2. Plot the data.
3. If there is a great deal of seasonal variability, for comparison purposes, do seasonal and trend adjustments.
4. If there is no trend, use the mean of the series.
5. If there are seasonal fluctuations, use the moving average. Remember, the higher the order of the moving average, the greater the smoothing effect.

THE POLITICS OF FORECASTING

If forecasting on its own merits is a tricky business, forecasting for public policy can be even more problematic. Because a forecast may involve the livelihoods of many individuals and has the potential to cause huge monetary damages, a forecast should be of great concern. Take, for example, the case of Mammoth, a mountain resort town in the picturesque Eastern Sierra region in California. Similar to many other places in the state, this region is susceptible to earthquakes. To complicate the matter, Mammoth Mountain is a dormant volcano. In 1998 the Hollywood movie *Dante's Peak*, set in a mythical resort town meant to mimic Mammoth, showed the plight of the town when the volcano suddenly erupted. This sensational movie, along with some dire predictions from volcanologists, caused the ski town a great deal of anxiety as real estate prices threatened to fall faster

A CASE IN POINT

Fighting Over a Fiction? The Budget Surplus in the Presidential Debate

During the fierce 2000 presidential campaign one issue dominated the national debate: how to spend the $4.6 trillion national surplus projected over the next ten years.[1] Based on this rosy prediction George W. Bush wanted to give a third of the surplus back to the taxpayers and use the rest to pay down the national debt and spend on education and national defense. Al Gore wanted to pay down the public debt and spend on numerous other social and military programs. Gore promised to eliminate the federal debt by 2012; Bush claimed he would do the same by 2016.

While these candidates exchanged barbs and insults and promised the most judicious spending plan, some experts quietly questioned the veracity of the forecasts. Because the budget surplus was based on the performance of a hot economy in 1999, experts feared that if the economy did not keep up with exceptional years of growth, the projected surplus would quickly melt away. In fact, if the economy produced a lower surplus, or no surplus at all, any ambitious spending plan would take the economy back to the days of deficit spending and the consequent burgeoning public debt.

To make the situation worse, the Congressional Budget Office warned that after the next ten years the government would face a funding crunch from Social Security, Medicare, and Medicaid that could "drive federal debt to unsustainable levels." As the aging baby boomers demand increasingly more health care and other social service dollars, around the year 2020 the federal budget may be overwhelmed by these limitless demands.

And it could get worse. The projected surplus is divided in two parts: $2.4 trillion in the Social Security program and $2.2 trillion in the rest of the budget. The analysts are comfortable with the projection for Social Security because it is based on relatively stable demographic data. However, it is the surplus in the rest of the federal budget that worries independent observers. Based on a different set of assumptions, the Center on Budget and Policy Priorities, a liberal group, estimated that the ten-year surplus outside Social Security would come closer to $700 billion. The Brookings Institution, a more centrist think tank, estimated that the figure might be as low as $352 billion. If these lower projections come true, the budget surplus would not be much of an issue to fight over.

Note

1. Ken Moritsugu and Jackie Koszczuk, "Surplus Could Be a Figment of Faulty Estimates," *San Diego Union Tribune,* October 7, 2000, A-2.

Discussion Points

1. Why do experts differ on forecasts?
2. What are the political pitfalls of public policy forecasting?
3. Can you ensure an "unbiased" forecast when it comes to public policy?

than skiers did on its slope. David Hill, chief scientist with the U.S. Geological Survey and a longtime observer of the region, calmed frayed nerves with his prediction that the odds of a sudden volcanic eruption were grossly overstated.[3]

Although forecasts are supposed to be an accurate description of the future, the power they hold in the area of public policy can often make them tools of special interest groups. The current debate on forecasts relating to global warming provides an example of the issues involved. If the cause of global warming could be pinned to the emission of hydrocarbon and other man-made gases, public policies would severely crack down on these polluting agents. Since such agents, in the form of large corporations, are concentrated in the industrial West, such a forecast can be highly significant for its economy.

Forecasts can also be used by scientists and environmentalists for the purpose of raising awareness. In the late 1950s a group of environmentalists became engaged in studying the entire world as one single socioeconomic and environmental system.[4] Their work alerted a generation of young scientists and environmental activists about the dangers of relying on dwindling natural resources. Despite the fact that the claims of a catastrophe were clearly overblown (and were realized as such at the time of their study), their research was instrumental in educating people about the risks of unrestrained growth. (For a report on how forecasting has affected the debate over the budget surplus, see "A Case in Point: Fighting Over a Fiction? The Budget Surplus in the Presidential Debate.")

Key Words

Catastrophic trend (p. 231)
Cyclical trend (p. 228)
Exponential trend (p.230)
Horizontal trend (p. 227)
Lagging (p. 236)
Linear trend (p. 226)
Logistic trend (p. 230)
Moving average (p. 236)
Naive projection (p. 236)
Negative trend (p. 226)

Positive trend (p. 226)
Projecting by the mean (p. 238)
Quadratic trends (p. 229)
Random errors (p. 226)
Seasonal adjustment factor (p. 233)
Seasonal trend (p. 227)
Stationary series (p. 227)
Trend adjustment factors (p. 234)
Trend analysis (p. 231)

Exercises

1. Write an essay on trend analysis when the past behavior is known. Give examples from real life for the various kinds of trend patterns discussed in this chapter.
2. A typical time series contains wide-ranging fluctuations. Explain, with examples, various sources of fluctuations in a data series. How can you adjust for such fluctuations?
3. In 1987 several states increased the speed limit on their highways in sparsely populated areas. A county analyst is trying to see if the change caused a discernible change in the accident fatality rate. She has compiled a table of quarterly fatality data.

Table 10.A

Quarter	1985	1986	1987	1988
I	85	76	88	92
II	43	42	52	48
III	51	57	71	78
IV	98	97	110	121

What conclusions can you draw for policy prescription?

4. You are in charge of investing your agency's liquid cash. You are considering investing in a particular security portfolio that has yielded the monthly returns shown below. How would you predict its behavior for the next three months?

Month	Yield
1	7.0
2	3.7
3	1.8
4	0.5
5	9.5
6	0.1
7	2.3
8	6.3
9	3.2
10	0.9
11	4.1
12	9.3
13	7.3
14	7.8
15	6.6

5. The list below shows the number of auto thefts in the city of Masters for the last fifteen years. Use the moving average technique to discern the overall trend and predict the number of auto thefts for the coming year. In this context, explain your choice of lag period.

Year	Auto thefts
1	98
2	87
3	110
4	112
5	108
6	121
7	132
8	125
9	127
10	130
11	145
12	153
13	148
14	151
15	149

6. Collect a series of data on any event of national, state, or local importance. Write a report on its trend pattern and predict its value for the next period.

Notes

1. Also, in reality, a series can assume a much more complex trend pattern. For a more detailed discussion, see Spyros Makridakis, Steven Wheelwright, and Victor McGee, *Forecasting: Methods and Application* (New York: Wiley, 1983).
2. To look at the use of moving average in discerning the underlying trend (and to help you forecast the future trend), log on to the Web page of any Wall Street brokerage firm (for example, Charles Schwab at http://www.schwab.com/). By choosing the box for a particular company (say, IBM), you can readily see the use of moving average as an aid to mental forecasting of stock prices.
3. See Robert Lee Holtz, "Southland's Quake Danger Forecast Is Cut," *Los Angeles Times*, March 18, 1998.
4. See Donella Meadows, Dennis L. Meadows, Jorgen Randers, and William W. Behrens III, *The Limits to Growth* (New York: Signet Books, 1960).

11

PROJECTION TECHNIQUES: THE METHODS OF SIMPLE AND MULTIPLE LEAST SQUARES

Forecasting is integral to the process of planning. In the previous chapter we discussed the problem of projecting a trend when a long history is unavailable. However, in the current information age, we frequently encounter a long series of past information. When such information is available, forecasting becomes much more systematic, or "scientific" if you will, than forecasting on the basis of a single rate of growth or on subjective judgment.

We do not have to look far to find examples of forecasting in the public sector. State and federal governments routinely forecast revenues from various sources for the preparation of budgets. Local governments, unless they are extremely large, depend primarily on state governments to provide them with such information and do not generally get involved in projecting tax revenues. However, local government agencies frequently engage in forecasting needs for their services. The financial management department may seek permission to raise money from a bond issue for enlarging the children's recreation facilities. This may call for a forecast of the number of children in the community for the next five years. In addition to government agencies, branches of the federal reserve banks, research institutes, information consultants, and many other groups get involved in the business of forecasting the future.

We discussed the difference between a trend projection and causal analysis in chapter 9. In this chapter, we will examine one of the most commonly used techniques of trend projection based on a series of data over time (called a time series): the **method of least squares,** or regression models.[1] In a straight or linear trend, we use time as a single independent variable. If you plot the per capita GDP of the United States, you will see that the series shows a fairly steady linear trend pattern. I have plotted the data in Figure 11.1. In cases in which there is a linear trend, we use a **simple regression** model, which has only one independent variable (in our example, time). However, at times the series may exhibit a complex nonlinear trend pattern. In such cases, you may have to use a nonlinear model with more than one independent variable. These are called **multiple regression** models. The focus of this chapter is on the effects of time. Hence, we will discuss multiple regression within the context of a more complex time pattern in the second half of the chapter. The discussion of multiple regression will continue in chapter 12 as a part of building causal models.

THE LOGIC OF LEAST SQUARES METHOD

The task of forecasting becomes considerably easier when we have long time-series data that allow us to see if there is a definite trend. When the trend is readily apparent, we can build a model that will help us forecast the future. For example, we can hypothesize from Figure 11.1 that GDP per capita is growing in a linear trend pattern over time. In other words, the elapsed time since the beginning of the study period determines the level of per capita income. The straight line drawn through the yearly data approximates the trend line. By our model we hypothesize that the per capita GDP of the country will continue to grow along this line and, by extending it into the future, we can forecast the future levels of per capita GDP.

Figure 11.1 U.S. Gross Domestic Product Per Capita (in 1972 constant dollars)

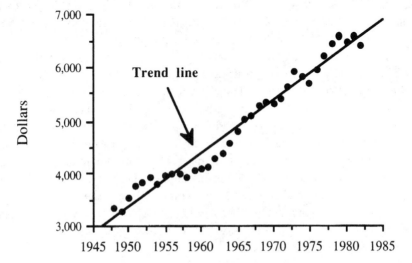

In building a model for the projection of trend, we hypothesize that the fundamental direction in a data series can be explained by the functional relationship proposed by the model. I can best explain the basic idea of a regression model with the help of Figure 11.2. The model in this figure shows the dependent variable (in this case, per capita income) as an input being transformed by the internal logic (or the functional relationship) of the system. An input stimulus (a change in the independent variable—in this case, the passage of time) produces the output (the new level of per capita GDP). At this point, it is extremely important to remember that when we are including "time" as the independent variable, we are, in fact, claiming to be agnostic regarding the true causal relationship that is propelling the direction of the dependent variable. Thus, multiple factors could affect the growth of the per capita GDP of a nation, including world business cycles, the invention of new technologies, and new areas of trade and commerce (for example, in the case of the United States, trade with a more open China and the former communist nations). War, revolution, or cataclysmic natural disasters, such as earthquakes and hurricanes, are also likely to affect the growth of national domestic products. The basic assumption of a time-series model is that the simple passage of time embodies within it all these complex events, resulting in a steady discernible pattern, which we call a trend.

Despite our hypothesis regarding a simple linear trend, as you can clearly see in Figure 11.1, not all the actual observations fall on the trend line. If they did, we would have a perfect relationship, offering a perfect forecast of the future values. However, one rarely sees a perfect relationship in the realm of social sciences. When some of the data points do not fall on this line, we claim that the disparity between our forecast and the actual observation is caused by **random errors.** These random events are defined as the effects of those independent variables that we did not include in our model.

Therefore, we assume that the observed system contains two components: the explained and the unexplained. That is,

$$\text{Data} = \text{trend} + \text{error.}$$

The primary purpose of trend analysis is to uncover the pattern that allows us to project it into the future. In this endeavor, we look for the "best line" that approximates

Figure 11.2 Time-Series Model

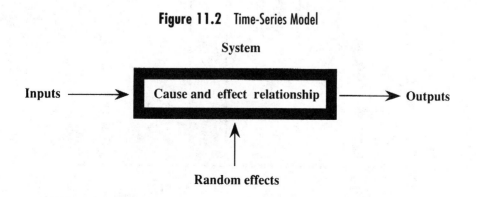

the trend in a data series. In Figure 11.3, for example, we are measuring the values of the dependent variable Y on the vertical axis, while the horizontal axis measures the independent variable X. The plotted observations show a linear trend pattern. By extending the trend (shown by the dashed line), we can project the future value of Y based on X. Then the question becomes how to derive the trend line. It should be obvious that to obtain the line that best explains the trend, we must find the one that *lies closest to the observations,* or leaves us with the least amount of unexplained error. Errors are the differences between the projected trend line and the observed datapoints.

Suppose we have five observations on the dependent variable, Y, the trend of which we are trying to estimate by deriving a line as close as possible to the data points. Suppose we have obtained the trend line for the data series. The points on the trend line are the estimated values. For the first observation Y_1, we estimate it to be $\hat{Y}_1$ (called "Y hat one"). Since our estimate falls short of the actual value, the difference between the actual and the estimated value is the random error, or the error of estimation, which we call ϵ_1.

It is obvious that drawing the line of estimation by hand (as in Figure 11.3) will not do because we can never be sure that it is, in fact, the closest line to the data. However, we can understand intuitively that the best possible line to fit a data set will have to be the least distance from the mean of the series. Consider the following datapoints:

$$X = 1, 2, 3, 4, 5$$
$$Y = 4, 6, 7, 9, 10$$

Figure 11.3 Errors of Estimation

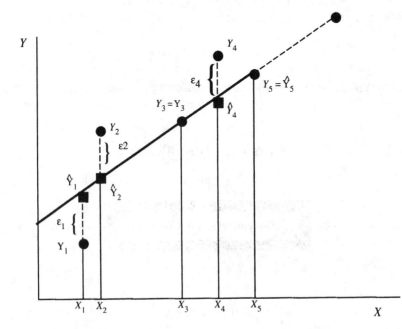

If you plot these points on graph paper, you can see that any line that does not go through the point (3, 7.2)—3 being the average of the X variables and 7.2 being the average of the Y variables—cannot be considered closest to the data points.

However, our problem does not go away when we draw a line through the mean values of the two series. Since the deviation from the mean is always the least, the sum total of deviation from the mean is always equal to 0. Therefore, in some cases this rule will not allow us to identify the "best" line. This problem can be shown with the help of Figure 11.4. Suppose I have only two observations and I want to draw the line to lie closest to these two points of observation. Clearly, as shown in Figure 11.4 (a), the line drawn through the two points will be the best line because for each observation the error terms are equal to 0. However, suppose I draw this line in the opposite direction, as shown in Figure 11.4 (b). Let us assume that the distances from the trend line to the observed points are +3 and –3, respectively. The problem with simply summing the errors is that the positive errors cancel out the negatives. If we want to choose the best line on the basis of the least amount of errors, we are at a loss to choose between these two lines, because the sum of errors for both of them is equal to 0. How do we choose between them?

In chapter 7 we discussed the problem of deviations from the mean being equal to 0. Recalling our discussion, we can see that this problem can be avoided if we *square the deviations* from the line. By following this method, the line in Figure 11.4 (a) still gives us an error value of 0, whereas the sum of the squared deviations for the second line is $(+3)^2 + (-3)^2 = 18$. Clearly, now we can choose the first line over the second.

Therefore, we can lay down our criterion for choosing the best line as *the one that gives us the least amount of squared deviation from the observed points.* This is the notion behind the method of least squares.[2] The equation derived through the method of least squares is called the **regression equation.**

Figure 11.4   The Problems of Summing the Errors

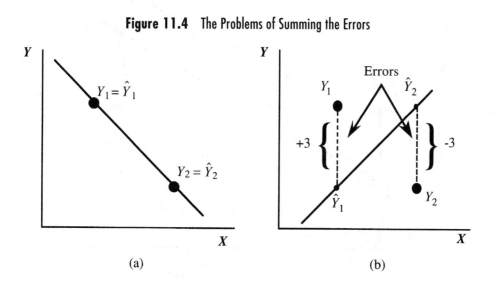

(a)   (b)

LINEAR TIME TREND: SIMPLE REGRESSION MODEL

The regression model for a straight line is given by the following equation:

$$Y = \alpha + \beta X + \epsilon \qquad (11.1)$$

where Y is the **dependent variable** (the one to be explained), α is the **intercept,** β is the **coefficient for trend** (or slope), X is the **independent variable** (the one that explains the dependent variable), and ϵ is the error of estimation (or the residual difference between actual Y and estimated Y).

Figure 11.5 is an explanation of the meaning of a straight-line equation. The intercept term (α) measures the point at which the trend line meets the vertical axis. Quite often, the intercept term has interesting interpretations. For example, in fitting a Keynesian aggregate consumption function (the relation between consumption and income), the intercept term measures the level of consumption one must have even when income is zero. This is the subsistence level of consumption, which presumably must be met either through government transfer (welfare payment) or private charity.

The trend coefficient β measures the magnitude that a one-unit change in the independent variable causes in the dependent variable. Thus a higher value of β' would signify a steeper line—implying that a small change in the independent variable will cause a great deal of change in the dependent variable. The reverse will be true for a smaller trend coefficient (β'').[3] A positive trend coefficient implies an upward slope; a negative coefficient, a downward slope; and a 0 coefficient implies the absence of any relationship between the dependent and independent variable.

Figure 11.5 Explanation of a Straight-Line Equation

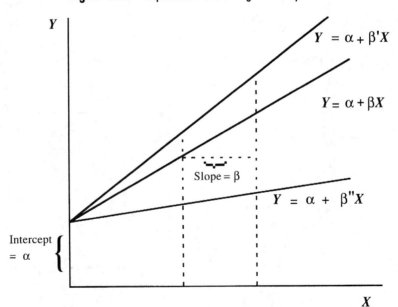

An estimated equation for a straight line contains three components: the coefficient (also known as the constant or parameter) for the intercept, the coefficient for the slope, and the error term:

$$\hat{Y}_i = a + b\hat{X}_i \tag{11.1a}$$

where $\hat{Y}_i$ is the estimated value of Y_i, a is the estimated intercept coefficient, and b is the estimated slope coefficient.

It is important to note the difference between the "true" coefficients and their estimated values. The true values are conceptual in nature and, as such, cannot be known. The best we can hope for is to obtain their closest estimated approximation. To help in the understanding of this important difference, I have denoted the true values with Greek letters and their estimated values with Roman letters.

The **error term** is the difference (the residual) between the *actual* and the *estimated* values of Y: $e_i = Y_i - \hat{Y}_i$. By replacing $\hat{Y}_i$ with $a + bX$ (from equation 11.1a), we get:

$$e_i = Y_i - a - bX_i \tag{11.2}$$

As I have explained earlier, by the method of least squares we estimate the coefficients of a and b such that we minimize this sum of errors:[4]

$$\text{Minimize} \sum_{i=1}^{n} (e_i)^2 = \sum_{i=1}^{n} (Y_i - a - bX_i)^2 \tag{11.3}$$

From the preceding expression (11.3) we can devise the following formula for the estimated coefficient of b:

$$b = \frac{\sum \left(Y_i - \overline{Y} \right)\left(X_i - \overline{X} \right)}{\sum \left(X_i - \overline{X} \right)^2} \tag{11.4}$$

where $\overline{Y}$ and $\overline{X}$ are the means for Y_i and X_i variables.

The intercept term is estimated by:

$$a = \overline{Y} - b\overline{X} \tag{11.5}$$

Let us consider the following example. Suppose for the purpose of long-term planning that we would like to estimate the future population of a small town. The population figures for the past five years are shown in Table 11.1. By plotting this series (see Figure 11.6) we can detect the existence of a steady linear trend. We then decide to forecast the future population size by using a linear equation form, shown in equation 11.1.

To estimate the coefficients a and b, for a straight-line equation, we need to work out Table 11.2.

Table 11.1   Population Over Time

Population (000)	Year
5	1
8	2
10	3
15	4
17	5

Recalling the formula for calculating b:

$$b = \frac{\sum \left(Y_i - \overline{Y} \right)\left(X_i - \overline{X} \right)}{\sum \left(X_i - \overline{X} \right)^2}$$

we can calculate the value of b by inserting the numbers from Table 11.2. Thus, we estimate

$$b = \frac{31.00}{10.00} = 3.1.$$

Similarly, we can calculate the intercept term a as:

$$a = \overline{Y} - (b\overline{X}) = 11 - (3.1 \times 3) = 1.7$$

Therefore, we can write the estimated equation as:

$$\text{Population } (\hat{Y}) = 1.7 + 3.1 \text{ Year } (X). \tag{11.6}$$

The plot of the actual data and the trend line are shown in Figure 11.6.

We have plotted the estimated and actual values of population in Figure 11.6. From this derived equation we can project the future population of the city. For example, we can estimate the population for the sixth year (6) by:

$$1.7 + 3.1 \times 6 = 20.3.$$

Table 11.2   Calculations for a Straight-Line Regression Equation

Population (Y_i)	Year				
	(X_i)	$(Y_i - \overline{Y})$	$(X_i - \overline{X})$	$(X_i - \overline{X})^2$	$(Y_i - \overline{Y})(X_i - \overline{X})$
5	1	−6	−2	4	12
8	2	−3	−1	1	3
10	3	−1	0	0	0
15	4	4	1	1	4
17	5	6	2	4	12
Total		0	0	10	31

Note: $\overline{Y} = 11.0$ and $\overline{X} = 3.0$.

Figure 11.6   Population Trend

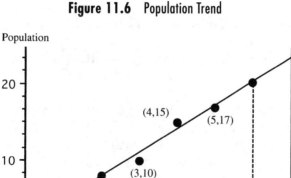

Similarly, to obtain the projected figure for the seventh year, we must substitute 7 as the value for the independent variable (*X*). This arithmetic calculation yields 23.4, the projected population figure for the seventh year.

Accuracy of the Results

Having estimated the trend line, you can legitimately ask, "How good are my results?" This question has two interrelated parts: First, you may ask whether your model is offering a significant explanation of the variations within the series. Second, you would want to explore how confident you feel about your estimation of the coefficients. That is, are the estimated values reflective of the "true" relationship between the dependent and independent variables, or did you obtain a correlation by chance—a spurious correlation?

Please recall Figure 11.3. While estimating the relationship between the dependent and independent variables, we can see that we can explain part of the series through estimation, whereas the remainder (the difference between the observed and the estimated values) is unexplained. A perfect explanation explains all the variations within a series. In contrast, in the absence of any relation between the two variables, none of the variations will be explained. Hence, the measure of goodness of fit is the proportion of explained variance within the total variance. Again, since we want to get rid of the problem of having to add positive deviations with negative deviations, we square the deviations and then sum the results.[5] This ratio is called the **coefficient of determination,** or R^2, and is written as:

$$R^2 = \frac{Squared\ sum\ of\ explained\ variations\,(ESS)}{Squared\ sum\ of\ total\ variations\,(TSS)} = \frac{\sum\left(\hat{Y}_i - \overline{Y}\right)^2}{\sum\left(Y_i - \overline{Y}\right)^2} \qquad (11.7)$$

where

Y_i represents the actual values for Y observations,

$\bar{Y}$ is the mean of Y, and

$\hat{Y}_i$ represents the predicted values of Y_i on the basis of the regression line (calculated by using the estimated equation, $Y = a + bX_i$)

You may note that when all the Y_i values are correctly predicted, then the predicted values are the same as the actual values. In that case, $\hat{Y}_i$ is equal to Y_i, which means that the numerator is equal to the denominator, or the value of R^2 is equal to 1. This is a perfect explanation. When a model cannot explain any variation (or when the variations are completely random), however, the values of $\hat{Y}_i$ form a horizontal line (such as the one shown in the previous chapter in Figure 10.3) that goes through the average value of the distribution. In such a case, $\hat{Y}_i$ is equal to $\bar{Y}$, which makes the numerator equal to 0 and consequently, $R^2 = 0$. Therefore, the value of R^2 will always fall within the limit 0 (no explanation) and 1 (perfect explanation):

Let us calculate the R^2 for our example from Table 11.3.

We can calculate R^2 by using equation 11.7:

$$R^2 = \frac{96.1}{98.0} = 0.981$$

In other words, our model is predicting slightly over 98 percent of the variations.

High R^2

There is no universally acceptable answer to the question of what a high R^2 is. Generally speaking, if you are dealing with *economic time-series data,* you are likely to find a high degree of correlation because most of the economic variables tend to move in the same direction. In times of prosperity all the good indicators tend to go up (for example, savings, investment, employment, housing construction). The reverse takes place during economic recession. In an interesting study Ames and Reiter showed that even when unrelated time series data were chosen at random and regressed

Table 11.3 Calculation of R^2

Population (Y_i)	Year (X_i)	Projected values ($\hat{Y}_i$)[a]	$(Y_i - \bar{Y})^2$	$(Y_i - \bar{Y})^2$
5	1	4.8	38.44	36.0
8	2	7.9	9.61	9.0
10	3	11.0	0.00	1.0
15	4	14.1	9.61	16.0
17	5	17.2	38.44	36.0
Total			96.10	98.0

[a] Note that the projected values are calculated with the help of the estimated equation 11.6.

against each other, R^2 values exceeded 0.5.[6] The lesson of their study is that since correlation between two variables only measures co-occurrence and does not necessarily establish a causal linkage, a high value of R^2 should not give cause for celebration, unless such a relationship can be backed up by solid theoretical reasoning.

You should also note that for cross-section data the R^2 values are typically smaller than those for the time-series data. Also, because of a greater complexity in their interrelationships, the correlation coefficients are often much smaller for sociological or political data than those for economic or financial data.

Relevance of the Estimated Coefficients

Now that we have determined how much of an explanation of the data the model is providing, we may want to know the following: How relevant are the *individual coefficients,* and how relevant are the coefficients *taken as a whole?* To answer these questions, we need to look back at the development of theoretical statistics. One of the most remarkable theorems of the entire field of mathematics and mathematical statistics was derived nearly two hundred years ago and provides the basis for hypothesis testing. Suppose you know the average (mean) height of the American male population (μ) and the standard deviation (σ). You are conducting a random survey, whereby you are collecting groups of men, noting their average height. At every try, you are getting this small sample group together and are noting their average height, subtracting it from the **population mean** (μ), and dividing by the **population standard deviation** (σ).[7] You continue with this process, which symbolically can be written as

$$\frac{\left(\overline{X_i} - \mu \right)}{\sigma} \tag{11.8}$$

As discussed in chapter 7, if you repeat your experiment, the plotted results will approach a normal distribution. This distribution will have a mean equal to 0 and a standard deviation equal to 1. The remarkable aspect of this theorem is that it does not matter what the distribution of the variable X_i is. Unless there are some systematic biases (like measuring only basketball players to arrive at the average height of the general public), repeating this procedure will give us the normal distribution as the number of samples increases. This theorem is known as the law of large numbers (see chapter 7). By the property of this standardized distribution we know how much of the values will fall within what range, which makes the derivation of a normal distribution particularly fortuitous. For example, we know that approximately 95 percent of all the values will fall within +1.96 standard deviation, and nearly 99 percent of all values fall within ±2.57 standard deviation. Therefore, in our example, suppose we come across a group of Pygmies with an average height that is more than 1.96 standard deviations below the average for men from the United States. Then we can state with a 95 percent level of confidence that the members of this particular sample are not Americans. Let me explain this with the help of Figure 11.7.

Figure 11.7   Curve of Normal Distribution

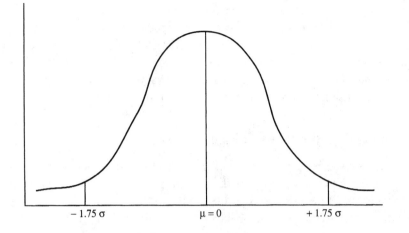

$$-1.75\,\sigma \qquad\qquad \mu=0 \qquad\qquad +1.75\,\sigma$$

You may notice, however, that I have emphasized the term **"random."** One of the most important assumptions of a regression model is that the model includes all the relevant explanatory variables. Therefore, the variation in the observed data that is not explained is caused by random factors, which are distributed normally around the mean of 0. A variable is considered random if its values are determined by the outcome of a "chance experiment." That is, in our example, if we confined our search to a particular ethnic group, or a group of basketball players, then the outcomes are not being determined by chance. Whether the selection is by design or by some unrecognized bias on the part of the researcher, this theorem of the law of large numbers will not apply; the resulting distribution will not approximate a normal distribution regardless of the number of experiments. As a result, none of the results described below will hold true. We will discuss the implications of this bias in detail in chapter 12.

The Significance of Individual Coefficients

As can be seen in Figure 11.7, a group average sufficiently different from the mean may indicate that the two populations are indeed different. Hence, this theorem serves as the basis for testing the validity of hypotheses. For our purposes, we can use this result to test the null hypothesis that our coefficients are results of chance and, in fact, there is no relationship between the dependent and the independent variables. For example, the level of statistical significance for our estimated trend coefficient (b) can be calculated by

$$\frac{b-\beta}{\sigma} \qquad\qquad (11.9)$$

where b is the estimated coefficient, β is the true coefficient, and σ is the true standard deviation of the distribution. Since we are testing the null hypothesis that there is no correlation between the dependent and independent variables, we set β equal to 0. Also, since we do not know what the true standard deviation is for population, we approximate it within the estimated standard error of coefficient, which we may call SE_b. Therefore, the expression 11.9 can be written as

$$t_b = \frac{b}{SE_b} \qquad (11.10)$$

Similarly, for testing the statistical significance of the coefficient a, we need to calculate the t ratio given by

$$t_a = \frac{a}{SE_a} \qquad (11.11)$$

From equations 11.10 and 11.11, we can see that the larger a coefficient is in relation to its standard error of estimate, the farther out the calculated ratio will be on our normal distribution chart. The farther out it is, the more convinced we will be that the coefficients are not equal to 0. Therefore, the value of this ratio will tell us that the coefficients are **statistically significant.**

Before we get into the process of actually testing the null hypotheses regarding the validity of the coefficients, I would like to repeat a few important properties of hypothesis testing from our discussion in chapter 6 (see pages 129–137). First, as the name suggests, by the law of large numbers the normal distribution is achieved only when the number of observations becomes extremely large. In such cases one can use the Z table for testing hypotheses. However, when the number of observations is relatively small, an approximation of the normal distribution is used to ascertain the critical values. This is called **Student's t distribution,** named after a statistician who used to write under the pseudonym *Student*.

Since we do not know the true standard deviation of an estimator (an estimated coefficient), we need to approximate it with our sample results. Let us take a concrete example. In our population projection, we estimated two coefficients: $a = 11.0$ and $b = 3.1$. On the basis of that result, we can use the following sample estimate of the true variance σ^2:

$$SE^2 = \frac{\sum e_i^2}{N-2} = \frac{\sum \left(Y_i - a - bX_i\right)^2}{N-2} \qquad (11.12)$$

where SE is the standard error of estimate.

You can see that the numerator of equation 11.12 is the sum of squared errors of estimate. This sum is being divided by $N-2$ (the number of observations minus 2) to approximate the true variance.[8]

With an estimate of $\sum e_i^2$, we can estimate the variance associated with the estimated coefficients, a and b. The respective standard errors are calculated by

$$SE_a = \sqrt{SE^2 \frac{\sum X_i^2}{N \sum \left(X_i - \overline{X}\right)^2}} \tag{11.13}$$

and

$$SE_b = \sqrt{\frac{SE^2}{\sum \left(X_i - \overline{X}\right)^2}} \tag{11.14}$$

From the preceding formulas, we can see that to calculate the standard errors of the coefficients, we need to add a few more columns to Table 11.2 (see Table 11.4).

From equation 11.12 the estimate of $SE^2 = 1.9/3 = 0.63$. Substituting the numbers in equations 11.13 and 11.14, we derive the estimated standard error of coefficients a and b as

$$SE_a = \sqrt{.63 \left[\frac{55}{5 \times 10}\right]} = 0.83$$

$$SE_b = \sqrt{\frac{.63}{10}} = 0.25$$

Substituting the respective values in equations 11.10 and 11.11, we get

$$t_a = \frac{1.7}{0.83} = 2.05 \tag{11.13a}$$

$$t_b = \frac{3.1}{0.25} = 12.4 \tag{11.14a}$$

For an interpretation of these results, we can resort to Figure 11.7. We noted that if the estimated coefficient is located farther away from its critical value, we can be reasonably certain that the estimated value is different from the true value proposed by our null hypothesis.

Table 11.4 Calculations for Tests of Significance

Population (Y_i)	Year (X_i)	Projected values ($\hat{Y}_i$)	$(Y_i - \hat{Y}_i)^2$	$(X_i - \overline{X})^2$	X_i^2
5	1	4.8	0.04	4	1
8	2	7.9	0.01	1	4
10	3	11.0	1.00	0	9
15	4	14.1	0.81	1	16
17	5	17.2	0.04	4	25
Total			**1.90**	**10**	**55**

These values (t_a and t_b) are distributed as t, with $N-2$ degrees of freedom (see definition in chapter 6). Since we have five observations, our degree of freedom is $5-2=3$. By checking a t table for three degrees of freedom, we see that for a 0.05 level of significance (95 percent confidence level), the t ratio is equal to 2.353. Therefore, if the ratios are greater than this number, we can state with a great deal of confidence that our estimated coefficients are indeed significantly different from zero. In other words, there is a significant relationship between the dependent and the independent variables.

Because the intercept term is less than this critical number (2.1), we cannot reject the null hypothesis that the intercept is equal to 0. In contrast, because the t ratio for the slope (b) is greater than this number, we can be sure that this number is statistically significant.

Presentation of Estimation Results

Once a regression equation is estimated, the results have to be presented to the policy makers. There are, of course, many ways of presenting this information. I suggest the following:

$$\text{Population} = 1.7 + 3.1\,\text{Year} \qquad\qquad (11.15)$$
$$t = (2.037)\ (12.32)^*$$
$$R^2 = 0.98$$
$$\text{Adjusted } R^2 = 0.97$$
$$N = 5$$
$$F(1,3) = 151.74^*$$

* Significant at 0.05 level.

The numbers within the parentheses in the estimated equation 11.15 above are the respective t values for the individual coefficients. The asterisks (*) point out the significant t values and F value. You may notice that the t value for the slope coefficient and the F statistic are significant, but the t value for the intercept term is not significant at the 0.05 level. An estimated equation with a high R^2 and significant slope coefficients but an insignificant intercept may seem a bit confusing to you. It may happen for two reasons. First, it may be that the "true" intercept is too close to 0, and thus the regression equation is unable to determine its estimated value. Or it may mean that you have left out some important independent variable in your construction (technically, "specification") of the model. We will discuss the problem of misspecification (incorrect formulation) of a regression model in chapter 12.

The Number of Observations

A series with five observations occurs in my example of population growth. You may ask, what is the minimum number of observations I need to establish a proper relationship between the dependent and the independent variables?

Remembering the law of large numbers, we can see that as the number of observations increases, so does the accuracy of the estimated coefficients. In Figure 11.8 I have shown how the estimated coefficients tend to converge on the "true" coefficients as the number of observations becomes very large (and, consequently, the sample distribution approaches a normal distribution). You may also note that with a larger number of observations, not only do the estimated coefficients come closer to the actual number, but their deviation gets smaller. That is, we are increasingly confident that our estimated **regression coefficients** represent their "true" values. Finally, no number can be considered sufficiently large to estimate the "true" value of the coefficient, so I have drawn the estimated coefficient b, with one hundred observations, close to its true value of β, but they are still not equal.

In sum, because there is no definition of a "very large number," as a rule of thumb you should not have fewer than ten observations in a regression model. My examples of the estimated equation have fewer than ten observations solely for the ease of computation.

TREND CHANGES: BUILDING MULTIPLE REGRESSION MODELS

In a straight-line model we hypothesize that the trend has remained unchanged during the period under study. However, it is entirely possible that the data may reflect a changing pattern. This change can be abrupt or can be part of a gradual process. An abrupt change in trend can result from sudden catastrophic events like war, the changing of a law, a significant invention resulting in a change in technology, or a change in policy resulting from a change in political leadership. These

Figure 11.8 Increasing Accuracy of Estimated Coefficients

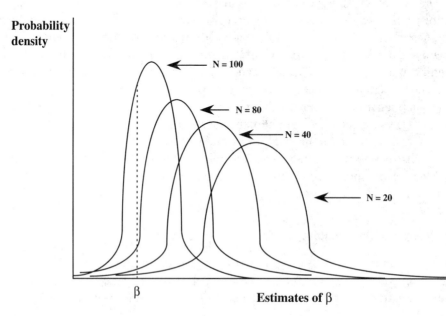

events introduce a **qualitative change** in a series. For example, if we note the trend of per capita GDP in a country like Iraq, we may notice dramatic downward shifts in trend following Iraq's two devastating wars with Iran and the coalition led by the United States. Similarly, several data series (such as national debt) for the United States will show signs of abrupt changes brought about by significant wars. A study of immigration patterns will clearly show the results of changes in the law. Similarly, the invention of many modern drugs, such as penicillin, caused shifts in the trends of infant mortality in the late 1940s and 1950s.

Abrupt Changes in Trend

Suppose we are studying the trend in per capita expenditure by the local government in a community that incorporated itself as a new city in 1996. The achievement of its city status has enabled it to access more state and federal grants, which has caused a vertical shift in the series. Table 11.5 provides the series of per capita government expenditures.

This abrupt change in trend is shown in Figure 11.9. You may notice that the vertical shift that takes place during the middle of the series (in 1996) does not affect the trend pattern itself.

These sorts of shifts are typical of series in which an extremely important external event has taken place or there is a large gap in the data set. It is clear from this figure that a broken trend line would produce fewer errors of estimation than would an unbroken straight line fitted through the entire series.

For a better visual presentation, I replotted the data shown in Figure 11.9 (see Figure 11.10). In this figure we can see the result of a vertical shift. We can account for this vertical shift if we draw a trend line based on our pre-incorporation (before 1996) data and then add a constant to the estimated values for the post-incorporation data (1996 and after). This can be done if we have *two* intercept terms, one for before and one for after the incorporation. We can accomplish this with a trick: We can introduce what is known as an **intercept dummy** variable.

Table 11.5   Per Capita Federal Grant Expenditures

Year	Expenditure (constant $)
1991	105.0
1992	110.0
1993	116.0
1994	120.0
1995	125.0
1996	180.0
1997	187.0
1998	193.0
1999	200.0
2000	213.0

Figure 11.9 Abrupt Shift in a Series

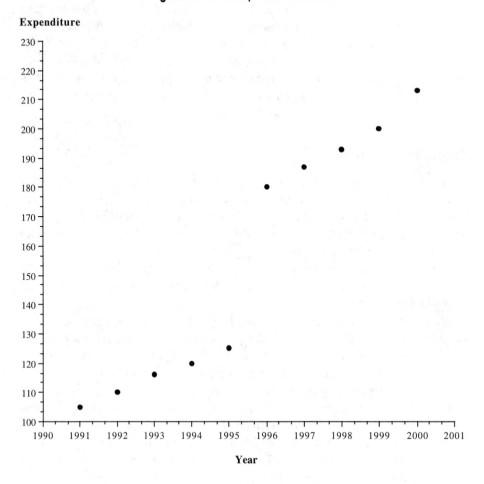

An intercept dummy introduces an additional intercept term to account for this kind of a shift. This takes the form of adding an extra independent variable, which has 0 for the observations prior to the time of shift and 1 for periods afterward. Therefore, the equation to be estimated is written as

$$Y_i = a + a' + bX_i + e_i \qquad (11.16)$$

where a' is the dummy variable, which is 0 for years prior to the shift (1991–1996 in our example) and is 1 for the years after (1996–2000).

Let us proceed with the example of our newly incorporated city. Since we want to introduce an additional independent variable a', we have to add a new column to Table 11.5 as seen in Table 11.6.

You may realize now that as we introduce an additional independent variable a', we will be using multiple regression instead of simple regression. The estimation of the coefficients of multiple regression is a bit too complicated to be calculated by

Figure 11.10 Shift in Expenditure Pattern

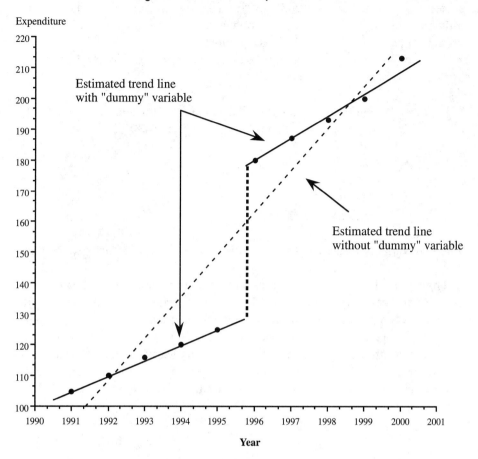

Table 11.6 Setting Up an Intercept Dummy Variable

Year	Expenditure (constant $)	Dummy (a')
1991	105.0	0.0
1992	110.0	0.0
1993	116.0	0.0
1994	120.0	0.0
1995	125.0	0.0
1996	180.0	1.0
1997	187.0	1.0
1998	193.0	1.0
1999	200.0	1.0
2000	213.0	1.0

hand. Even though generations of students of statistics and econometrics were subjected to this torturous exercise, the proliferation of computers has made the estimation rather simple. Therefore, you will want to use suitable statistical software to derive the coefficients for this equation.

The use of this dummy variable gives us an excellent predictive model as shown by the results of the estimated equation:[9]

$$\text{Expenditure} = -12{,}739.65 + 6.45\,\text{Year} + 47.15\,\text{Dummy} \qquad (11.17)$$

t ratio $\qquad\qquad (-9.768)^* \quad (9.857)^* \quad (12.543)^*$

$R^2 = 0.996$

Adjusted R^2 $(\overline{R^2}) = 0.995$

$N = 10$

$F(2,7) = 968.7^*$

* Significant at 0.05 level.

where the dummy variable is 0 for years prior to 1996 and 1 for the years 1996 and after.

I have placed the calculated t ratios under the corresponding regression coefficient. As you can tell from this equation, we are explaining 99.5 percent of total variance in the series. The dummy variable tells us that as a result of incorporation, an average resident of the city gained $47.15 in government funding. The coefficient for the variable "Year" tells us that every year, the federal contribution has gone up by $6.45 per city resident. If we want to predict the level of per capita government expenditure for 2001, we will have to write the equation as follows:

$$\text{Projected Expenditure (2001)} = -12{,}739.65 + 6.45 \times 2001$$
$$+ 47.15 \times 1.0 = 213.95$$

For estimating values for years prior to 1996, we will have to set the dummy variable equal to 0, and therefore the equation will contain only the intercept and the slope terms. Thus, we may estimate the value for 1993 as follows:

$$\text{Estimated Expenditure (1993)} = -12{,}739.65 + 6.45 \times 1993$$
$$+ 47.15 \times 0.0 = 115.2$$

We have plotted the predicted versus the actual values of expenditure in Figure 11.10. The estimated line with the dummy variable has been drawn with a solid line, whereas the straight-line equation has been drawn with a dotted line. You may notice the close approximation of the actual values as a result of the use of the dummy variable. For example, if you estimate the equation without the dummy variable, you get the following result:

$$\text{Expenditure} = -26{,}971.81 + 13.59 \times \text{Year} \qquad (11.17a)$$

t value $\qquad\qquad (-9.26)^* \quad (9.31)^*$

$R^2 = 0.915$

Adjusted R^2 ($\overline{R^2}$) = 0.905
$N = 10$
$F(2,7) = 86.67$*
* Significant at 0.05 level.

Although this equation looks excellent on its own, the use of the dummy significantly improves the quality of the estimated equation.[10]

Abrupt Changes in Slope

In the previous example, we discussed the situation in which there is a parallel shift in the trend line. In reality there can also be an abrupt change in the slope. This change is more dramatic because this new situation has altered the entire direction of the trend line. There are many examples of this abrupt change in trend. The discovery of gold in California in 1849 caused a huge population influx; the initiation of the Great Society program caused a sudden increase in the trend of social expenditure; the successful launching of the Soviet Union's *Sputnik* caused a big increase in expenditure for NASA for a decade; during the presidency of Ronald Reagan, federal assistance to state and local governments took an abrupt change in the opposite direction. Let us consider a hypothetical example of government expenditure on drug rehabilitation programs for a period of fifteen years. Assume that owing to heightened awareness and a change in political leadership during the eighth year of the study, society decided to spend increasing amounts on drug rehabilitation programs (see Table 11.7 and Figure 11.11).

The plot in Figure 11.11 makes it clear that the trend pattern changed after the seventh year. Whereas for the first seven years of the study government expenditure

Table 11.7 Expenditures on Drug Rehabilitation Programs

Year	Expenditure (in $000)
1	76
2	75
3	78
4	76
5	80
6	81
7	80
8	96
9	97
10	102
11	109
12	114
13	116
14	125
15	129

Figure 11.11 Plot of Trend in Government Expenditure for Drug Rehabilitation

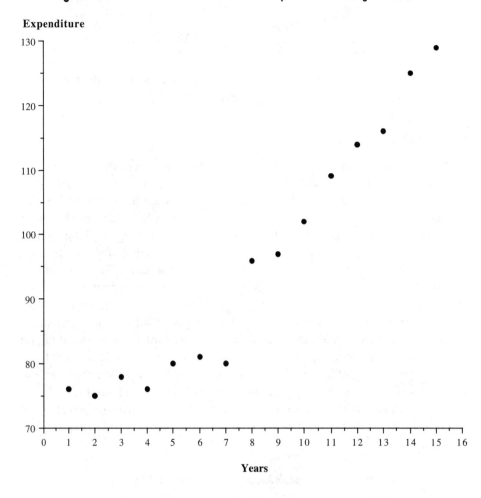

was increasing at a slow rate, the rate of change accelerated greatly from the eighth year on. This change in trend cannot be accommodated simply by adding an intercept dummy. Therefore, in our projection of trend, we need to account for this change. This abrupt change can be captured adequately by using dummy variables for the two different slopes. Imagine holding a stick at an angle approximating the trend shown at the beginning of a data series. We can visualize the change in trend if we break the stick at the point where the change took place. To split the series into two distinct trend lines, we introduce two dummy variables, D_1 and D_2, with D_1 having the value 1 for all the points for which the old trend applies and 0 for the rest. D_2 has 0s and 1s in the reverse order. Then, by multiplying the independent variable by these two dummy variables, we can create two new sets of independent variables. By running a multiple regression on the dependent variables against these two newly created variables, we can estimate the equation containing two different slopes (Table 11.8).

Table 11.8 Setting Up Slope Dummy Variables

Year	Expenditure	D_1	D_2	$D_1 \times Year$	$D_2 \times Year$
1	76	1	0	1	0
2	75	1	0	2	0
3	78	1	0	3	0
4	76	1	0	4	0
5	80	1	0	5	0
6	81	1	0	6	0
7	80	1	0	7	0
8	96	0	1	0	8
9	97	0	1	0	9
10	102	0	1	0	10
11	109	0	1	0	11
12	114	0	1	0	12
13	116	0	1	0	13
14	125	0	1	0	14
15	129	0	1	0	15

By using the data shown in Table 11.8, we estimate the trend equation for government expenditure, which yields the following results:

$$\text{Expenditure} = 70.61 + 1.663 \, (D_1 \times Year) + 3.568 \, (D_2 \times Year) \quad (11.18)$$

t value   (27.5)*   (2.8)*   (15.0)*

$R^2 = 0.974$

Adjusted R^2 ($\overline{R^2}$) = 0.969

$N = 15$

$F(2,12) = 222.75*$

* Significant at 0.05 level.

From this equation, we can see that the trend coefficient for the second period (3.568) is 2.15 times larger than that for the first period (1.663). This equation can be used to estimate the amount of government expenditure for every year within the study and can be used for predicting the values for future time periods.

If you estimate an equation with a **slope dummy,** you may run into a problem when you attempt to forecast. If you estimate an equation with two slope dummies to account for the two phases of a trend, you may have to include an intercept dummy in your model. If you do not include an additional intercept dummy, the model will force each slope to compromise on a common intercept, which will make both the slope lines deviate from their true positions. If, however, you allow for the slope dummies to have their own intercepts, the estimated results will be far superior.

Consider once again the estimated equation (11.18). We can significantly improve the model by including an intercept dummy D_1. The model is estimated as

$$\text{Expenditure} = 53.77 + 20.51 \, D_1 + 0.929 \, (D_1 \times Year) + 4.976 \, (D_2 \times Year) \quad (11.19)$$

t value   (18.05)* (6.24)*   (2.98)*   (19.58)*

$R^2 = 0.994$
Adjusted R^2 ($\overline{R^2}$) = 0.993
N = 15
F(2,12) = 630.47*
*Significant at 0.05 level.

If you compare the estimated results of equation 11.18 with those of equation 11.19, you will notice that all the statistics have improved. However, the real improvement can be seen when the predicted values based on the two equations are plotted side by side against the actual values. In Figure 11.12, I have drawn the predicted values of actual expenditure based on the two models. You can see that the line with a dummy variable is clearly superior (closer) to the actual values. You may also note that the slope of the second phase (4.976) is nearly 5.4 times the slope of the first phase (0.929). I have presented the estimated data in Table 11.9.

Figure 11.12   Comparison of Estimated Trend Lines

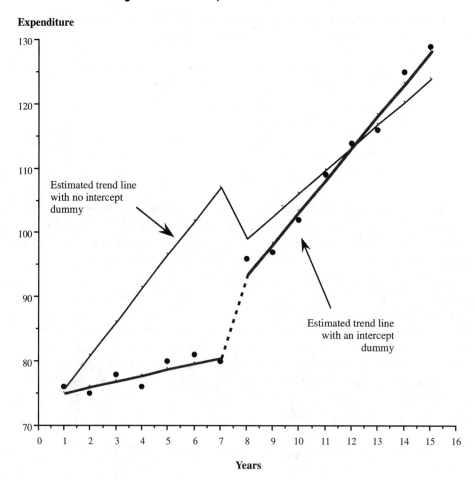

Table 11.9 Comparison of Estimated Data

Actual observations	Estimated values (without intercept dummy, eq. 11.18)	Estimated values (with intercept dummy, eq. 11.19)
76	72.27	75.21
75	73.94	76.14
78	75.60	77.07
76	77.26	78.00
80	78.93	78.93
81	80.59	79.86
80	82.25	80.79
96	99.16	93.58
97	102.72	98.56
102	106.29	103.54
109	109.86	108.51
114	113.43	113.49
116	116.99	118.46
125	120.56	123.44
129	124.13	128.42

GRADUAL CHANGES IN TREND: ESTIMATION OF NONLINEAR TRENDS

Many data series relating to society and economy can be approximated by a straight line. When the trend is fundamentally nonlinear, however, the use of a straight line will cause severe problems in forecasting. Many nonlinear forms can be captured by regression equations (thanks to advancements in computer technology) without a great deal of computational problems. Some of the nonlinear trends can be estimated easily by transforming the data, in which case we do not need to use any special nonlinear estimation techniques (which are beyond the scope of this book). Let us consider a few examples.

Polynomial Forms

A polynomial form expresses a dependent variable as a function of a number of independent variables. Some of these independent variables may be raised to powers greater than 1. The degree of a polynomial is known by the highest power among the independent variables. Thus, a quadratic form, expressed as $Y_i = a + b_1X_i - b_2X_i^2$, is called a second-degree polynomial, the equation $Y_i = a + b_1X_i - b_2X_i^2$ $Y_i = a + b_1X_i - b_2X_i^2 + b_3X^3$ is called a third-degree polynomial, and so on.

It is common to find examples of a quadratic relationship in nature. For example, as we apply fertilizer to plants, they grow at a rapid rate, and we get more flowers, fruits, and vegetables. However, after a certain point, the application of more fertilizer damages their growth. Or, after an initial period of decrease in the cost per flower, we increase our scale of operation. But at a certain point, inefficiency creeps in and unit costs start climbing. As another example, if we start consuming something we highly desire, our satisfaction goes up, but after a point of satura-tion, we tend to lose interest. These are all examples of quadratic relationships as discussed in chapter 10 (see pages 229–230). A quadratic form can be U shaped or inverted U shaped.

The quadratic equation is specified as

$$Y_i = a + b_1 X_i - b_2 X_i^2 \qquad (11.20)$$

for a U-shaped relationship, and

$$Y_i = a - b_1 X_i + b_2 X_i^2 \qquad (11.21)$$

for an inverse U–shaped relationship.[11]

Let us see how these nonlinear forms are estimated. Consider the data series for the federal budget deficit as a percentage of GDP shown in Table 11.10. Note that I have used five-year averages. You may also note that I have replaced the indepen-dent variable with a new column, "Time."

During the first twenty years, between 1970 and 1985, the federal budget deficit as a percentage of U.S. GDP showed a trend of steady increase. However, this trend reversed itself in the next decade. Therefore, if we try to fit a straight-line trend, the approximation of the actual data will be rather poor. This is demonstrated when a linear estimation gives us the following result:

$$\text{Percentage deficit} = 2.52 + 0.237 \, \text{Time} \qquad (11.22)$$
$$t \, \text{value} \ (1.52) \quad (0.56)$$
$$R^2 = 0.072$$

Since the critical value for t at a 0.05 level of significance with 5 degrees of free-dom is 2.05, we cannot reject the null hypothesis that the coefficients are, in fact, equal to 0. As you can clearly see in Figure 11.13, the line fitted through the data does not give us a good prediction. The situation changes dramatically, however, when we try a quadratic fit. To do that, we need to add one more column of inde-pendent variables, "Time^2" (see Table 11.11).

Table 11.10 Budget Deficit as a Percentage of GDP (five-year average)

Year	Percentage of GDP	Time
1970–1974	1.5	1
1975–1979	2.8	2
1980–1984	3.9	3
1985–1989	5.4	4
1990–1994	4.9	5
1995–1999	1.6	6

Figure 11.13 Publicly Held Federal Debt as a Percentage of GDP: Linear Estimation

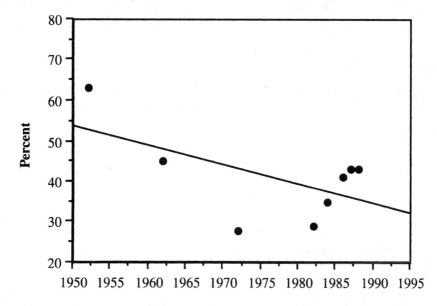

Source: Economic Report of the President (Washington, D.C.: Government Printing Office, 1989).

Now that we have made the necessary data transformation, we can estimate the desired equation. In the same way we estimated the straight-line equation, we can use our computer software to estimate the three coefficients (*a, b,* and *c*). In this case, we will have to indicate that we have two independent variables ("Year" and "Year^2") instead of one.

The estimated values of the coefficients are

$$\text{Percentage deficit} = -2.38 + 3.91\ \text{Time} - 0.525\ \text{Time}^2 \qquad (11.23)$$
$$t\,\text{value}\quad (-1.481)\quad (3.72)^*\qquad (-3.57)^*$$
$$R^2 = 0.823$$
* Significant at 0.05 level.
The critical value for *t* at a 0.05 level of significance = 2.0.

Table 11.11 Transformation of Data for the Estimation of a Quadratic Equation Form

Year	Percentage of GDP	Time	Time^2
1970–1974	1.5	1	1
1975–1979	2.8	2	4
1980–1984	3.9	3	9
1985–1989	5.4	4	16
1990–1994	4.9	5	25
1995–1999	1.6	6	36

As you can see from Figure 11.14, the estimated quadratic equation (11.23) is clearly superior to the straight-line equation (11.22). From this equation, we can estimate the value for 1982 to be 29.81 percent, much closer to the actual figure.

Higher-Order Polynomials

Although the regression results indicate that the quadratic form (equation 11.20) seems to be a definite improvement over the linear form (equation 11.17), can we not improve the results even more by using a third-degree polynomial? If we run a third-degree equation, we get the following result:

$$Y = 17,704,000 + 271,050\,\text{Year} - 13.83\,\text{Year}^2 + 3.0\,\text{Year}^3 \qquad (11.24)$$
$$R^2 = 0.983$$

Indeed, as equation 11.24 and Figure 11.15 indicate, the third-degree polynomial is a better fit than a second-degree. In fact, if we keep increasing the degree of polynomial, the resulting curve will get closer and closer to the observed points and, when we use $n - 1$ (the number of observations minus 1) degree, there is no residual. A perfect fit! Unfortunately, such an exercise reduces our result to a mathematical tautology. In fact, it is extremely rare for researchers in social sciences to use higher than a second-degree polynomial. Apart from the tautological reasoning, the use of a higher-degree polynomial imposes undue restrictions on the data. For example, in a third-degree polynomial the predicted values of Y may increase

Figure 11.14 Publicly Held Federal Debt as a Percentage of GDP: Quadratic Estimation

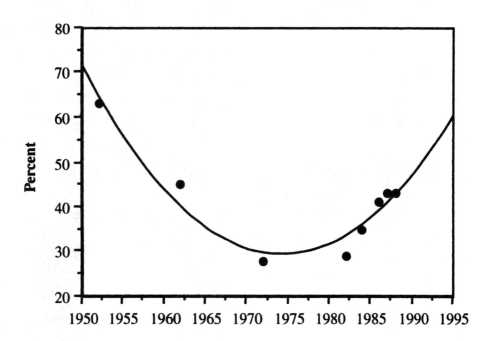

for the initial range of the value of X, then decrease rapidly, and finally increase at a dramatic rate. In the final stage, when the coefficient of the extremely large third-degree term becomes dominant, predictions outside the sample range will give a highly inflated figure, as you can see in Figure 11.15.

Even the simpler quadratic form is not free from structural biases. Its strict mathematical structure forces a symmetric specification, which can lead to faulty predictions. The result of this bias is shown in Figure 11.16. If the dependent variable shows a symmetric distribution, then you are safe. If the distribution is skewed, however, the predictions will be suspect. Unfortunately, this bias may not be apparent from the regression results, which will show a fairly decent fit. Yet if you plot the actual observations against the predicted values, the quadratic form will reveal its shortcomings.

Log-Transformed Forms

In the segment of social science research that uses **regression analysis,** perhaps the most common functional specification after the linear form is the log-log form. To understand log-log functions, you should know what a log, or logarithm, is.

A log transformation expresses a number by the exponent of its base. That is, suppose we are using 10 as the base. Since 1,000 is 10^3, we write $\log(1,000) = 3$. By following this logic, $\log(100) = 2$, $\log(10) = 1$, and because any number raised to the power 0 is equal to 1, $\log(1) = 0$. For numbers less than 1, their log values

Figure 11.15   Prediction with a Third-Degree Polynomial

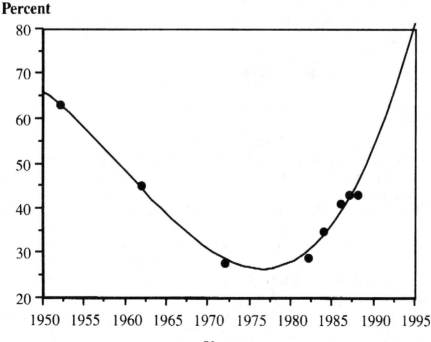

Percent / Year

Figure 11.16 Symmetry Forced by a Quadratic Form

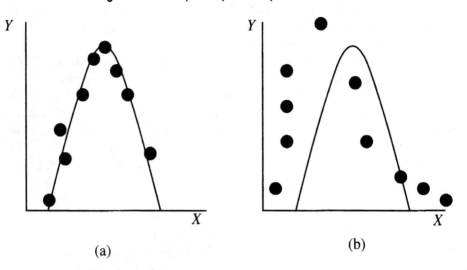

become less than 0, or negative. However, as the logs of numbers come close to 0, they produce large negative numbers and, therefore, the log of 0 is an infinitely large negative number. *So you cannot take the log of 0.* Logs can have any base, but the most commonly used base is 10. Hence, it is called the **common log.** If the base of a log is *e* (a commonly used number in mathematics, which is equal to 2.71828), it is called a **natural log.** If you want to get the original values from the log-transformed values, you have to use an **antilog.** Thus, the common log of 10 is 1, and the antilog of 1 is 10. The common log is written as **log,** whereas the natural log is expressed as **ln.** For a better understanding of logarithm, you may try log transforming a few numbers with the help of your hand calculator.

Although you can use either 10 or *e* as the base, in statistics it is more common to use the *e*-based natural log. Therefore, in this section, we will use the expression ln for log-transformed variables. By log transforming the dependent and independent variables, a log-log functional form is written as

$$\ln (Y_i) = a + b \ln (X_i) + e_i \qquad (11.25)$$

The log transformation of the data offers us a few attractive features. First, a series may exhibit a nonlinear form such as the ones shown in Figure 11.17 (a). If the coefficient *b* is greater than 1, the series would grow exponentially. Although it is hard to find examples of a series with such an explosive growth pattern in the realm of social sciences, over a short period of time a series may exhibit such a pattern (for example, housing prices in the boom areas of the United States). Many series in the social sciences come close to the lines shown where $0 < b < 1$. For example, cross-national data show that as nations become affluent, their aggregate rate of growth, after a period of rapid expansion, tends to slow. Also, it is relatively easy to find examples where *b* is negative (< 0). For example, we know that as nations become affluent, their population numbers register a steady rate of

Figure 11.17   Double-Log Functional Forms

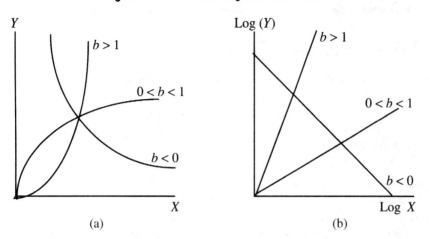

(a)   (b)

decline. In such cases log-log functions offer a better fit than linear forms. If you plot the data on a log-log form, they will show linear patterns, as in Figure 11.17 (b).

Second, the log transformation of a very large number makes it small; for instance, the ln $(85,790) \cong 11.36$. Therefore, the log transformation gives a better-fitted equation for data that vary a great deal (which often is the case when the numbers are large). Note, however, that if you estimate a log-log curve, the predicted values will be in log forms. To change to actual numbers, you will have to take their antilog.

Inverse Forms

The inverse functional form expresses Y as a reciprocal (or inverse) of the independent variable X. An inverse functional form can show a positive or a negative relationship between the dependent and independent variables. You may notice that because it is an inverse relationship, the following expression will give you a negative relationship:

$$Y_i = a + b\frac{1}{X_i} + e_i \tag{11.26}$$

whereas

$$Y_i = a - b\frac{1}{X_i} + e_i \tag{11.27}$$

will show a positive relationship, as shown in Figure 11.18. While using an inverse form, you should remember that since you cannot divide any number by zero, there must be no zeroes in the data series for the independent variable.

You should use the inverse functional form when the value of the dependent variable falls (or rises) sharply and then approaches a certain number without actually ever being equal to it as the value of the independent variable gets larger. Figure 11.18 illustrates the asymptotic nature of a typical inverse functional form.

The Problem of Irrelevant Independent Variables: Adjusted R^2

Although R^2 is widely used as a measure of goodness of fit and as a measure for choosing among the alternate specifications, it contains some important drawbacks. The most important problem with R^2 is that it measures how much of the total variation is being explained by the model. Therefore, in a multiple regression model, if one keeps on adding variables that are only marginally relevant, the total amount of explained variation will go up (or, at the very least, when a variable is absolutely irrelevant, the amount will remain unchanged). Thus, in a model, if we include an independent variable that adds nothing to the explanation of the dependent variable, the R^2 measure *will not go down* to reflect the inclusion of an irrelevant variable. To correct this problem, we use **adjusted,** or corrected, **R^2**. The adjusted R^2 is written as $\overline{R^2}$ ("R-bar squared") and can be calculated either independently or from the calculated value of R^2. Because it is easier to calculate it from the calculated value of R^2, I provide the following formula:

$$\overline{R^2} = 1 - (1 - R^2)\frac{N-1}{N-K} \tag{11.28}$$

where
N is the number of observations, and
K is the number of coefficients in the regression equation.

Note the following features in this formula:

1. There is just one independent variable, that is, $K = 1$, $R^2 = \overline{R^2}$. Otherwise, R^2 will always be greater than $\overline{R^2}$ when there is more than one independent

Figure 11.18   The Inverse Form

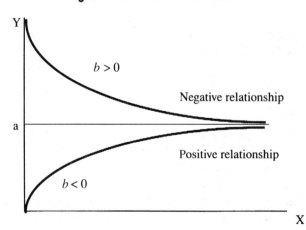

variable $(K > 1)$. You can have only one independent variable if you run a regression equation without the intercept term, that is, if you are estimating an equation $Y = bX + e$. This is a special form of equation that makes a rather stringent assumption that the intercept term is equal to zero. Although special reasons to formulate such a model may arise, in general you should not specify a model without the intercept term.

2. If you include an additional independent variable in the model, unlike the R^2, $\overline{R^2}$ may go *up* or *down*. If you think about it, this makes sense. Consider once again, for instance, the case of GDP per capita in Figure 11.1. The trend line appears to be linear. However, we want to see if there is a shift in trend. In that case, when we introduce the second independent variable (a dummy variable), the squared value of time, the inclusion is either going to add significantly to the explanation or it will be an irrelevant independent variable. If it adds significantly to the explanation, the value of R^2 will increase more than the offsetting effects of an increase in the number of independent variables. As a result, the value of the $\overline{R^2}$ will increase from the previous estimation. In contrast, if the improvement in explanation as a result of the inclusion of an additional independent variable is less than the dampening effects of an additional variable, $\overline{R^2}$ will register a decline.

Suppose that five years ago your city introduced tough youth crime legislation requiring mandatory punishment for gun-related crimes. You have been asked to see if the action has resulted in a change in the city's crime rate. By using a simple time-series regression $(K = 2)$ on the data for the last twenty years $(N = 20)$, your model explains 60 percent of the total variation $(R^2 = 0.6)$, showing a gradual rising trend. From this information you calculate the adjusted R^2 as follows:

$$\overline{R}^2 = 1 - (1 - .6)\frac{20 - 1}{20 - 2} = 0.58 \tag{11.29}$$

Now you have included a dummy variable starting the year the legislation was passed. By re-estimating your equation with two independent variables, you can attempt to provide evidence for the efficacy of the legislation. Let us suppose the new equation shows an R^2 value of 0.62, or a 2 percent improvement in your over-all explanation of the city's crime rate. You can now calculate the adjusted R^2 for the new equation:

$$\overline{R}^2 = 1 - (1 - .62)\frac{20 - 1}{20 - 3} = 0.57 \tag{11.30}$$

As you can see, since the addition of the dummy variable did not improve the overall explanation significantly to offset the dampening effects of fraction $[(N - 1)/(N - K)]$, the $\overline{R^2}$ value actually went down, leading you to conclude that there is no significant statistical evidence to suggest that the passage of the legislation has had an effect on the city's crime rate.

The Significance of Coefficients Taken Together

A multiple regression model contains many independent variables, most of which are statistically significant on an individual basis. However, questions may still be raised as to their significance as a set. For this test, we test the null hypothesis that none of the explanatory variables helps to explain the variation of the dependent variable around its mean (that is, $b_0 = b_1 = b_2 = \dots b_n$). In our previous attempt to establish statistical significance of individual coefficients, we used the t distribution. For this test, known as the joint probability test (since we are testing the collective significance of all the independent variables), we have to use the F distribution. We calculate the F value for the equation by

$$F_{(K-1,\,N-K)} = F_{(1,3)} = \frac{R^2}{1-R^2} \frac{N-K}{K-1} \tag{11.31}$$

The F test is closely linked to the R^2 in that, while testing the null hypothesis that none of the independent variables is relevant, the F test, in fact, is testing the null hypothesis that $R^2 = 0$. Therefore, for a two-variable linear equation, the null hypothesis is that the slope of the regression line is horizontal (such as in Figure 10.3 in the previous chapter).

From our example, we can calculate the F statistics as follows:

$$F_{(2-1,\,5-2)} = F_{(1,3)} = \frac{0.9806}{\left(1-0.9806\right)} \frac{5-2}{2-1} = 151.64$$

The subscript for $F\,(K-1,\,N-K)$ denotes the degrees of freedom. You will see that the F table (Appendix C) is arranged in a matrix form, where the coordinates are specified by the row and column numbers. For our test, the first number of the subscript $(K-1)$ refers to the numerator (the column), and the second number $(N-K)$ refers to the denominator (the row) of the table. By consulting the table (Appendix C), we can find that the critical value for $F_{(1,3)}$ at a 5 percent level of significance is 10.1. Since our F value 151.64 is greater than 10.1, we can reject the null hypothesis and conclude that the model is indeed relevant.

Choosing the Correct Functional Form

So far we have discussed quite a few functional forms for regression models. When it comes to choosing the correct functional form, essential for good forecasting, the books on econometric theory are of little use to a researcher. However, I can offer these words of advice: *Unless theory, common sense, or your experience tells you otherwise, use a linear form.* Before using any model, read theoretical literature on its behavior, plot the data to see if there is any reason to believe that a form other than a linear one is more appropriate, and draw on your or an expert's experience in choosing the functional form.

Imagine that you have been asked to project the property tax revenue for your county. After plotting the data you detect a slight upward trend that may tempt you to go for a second-degree polynomial fit. However, you should be careful, because the trend may be the result of a recent economic boom and its effects may be temporary. Therefore, although the estimated equation with a quadratic form is giving you better R^2 and adjusted R^2 values, your estimations may be too optimistic, particularly when the economy slows down.

FORECASTING AND ITS PROBLEMS

The purpose of estimating a regression equation is to forecast. We depend on forecasting in every facet of modern life. The stock market reacts to the projected future of the economy, revenue and expenditures are forecasted for government budgets, students often choose their career based on the expected remuneration, orders are placed on the basis of forecasted demand, and investments are made on the basis of expected future trends in the market. Therefore, from private decisions to public policies, forecasting has become an integral part of our lives. However, you often hear such ironic comments as, "It is extremely difficult to predict, especially the future." Indeed, there is a great deal of truth to this cynicism. However, since we are in the business of forecasting, let us go about it in a more systematic fashion.

A projected forecast is a quantitative estimate of the likelihood of an event taking place in the future, based on available data on past history. There are two kinds of forecasts. A forecast can be either a **point forecast** or an **interval forecast.** A point forecast predicts a particular value for our dependent variable, which is likely to take place at a certain future point in time. An interval forecast, in contrast, indicates a band within which the future value is likely to lie.

Point Forecasts

We tend to prefer to offer single numbers rather than ranges, so most of our predictions turn out to be point forecasts. Interval forecasts make clear the probability factor associated with the predicted value, but point forecasts do not always do so. However, whether explicit or not, all forecasts contain an element of probability. Thus, when we forecast the government revenue to be $1.6 trillion for the year 2005 or the population of a city to be 123,758, despite the apparent precision to the last decimal point, we are predicting a probable occurrence by extrapolating from a past trend. In a sense, an economic forecaster has a certain handicap compared with a weather forecaster. We associate weather forecasting with probabilistic outcome, even though the actual outcome is always binary—either it is going to rain or it is not. Thus, when we are told that there is a 40 percent chance of showers, we are not terribly disappointed with the forecaster when it does not rain. Yet the results of forecasts based on a regression model, with its numerical precision and its omission of the probability factor, convey a certain sense of determinism and thus can be extremely deceiving. Therefore, it is important to inquire into the factors that make a forecast good or poor.

The worth of a forecast is in its accuracy. Yet it is possible to have a good predictive model provide an inaccurate prediction, or a prediction based on a poor model turn out to be astonishingly close to reality. However, before we delve deeply into the questions of accuracy and sources of possible error, it is important to clarify certain useful terminology.

Forecasting can be either **ex post** or **ex ante.** Suppose we are predicting on the basis of a series of past data, which ends last year. We know the value of the dependent variable for this year, so we may compare the accuracy of our prediction against this known data. This is called an ex post prediction, in which we know with certainty the values of the dependent and independent variables. It is still a prediction because the model is providing us with values outside of the study period (which had ended the previous year). It is called *ex post,* or "after the fact," because the event has already taken place. In contrast, an *ex ante* forecast predicts values that are not yet known.

We can also distinguish between **conditional** and **unconditional** forecasts. An unconditional forecast is made when we know with certainty the values of all the independent variables. If we are predicting on the basis of time alone, measured in years, we know the value of the independent variable in a forecast for the next year. However, if we do not know the values of the independent variables with any certainty, the forecast is called conditional. An ex post forecast is always an unconditional forecast because we know the values of the dependent and independent variables. But an ex ante forecast may be either conditional or unconditional. Clearly, if we do not know for sure the values of the independent variables in the future, this will be an example of both an ex ante and unconditional forecast. However, like the example of time series for a future year, or when the independent variable is the past year's dependent variable (for example, when we hypothesize that how we will perform next year will depend on how we do this year), then a forecast can be both ex ante and conditional.

Interval Forecasts

An interval forecast is made when a boundary or band is provided, within which the actual value is likely to lie. For this kind of forecast, we need to use the law of large numbers again. We discussed earlier that we can test the validity of our null hypothesis by calculating how many standard deviations away the estimated parameter is from its "true value." By using the same logic, we can predict with a given level of certainty that the actual value of the predicted variable will fall within a particular range. Thus, for example, we are testing at a 0.05 percent level of confidence the null hypothesis that our estimated parameter b is the same as the "true" parameter β. We write this as

$$-t_{0.05} \leq \frac{b - \beta}{\sigma} \leq t_{0.05} \tag{11.32}$$

where $t_{0.05}$ is the value of the t ratio (derived from the t table) at a 0.05 percent level of confidence, and σ is the standard deviation.

We reject the hypothesis if the calculated value of this ratio is greater than or equal to, or less than or equal to, the critical value of the t ratio. Now it is easy to see that we can use the same logic to state that

$$b - \sigma\, t_{0.05} \leq \beta < b + \sigma\, t_{0.05}. \tag{11.33}$$

The preceding equation states that we are 95 percent confident that the actual value of the parameter β is going to be between $b \leq \sigma\, t_{0.05}$. Therefore, we can use the same technique to derive the band within which we predict with a certain degree of confidence what the future value of our dependent variable will be. This is given by

$$\hat{Y} - \sigma_f t_{0.05} \leq Y_f \leq \hat{Y} + \sigma_f\, t_{0.05} \tag{11.34}$$

where
   $\hat{Y}$ is the predicted value of Y,
   σ_f is the standard deviation associated with forecasting, and
   Y_f is the future value of Y

This formula would provide us with the necessary interval for our predicted value if we knew the value of σ_f. Since we do not know this value, we estimate it. For estimating the errors associated with prediction (S_f^2), we need to adjust the standard error of estimation (SE^2) derived in equation 11.34 with the following factor:

$$S_f = \sqrt{S_f^2} = \sqrt{SE^2\left[1 + \frac{1}{N} + \frac{\left(X_{t+1} - \overline{X}\right)^2}{\sum\left(X_i - \overline{X}\right)^2}\right]} \tag{11.35}$$

where X_t is the terminal period of the study. If our study period includes 25 years, then X_t is 25, and when we predict for the next year, X_{t+1} is 26. Therefore, by using this measure, we can rewrite equation 11.35 as

$$\hat{Y} - S_f t_{0.05} \leq Y_f \leq \hat{Y} + S_f t_{0.05} \tag{11.36}$$

It is interesting to note from the formation of equation 11.35 that because of the expression $(X_{t+1} - \overline{X})^2$, as the prediction moves away from the mean ($\overline{X}$), the error of prediction flares out in an exponential manner. In other words, the farther into the future we want to predict, the greater our chance of committing an error and, therefore, the larger the band of prediction interval. This is shown in Figure 11.19.

Looking back at our first example of forecasting population for a small city, we had already calculated the values of S (which is 1.9) and $\sum\left(X_i - \overline{X}\right)^2$ (which is 10). Hence, for us, the standard error of prediction is

Figure 11.19   Errors of Prediction

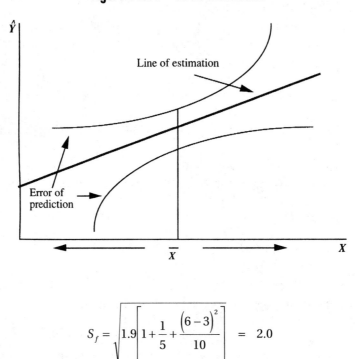

$$S_f = \sqrt{1.9\left[1 + \frac{1}{5} + \frac{\left(6-3\right)^2}{10}\right]} \;=\; 2.0$$

This error of prediction is distributed with $N-2$ degrees of freedom. Since we had five observations, the relevant t value is 3.182. We can derive the prediction for the sixth year from our estimated equation, which is 20.3. Therefore, the interval of prediction is given by

$$20.3 - 2 \times 3.182 \le \hat{Y}f \le 20.3 + 2 \times 3.182$$

or

$$13.94 \le \hat{Y} \le 26.66.$$

We are 95 percent confident that the future population for the sixth year will fall between the band 13.94 and 26.66. To check out the flaring effect of the prediction errors, you may calculate it for a few more years in the future.

EXPLAINING THE PRESENT WITH THE PAST: LAGGED DEPENDENT VARIABLES

In the real world, once an incident has taken place its effects linger for a considerable amount of time. We can argue that the level of crime that a city is presently experiencing will largely be dependent on the extent of criminal activities last year. This kind of a lingering relation is particularly true when the relation between the dependent and independent variables is shaped by long-term factors such as culture, poverty, or education. Therefore, it may be true that for a forecast of a city's future crime rate, we have to look at past records of criminal activities. In econometric analysis, this is accomplished by running a regression treating the past year's observation as the independent variable for this year. Thus,

$$Y_t = a + Y_{t-1} + e_t \tag{11.37}$$

In technical terms, this use of the past year's data as the independent variable is called a **lag dependent variable** or an **autoregressive model**. An example may clarify this model for you. Suppose we are trying to forecast the number of violent crimes for future years. We have the data presented in Table 11.12.

In Table 11.12 the yearly crime statistics for the city (Y_t) are presented under the heading "Current year's crime rate." In the column labeled "Previous year's crime rate," the data are lagged by one period (Y_{t-1}). Using this information in equation 11.38, we estimate that the model for the lagged dependent variable will be

$$Y_t = 2.192 + 0.981\ Y_{t-1} \tag{11.38}$$

t value   (1.26)   (12.53)*

$R^2 = 0.929$

Adjusted R^2 $(\overline{R^2}) = 0.923$

$N = 14$

$F(1,12) = 156.83*$

* Significant at 0.05 level.

Table 11.12   Yearly Crime Statistics

Year	Current year's crime rate (Y_t)	Previous year's crime rate (Y_{t-1})
1	10	—
2	13	10
3	13	13
4	16	13
5	15	16
6	18	15
7	19	18
8	25	19
9	24	25
10	26	24
11	27	26
12	29	27
13	30	29
14	31	30
15	35	31

You may notice that as a result of lagging, we are missing the first year's data. Hence, the number of observations has become 14 instead of 15. You may also notice that the results of this equation can be used to forecast the future year's crime rate. For instance, for the sixteenth year, we need to plug in the data for the fifteenth year in the equation. That is, the estimated figure for the sixteenth year is

$$\hat{Y}_{t+1\,(16th\ year)} = 2.192 + 0.981 \times 35 = 36.52$$

This equation can be used ad infinitum to generate future forecasts. For the seventeenth year, we need to plug in the forecast for the sixteenth year; for the eighteenth year, we need the forecast for the seventeenth year, and so on. As we discussed in the previous section, the farther we move into the future years (and, therefore, away from the mean of the actual series), the progressively larger will be the errors of estimate.

The use of a lagged dependent variable in a regression equation carries some rather important implicit assumptions. Be aware that by accepting the previous year's observation as the independent variable, you are assuming that all the external forces that shaped last year's crime rate will continue to have the same impact in determining future values.

Forecasting by Curve Fitting: A Step-by-Step Approach

- *Review the literature.* Understand the underlying relationship linking the dependent variable with the independent variables. If there is no literature available, prepare the appropriate arguments for your postulated hypothesis.
- *Collect data.* Collect data arranged in a series. Make sure there are no missing or otherwise "contaminated" data.
- *Plot the data.* A scatter plot will show you the nature of the underlying trend.
- *Formulate a projection model.* Decide on the appropriate model of forecasting. When in doubt, use parsimony as the guiding principle. If there is a strong quadratic or exponential trend, use an appropriate nonlinear form. If in doubt, use a linear form. If there are a number of distinct trend patterns or many fluctuations in the series, use the moving average model.
- *Estimate the model.* Use appropriate computer software to estimate the parameters. Present your findings with all the estimated parameter values and their corresponding *t* values. Report the R^2 and the *F* statistic. Then verbally explain the full implications of the estimated model. If the report is to be read by a nontechnical person, consider placing the results of your estimation in a footnote or in the appendix. Make sure that the reader is fully aware of your methodology, assumptions, and the data.

For using a trend model, you must remember that the trend method assumes the existence of a continuing trend and therefore cannot predict turning points. If the trend pattern changes or is expected to change, you are better off using a causal model of prediction.

Key Words

Adjusted R^2 (p. 276)
Antilog (p. 274)
Autoregressive model (p. 283)
Coefficient for trend (slope) (p. 250)
Coefficient of determination (R^2) (p. 253)
Common log (p. 274)
Conditional forecasting (p. 280)
Dependent variable (p. 250)
Error term (p. 251)
Ex ante forecasting (p. 280)
Ex post forecasting (p. 280)
Independent variable (p. 250)
Intercept (p. 250)
Intercept dummy (p. 261)
Interval forecast (p. 279)
Lag dependent variable (p. 283)
ln (p. 274)

Log (p. 274)
Method of least squares (p. 246)
Multiple regression (p. 246)
Natural log (p. 274)
Point forecast (p. 279)
Population mean (p. 255)
Population standard deviation (p. 255)
Qualitative change (p. 261)
Random (p. 256)
Random errors (p. 247)
Regression analysis (p. 273)
Regression coefficients (p. 260)
Regression equation (p. 249)
Simple regression (p. 246)
Slope dummy (p. 267)
Statistically significant (p. 257)
Student's t distribution (p. 257)
Unconditional forecasting (p. 280)

Exercises

1. The county health authority data show a 3 percent annual increase in the number of indigent emergency care cases. According to a recent survey of area hospitals, there were 3,500 such cases last year. Using a single-factor forecasting model, estimate the number of cases of indigent emergency care in your county for the next five years. If the county is paying $1,500 per case for treatment, estimate the total money requirement during this period of time. Having made the estimate, comment on the reliability of your results.

2. A similar method can be used to estimate the number of homeless people, teenage pregnancies, illegal immigrants, and the like. As a part of your project, select a specific issue in your city or state and forecast its course for the next three years.

3. The table below presents three different distributions, all showing a quadratic structure. Explain which one (Y, K, or Z) will be best explained by a quadratic specification.

Dependent variables		Independent variable	
Y	K	Z	Time
2	2	2	1
4	3	10	2
7	5	15	3
10	12	8	4
8	16	4	5
3.5	10	3	6
2	2	2	7

4. Consider the hypothetical yearly data of garbage collection for the town of Masters, Pennsylvania. Estimate the tonnage of garbage collection for 2002 and 2003. Use

various models of forecast. Which one of these models would you choose and why? Explain fully your choice of forecasting technique.

Collection of Garbage in Masters, Pennsylvania (in 000 tons)

Year	Garbage
1980	1,325
1981	1,356
1982	1,386
1983	1,402
1984	1,435
1985	1,495
1986	1,550
1987	1,597
1988	1,645
1989	1,701
1990	1,756
1991	1,810
1992	1,899
1993	1,967
1994	1,998
1995	2,030
1996	2,780
1997	3,134
1998	3,753
1999	4,004
2000	4,139
2001	4,356

5. The crime rate in the United States has gone down steadily every year since 1990. The city of Masters is no exception. The following table shows the burglary rate per 1,000 population. Use an inverse functional form to estimate the burglary rate for the years 2001 and 2002.

Burglary Rate in Masters, Pennsylvania (per 000 population)

Year	Burglary rate
1990	2.95
1991	2.65
1992	2.42
1993	1.99
1994	1.90
1995	1.85
1996	1.81
1997	1.78
1998	1.76
1999	1.74
2000	1.74

6. The following table shows per capita chicken consumption (in pounds) for the period 1986 through 2000. On the basis of this information, forecast the per capita

demand for the years 2001, 2002, and 2003. For these years, assume that the actual numbers were 51.6, 53.0, and 53.8. Comment on the accuracy of your model.

Year	Consumption
1986	35.6
1987	36.5
1988	36.7
1989	38.4
1990	40.5
1991	40.3
1992	41.8
1993	40.4
1994	40.7
1995	40.1
1996	42.7
1997	44.1
1998	46.7
1999	50.6
2000	50.1

7. Predict the value of Y for X equal to 16, 17, 18, 19, and 20.

X	Y
1	35
2	28
3	25
4	20
5	18
6	16
7	15
8	16
9	21
10	27
11	32
12	35
13	39
14	45
15	53

8. Collect any time-series data (for example, government debt as a percentage of GDP, population, sales tax revenue), and with the help of a regression model, project it for the next five years. Estimate the errors of projection for each year's projection and calculate the confidence intervals.

9. The passage of the Property Tax Limitations Act (Proposition 13) in California in 1978 caused a dramatic shift in local government finances for the state. The following are the property tax rates per $100 of assessed valuation for the city of San Diego. Estimate the tax rate for 1991 and 1992. Also estimate the intervals for those two years.

Year	Tax rate	Year	Tax rate
1971	1.959	1981	0.0860
1972	1,809	1982	0.0195
1973	1.774	1983	0.0170
1974	1.753	1984	0.0160
1975	1.753	1985	0.0147
1976	1,733	1986	0.0130
1977	1,548	1987	0.0117
1978	1.357	1988	0.0112
1979	0.131	1989	0.0103
1980	0.088	1990	0.0099

Notes

1. Numerous books are available on regression analysis and the method of least squares. For one of the best explanations, see Peter Kennedy, *A Guide to Econometrics,* 2d ed. (Cambridge: MIT Press, 1985).
2. The method of least squares has a long history, with the names of some of the most illustrious mathematicians attached to its development. This method was first proposed in 1806 by Adrien-Marie Legendre. Shortly afterward, Pierre-Simon de Laplace and Carl Friedrich Gauss justified its use and demonstrated some of its useful properties. In 1812 Laplace offered proof that every unbiased linear estimator is asymptotically normal when the number of observations tends to infinity. Further, Laplace demonstrated that for the least squares estimators the asymptotic variance is minimal. In a series of articles (1821–1823) Gauss showed that among all unbiased linear estimates, the least squares estimators minimize the mean square deviations between the true value and the estimated value. Most important, Gauss established that this relationship holds for any distribution of the errors and for any sample size. Later corroboration of his findings came through the work of Andrey Markov (1912). Subsequent developments in the least squares method were the work of mathematicians such as Aitkens and Fisher from the late 1920s through the 1940s. This method forms the basic building block of the field of econometrics.
3. If you are not well versed in the algebra of a straight-line equation, you may engage in the following exercise. Consider two sets of equations: (a) $Y = 2 + 0.5X$ and (b) $Y = 2 + 2.5X$. By substituting values of 0, 1, and 2 for X, you can see the implications of the intercept and trend coefficient. [Y is equal to 2, 2.5, 3 for (a) and 2, 4.5, 7 for (b)].
4. For those of you who are interested in the logic of derivation of the formulas for a and b, they can be derived by the use of differential calculus. Thus, we are trying to minimize

$$S = \sum_{i=1}^{n}\left(e_i\right)^2 = \sum_{i=1}^{n}(Y_i - a - bX_i)^2 .$$

Therefore, the sum of squares is minimized with respect to the values of a and b. Hence, we have:

$$\frac{\delta S}{\delta a} = -2\sum(Y_i - a - bX_i) \tag{11.3a}$$

$$\frac{\delta S}{\delta b} = -2\sum X_i(Y_i - a - bX_i)$$

(11.3b)

By setting equations 11.3a and 11.3b equal to 0, we can get two equations that can be solved for two unknowns, *a* and *b*. By solving these two equations, we get equations 11.4 and 11.5 for estimating the two parameters.

5. The squared sum of explained variations is also known as the error sum of squares (ESS), and the squared sum of total variation is also referred to as the total sum of squares (TSS).

6. E. Ames and S. Reiter, "Distributions of Correlation Coefficients in Economic Time Series," *Journal of American Statistical Association* 56 (1961): 637–656.

7. Once again, note that we are using two different sets of symbols for mean and standard deviations. They are μ and $\bar{X}$ for mean and σ and S for standard deviation. This is because we want to distinguish between the population, or the "true," mean and standard deviation and between the sample, or "observed," mean and standard deviation. The true values have only conceptual validity because we can never observe them. Yet, in statistical theory, theorems such as the one shown by equation 11.8 are valid only when we have the true values. Therefore, to get around the problem, we use the estimated or sample values with some necessary modifications.

8. The theoretical justification of dividing the sum of squared errors by $(N-2)$ lies in the fact that there are N data points in the estimation process but the estimation of the intercept and the slope introduces two constraints on the data. This leaves $N-2$ unconstrained observations with which to estimate the errors of estimate. Hence, the number $N-2$ is referred to as the number of degrees of freedom.

9. You may notice that here we have estimated the time trend by using the actual values of the years (such as 1991) as the independent variable. For ease of computation, you may also use numbers 1, 2, 3, and so forth for the actual values of the year. This will not change the basic relationship between the dependent and the independent variables; only the values of the estimated coefficients will change. On a computer, try estimating the same equation both ways, and then calculate the predicted or estimated values for the dependent variable. They will not change.

10. By using the two equations, you can compute the values of the dependent variables and examine the relative efficiency of the two models.

11. To see how these equations specify a quadratic relationship, consider the following two equations:

(a) $Y = 10.0 - 2.0X + 0.5X^2$ and
(b) $Y = 2.0 + 2.0X - 0.5X^2$.

If you start substituting values 0, 1, 2, 3 for X (and squaring them for X^2) and then calculating and plotting the resulting values of Y, you will see the shapes of quadratic curves.

12

MODELS OF CAUSAL PREDICTION: MULTIPLE REGRESSION

If you are interested in forecasting an event you may do so by extending the trend or by examining the event's root causes. Forecasting based on trend was covered in the previous chapter. In this chapter we will discuss causal prediction, the method to be used when models of trend projection may be inappropriate.

As you have learned, trend projection models assume that the present trend is going to continue, at least for the period of prediction. The problem with an assumption of continuity is that a past trend may not hold true for any length of time. Or the data may not show any obvious trend pattern. In these cases we must think about the causal relations that may link the dependent variable with a set of independent variables.

Causal models based on multiple regression techniques have been used in public policy analyses in many different ways. Many local governments depend on multiple regression models for assessing property taxes.[1] Property tax is assessed on its market value. However, we cannot know the value before a property is sold, so an assessor must estimate, or forecast, the market price.[2] Because a high assessment means a high property tax for the homeowner, property tax assessments have been a source of conflict in many communities across the nation. How do you forecast a property's market price? Let us look at a hypothetical example. Suppose your town's appraiser has assessed the value of a custom-built home at $265,000, which the owner is challenging as far above its market value. Your job is to determine the validity of the owner's claim. You will have to build a causal model for predicting the market value of the property. The distinction between a trend projection and a causal model is further explained in "A Case in Point: Base-line Estimation of Government Revenue."

BUILDING A CAUSAL MODEL

The first step in building a causal model requires establishing the causal linkage between a dependent variable and a set of independent variables. Once we have inquired into the causes of a specific event (the dependent variable), we begin our analysis by selecting the independent variables. After preparing a list and collecting data, we determine how these independent variables relate to the dependent variable. These two steps comprise the **specification of the model.** At this stage, the difference between a time-series model and a causal model comes into sharper focus. For building a model in which the only explanatory factor is the trend over time, we do not need to understand the causes of a change. However, in specifying a model for causal analysis, we must develop a deep understanding of the change's causes.

Let us return to our example of predicting the price of a house. As the first step toward specification, we hypothesize that the price of a house depends on the following independent variables: the type of structure and its location. We assume that the type of structure has only one component: the size of the covered area. The location factors include two separate variables: whether the house has a view and whether it is located on a cul-de-sac. You can write your model as

$$\text{Price} = f(\text{Area}, \text{View}, \text{Cul-de-Sac}) \tag{12.1}$$

The expression (12.1) is read as "price is a function of (or depends on) area, view, cul-de-sac." This expression is also known as an **implicit function** or **implicit model.** It is called implicit because we are not making any explicit hypotheses regarding the nature of the relationship between the dependent variable and the independent variables. If we express the model by specifying the relationship, the expression is called an **explicit function** or **explicit model.** Thus, the implicit function written in (12.1) can be made explicit by writing

$$\text{Price} = \beta_0 + \beta_1 \, Area + \beta_2 \, View + \beta_3 Cul - de - Sac + \varepsilon \tag{12.2}$$

where the β_i's are the coefficients for the independent variables, and ε is the error term.

A CASE IN POINT

Base-line Estimation of Government Revenue

All governments want to know the estimated economic impact of proposed tax or expenditure legislation. When considering a proposal to lower the capital gains tax, grant a $500-per-child tax credit, or reduce the so-called marriage tax (the higher tax bracket for married couples due to their combined incomes), the government must know the fiscal impact of these actions. In 1990, facing the specter of an unrestrained federal deficit, Congress imposed a mandatory requirement known as PAYGO (pay as you go) as part of the Budgetary Enforcement Act (BEA). The act requires that every piece of revenue or expenditure legislation demonstrate that its impact will remain within the federal budget's deficit targets.[1] This requirement mandates forecasts of the proposed legislation's effects.[2] The Congressional Budget Office prepares the PAYGO estimates for the federal government, and the Joint Committee on Taxation prepares the revenue proposal estimates for congressional committees. For most states, the legislative staff does fiscal estimates. Estimates for other states come from a state budget agency or the state tax department. Most local governments rely on the state to provide them with revenue estimates.

The process of estimating fiscal impact can help us understand the main ideas of this chapter. Suppose the government is considering a proposal to lower the capital gains tax. Its impact can be estimated in one of two ways:

1. *Static or trend component.* Static estimates presume that taxpayers do not alter their economic behavior in the face of a new tax structure. A static analysis may examine sample tax return data and estimate the impact of loss of revenue based on the average capital gains of the population. We can use a time-series analysis, extending the past trend to estimate the future impact.
2. *Dynamic or causal component.* In contrast to the static estimate, this component assumes that people change their behavior when confronting new tax laws. A lower capital gains tax may prompt many to sell their properties and collect capital gains sooner than they would have under the previous law. Such rapid turnover may create an atmosphere for a more vibrant real estate market, with many more producers and consumers entering the market. These new activities may, in fact, compensate for the loss of capital gains tax revenue forecasted by a static or trend-based analysis. For the dynamic component, we must use causal models based on multiple regression analysis.

Notes

1. Richard Doyle and Jerry McCaffrey, "The Budget Enforcement Act of 1990: The Path to No Fault Budgeting," *Public Budgeting and Finance* 11 (1991): 25–40.
2. John Mikesell, *Fiscal Administration: Analysis and Applications for the Public Sector,* 5th ed. (Fort Worth, Texas: Harcourt Brace, 1999), 490–492.

Discussion Points

1. How is a forecast based on trend projection different from one derived from a causal model?
2. Suppose you are a congressperson sponsoring a bill that would grant an income tax credit for college tuition. Explain how you would use the two methods of forecasting to evaluate this proposal.

The explicit model (equation 12.2) states that we expect the price to go up with the size and relative desirability of the area and location factors. Also, the model states that we are hypothesizing a linear relationship between price and the other independent variables.

CAUSALITY VS. CO-OCCURRENCE

One of the most difficult problems of statistical analysis based on regression or a correlation coefficient is that the results can never establish **causality;** they can only demonstrate **co-occurrence.** That is, the empirical results can establish that the dependent and the independent variables moved in the same direction, but they cannot say whether one caused the other. The actual causality must be established by a theoretical explanation of human behavior. Policy researchers develop their hypotheses by thoroughly reviewing the literature on the theories of human social interactions.

An example may clarify this point. Data show that productivity in the United States, measured in per capita GDP and adjusted for inflation (real per capita GDP), is increasing steadily over the years. So is the population of Lima, Peru. If we regress U.S. per capita GDP against the population of Lima, we will find a high degree of statistical significance, leading to the claim that an increase in Lima's population adds to U.S productivity. Yet it is obvious that no such causal connection exists. On the other hand, if you study the literature on economic growth, you find that the accepted theories explain growth in national per capita GDP by pointing to a combination of expenditure on financial capital (total national capital formation) and spending on human capital (for example, education, health care, or research and development).

The issues of causality and correlation are central to our understanding of the methods of scientific research. Hardly a day passes without medical researchers linking some food or personal habit with some human ailment. Many of these findings, of course, cannot claim causality and instead point out close association. Sometimes researchers misuse these findings by asserting a causal connection where there is none. In contrast, some people take advantage of the fact that these results do not *prove* causality and deny a significant relationship. Lobbyists for the tobacco industry have tried to dismiss the results linking lung cancer with smoking as mere co-occurrences. However, in the face of overwhelming evidence, increasing public awareness has prompted public policies that limit tobacco use.

Other than mistaking co-occurrence for causality, we may make significant mistakes by using trivial variables to find a causal linkage. Suppose we want to develop a model for explaining the difference in criminal justice expenditures among cities of similar size. If we include in the model the number of law enforcement officers as an independent variable, we will be engaging in a trivial pursuit, since it is obvious that when we hire more officers, the size of our budget goes up. Instead, we should use variables such as crime rate, population density, and per capita city income. Of course, when trying to exclude trivial independent variables, lines tend to blur. A deep understanding of human behavior, not statistical manipulation, helps you see that link between the dependent and independent variables.

ESTIMATION OF THE MODEL

After specifying a model, we estimate the relevant coefficients. For this step we need to determine how each of the variables is to be quantified or **operationalized.** Thus, in our example, we can operationalize housing quality as an explanation of price with the help of our independent variables: the size of a house expressed in square feet of covered area, the presence or absence of a view, and the location on or off a cul-de-sac (which is desirable for privacy and the absence of fast-moving traffic). We expressed each location variable (View and Cul-de-Sac) as an intercept dummy, with a value of one if a particular house has a view and one if it is located on a cul-de-sac. If, on the other hand, it has no view and is not on a cul-de-sac, each location variable gets a value of zero.

Suppose the assessor's office has provided you with information on thirty houses in the neighborhood sold during the last six months. The information is presented in Table 12.1. You can estimate the model with this data.[3]

Using information from Table 12.1, you can write the estimated equation as follows:

$$\text{Price} = 6{,}767.87 + 100.04\,\text{Area} + 40{,}603.07\,\text{View} + 42{,}607.31\,\text{Cul-de-Sac} \qquad (12.3)$$

t value (0.233)   (8.18)*   (3.23)*   (3.38)*

$R^2 = 0.786$ Adjusted $R^2 = 0.761$

$F(3,26) = 31.77*$

$N = 30.$

* Significant at 0.05 level.

The estimated equation (12.3) tells an interesting and convincing story about how home prices are determined. It states that each square foot adds $100.04 to the price of a home. The estimated results also point out that locational variables contribute heavily to the determination of price. If the property is located on a piece of land with a view, the price increases by $40,603.07, while sitting on a cul-de-sac boosts the price by another $42,607.31.

The interpretation of the intercept term is often problematic in a regression equation. Equation 12.3 indicates that even if there is not a single square foot of

Table 12.1   Housing Prices and Characteristics

	Price	Area (square feet)	View	Cul-de-Sac
1	$310,000	2,200	1	1
2	233,000	1,800	0	0
3	400,000	3,500	1	0
4	430,000	3,200	1	1
5	210,000	1,800	0	0
6	240,000	1,700	1	1
7	300,000	2,200	0	1
8	350,000	2,100	1	1
9	385,000	2,600	1	1
10	368,000	3,000	0	0
11	200,000	2,000	0	0
12	298,000	1,750	1	1
13	275,000	1,900	0	1
14	198,000	1,800	0	0
15	253,000	2,200	1	0
16	278,000	2,100	1	1
17	320,000	2,170	1	1
18	178,000	1,200	1	1
19	225,000	2,000	0	0
20	212,000	1,900	0	1
21	288,000	2,800	0	1
22	315,000	2,300	1	1
23	255,000	2,600	0	1
24	284,000	2,700	1	0
25	189,000	1,640	1	0
26	220,000	2,600	0	0
27	248,000	1,900	1	0
28	276,000	2,000	1	1
29	210,000	2,300	0	0
30	205,000	2,200	0	0

covered area, there is still a price. Therefore, the temptation to interpret the intercept term as the price of land is great. Using this logic, we can state that if a parcel of vacant land (square feet = 0) does not have a view (View = 0) and is not located on a cul-de-sac (Cul-de-Sac = 0), it will still carry a price of $6,767.87. With a view, this price will change to $47,370.94. If the land is located on a cul-de-sac but has no view, it is worth $49,375.18. Finally, when a plot of land in this particular neighborhood has a view and is located on a cul-de-sac, it should command a price of $89,978.25. The danger in such an assertion is that we can interpret the intercept term to be the land price if we accept the model to be perfectly specified. If not, we may have left out one or more significant independent variables, the impact of which will then be captured by the intercept term. For example, we did not use the lot size (or the total land area) for the houses. Since this is a potentially important variable, we cannot readily interpret the intercept term. Therefore, unless the model is fully specified (includes all important variables), any interpretation of the intercept becomes questionable.

The estimated results indicate that the four independent variables explain 78.6 percent of the variations (R^2). Since there are thirty observations, at 29 degrees of freedom, the relevant t value for evaluating the significance of the four estimated coefficients (including the constant) at a 95 percent level of confidence is 1.697. All coefficients except for the constant have t values greater than this number, so all are statistically significant. The critical F value at 3 and 26 degrees of freedom is 2.76. Since the calculated F value is 31.768, we can safely conclude that the equation as a whole is statistically significant.

Now that you are satisfied with the quality of the estimated model, you can predict the price of the house in dispute. The equation states that each square foot of housing area adds $100.04 to the base price of $6,767.87 (value of the intercept). Also, if a house has a view its price goes up by $40,603.07. Finally, its location on a cul-de-sac increases its value by $42,607.31. This particular house has 2,200 square feet of covered area and, although it does not have a view, it is located on a secluded cul-de-sac. Armed with the information derived from the estimated model, you can forecast the market price as follows:

$$\text{Estimated price} = 6{,}767.87 + 100.04 \times (2{,}200) + 40{,}603.07$$
$$\times (0) + 42{,}607.31 \times (1.0).$$

Notice that since this house does not have a view, the value of the dummy variable is zero. But because the house is located on a cul-de-sac, the dummy value of this variable is 1. Using this equation, we calculate the estimated price of the property to be approximately $269,463. Therefore, according to your estimation, the owner does not have a strong case. In fact, from the estimated result we learn that the property has been appraised at a value lower than its estimated market price.

HOW GOOD IS THE MODEL?

Because of its mathematical elegance and ease of explanation, multiple regression is probably the most commonly used technique of statistical research and econometric prediction. Although regression analysis offers a powerful tool for prediction, its quality depends on the model and how close it is to the "true" relationship. Again, as we have mentioned before, we cannot observe the "truth." Therefore, we have no objective way of knowing whether we are sufficiently close to a desired specification. Since the process of specification contains two separate parts—(1) choosing the right set of independent variables and (2) postulating the correct functional form—let us discuss both parts in detail, beginning with the problem of selecting the right set of independent variables.

Choosing Independent Variables

When choosing the independent variables, we might omit important variables or include some that are irrelevant. The error of omitted variables occurs because of our lack of understanding of the underlying factors that produce the dependent variable. Such lack of understanding may result from a general dearth of theoretical insight into a particular aspect of social behavior or from a paucity of data. If we want to determine the reasons why kids engage in random school shootings, we may find out that there is neither a strong theoretical explanation of this puzzling behavior, nor a good deal of data on potential offenders to specify a causal model. Therefore, if we attempt to build a model, we are likely to encounter the problem of misspecification and are apt to leave out important explanatory variables or include irrelevant ones. Either error leads to some rather serious problems of estimation. Let me explain. The basic idea of a multiple regression is illustrated in Figure 12.1.

As you can see, I have explained the dependent variable Housing Price with the help of two independent variables, View and Area. The intersecting parts of the Venn diagram show which aspects of the dependent variable are explained by the two independent variables. The regression model explains the area where the dependent and independent variables overlap. As you can see, the area of overlap is divided into three segments. The area V signifies the price difference among the houses explained by the presence or absence of a view. Segment A is the price that is explained by the size of the structure (Area). However, there is also an area of correlation between the size of the house *and* the view. The correlation may be high since the lots with prime views tend to attract larger homes. This area is designated VA. The R^2 derived from the estimated equation is a ratio of the total area of these three sections to the total area of the dependent variable [(A + V + VA)/Housing Price]. A high R^2 would mean that these overlapping areas cover

Figure 12.1   Visual Explanation of Multiple Regression

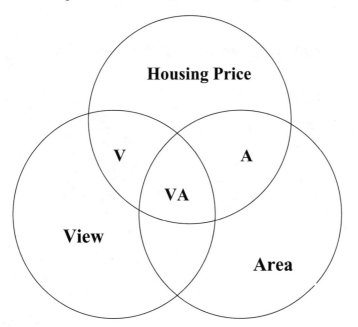

most of the dependent variable, and a low R^2 would imply a small area of intersection.

We would misspecify a model if we excluded an important variable and/or included an irrelevant one. Thus, in the case of estimating housing prices, if we leave out either the area or the view, we will run into the problem of misspecification. A small R^2 value is the first indication of **misspecification** (incorrect construction of a regression model) due to an omitted variable.

On the other hand, if we include irrelevant variables, the overall explanation of the dependent variable will not improve. In Figure 12.2 the irrelevant variable (Time) is shown with a dotted line. You may notice that compared with the other two independent variables, this one explains very little of the dependent variable (Housing Price). Therefore, its inclusion has little or no effect on the total explanation (R^2) of the model. Also, when we compare the adjusted R^2 of the new model with that of the old model (without the variable Time), the adjusted R^2 of the expanded model turns out to be smaller than that of its properly specified predecessor.

Let me now explain the impact of misspecification on t values. Suppose in our housing price example that the true relation is captured by the specification of equation 12.2; that is, housing prices depend on these three variables: Area, View, and Cul-de-sac. In this case the estimated coefficients will reflect their true values. For the purpose of exposition, let us say that we did not include the independent variable Area. As a result, equation 12.2 is improperly specified and is written as

$$\text{Price} = \beta_0' + \beta_1' \; View + \beta_2' \; Cul\text{-}de\text{-}Sac + \varepsilon \qquad (12.4)$$

Since the true relationship includes Area (see equation 12.3), the effects of the omitted variable will be distributed among the remaining independent variables

Figure 12.2   Visual Explanation of Irrelevant Variable

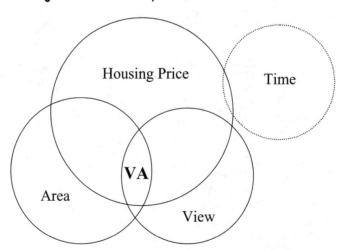

and error term. This situation will create two problems. First, the estimated coefficients for the independent variables, by illicitly incorporating fractions of another coefficient, will deviate from their true value. Second, the error term will now contain bias due to contamination by the residual factors of the omitted variable, causing the regression to violate the precepts of the classical least squares method. Moreover, the estimated coefficients will not be the best, linear, unbiased estimators. Let us see what happens to our estimated equation as a result of errors of omission. First we will omit an important explanatory variable, and then we will include an irrelevant one. We have reestimated equation 12.4 by omitting the variable Area from equation 12.3, with the following results:

$$\text{Price} = 230,560.4 + 43,030.87 \text{ View} + 34,230.87 \text{ Cul-de-Sac} \qquad (12.5)$$

t value $(12.72)^*$ $(1.84)^*$ (1.47)

$R^2 = 0.234$ Adjusted $R^2 = 0.177$

$F(2,27) = 4.11^*$

$N = 30$

*Significant at 0.05 level.

If you compare the estimated results of equation 12.5 with those of equation 12.3, you can see the obvious differences. First, both the R^2 and the adjusted R^2 have dropped significantly, implying that less is explained by the new model. Second, quite significantly, the variable Cul-de-Sac is no longer statistically significant. To a researcher, these are the telltale signs of a poorly specified model. Therefore, any prediction based on such a model would be erroneous.

The errors of specification, however, are the most difficult to detect. If you have omitted some important explanatory variables, the first indication may be a lower than expected R^2 value. Because R^2 measures the percentage of explained variance, leaving out important explanatory variables will cause it to be low.

As we have seen, the omission of an important variable also causes its effect to be absorbed by the error term. The second probable sign of omission is a high **serial correlation,** in which the error terms of one period are correlated with those of previous periods. The problem of serial correlation will be discussed later in this chapter, but it may suffice at this time to point out a few important facts. You may recall that one of the fundamental assumptions of the least squares method is the random distribution of error terms. Now suppose that the properly specified model for determining housing prices consists of the three independent variables Area, View, and Cul-de-Sac but that we have failed to include Cul-de-Sac. In that case, the misspecified model is

$$\text{Price} = \beta_0'' + \beta_1'' \, Area + \beta_2'' \, View + \varepsilon \qquad (12.6)$$

Since I have omitted Cul-de-Sac, its effects are now incorporated in the error term (ε), which, in effect, has become ($\varepsilon + \beta_3''$ *Cul-de-Sac*). As you can imagine, because the variable Cul-de-Sac is causally linked with price, the effects of its omission will not be random, and its inclusion in the error term will cause a bias.

This bias in the error term causes serial correlation. If there is evidence of a high degree of serial correlation, you should look for important explanatory variables that you may have inadvertently left out.

Let me repeat, the error of omitted variables can be corrected not by resorting to any statistical technique but through an understanding of the nature of the dependent variable. This understanding must come from the theoretical literature. If we are trying to build a model to predict the crime rate of a city, we must have a deep understanding of the sociological factors that determine the overall crime rate. For forecasting revenue for the state government, we must look into economic theory and understand the state's fiscal structure.

We noted earlier that the second source of specification error is the inclusion of **irrelevant variables** in a model. What happens when we include independent variables that do not explain the dependent variable? This error is easier to detect than an error of omission and even simpler to correct (by eliminating irrelevant variables from the model). Let us see what happens when we include irrelevant variables in the model.

Suppose that in estimating housing prices we decide to include a fourth independent variable, which measures the ease of access from a house. This variable, shown in Table 12.2, is measured by the minutes of travel time to reach the nearest highway.

When we include this new variable and re-estimate our model, we get the following results:

Price =
9,291.11 + 99.78 Area + 41,496.06 View + 43,182.0 Cul-de-Sac − 180.5 Time (12.7)
t value
(0.30)   (8.0)*   (3.15)*   (3.32)*   (−0.29)
$R^2 = 0.786$ Adjusted $R^2 = 0.752$
$F(4, 25) = 23.01$*
$N = 30$
* Significant at 0.05 level.

As you can see from the preceding results, the new variable turns out to be statistically insignificant. This lack of statistical significance may be due to some people preferring easy access to the highway, while others prefer seclusion and distance from it. Therefore, these conflicting preferences do not show up in the determination of demand for housing. Returning to Figure 12.2, you can see that when we include an irrelevant variable (Time), the area of explanation (where Time overlaps Housing Price) is rather small, and hence its inclusion does not increase significantly the R^2 value.

The inclusion of irrelevant variables poses less of a specification problem than the omission of important variables. Thus, if the new variable is totally random, it will impose no bias on either the estimated coefficients or the error term. However, unless you are deliberately choosing a random series, few data sets in nature will be randomly distributed with respect to another, especially when a researcher

Table 12.2 Variables for Determining Housing Price

Price	Area (square feet)	View	Cul-de-Sac	Time (minutes)
$310,000	2,200	1	1	25
233,000	1,800	0	0	3
400,000	3,500	1	0	17
430,000	3,200	1	1	8
210,000	1,800	0	0	2
240,000	1,700	1	1	35
300,000	2,200	0	1	7
350,000	2,100	1	1	33
385,000	2,600	1	1	35
368,000	3,000	0	0	21
200,000	2,000	0	0	10
298,000	1,750	1	1	1
275,000	1,900	0	1	15
198,000	1,800	0	0	4
253,000	2,200	1	0	15
278,000	2,100	1	1	13
320,000	2,170	1	1	9
178,000	1,200	1	1	32
225,000	2,000	0	0	22
212,000	1,900	0	1	25
288,000	2,800	0	1	1
315,000	2,300	1	1	7
255,000	2,600	0	1	19
284,000	2,700	1	0	20
189,000	1,640	1	0	20
220,000	2,600	0	0	4
248,000	1,900	1	0	3
276,000	2,000	1	1	15
210,000	2,300	0	0	10
205,000	2,200	0	0	25

has reason to believe that there is *some* causal link between the dependent and the independent variables. This largely irrelevant variable will impose some biases and can be detected. To locate this variable, look for the following results:

1. If the included variable is not significantly correlated with the dependent variable, this lack of correlation will show up as an insignificant t value for the included variable's estimated coefficient. As can be seen (equation 12.7) the variable Time has a statistically insignificant t value.

2. Although R^2 will remain unchanged or may even go up slightly, the adjusted R^2 will register a decline. You may recall our discussion of R^2 and adjusted R^2 in chapter 10. The R^2 is the measure of total explanation. Therefore, even if you add an utterly irrelevant variable, the worst it can do is to add nothing to the explanation. In this case R^2 will remain the same (unchanged) when

you include this variable in the original list of independent variables. However, you may recall that the formula for adjusted R^2 states

$$\bar{R} = 1 - \left(1 - R^2\right) \frac{N-1}{N-K}$$

So unless the new variable adds more to the value of R^2 than does the correction factor $[(N-1)/(N-K)]$ made for the inclusion of an additional variable, the value of R^2 will decline. By comparing the estimation results of equation 12.3 with those of equation 12.7, we can see that the R^2 value has remained unchanged at 0.786 with the inclusion of the irrelevant variable, Time. However, since this marginal increase could not compensate for the adjustment factor, the adjusted R^2 has declined from 0.761 to 0.752.

3. The inclusion of irrelevant variables tends to increase the variance of the estimated coefficients. This increased variance reduces the t values of the coefficients. As you can see, the inclusion of an irrelevant variable has caused a slight reduction in the t values of all three independent variables.

4. An irrelevant variable may mean that the new variable is measuring the same phenomenon as one of the other independent variables. In this case, the analysis suffers from multicollinearity, a problem discussed at greater length later in this chapter.

Searching for the Proper List of Independent Variables

One of the greatest beneficiaries of this technological advent in computer hardware and software has been the econometrician. Thanks to the increased computing capabilities of modern computers, the most sophisticated techniques of estimation are available to prospective users at the touch of a button. As a result, the temptation to forgo the thoughtful but time-consuming effort required to build a theoretically sound model and to settle for a model of empirical convenience is strong. Yielding to it can often lead to serious but undetected problems of specification error. To underline the fact that there is no substitute for the deep understanding of the causal interrelationship, I will discuss some of the most commonly misused techniques for solving specification problems.

Suppose I am trying to build a causal model for forecasting a complex sociological phenomenon: drug abuse cases among high school students. An industrious researcher, I have found information on various social and economic characteristics of the general population in the surrounding areas of the school district. However, lacking familiarity with the scholarly literature on the subject, I do not have a clue about which variables are important and which are not. But it is easy to run a regression equation when the data are already in the machine, so there is no stopping me. I proceed to run a large number of equations and then choose the combination that gives me the highest R^2 and best t values. This approach is called a **fishing expedition** or **data mining.** The problem is that since the model has been built without a profound comprehension of the causal linkages, what we may be observing is a simple case of co-occurrence. Therefore, this model is likely to give us misleading forecasts, as the future development of these less-than-relevant independent variables will have little bearing on the course of the dependent variable.

Stepwise regression is a statistical technique that minimizes the tedious job of having to choose manually the best set of independent variables. Given a list of variables, this technique will search for the variable that gives the highest R^2. After that, it will pick from the list the second variable that adds the most to this R^2 value, and then go to the third, and so on. Many of the statistical packages come with this stepwise option. The problem with stepwise regression is that it selects independent variables based solely on the strength of association and not on causality.

Predicting on the Basis of the Wrong Functional Specification

Even after we have selected the "correct" set of independent variables, serious errors can arise if we do not choose the right functional form. For example, suppose we have a data set in which the true relationship is a quadratic one. If we assume that the relationship is linear and fits a straight line, we will get a terribly inaccurate predicted value (see Figure 12.3). I have discussed this problem in the previous chapter.

The only way to avoid the problem of misspecifying the functional form is to graph each independent variable against the dependent variable. Although a linear form is recommended over a more complicated nonlinear one, you cannot always use the linear functional form. If the data are arranged in a way that quickly reveals, say, a quadratic form, you may not have to spend time plotting the data.

Figure 12.3   Errors of Functional Misspecification

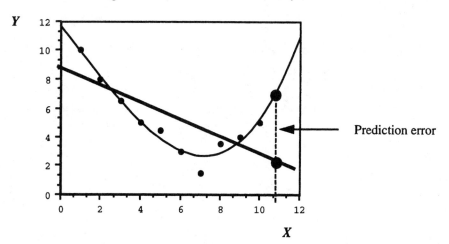

Note: Figure shows a huge error in prediction due to the misspecification of the functional form. Clearly, in this case, the polynomial form is more appropriate. The choice of a straight line causes prediction error.

However, in most cases you cannot be sure until you have plotted them. Consider the two sets of data presented in Table 12.3. Series A presents citywide survey results showing support for a public roller-skating park. The data clearly show that support for the project increased rapidly over the years and then, as the roller-skating fad diminished, the support waned. The data are presented in a way (in this case, over time) that makes the nature of the relationship between the two variables obvious. However, the results of another series may not be arranged so conveniently for the researcher to discern the shape of the relationship. Take Series B, which shows a cross-section of support among community residents for the same project in 2001. Since the dependent and independent variables are not arranged in any order, you may not be able to grasp their relationship simply by looking at the data. However, I have plotted the two variables in Figure 12.4, which clearly shows a quadratic relationship between them, with support for the park coming solidly from the middle income neighborhoods. In contrast, the poor and wealthy show a distinct lack of interest.

Although Figure 12.4 strongly suggests a nonlinear relationship, we have not solved the problem completely. You may still be undecided about the type of polynomial to use. You could try a quadratic or a second-degree polynomial.

The estimation of the second-degree polynomial gives us the following result:

$$P = -24.92 + 3.71\ Y - 0.056\ Y^2 \tag{12.8}$$

t value $\qquad\qquad (-0.92)\ (2.37)^*\ (-2.80)^*$

$R^2 = 0.69$ Adjusted $R^2 = 0.61$

$F(2,7) = 7.91^*$

$N = 10$

* Significant at 0.05 level.

where P = percentage of support for the project within the community in 2001 and Y = median income of the community.

Table 12.3   Detecting the Relationship between Variables in a Series

| | Community support for roller-skating park | | |
| | Series A (1991–2000) | Series B (2001) | |
Year	Community support (percent)	Household median income ($000)	Community support (percent)
1991	3	60	5
1992	5	19	30
1993	10	25	35
1994	15	30	50
1995	25	52	3
1996	35	36	35
1997	20	17	9
1998	18	58	7
1999	13	28	40
2000	6	45	20

Figure 12.4 Community Support for Roller-skating Park, 2001

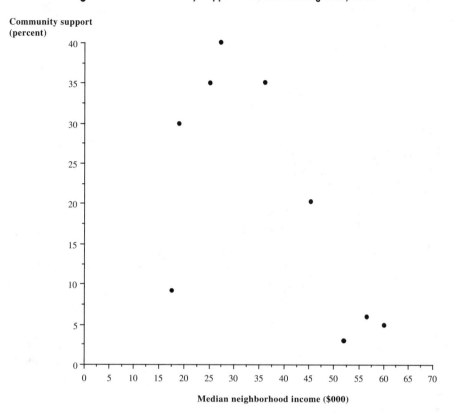

The estimated results look fine, with high R^2 and significant t and F values. The estimated curve has been plotted with a heavy line in Figure 12.5.

However, we may also be tempted to try a third-degree curve, since the series shows some sign of turning the corner and going up again. In that case, the results are as follows:

$$P = -192.78 + 19.69\,A - 0.515\,Y^2 + 0.004\,Y^3 \tag{12.9}$$

t value $\qquad\qquad\quad$ (4.9)* $\quad$ (5.45)* $\quad$ (5.06)* $\qquad$ (4.54)*

$R^2 = 0.93$ Adjusted $R^2 = 0.90$

$F(3,6) = 26.88$*

$N = 10$

* Significant at 0.05 level.

The preceding results indicate that although the second-degree curve gives us a good fit, the third-degree one gives us an even better fit. I have plotted the expected values based on the preceding formulations (equations 12.8 and 12.9) in Figure 12.5. Not only do the two models give us different estimated results for the observations within the sample range, but also the problem of model specification

Figure 12.5 Projection and Model Specification

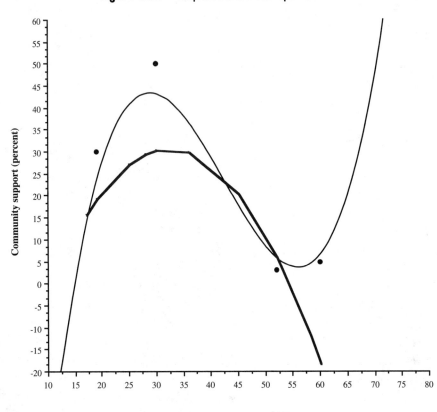

becomes truly critical when we attempt to project outside the sample range. For example, if we want to project for $Y = 75$, the expected value for the quadratic form is –62.42, while for the third-degree polynomial it is 74.6.[4]

It is important to remember that the functional form you choose may give you forecasts that are significantly different from one another, especially for the independent variables *outside the sample range considered in the model* (the range between the highest and the lowest values of the independent variable). In that case, you may not have any objective way of choosing among the different functional forms.

However, even if a higher-order functional form gives you an apparently good fit, there are few, if any, instances in the social sciences that conform to the explosive growth of a higher-order polynomial. Therefore, to repeat my previous suggestion, always use a linear form when in doubt, and never use a functional form higher than the second order.

Returning to our example of predicting housing prices, to specify the functional form, we plotted Price against Area in Figure 12.6. From the plotted data, we decided that the linear form was the best functional form.

Figure 12.6   Relationship between Housing Prices and Covered Area

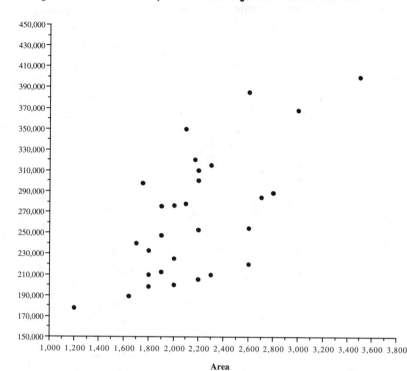

WHEN REGRESSION RESULTS ARE SUSPECT: THE ERRORS OF ESTIMATION

While using regression analyses, a researcher, like the heroes of the Greek epics, can be misled by a number of different errors or may forfeit sound reasoning and be seduced by empirical results that appear to be gorgeous at first glance. However, more careful scrutiny reveals their deceptive nature. Let us discuss the major errors of regression analysis.

Identifying Multicollinearity

One of the premises of the classical least squares method is that the independent variables are not *collinear* (not correlated). In statistical terms this lack of correlation is called *orthogonal*. Take any series of numbers (for example, the square-feet measurements of the various houses in our example). If another variable is created by adding, multiplying, dividing, or subtracting a constant, then these two variables are perfectly correlated and are called perfectly collinear with each other. Hence, in our housing price equation, if we add another variable that measures the covered area in square meters, then we have created a situation of perfect **multicollinearity,** since this new variable is a multiple of the old variable. The presence of perfect multicollinearity prevents us from deriving any estimate of the slope coefficients.[5] Let me explain why. Let us suppose that we are trying to estimate the following equation:

$$Y = a + bX + cZ + \varepsilon \qquad\qquad (12.10)$$

where X and Z are two highly correlated (collinear) independent variables.

You may visualize the effects of multicollinearity with the help of the Venn diagram in Figure 12.7.

Let us go back to our example of estimating housing price. Suppose that we have included two independent variables: the square feet of the house (Area) and the number of bathrooms (Bathrooms). As you can see from this diagram, the two independent variables explain the dependent variable. The parts of Housing Price that are explained by the two independent variables are the overlapping areas. However, if you compare this figure with Figure 12.2, you will see that in this case the problem is that the two independent variables overlap each other to a large extent. This result is caused by the simple fact that the larger a house is, the more bathrooms it is likely to have. This is the problem of multicollinearity.

To explain the problem, I have marked the areas of intersection separately. The part of Housing Price that is explained exclusively by each of the two independent variables, Area and Bathrooms, is labeled A and B, respectively. The segment that is jointly explained is marked a + b. Finally, the portion of the figure that is a simple overlap between the two independent variables, without any implication for the explanation of Housing Price, is labeled A' + B'. As we have seen before, R^2 is measured by the ratio [A + (a + b) + B] / (total area of Housing Price).

The problem of multicollinearity shows up in the estimation of the coefficients. If there is a high degree of multicollinearity among the independent variables, we encounter two significant problems: First, we face the problem of estimating the "true" coefficients of the individual independent variables. Thus, in Figure 12.7, while calculating the relation between Housing Price and Area, regression analysis

Figure 12.7   Multicollinearity and Its Effects on R^2

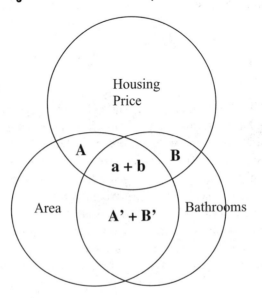

concentrates only on segment A. Because it cannot disentangle the area (a + b) co-explained by the two independent variables, the regression model ignores area (a + b). As a result, *the estimated coefficients turn out to be smaller and more statistically insignificant than they would be if only one of these variables were introduced without the other.*

Second, multicollinearity enlarges the standard error of the estimated coefficients. *As a result the calculated* t *values can become highly questionable* (see Figure 12.8).

Computing a multiple regression is extremely time consuming, so the formulas for calculating regression coefficients for multiple regression models are not included in this book. However, for the purposes of exposition, I would like to point out that when there is more than one independent variable, the estimated standard error of slope coefficients is obtained with the following formula:

$$ SE(b) = \sqrt{\frac{\sum_{i=1}^{n} e_i^2 / (N-K)}{\sum_{i=2}^{n} \left(X_i - \overline{X}_1\right)\left(1 - r^2_{XZ}\right)}} \qquad (12.11) $$

where e_i^2 is the error sum of squares,

N is the number of observations,

K is the number of independent variables, and

r^2_{XZ} is the square of the correlation coefficient between the two independent variables, X and Z.

From the preceding formula you can see that when there is no correlation between X and Z (that is, when $r^2_{XZ} = 0$), the term $(1 - r^2_{XZ})$ in the denominator is equal to 1. Therefore, the estimated standard error of the estimated regression coefficient b is at its minimum.

Figure 12.8   The Effects of Multicollinearity on the Standard Errors of Estimation

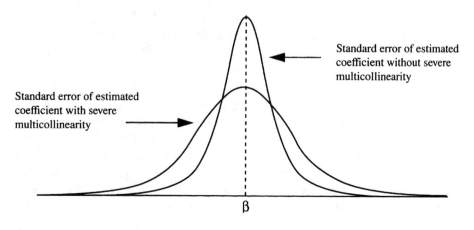

Standard error of estimated coefficient without severe multicollinearity

Standard error of estimated coefficient with severe multicollinearity

β

However, as the correlation between X and Z becomes stronger, the correlation coefficient, r^2_{XZ}, approaches 1. If there is a perfect correlation, this term equals 1. In that case the denominator of the estimated standard error equals 0, which makes the standard error infinite. This result makes the estimation of the standard error of the regression coefficients impossible.

In real life we seldom encounter perfect collinearity between two independent variables unless they are the same variable, simply expressed in two different measurement units. If we accidentally use two perfectly collinear independent variables, our computer software will warn us by posting an error message. What the software cannot tell us, though, is where there is less than perfect correlation. This situation, as we can deduce from the preceding equation, will make our estimated standard error more widely dispersed, as shown in Figure 12.8.

What is the immediate effect of this increasing dispersion of the error term of the estimated coefficients? As you may recall, the t values for the estimated coefficients are calculated by dividing the coefficient by its standard error (see equation 11.11 in the previous chapter). Therefore, this increase in the error term will reduce the t value, causing the researcher to reject an otherwise significant independent variable as insignificant.

You may note that despite multicollinearity, the estimated coefficients will remain unbiased, as Figure 12.8 indicates. In other words, in our example of housing prices, we estimated the regression coefficients with the help of thirty observations. This calculation gave us an estimate of the true value of β. If we considered another sample group of houses and re-estimated the same equation, we would get another estimate of this elusive β. If we continued to repeat this experiment, the distribution of the estimated values of β would have a mean, which would get closer and closer to the true value of β. You may recall that this is the property of unbiasedness in the classical least squares method. The presence of multicollinearity does not make our estimated coefficients biased. Therefore, this property of least squares is not violated.

Since the variance of the distribution of the estimated coefficients goes up with increasing levels of multicollinearity, including a collinear variable will cause the estimates to fluctuate widely. If we include an independent variable that is highly correlated with another independent variable in the model, the variables' estimated coefficients will become extremely sensitive and will change dramatically each time the equation is run with a slightly different set of independent variables. *However, this extreme sensitivity will not affect those independent variables that are not highly correlated with this new variable.*

The presence of multicollinearity does not affect the measures of overall goodness of fit. That is, R^2 and F values in an equation with a high degree of multicollinearity will be unaffected. Consider our example of estimating home prices. Suppose we include two other variables in the model, the number of bathrooms (Bathrooms) and the total, as opposed to covered, land area (Land). Suppose that these homes are all located in the same tract-home development and therefore the total land area is highly correlated with the covered area. So is the number of bathrooms. These new variables are presented in Table 12.4. Let us explore the

Table 12.4 Housing Prices and Multicollinearity

Price	Area (square feet)	Bathrooms	View	Cul-de-Sac	Land (square feet)
$310,000	2,200	3.5	1	1	4,170
233,000	1,800	2.5	0	0	3,330
400,000	3,500	5.0	1	0	6,175
430,000	3,200	4.0	1	1	6,000
210,000	1,800	2.0	0	0	3,330
240,000	1,700	2.0	1	1	3,045
300,000	2,200	3.0	0	1	4,090
350,000	2,100	3.0	1	1	3,885
385,000	2,600	4.5	1	1	4,810
368,000	3,000	4.5	0	0	5,650
200,000	2,000	2.5	0	0	3,777
298,000	1,750	2.0	1	1	3,237
275,000	1,900	2.5	0	1	3,500
198,000	1,800	1.5	0	0	3,330
253,000	2,200	3.0	1	0	4,100
278,000	2,100	3.0	1	1	3,885
320,000	2,170	3.5	1	1	3,999
178,000	1,200	1.0	1	1	2,220
225,000	2,000	3.0	0	0	3,700
212,000	1,900	2.0	0	1	3,515
288,000	2,800	3.5	0	1	5,280
315,000	2,300	4.0	1	1	4,255
255,000	2,600	3.0	0	1	4,810
284,000	2,700	3.5	1	0	4,995
189,000	1,640	2.0	1	0	3,034
220,000	2,600	3.0	0	0	4,810
248,000	1,900	2.5	1	0	3,515
276,000	2,000	3.5	1	1	3,700
210,000	2,300	3.0	0	0	4,255
205,000	2,200	2.5	0	0	4,070

effects of including these highly correlated independent variables in the model. The results of the newly estimated equation are as follows:

Price =
33,268.056 + 29.92 Area + 30,137 View + 38,598.56 Cul-de-Sac
$$+ 10.24 \text{ Land} + 31,879.62 \text{ Bathrooms}$$
$$(12.12)$$

t value
    (1.10)   (0.19)   (2.24)*   (3.15)* (0.12)*   (2.29)
$R^2 = 0.825$ Adjusted $R^2 = 0.788$
$F(5,24) = 22.58*$
$N = 30$
* Significant at 0.05 level.

By comparing the results of equation 12.12 with those of equation 12.3, we can see the impact of severe multicollinearity. The most affected variable is Area, which is highly correlated with the newly introduced variables Land and Bathrooms. Although the estimated coefficients and their respective *t* values for the other two independent variables (View and Cul-de-Sac) remained relatively unchanged, the estimated coefficient for Area was significantly reduced, and its error term greatly increased, causing a precipitous drop in the *t* value. You also may notice that the R^2 value was not affected by including the highly correlated independent variables.

Once you understand the problems caused by multicollinearity, the question becomes how to detect it and what to do about it. You should note that multicollinearity should be suspected if you have *high R^2* values but lousy *t* values.

To detect which independent variables are collinear, you should calculate the correlation matrix among the independent variables. Most software packages can provide you with the matrix of correlation coefficients shown in Table 12.5.

Each entry in the table shows the correlation coefficient between the row and column variables. For example, the correlation between Bathrooms and Area is 0.867. The diagonal numbers are all 1.000 because, by definition, each variable has a perfect correlation with itself. You can see that three of the independent variables—Area, Bathrooms, and Land—are highly correlated with each other. This would account for the multicollinearity in the estimated equation.[6]

Resolving Multicollinearity

Multicollinearity poses a dilemma for the analyst. If there is severe multicollinearity between two independent variables, one of the best ways to resolve the problem is to eliminate one of the variables. However, if the eliminated variable happens to be an important variable in explaining the dependent variable, then by eliminating it we will cause specification error with its accompanying problems. Further, as we have noted, multicollinearity among a partial list of independent variables will not affect the other variables, nor will the error term be biased.

Researchers often choose not to do anything about multicollinearity unless the problem is acute. Looking at the correlation coefficients of our previous example,

Table 12.5 Correlation Matrix

	Area	*Bathrooms*	*View*	*Cul-de-Sac*	*Time*	*Land*
Area	1.000					
Bathrooms	0.867	1.000				
View	−0.003	0.208	1.000			
Cul-de-Sac	−0.078	0.060	0.330	1.000		
Time	−0.079	0.035	0.289	0.237	1.000	
Land	0.997	0.864	−0.022	−0.069	−0.092	1.000

I would be inclined to include the number of bathrooms in the model because it happens to be one of the vital considerations in determining the price of a home. On the other hand, I would reason that with a correlation coefficient of 0.997, Land is not adding much to the explanation of market price beyond that provided by Area. I would specify the model by including Bathrooms but eliminating Land. As you can tell, this decision is purely a line call based on subjective judgment.

Econometricians have tried to walk the tight rope between being comprehensive—including all the important information—and avoiding severe multicollinearity. Although balancing these competing objectives is a matter of subjective judgment and comes through years of practice, you can improve your chances of success immediately by following these practical steps for eliminating multicollinearity among the independent variables:

1. *In certain circumstances the two independent variables can be added together.* This newly created variable will contain information from both variables and may add to the explanation without contributing the problems of multicollinearity. This trick may work provided the two variables do not have opposite expected signs or are not significantly different in magnitude. Suppose we are adding two highly correlated independent variables, X and Z, to form a new variable. If X is positively related to the dependent variable Y while Z is negatively related (X and Z are negatively correlated with each other), the newly created variable will have little explanatory capability because the positive relation will be offset by the negative one. Adding independent variables also will not work if one of the variables has a substantially higher mean than do the others. In this case the smaller variable will be lost in the larger variable, and the linear combination of the two will not provide any more insight into the variation of the dependent variable. Further, the newly created variable may not have any intuitive meaning. For example, for a completely different purpose, economist Arthur Okun created an index by adding the unemployment rate and the rate of inflation, calling the sum the "misery index." This composite measurement has a readily understandable meaning. In contrast, if we add Area and Land, this composite variable may not convey any definite meaning to policy makers (in this case, the property owners).

2. *For time-series data, the problem of multicollinearity can also be solved if you take the first difference.* That is, you create a new variable by subtracting the preceding time period's data from those of the current period. Suppose we are trying to forecast the sales tax revenue for a state government. We have chosen as independent variables the growth rate of per capita state income and the rate of unemployment. But in formulating our model we find that there is a strong negative correlation between these variables (that is, during prosperous times, when the income growth rate is high, unemployment is low, and vice versa). Therefore, we cannot add these two variables together. A way out may be to use the yearly difference in the unemployment rate, which may not have as strong a correlation with the growth rate of per capita income as does the absolute level of unemployment. However, even this method is not a panacea for correcting multicollinearity. Similar to the problem of creating a composite variable, using the yearly difference of a

variable may not have the same meaning (or even any meaning) as an independent variable. Even after getting a high t value and R^2, we may be at a loss to explain our results in a meaningful way.

3. *Finally, another (and probably the least controversial) way of dealing with multicollinearity is to increase the sample size.* If doing so is a viable alternative, it is certainly worth pursuing. If the two variables are not simply multiples of each other (perfectly correlated), then as the number of observations increases, the natural variations within the series will sufficiently distinguish themselves and allow the proper estimation of the model. In our example of housing prices, if we can increase the sample size from thirty to, say, three hundred, the variations within the two series may distinguish themselves enough to allow us to estimate the model properly.

Identifying Serial Correlation

Serial correlation (also known as **autocorrelation**) means that the order in which the observations are arranged has some effect on the estimation of the regression coefficients. In other words, serial correlation exists if the error of one observation depends on that of the previous one. An example may clarify the point. Many cities across the nation want to reduce lawsuits stemming from work-related injuries. The job of a risk manager is to curtail such lawsuits by offering adequate training to his or her workers. However, the training programs are expensive, so some cities establish a benchmark for the amount of workers' compensation paid out each year. If a city pays more than the specified amount this year, it will invest more money in the training program next year. On the other hand, if the city pays less than this benchmark amount, less money will be allocated for training the following year. Before initiating this benchmark program, the allocation of money followed other guidelines, and the error term from the equation explaining expenditure on training showed a random pattern. I have shown the hypothetical distribution of the error term in Figure 12.9, in which the trend line over time is a flat horizontal line.

However, after introducing the benchmark program, the error terms were correlated with the past year's term. That is, if the yearly compensation overshot the target, more money flowed into the training program; if it undershot, money was taken away from the program. Situations such as these, in which the current year's performance is predicated upon that of the previous year, show serial correlation. In contrast to Figure 12.9, in which the error terms are randomly distributed, Figure 12.10 shows two kinds of serial correlation: **positive** and **negative.** If the current period's error term generally shows the same sign as error terms of previous periods, then the series is said to have a positive serial correlation. Thus, if a public policy affects the course of the economy for a number of years (as did Proposition 13, the California initiative that cut property taxes and restricted the abilities of local governments to raise and spend money), the series shows positive serial correlation.

In contrast, if a series shows alternately positive and negative error terms, it demonstrates negative serial correlation. In this case the error terms oscillate back

Figure 12.9 Distribution of Errors Showing No Serial Correlation

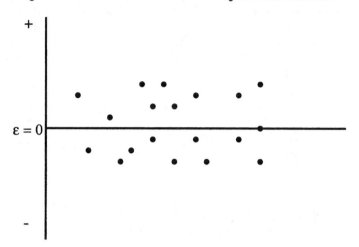

and forth like a pendulum. The equation explaining spending on the benchmark program may exhibit a negative serial correlation.

A correlation between successive error terms violates one of the fundamental principles of the least squares method. The most widely used method for detecting serial correlation is the **Durbin-Watson** *d* test.[7] This test applies only in the following cases:

1. The regression model includes an intercept term.
2. The error terms have a first-order correlation, meaning that each year's error is correlated only with that of the preceding year and not with the errors of the previous two or three years. In symbolic terms this can be written as

$$e_t = \rho e_{t-1} + \varepsilon \tag{12.13}$$

Figure 12.10 Serial Correlation

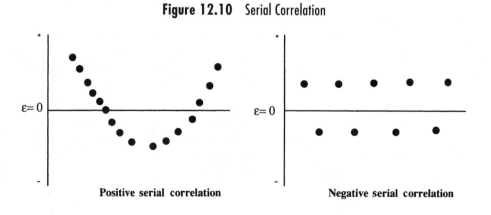

Positive serial correlation   Negative serial correlation

where e_t is the residual (estimated error term) in year t,

e_{t-1} is the residual (estimated error term) in the previous year $(t-1)$,

ρ is the correlation coefficient, and

ε is the true random error term.

3. The regression model does not include a lagged dependent term.

The Durbin-Watson d statistic is defined as

$$d = \frac{\sum_{t=2}^{n}(e_t - e_{t-1})^2}{\sum_{i=1}^{n}e_t^{\,2}}$$

(12.14)

The d statistic varies between 4 and 0. If there is perfect positive serial correlation ($\rho = 1$), e_t is the same as e_{t-1}, and the numerator becomes zero. In other words, with a perfect positive correlation the d statistic $= 0$. If, on the other hand, there is perfect negative correlation ($\rho = -1$), then the numerator becomes $4\sum e_t^{\,2}$. In that case equation 12.14 becomes

$$\frac{4\sum e_t^{\,2}}{\sum e_t^{\,2}} = 4.$$

If there is no serial correlation at all, the d statistic is equal to 2. Hence, if the d statistic is close to either 0 or 4, you should suspect serial correlation.

Unfortunately, the correction for serial correlation is beyond the scope of this introductory textbook. If you are interested in knowing more about these problems, you may consult one of many excellent texts on econometrics.[8]

Heteroskedasticity: The Problem of Scaling Variables

One of the important conditions for the least squares method is that the variability (standard deviation) of the error term of the observations does not vary with the size of the dependent variable. This is the condition of **homoskedasticity.** Figure 12.11 demonstrates the implication of this assumption.

As you can see, the variance of the error term corresponding to the three observations of the dependent variable X falls within the same band. However, this happy situation may not hold true if the independent variables vary a great deal with the size of the dependent variable. In that case, as the scale of the dependent variable increases, so does the variability of the error term. This situation of increasing variability of the error term is called **heteroskedasticity** and is shown in Figure 12.12.

Heteroskedasticity, therefore, is caused essentially by mixing apples with oranges in the data set, and is typically encountered in cross-section models. Suppose we are trying to account for urban crime in America. If our data set contains the number of high crimes committed in large cities, along with those perpetrated

Figure 12.11 Homoskedastic Distribution of Errors

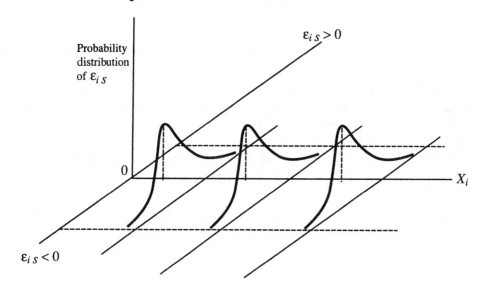

in small towns in primarily agricultural states, we are likely to encounter heteroskedasticity. If the model is not properly specified, then differences in the variance of the error terms may result. This is called **impure heteroskedasticity.** If, on
the other hand, despite the best specification of the model, the error terms show
signs of heteroskedasticity, this is known as **pure heteroskedasticity.**

Figure 12.12 Heteroskedastic Distribution of Errors

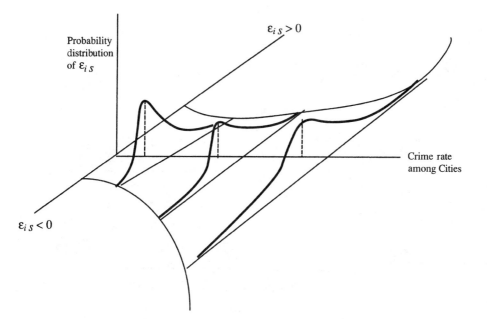

Detecting Heteroskedasticity

Heteroskedasticity can be visually inspected by plotting the error terms. If we do not have heteroskedasticity, the errors will be distributed randomly around 0.0. However, if it is present, the errors will show a flaring-out pattern, as in Figure 12.13.

To explain the point, let us return to our example of estimating housing prices. Using the results of equation 12.3, we have obtained the predicted value for each of the homes in the sample. The difference between the actual and the predicted value is the error term. The error terms of the housing price data have been plotted in Figure 12.14.

The plot in Figure 12.14 does not indicate overwhelming heteroskedasticity since the housing prices are fairly close to each other. Now suppose we included in

Figure 12.13   Hypothetical Errors Showing Presence and Absence of Heteroskedasticity

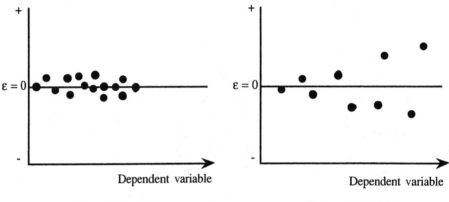

Figure 12.14   Error Terms of Housing Price Data

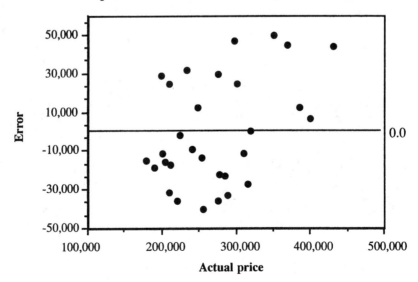

the sample data an adjoining but dissimilar neighborhood. Whereas the original sample contains data from an upper-middle-class area, the next sample is from a decidedly more affluent one.

The expanded data set, with ten new entries of extremely high-priced homes, is presented in Table 12.6. In this table we have included a column of predicted

Table 12.6 Housing Prices with Data for a Dissimilar Neighborhood

Observations	Price	Predicted price	Error (residuals)
1	$310,000	$320,733	−10,733
2	233,000	168,067	64,933
3	400,000	422,349	−22,349
4	430,000	436,803	−6,803
5	210,000	168,067	41,933
6	240,000	262,698	−22,698
7	300,000	263,770	36,230
8	350,000	309,126	40,874
9	385,000	367,161	17,839
10	368,000	307,351	60,649
11	200,000	191,281	8,719
12	298,000	268,501	29,498
13	275,000	228,949	46,051
14	198,000	168,067	29,933
15	253,000	271,458	−18,458
16	278,000	309,126	−31,126
17	320,000	317,251	2,749
18	178,000	204,663	−26,663
19	225,000	191,281	33,719
20	212,000	228,949	−16,949
21	288,000	333,412	−45,412
22	315,000	332,340	−17,340
23	255,000	310,198	−55,198
24	284,000	329,493	45,493
25	189,000	206,458	−17,459
26	220,000	260,923	−40,923
27	248,000	236,637	11,363
28	276,000	297,519	−21,519
29	210,000	226,102	−16,102
30	205,000	214,495	−9,495
31	535,000	548,433	−13,433
32	648,000	640,217	7,783
33	656,000	606,468	49,532
34	802,000	814,322	−12,322
35	735,000	724,313	10,687
36	546,000	658,699	−112,699
37	762,900	944,846	−181,946
38	485,000	546,637	−61,637
39	942,000	979,667	−37,667
40	1,250,000	898,418	351,582

values of house prices by using the specification of equation 12.15 and adding a dummy variable for the two communities. The newly created dummy variable for the moderately priced community (Com) is 0, and it is one for the wealthy community. The estimated equation is as follows:

Price =
–40,859.71 + 116.07 Area + 56,963.41 View + 49,275 Cul-de-Sac + 275,903.98 Com
t value   (12.15)
  (0.94)   (6.20)*   (2.11)*   (1.88)*   (6.73)*
R^2 = 0.905 Adjusted R^2 = 0.894
$F(4,35)$ = 83.57*
N = 40
* Significant at 0.05 level.

The column "Predicted price" was created using this formula. The error terms were calculated by subtracting the predicted price from the actual price (Price).

The terms shown in the "Error" column of Table 12.6 have been plotted against Price in Figure 12.15. By comparing this figure with the previous one (Figure 12.14), you can clearly see that the introduction to the sample of high-priced homes has created heteroskedasticity.

Effects of Heteroskedasticity

Pure heteroskedasticity can increase the variance of the estimated coefficients in a way that will cause the t and F values to come out stronger than what is warranted by the data. Therefore, though the estimates will remain unbiased, all the measures of hypothesis testing will be suspect. On the other hand, if there is impure heteroskedasticity resulting from a poor specification of the equation, its impact on the estimators will be similar to the effect of serial correlation discussed earlier.

Correcting Heteroskedasticity

The error of heteroskedasticity is primarily caused by a variable that is too diverse. For that reason, heteroskedasticity should be suspected in cross-section data with samples varying greatly in size. Time-series data stretching over a long period of time is also suspect, as are data series in which the magnitude of the dependent variable is increasing with time at a very high rate. If we are trying to predict the number of homicides in our city based on the number of homicides committed this year in a large number of diverse cities and towns, we are likely to encounter heteroskedasticity. Also, it is likely to exist in time-series data showing the number of individuals infected with the deadly and rapidly spreading AIDS virus, since the actual number of infected individuals keeps increasing every year.

Heteroskedasticity can be detected with the help of some of the more sophisticated tests, which are beyond the scope of this introductory book. However, we may say a few words about correcting heteroskedasticity at this point. First, if het-

Figure 12.15   Error Terms Showing Heteroskedasticity

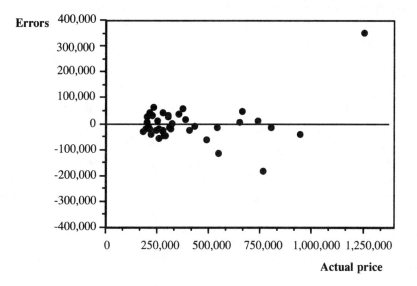

eroskedasticity is impure, it can be corrected simply by specifying the model better. To repeat our discussion of proper specification, developing a better model requires a great deal of hard work in thinking through the proper theoretical structure.

If, on the other hand, heteroskedasticity is pure, the very nature of the data causes the variance of the error terms to change, and we need to think about the dependent variable. For example, if we encounter strong heteroskedasticity in trying to work with data on the number of homicides in cities and towns across the nation, we may separate the sample into two groups: large cities and small towns. Or we may express the absolute numbers in ratios, such as homicide rate per one thousand inhabitants. Sometimes these kinds of data transformation can reduce the variance to such an extent that heteroskedasticity can be significantly reduced.

When the Data Are Imperfect

Finally, in forecasting with regression models, serious errors occur when the data are spurious. In statistics this situation is known as the **error in variable,** or the measurement problem. The problem can creep in because of various factors. Many sociological data, when available, often contain severe measurement errors. Thus, information on child and wife abuse, rape, and incest are significantly underrepresented. Even economic data, such as unemployment or inflation figures, are often criticized for containing biases of all sorts. Unemployment data are typically collected by adding the numbers of all those who registered at unemployment offices. This list, then, does not include those whose unemployment benefits have run out, students or homemakers seeking employment for the first time, or the underemployed (those who are working at levels far below their capabilities, such as an engineer working as a waiter in a restaurant). The data on inflation are computed by comparing the prices of items in a basket of goods a "typical" consumer would buy. Because of wide differences in consumption habits, the inflation figures published by the Bureau of Labor Statistics are likely to affect individuals differently.

Therefore, when data containing biases are used in a regression model, the accuracy of statistical explanation and prediction is affected. Errors can occur if the dependent variable is biased or if there is measurement error in the independent variable as well. If the dependent variable contains measurement error but the independent variable is generally free of it, and the bias is random, then the measurement error will increase the errors of prediction while the estimated coefficients remain unbiased. Thus, the predicted results will have more variation, although the estimated coefficients will be unbiased. In other words, if we were to repeat the experiment a sufficient number of times with different samples, the average of all the estimated coefficients would approach the actual coefficient. Theoretically at least, this is a lesser problem than the one caused by an error in the independent variable.

If the independent variables contain measurement biases, bias spreads through the error term (e) in the estimated equation, and this problem cannot be corrected easily. In effect, this bias in the independent variable will cause the independent variable to be correlated with the error term (e).[9]

Beta Coefficient: Measuring the Relative Strength of the Independent Variables

The regression coefficients measure the slope of the independent variable in explaining the dependent variable. However, the size of the coefficient depends on the relative size of the independent variable. If you use actual years as independent variables (for example, 2001, 2002, 2003, and so on) the estimated coefficient will be much smaller than if you use time (1, 2, 3, and so forth). This change does not affect the R^2 or the t and F values. It simply adjusts the absolute size of the coefficient to fit the relationship. Thus, when we estimate a quadratic relationship ($Y = a + bX + cX^2$), the estimated coefficient c turns out to be a lot smaller than b.

This dependence of the coefficients on the size of the independent variables may pose a problem for someone interested in finding out the relative strength of the independent variables in explaining the dependent variable. One way to determine this relative strength is to **standardize** the variables. You can standardize a variable by calculating

$$SD\left(X_i\right) = \frac{X_i - \overline{X}}{S} \tag{12.16}$$

where
$SD(X_i)$ = the standardized values of the variable X,
$\overline{X}$ = the mean of X_i, and
S = the standard deviation of X_i.

A CASE IN POINT

Exploring the Effects of Red Tape on Caseworkers' Behavior

Although we mention death and taxes as the only two certainties in life, we might safely claim a third—bureaucratic red tape. A study exploring the impact of red tape on a client's benefits claims yielded interesting conclusions.[1] The data for the study were based on a simulated training session for newly hired caseworkers in a local public assistance agency. The subjects—a group of forty-nine graduate students and forty-seven social workers—were given "background case histories" of four hypothetical clients seeking public assistance. Using these materials, they recommended benefits for each of the clients. The subjects met in small groups. After familiarizing themselves with the requirements and mission of a social service agency, they were asked to review the clients' needs.

To isolate the effects of red tape, the subjects were randomly assigned high or low procedural requirements. Subjects receiving high requirements (red tape) were asked to fill out separate forms for each supplemental benefit or service they recommended. Moreover, the subjects were required to provide a narrative justification for their recommendations. In contrast, those who received the low red tape cases were required to fill out a simple checklist of recommended benefits with corresponding dollar amounts. Clients who had to go through high red tape were assigned the value of one, whereas those who did not were given a value of zero.

Besides being subjected to red tape, the subjects also were tested for "compassion." Each subject was given two pairs of male and female clients. Each pair was eligible for the same amount of benefits, but one pair's background was described in such a way as to evoke compassion, while the other's was written so as to elicit no compassion. Those clients whose history was designed to evoke compassion were assigned a value of one, and the others received a value of zero. Since there were two distinct groups of subjects, an independent variable called Professional Field was created by assigning zeros to the public administration students and ones to the professional social workers. Finally, the male subjects were scored as zeros and the females as ones.

Researchers wanted to know how individuals make decisions, so they specified the model fully by considering several characteristics of the subjects, such as education (years after high school). Also, using a rating scale, researchers gave each subject scores for altruism (the higher the score, the greater the subject's tendency toward sympathy and concern for others), locus of control (personal efficacy and interpersonal and sociopolitical control), and rule orientation (tendency to strictly follow the letter of the law).

Researchers regressed these eight independent variables against the dependent variable, the total dollar value of the benefits granted by subjects to clients. The table shows the regression results, which were computed separately for female and male clients.

From the table you can draw the following conclusions:

- You should consider only the statistically significant coefficients, Red Tape and Compassion.

Independent variables	Female clients			Male clients		
	Unstandardized coefficient	Standardized coefficient (beta)	t value	Unstandardized coefficient	Standardized coefficient (beta)	t value
Red Tape	−261.34	−0.36	−5.28**	−175.07	−0.40	−5.88**
Compassion	245.93	0.34	5.35**	92.80	0.21	3.35**
Professional Field	87.89	0.12	1.66	57.93	0.13	1.82
Years of Education	19.92	0.11	1.53	14.76	0.14	1.88
Altruism	2.28	0.07	1.03	1.74	0.09	1.30
Locus of Control	0.71	0.03	0.48	0.11	0.01	0.12
Rule Orientation	−2.21	−0.04	−0.59	2.12	0.06	0.93
Gender	11.81	0.02	0.023	11.81	0.08	1.16

Notes: Dependent variable is total dollar value of assistance granted. Adjusted R^2 is 0.25 for females, 0.22 for males.
** Significant at 0.05 level.

- The absolute size of the beta coefficients suggests that the most important independent variable is Red Tape, followed by Compassion.
- The coefficients for Red Tape tell us that, on average, tedious bureaucratic formalities reduce allocations to female clients by $261.34 and those to males by $175.07.
- However, if a female client evokes compassion, she receives $245.93, whereas for males the corresponding figure is $92.80.
- The regression results highlight the subjective nature of decisions on allocating resources, even decisions made by professional social service workers.

Note

1. Patrick G. Scott and Sanjay K. Pandey, "The Influence of Red Tape on Bureaucratic Behavior: An Experimental Simulation," *Journal of Policy Analysis and Management* 19 (2000): 615–633.

Discussion Points

1. What are the policy implications of the estimated results?
2. Given that only two out of eight independent variables turned out to be statistically significant, what conclusions can you draw about the specification of the equation?

Most statistical software packages provide you with the beta coefficient along with the estimated coefficients of the nonstandardized variables. To learn about real-world application of beta coefficients, see "A Case in Point: Exploring the Effects of Red Tape on Caseworkers' Behavior."

SUMMARY: STEP-BY-STEP SUGGESTIONS FOR BUILDING A MODEL OF CAUSAL PREDICTION

1. **Develop a theory.** The first step toward building a causal model is to have an excellent understanding of causality. Do a thorough job of reading the existing literature on the issues. Then, based on your theoretical understanding of the relation between the dependent and independent variables, develop your hypothesis in terms of an implicit model.

2. **Operationalize variables.** Having developed your hypothesis, think of how you can measure the relevant variables. You have to make sure that you are measuring what you intend to measure and nothing else.

3. **Collect clean data.** If there are built-in biases, make sure you are aware of them and can make the necessary adjustments to your model.

4. **Plot the dependent variable against each independent variable.** To formulate the explicit functional form, plot the dependent variable against the independent variables. Determine which form is most appropriate.

5. **Estimate** the regression equation and make necessary adjustments to omit unnecessary variables and include necessary ones.

6. **Check for multicollinearity.** Calculate the correlation matrix. If the problem of multicollinearity is not acute, leave it alone. Otherwise, see if you can pick one variable from the collinear ones to represent the set. Also see if adding the variables or taking the first difference makes theoretical sense.

7. If there is reason, **check for heteroskedasticity.**

8. **Check for serial correlation.** Use Durbin-Watson statistics, if available.

9. **Present estimation results clearly** and draw conclusions.

10. **Explain all the assumptions** and point out the possible sources of biases in your conclusions.

Tips: Go for parsimony. If two models explain approximately the same amount, choose the one with fewer variables. Moreover, **keep it simple.** Unless a more complicated functional form is truly necessary, choose the simpler one. While forecasting the future, remember that the error of estimation will flare out as you move away from the sample mean. Therefore, the difficulty of making accurate predictions increases exponentially as you go farther into the future.

Key Words

Operationalize (p. 294)
Positive serial correlation (p. 314)
Pure heteroskedasticity (p. 317)

Serial correlation (p. 299)
Specification of a model (p. 291)
Standardized variables (p. 322)

Exercises

1. What is causal prediction? What are its advantages over trend projection? What are its relative shortcomings?

2. Refer to our estimated model of housing price in equation 12.3, then comment on the following four units presently on the market:

Area	View	Cul-de-Sac	Asking price
a. 2,500	yes	no	$295,000
b. 3,200	yes	yes	$325,000
c. 1,500	no	no	$162,000
d. 1,950	no	yes	$182,000

To explain housing prices more thoroughly, what are some other variables you would include in the model?

3. Suppose you have been asked to forecast the crime rate of your city. You have decided to use a cross-sectional model of fifty-five cities across the nation.

   a. What measure of the dependent variable would you use?
   b. Which variables would you include as the independent variables, and what signs for their coefficients would you postulate?
   c. What would be the source(s) of your information?
   d. Explain the various statistical problems that you would face while estimating this model.
   e. What actions would you take to correct these problems?

4. Suppose your state legislature is considering legalizing a state-run lottery. One aspect of the lottery that is under scrutiny is the demographic profile of the prospective players. A survey of total yearly purchases of lottery tickets by 500 participants in a neighboring state shows the following relation:

Total purchases = 10.51 − 0.086 PI + 1.23 Age − 0.162 Ed + 2.59 Min + 3.05 Male
t value   (6.78) (3.67)   (2.46)   (2.01)   (2.01)   (1.14)
R^2 = 0.68 Adjusted R^2 = 0.59
$F(5, 494)$ = 189.95
N = 500

where
PI = personal income (in $000),
Age = age of the lottery player,
Ed = years of education,
Min = dummy variable with minority = 1, nonminority = 0, and
Male = dummy variable with male = 1, female = 0.

a. Write a detailed report explaining the results.
b. What are the important policy implications that the legislators should be aware of?
c. What are some of the other independent variables that could have been included?
d. Based on this estimated model, how much are you expected to spend on lottery per month?

5. The water utility department of your town has estimated the following model of water use per capita:

PWU = 15.64 + 1.86 Y + 3.29 CH + 2.87 AD + 0.029 SQ + 0.009 LS
t value   (2.39) (7.85)   (3.99)   (1.99)   (2.53)   (2.01)
$R^2 = 0.76$ Adjusted $R^2 = 0.74$
$F(5, 344) = 189.95$
$N = 350$

where PWU = per capita water use (in gallons),
Y = income per household (in $000),
CH = number of children in the house,
AD = number of adults in the house,
SQ = square feet of covered area, and
LS = lot size (land area).

Interpret this equation and write a report explaining the significance of these findings.

6. What are the possible sources of bias in the estimation of a classical least squares method? Explain the terms *multicollinearity, heteroskedasticity,* and *serial correlation.* Discuss how you would detect them in an estimated relationship. What are some of the ways of eliminating multicollinearity and heteroskedasticity?

7. Suppose there are fifteen counties in your state. You are given the current year's sales tax revenue and a number of independent variables. Estimate the equation and, based on the projected growth of the independent variables, forecast the state's total sales tax revenue five years from now. Also, comment on the relative size of the beta coefficients. (Hint: Estimate the equation, examine it for various errors, and, based on the correct specification, re-estimate the equation. Using the revised equation, forecast each county's tax revenue and then add the county revenue figures to forecast the state's tax revenue).

	Current year's data				Forecasted data	
				Land area		
			Per capita	devoted to		
	Tax revenue	Population	income	agriculture	Population	Per capita
County	($million)	(000)	($000)	(percent)	(000)	income ($000)
A	38.7	50.0	23.2	60.0	52.0	24.0
B	156.0	75.0	32.8	20.0	86.5	36.2
C	115.9	151.1	22.1	75.0	153.0	22.8
D	98.7	45.6	36.9	15.0	54.0	39.7
E	68.3	98.0	24.1	62.0	101.0	24.9

F	220.8	94.0	36.0	18.0	99.0	38.6
G	75.2	102.9	23.0	62.0	105.0	23.2
H	268.8	91.7	41.0	3.0	110.0	46.2
I	32.1	65.0	21.9	82.0	61.0	22.1
J	69.2	47.1	34.6	59.7	49.5	33.6
K	199.9	98.0	35.6	21.0	106.0	37.8
L	86.0	110.0	23.8	58.0	111.8	24.3
M	112.8	202.0	25.0	66.0	198.0	25.0
N	209.0	85.3	40.1	5.0	96.7	46.5
O	116.0	66.0	39.0	22.0	121.0	41.2

Notes

1. For an excellent discussion of computer assisted mass appraisal of property value, see Glen Fisher, *The Worst Tax? A History of the Property Tax in America* (Lawrence: University of Kansas Press, 1996), 176–186. See also J. Richard Aronson and Eli Schwartz, *Management Policies in Local Government Finance*, 4th ed. (Washington, D.C.: International City/County Management Association, 1996), 211.
2. In most states property tax is 1 percent of the assessed value.
3. I did not write the formula for deriving multiple regression coefficients. The formula is complex, and calculating it is extremely time consuming. For estimating multiple correlation, you should familiarize yourself with available statistical packages. There are a number of excellent and "user-friendly" software programs, of which SPSS and Minitab are perhaps the most widely used.
4. Our problem has been compounded by the fact that we have a percentage measure as a dependent variable and are therefore restricted between zero and one. However, even without this restriction, higher-order polynomials can quickly ascend or descend to absurd levels of prediction, particularly for the values of the independent variable outside the sample range.
5. You may test this statement by creating a linearly dependent variable and then including both independent variables in a regression model. Most software will give you an error message stating that the coefficients cannot be computed. A few software programs will give you highly imprecise estimates due to rounding error.
6. The presence of multicollinearity is best determined by the test of variance inflation factor. However, this test is a bit too complicated for this book. See O. E. Farrat and R. R. Glauber, "Multicollinearity in Regression Analysis: The Problem Revisited," *Review of Economics and Statistics* (1967): 92–107; D. A. Belsley, E. Kuh, and R. E. Welsch, *Regression Diagnostics: Identifying Influential Data and Sources of Collinearity* (New York: Wiley, 1980). For an excellent overall discussion, see A. H. Studenmund, *Using Econometrics: A Practical Guide*, 2d ed. (New York: Harper Collins, 1992).
7. This test is based on J. Durbin and G. S. Watson, "Testing for Serial Correlation in Least-Square Regression," *Biometrica* (1951): 159–177.
8. See, for example, Harry H. Kelejian and Wallace E. Oates, *Introduction to Econometrics: Principles and Applications* (New York: Harper and Row, 1981); and Studenmund, *Using Econometrics*.
9. This situation will be close to the simultaneous bias. However, the bias of simultaneity has been deliberately left out of this introductory book. Without

explanation, I will simply state that this bias can be corrected by using the instrumental variable approach. If you are interested in learning more about this problem, see Peter Kennedy (1998). Also see Studenmund, *Using Econometrics,* or R. Pindyck and D. Rubinfeld, *Econometric Models and Econometric Forecasts* (New York: McGraw-Hill, 1981).

13

THE ELEMENTS OF STRATEGIC THINKING: DECISION TREE AND GAME THEORY

In March 1976 President Gerald Ford had a problem. Epidemiologists were concerned about a virulent form of the influenza virus, swine flu, which had broken out at Fort Dix, New Jersey. Experts feared that this new strain would hit the larger population of the United States in the fall, during flu season. Many scientists suggested that the flu was related to a strain that in 1918–1919 had caused a worldwide epidemic and had taken twenty million lives.

Quickly mutating flu viruses are nightmares for health care professionals. To counter the threat of influenza, manufacturers reproduce strains of the virus in laboratories, incubate them in eggs, and turn them into vaccines. When injected into humans, these harmless viruses become part of the shield that protects the body from natural viruses. But viruses play hide and seek with researchers by mutating, making them impervious to inoculation. To compound the problem, the protective virus must be reproduced *before* the actual infestation takes place. If people are already infected, there is not much a doctor can do. Therefore, President Ford needed to decide whether to do nothing or to start a massive inoculation program for the entire population, especially people who fall in the high-risk category (for example, the elderly and those with lung ailments or other chronic health problems). If he chose to do nothing, and the worst fears of the experts were realized, the nation would face a public health catastrophe of unparalleled proportions. But if the experts were wrong, the president would save a great deal of money. Massive inoculation programs carry high price tags, along with the risk that some people may die from complications related to the injection.

On the other hand, if the swine flu virus infiltrated the general population after the president had assumed the associated risks and ordered a nationwide inoculation program, the president would be admired for his prudence by a grateful public, and this gratitude would translate into a considerable amount of political goodwill for the president. However, if the threat failed to materialize, the president's policy would likely be widely ridiculed for wasting valuable public resources. Place yourself in the president's position. What would you have done? At the root of President Ford's problem was uncertainty. He did not know the future course of the virus. It is natural that a decision maker will frequently face uncertainty. So far, our discussion of how quantitative techniques aid the decision process has not addressed the question of uncertainty. Let us now see how introducing this quirk into the process affects our decisions.

GETTING A GRIP ON UNCERTAINTY

Making decisions about an uncertain future is basic to human existence. Without the benefit of hindsight, we cannot expect our decisions to be right on target. In fact, we will never have perfect or complete information about a future event. If we did, every public policy would be a success, and in the end there would be no distinction among the past, present, and future. Since the real world does not operate in this way, we must proceed strategically and establish a logical process for viewing uncertainty from an analytical perspective.

One way of looking at the unpredictable future is to follow the early work of the eminent economist Frank Knight.[1] In his seminal work Knight distinguishes **risk** from **uncertainty.** Risk is when one can calculate the probability of a future outcome, and uncertainty is when one cannot. When you buy car insurance, agencies use your age, education, and driving record to estimate the actuarial risk of covering the costs of probable accidents. However, when you encounter a unique event for which there is no probability estimate, you face an uncertain situation.[2] If you are judging the probability of an election result, a legislative outcome in Congress, or a future draft choice by a professional sports franchise in your town, you encounter uncertainty. As suggested by our discussion of probability in chapter 5, I can assert that for a future event, we can use the measures of objective probability to estimate risk, whereas for uncertainty, we must depend on subjective estimates.

You may ask, how does the concept of risk differ from that of uncertainty? The fundamental difference between the two rests on the availability of substantive knowledge. Simply put, risky events are not unique; they take place often enough for the researcher to recognize their pattern. Insurance companies, having covered hundreds of thousands of motorists, can calculate the risk of insuring an individual driver. For example, there is a pattern to how most twenty-one-year-old males drive, and insurers take their past behavior into account when setting rates. In contrast, if you want to know if I will be involved in an accident on my way home, you are dealing with uncertainty. This is because, as you may recall from our earlier discussion of probability (see chapter 6), the outcome of any single event is unpredictable; results are predictable only over a number of tries. That is, you cannot say for sure whether you will flip heads in a single coin toss, but you can predict a 50-percent outcome over a large number of tries.

The literature on uncertainty points out that there are four general sources of uncertainty, which are listed below.[3] You may notice that the first three of these depend on the researchers themselves. Luckily, we can use different strategies to reduce their impact. The last source, at the core of uncertainty, is something that we simply cannot avoid and must learn to live with.

THE INADEQUACY OF KNOWLEDGE. There are events that are not entirely unknowable but depend on the knowledge and expertise of the inquirer. If I am asked to ascertain the risk of ground water contamination from a waste treatment plant, without substantive knowledge in the field, I may fail to come up with a reasonable answer. However, if I am a properly trained expert, I am much better equipped to calculate risk levels. To reduce uncertainty, decision makers must look for the proper personnel to evaluate the odds of uncertain outcomes. If the necessary expertise cannot be found in house, they should look for outside consultants.

BIASES OF REASONING. Personal biases can cloud the mental process through which we analyze the future. These biases may crop up from a number of different sources (see chapter 4). A decision maker must be constantly on guard against such biases.

INTERDEPENDENCE OF HUMAN ACTIONS. In a society people work in groups. As a result, the final output does not depend on one individual but on a number of actors. Their joint efforts shape the ultimate outcome of a project. Traditional neoclassical economics assumes that people follow their self-interest independent of others. However, research in social psychology and other branches of the social sciences has shown that those around us fundamentally affect our behavior. In dealing with others, we can never be sure of their identity, ideology, group affiliation, or levels of commitment.[4] Harvey Leibenstein pointed out that any manager who assumes that employees will always work "according to the book" will soon be humbled.[5] Hence, a proper assessment of the future must include a deep understanding of human beings as social animals.

THE BASIC CORE OF UNCERTAINTY. The outcome of a future event depends not only on our knowledge and effort but also on factors that are completely beyond our control. Young Back Choi explains this obscured understanding with an old Chinese fable.[6] An old man goes into the field and finds a nice horse. "Lucky me!" he exclaims and gives it to his son. Unfortunately, his son falls off the horse and becomes lame. "This horse has brought me only misfortune," sighs the old man. Soon war breaks out with the dangerous barbarians, and the emperor's army takes away all the young men of the village to fight the enemy. But the army does not take the old man's lame son. The old man is thankful for finding such a lucky horse.

DECISION MAKING AND EXPECTED PAYOFF

The question of how to make the best possible decision under uncertain conditions has come under intense scrutiny. The first analytical breakthrough was derived by John von Neumann and Oscar Morgenstern, two mathematicians from Princeton University, and was developed further over the years by a great number of mathematicians and economists. Let me explain the basic precepts of their analysis. Suppose someone offers you a choice. If you predict correctly, you may win $2 in a coin toss or $5 in a roll of the dice. Which option do you choose? Theoretically, you should choose the coin toss because your chances of winning are 1/2 = 0.5. On the other hand, with the roll of the dice, your chances of calling the right number are 1/6 = 0.167. The **expected payoff** in a risky situation is calculated by the following equation:

$$\text{Expected payoff} = \text{probability of winning} \times \text{amount of reward}.$$

That is, in our case, the expected payoffs are

$$\text{Expected payoff for coin toss} = 0.5 \times \$2 = \$1$$

$$\text{Expected payoff for roll of the dice} = 0.167 \times \$5 = \$0.83$$

As you can see, you will be better off by betting on the coin toss—that is, unless you are a real gambler or risk taker. In this case, you may prefer the higher reward offered by the dice regardless of the chances of winning. For the moment, let us assume that you are neither an excessive risk taker nor an extreme risk averter; instead, you are a risk-neutral decision maker. If you want to maximize your chances of winning in the long run, you will be better off, given uncertainty, by following the law of rational decision making and choosing the option with the highest expected payoff. In fact, in every uncertain situation, including those involving gambling or card games, good players will depend primarily on the proper calculation of the odds. At blackjack tables in the casinos, the house realizes its profits solely by playing the odds, which are in its favor. Although there are winners among the players, the house always cleans up the table at the end of the day.

THE DECISION TREE

We can use the insights developed by von Neumann and Morgenstern to analyze the optimal course of action. The branch of social science and applied mathematics that is dedicated to the study of decision making under uncertainty is broadly called game theory. However, when a single decision maker evaluates the choice of action, he or she uses a **decision tree,** a diagram showing the sequence of events with their corresponding probability figures.

Let us go back to the uncertain public policy problem of President Ford. Suppose that the experts at the Center for Disease Control estimate the probability of the deadly virus's reaching the United States to be 40 percent. Also suppose that the president's political advisors appraise the benefits of his decision on a scale of +10 through –10, with +10 being the most desirable outcome and –10 being the most undesirable. Because we do not know President Ford's reasoning process, we must hypothesize that if he decides to do nothing and the epidemic becomes real, this outcome will be the least desirable of his options (scored as –10). But if he decides to take no action and the epidemic does not show up, then he has remained calm in the face of an unjustified doomsday prediction and has saved a considerable amount of public money. On his scale this result rates a +5.

On the other hand, if he decides to inoculate the population, the most desirable situation arises, from his perspective, if the threat of epidemic turns out to be real. In that case the president will be hailed as a savior—an outcome worth +10 in his rating. However, if the epidemic does not show up, the decision to start a mass inoculation program may turn out to be a political liability, which is assessed a –5 rating. Having put numerical values on the probabilities and payoffs, we can calculate the expected payoffs facing the president (see Table 13.1).

I have drawn the logical structure of President Ford's actions in the form of a decision tree (see Figure 13.1). The branches of a decision tree can be divided into **actions** and **outcomes.** Although actions are deliberate and reflect an individual's conscious decision, outcomes are uncertain. If you inspect Figure 13.1 closely, you will see that it contains four important elements.

1. *Decision nodes:* the points at which the decision maker must choose a possible course of action. In this particular case, President Ford has one decision node that shows two possible actions: do nothing or inoculate. I have drawn this node with a square.
2. *Chance nodes:* the points showing the probable outcomes of an action. After the president chooses an action, there are two possible outcomes: the

Table 13.1   Hypothetical Expected Payoff Matrix for President Gerald Ford

Action (1)	Situation (2)	Probability (3)	Payoffs (4)	Expected payoffs (5) = (3) × (4)
Do nothing (A)	Epidemic starts	0.4	–10	–4
	Epidemic does not show up	0.6	+5	3
Total		1.0	–5	–1
Start mass inoculation (B)	Epidemic starts	0.4	+10	4
	Epidemic does not show up	0.6	–5	–3
Total		1.0	5	1

Figure 13.1 Hypothetical Decision Tree on Swine Flu Threat

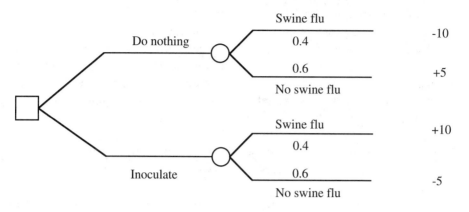

flu breaks out or it does not break out. The chance nodes are indicated with circles.

3. *Probabilities:* estimates of the possible outcomes. Probabilities can be determined either through observation in the case of objective probabilities or through the subjective assessments of experts.
4. *Payoffs:* consequent rewards and losses experienced by the decision makers. Payoffs can be estimated in monetary terms or, as in this case, in terms of some other agreed upon scale. These payoffs can be actual or perceived profits or losses.

In Figure 13.2 we can see that, facing an uncertain situation, President Ford had a choice between an expected payoff of –1 (for the "Do nothing" option) and +1 (for the "Inoculate" option). Therefore, given the logical construct, he should have chosen the option to inoculate the entire population against a probable swine flu infestation. As an anecdotal postscript to this analysis, we should note that President Ford did choose to inoculate, and the virus failed to show up in the United States.[7]

Figure 13.2 Decision Tree on Swine Flu

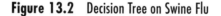
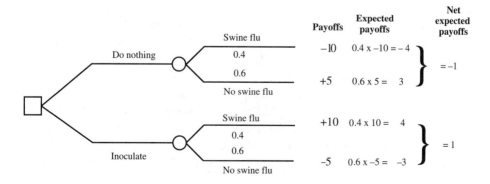

Structuring a Decision Tree

From the preceding rendition of a decision tree, you can see that a tree can be a powerful tool of logical reasoning when the outcomes are shrouded in risk. This exercise allows you to see the true nature of a problem more clearly by providing you with a deeper understanding of the role of chance as it relates to the alternative courses of action. Also, the very process of identifying the alternatives, their outcomes, and their sequential interaction with their respective probabilities can reveal more about the core of the problem than you may otherwise have known.

To be an effective tool of analysis, decision trees must be as exhaustive as possible in identifying every conceivable outcome. Thus, in the above example, I have identified two options for President Ford: to do nothing and to inoculate the entire population. If there were other options, such as inoculating only those who were at the highest possible risk, or restricting the inoculations to specific geographic areas, they also should have been fully explored. This process of identifying alternatives, then, should be **collectively exhaustive.** That is, no feasible option should be deliberately left out without an explicit justification for its exclusion.

Further, the options must be **mutually exclusive.** In other words, the options should be defined in ways that do not overlap. Let us say that we have defined the president's three options as (1) do not inoculate, (2) inoculate only the high-risk population, and (3) inoculate everyone. In this case, all options are mutually exclusive since you cannot meaningfully choose more than one option at one time. If I choose to inoculate only the high-risk segment of the population, that choice would preclude my choosing to inoculate everyone in the nation. However, suppose the president has another option: to immediately launch a research project investigating the causes of the pandemic. The decision tree would have four branches: (1) do not inoculate, (2) inoculate only the high-risk population, (3) inoculate everyone, and (4) start a research project. As you can see, launching a research project does not exclude the other three options, and you can conduct research along with any other action. Therefore, unless your action is predicated on the findings of the research project, you should not include the project in the decision tree.

Evaluating Flood Damage Reduction

Imagine that several neighborhoods in your town have serious problems with seasonal flooding. A recent study commissioned jointly by the Federal Emergency Management Agency (FEMA) and the U.S. Army Corps of Engineers (COE) shows that if your town is hit by a catastrophic hundred-year flood (with a corresponding probability of 1 percent, or 0.01), the damage may equal $150 million. However, the study also suggests that the construction of a floodwall may significantly reduce the damage from flooding. Table 13.2 presents the estimated damage figures corresponding to the various levels of flooding. The flooding we can expect every other year (with a probability of 0.5) is not likely to cause much damage. However, a more severe flood

Table 13.2 Estimated Flood Damage with and without Floodwall

Probability of flood	Estimated damage (in $ million)		Difference in estimated damage (in $ million)
	Floodwall	No floodwall	
0.50	0	0	0
0.40	0	18	18
0.30	10	20	10
0.20	19	25	6
0.10	23	40	17
0.01	87	150	63
Total	139	253	114

that inundates the town every five years (having a probability of 0.2) may cause up to $25 million of damage. Figure 13.3 plots the data presented in Table 13.2.

As a preventive measure, the town is considering the construction of a flood-wall. The COE estimates that the floodwall will cost the town $10 million. The town council is trying to decide whether to finance the structure with a municipal bond issue. I have represented the choices open to the town council in the form of a

Figure 13.3 Probability of Flood Damage

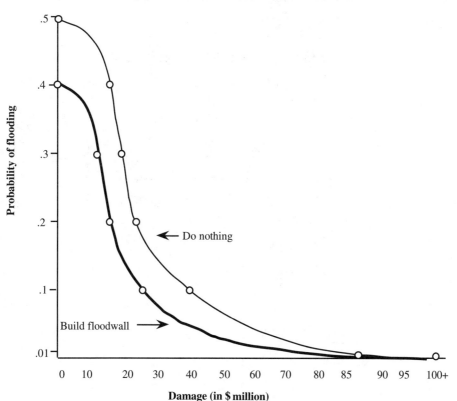

decision tree (see Figure 13.4). To make the diagram less complicated, I have elim-inated the most frequent flooding, which does negligible damage. As you can see, I have numbered the decision nodes and added letters to the chance nodes. The symbol ⊟ indicates the point in the decision process at which a fixed cost has been incurred. This symbol stands for the cost of constructing the floodwall, which we must add to the total expected flood damage.

If you look again at Table 13.2, you may be tempted to conclude that the total savings for the project is $114 million, the total difference in estimated damage, minus $10 million, the cost of building the floodwall. However, when you take into account the respective probability measures, you will see that the bulk of the sav-ings comes from limiting the damage of the most devastating flood, which is expected to occur every hundred years. Since the probability of such a monster flood is small (0.01), the expected payoff is puny. As you can see from Figure 13.4, the expected loss without the floodwall is $1.5 million, as compared with $0.87 million with the floodwall. The expected savings comes to $630,000. The total ben-efits of constructing a floodwall are still greater than those of not constructing it. If we go ahead with the construction, our expected damage is $9.97 million plus the cost of construction, $10 million, or a total of $19.97 million. Because this number is smaller than the expected damage of $23.7 million without the floodwall, we should go ahead with the project.

At this point you should note that since we find the "do-nothing" option decid-edly inferior to the construction of the floodwall, we have crossed it out with an

Figure 13.4 **Decision Tree on Flood Control**

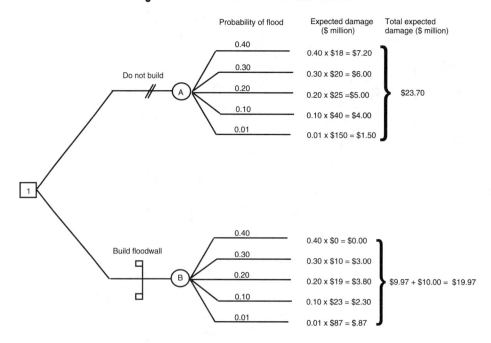

etch mark: //. This mark shows that we have considered this option and have rejected it in favor of another.

This example of a decision tree is relatively simple since it contains only one decision node. However, a decision tree can be much more complex and include many more decision nodes. Let us extend our example to include some additional decision options.

The COE study has come up with another flood control plan. It suggests that the town council consider building, in addition to the floodwall, a small levee of locally available impervious soil. This levee, to be constructed a few miles upstream, may divert enough water to significantly reduce the town's damages, particularly from the more frequent swells. However, there are a couple of caveats. First, the levee may turn out to be ineffective. In that case, the town will incur the same amount of damages as it would have sustained without this new construction. But if the levee is effective, the town will realize significant savings by constructing the floodwall. The COE estimates the construction cost for the levee to be $1 million. The agency further predicts that the probability of the levee proving effective is 70 percent.

The second caveat is that in the case of a catastrophic flood, the levee is likely to collapse. If it does, the damage from the flood will escalate even more than it would if the levee and floodwall had not been built (see Table 13.3). This caveat introduces new options. The town can still decide to do nothing, it can immediately start building a floodwall, or it can wait to see whether the earthen levee is effective. If the levee is ineffective, then it can consider constructing the floodwall. If the levee is successful, it may go ahead and build the flood control device or may decide not to build it after all (see Figure 13.5).

Table 13.3 presents the damage estimates for an effective levee. You may note that I have left out one option. I did not include the damage estimates for when the levee is ineffective. This is because these estimates are the same as those for no

Table 13.3 Estimated Flood Damage with Floodwall and Levee

Probability of flood	Estimated damage (in $ million)			
	Floodwall	No floodwall	Effective levee with floodwall	Effective levee without floodwall
0.50	0.00	0.00	0.00	0.00
0.40	0.00	18.00	0.00	0.00
0.30	10.00	20.00	0.00	15.00
0.20	19.00	25.00	5.00	20.00
0.10	23.00	40.00	10.00	40.00
0.01	87.00	150.00	180.00	150.00
Total expected flood damage (probability × damage)	9.97	23.70	3.80	14.00

Figure 13.5 Expanded Decision Tree on Flood Control with Levee Option

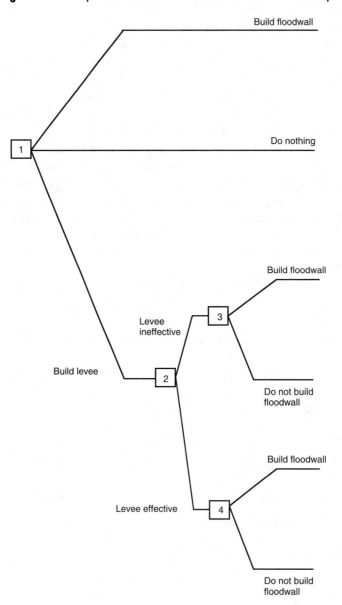

levee at all. Combining information from Table 13.2, Table 13.3, and Figure 13.5, we can build the decision tree shown in Figure 13.6.

When there are several decision nodes, the simplest way of working out a decision tree problem is *folding backwards*. In this case, the first two options of doing nothing and building the floodwall have to be evaluated against the option of constructing the levee first. In evaluating that option, we must consider decision nodes 2 and 3. For decision node 2, if the levee is ineffective, it stands to reason that the floodwall should be built, since the total estimated damage for the option

Figure 13.6   Decision Tree on Flood Control with Total Expected Costs

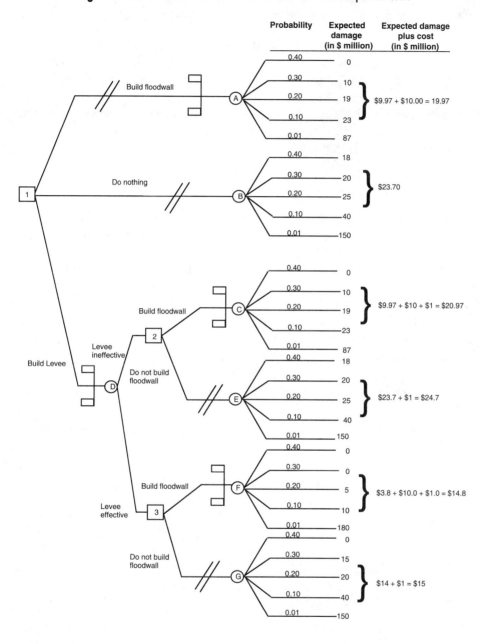

of "do not build" ($23.7 million + $1 million for levee = $24.7 million) is higher than that for the decision to construct the floodwall ($9.97 million + construction cost of $10 million + $1 million = $20.97 million).

If, on the other hand, the levee is found to be effective (at decision node 3), building the floodwall once again seems to be a better option than not building it. That is because the expected damage with an effective levee and a floodwall,

$14.8 million ($3.8 million of expected flood damage + $10 million for the flood-wall + $1 million for the levee), is lower than the expected cost of not building a floodwall, $15.0 million ($14.0 million + $1 million).

We are now in a position to evaluate the options: do nothing or immediately build the floodwall. As you can see, the estimated damage for the do-nothing option is $23.7 million, while the damage for the immediate construction of the floodwall is expected to be $19.97 million. Since these estimates are higher than those for building the floodwall whether or not the levee is effective, we should recommend that the town council build the levee and the floodwall. I have sum-marized the findings in Table 13.4.

Risk Tolerance and Expected Payoff

Each one of us views risk differently. I was recently watching a game show in which the contestant had two answer choices. If she gave the right answer, she would earn a $500,000 prize, doubling her current winnings of $250,000. But if her answer was incorrect, she would receive only $100,000. What would you do if you were in her position? Let us draw her options in the framework of a decision tree (see Fig-ure 13.7).

If her chances of choosing the right answer are 50–50, her expected payoff is greater than that of the sure-bet option (probability = 1.0) of taking the money she has already won. But would you be a cool statistician and risk losing $150,000? If you would, your behavior would be considered **risk neutral.** On the other hand, if you would choose the second, sure-bet option, your action would be regarded as **risk averse;** that is, you would prefer to avoid risk in decision making. In contrast, some people thrive on taking high risks. If you are only 30 percent sure that you

Table 13.4   Total Estimated Cost of Floodwall and Levee

| | Estimated damage (in $ million) | | | | | |
| | | | Ineffective levee | | Effective levee | |
Probability of flood	Floodwall	No floodwall	Floodwall	No floodwall	Floodwall	No floodwall
0.50	0.00	0.00	0.00	0.00	0.00	0.00
0.40	0.00	18.00	0.00	18.00	0.00	0.00
0.30	10.00	20.00	10.00	20.00	0.00	15.00
0.20	19.00	25.00	19.00	25.00	5.00	20.00
0.10	23.00	40.00	23.00	40.00	10.00	40.00
0.01	87.00	150.00	87.00	150.00	180.00	150.00
Total estimated damage	9.97	23.70	9.97	23.70	3.80	14.00
Cost of floodwall	10.00	0.00	10.00	0.00	10.00	0.00
Cost of levee	0.00	0.00	1.00	1.00	1.00	1.00
Total cost	19.97	23.70	20.97	24.70	14.80	15.00

Figure 13.7   Risk and Payoff in Television Game Show

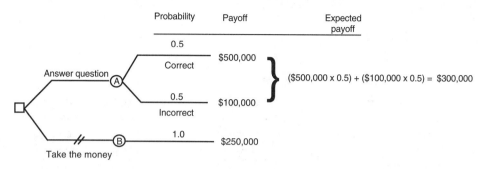

know the correct answer, the expected returns for attempting to answer are $220,000, $30,000 less than the returns expected for taking the money. In this case, if you still insist on chasing the high reward of half a million dollars, you will be considered a **risk lover.**

Is it then irrational to be anything but risk neutral? There is a problem with defining human rationality as risk-neutral behavior. As I have shown in chapter 2, the so-called Allais paradox demonstrates that people's preference for risk can vary across the range of probability and reward. From a policy perspective, it may be advisable to take risks as long as you can comfortably bear the consequences of the loss. Consider, for example, our hypothetical example of constructing a levee along with a floodwall. By following the rules of mathematical expectation, we have recommended the construction of both. However, if you examine the payoff matrix carefully, you will see that such a recommendation may be shortsighted. Building both flood control devices significantly lowers the risk with more frequent flooding, but it heightens the risk of damage associated with a cataclysmic flood. A huge increase in the water level may suddenly break the levee, and the breach could exacerbate an already catastrophic incident. The question is, can you afford a small risk that you will incur a devastating loss? After all, the hundred-year flood may not wait another hundred years to show up. If it occurs, the entire town may be wiped out. Given this possibility, can you blame the authorities for taking the less expensive and less risky option of building only the floodwall? For another example of how policy makers weigh risk against expected payoffs, see "A Case in Point: Risky Business."

TWO ACTIVE PLAYERS: GAME THEORY

The decision tree is a schematic representation of decision making under uncertainty. It falls under the more general area of study called **game theory.** Game theory is a mathematical technique to evaluate the strategic interaction between two or more opponents based on expectations about their possible moves. This technique is particularly useful when you are in a situation of active confrontation, must make strategic decisions, and are uncertain about the moves of your opponent(s). The

A CASE IN POINT

Risky Business: Orange County Bankruptcy

On December 6, 1994, officials of Orange County, California, one of the most affluent and fiscally conservative counties in the nation, declared bankruptcy, the result of risky investments made by county treasurer Robert Citron.[1] When the final tallies were made, the county had lost a total of $1.64 billion from its investment pool, which invested money for the county, its 31 cities, and more than 150 other, mostly single-purpose, government entities.

The primary guiding principles for local government investment pools are safety, liquidity, and yield. That is, when investing public money, pools must safeguard invested money and not take unacceptable risks. Fund managers should also make sure that the municipality has enough liquid cash on hand to meet its obligations. Finally, cash managers seek to maximize return on investment (yield).

Citron was the county treasurer for more than twenty years. He was widely considered a "financial guru" who could consistently earn returns vastly superior to those realized by other municipalities throughout the state and the nation. In fact, Citron had promised that a full 35 percent of the 1995 county revenue would come from interest income. As it turned out, Citron was paying more attention to the possibility of yield than to the reality, virtually ignoring the safety of his investments by choosing high-risk instruments called "derivatives." The problem with derivatives is that if the market follows your prediction, these securities give you extremely high returns, but if it does not, they can result in stratospheric losses.

To be sure, Citron did have his critics, who claimed that he was taking unacceptable risks. However, the county, like most other local governments in California, was strapped for tax revenues because Proposition 13 (a sweeping property tax reduction measure) had put the county in a financial straightjacket since its passage in 1978. Because these investments brought in huge sums of money—without requiring that the county impose higher taxes on the highly conservative electorate—such words of caution were ignored by the politicians who supervised Citron.[2]

Notes

1. For a comprehensive review of the problem, see Mark Baldassare, *When Government Fails: The Orange County Bankruptcy* (Berkeley and San Francisco: University of California and Public Policy Institute of California, 1998). In this section, I concentrate mostly on risk management. However, a number of studies, in addition to identifying the problem of assuming undue risks, point to fraud and criminal activities in this expensive fiscal fiasco. See, for example, Susan Will, Henry N. Pontell, and Richard Cheung, "Risky Business Revisited: White-Collar Crime and Orange County Bankruptcy," *Crime and Delinquency* 44 (1998): 367–387.

2. In the end, Robert Citron, the "financial wizard," was convicted of fraud. Most interestingly, during his trial, a neuropsychologist testified in his defense that she found extensive damage in Citron's frontal brain, which "allows you to think, analyze information, and be conscious." Echoing her findings, a clinical psychologist

compared him to "an empty bottle put out into the water." The experts claimed that Citron had suffered from brain damage throughout his life. See "Former Orange County Treasurer Had Brain Damage, Witnesses Say," *San Diego Union Tribune* via the Associated Press, Nov. 19, 1996, A-4.

Discussion Points

1. Does it always pay to be risk neutral when dealing with an uncertain future? Is it advisable to be a risk lover in certain situations? When?
2. From the standpoint of risk management, why did Orange County face a fiscal disaster?

---

literature on game theory is varied and rich. The beauty of this technique is that it can be used to explain strategies in a variety of scenarios, from chess games to corporate takeovers, from labor union bargaining to the negotiation of international treaties. Also, because it lends itself to mathematical modeling, literature about it varies from simple to extremely complex, from eminently practical to highly esoteric.[9] The rules of strategic decision making have been researched by psychologists (to study fallacies about uncertainty), international relations scholars (to predict the strategic moves of countries), and students of corporate strategies (to explore the ways in which corporations interact).[10] Students of negotiating and bargaining have tried to come up with rules for conflict resolution.[11] These diverse inquiries have significantly advanced our knowledge about strategic decision making and sometimes have inflated expectations beyond what these techniques can deliver.[12]

Let us start with a simple game with two players. Although decision trees are shown as diagrams, two-player games are usually written as matrices. Since game theory can explain the outcome of a confrontation between two or more parties, it is useful in analyzing policies of engagement. Let us assume that your city is engaged in a bitter labor dispute. The garbage collectors' union is threatening to go on strike during the busy Christmas season. The city has been in negotiation with the union for some time, but the parties remain far apart in their positions. The union believes that the conservative mayor wants to weaken organized labor and has little faith in her commitment to an acceptable negotiated settlement. The mayor, on the other hand, is up for reelection in February. She believes that the actions of organized labor are politically motivated and are designed to undermine her candidacy. The state mediators, unable to end the impasse, suggest binding arbitration, in which case an independent board reviews the situation and proposes a compromise binding on both sides. From the perspective of the union, there are two options: to accept arbitration and risk a less-than-acceptable contract, or to go on strike. Similarly, the mayor has two options. She can accept arbitration and run the risk of approving a contract that she believes might be fiscally irresponsible for the city, or she can hang tough and not negotiate with the garbage collectors' union. We can analyze the city's dilemma with the help of game theory. Table 13.5 shows the payoff matrix for the two parties.

Table 13.5 Payoff Matrix for Mayor and Garbage Collectors' Union

	Mayor's position	
Union's position	Accept arbitration	Hang tough
Accept arbitration	3, 2	0, 5
Strike	4, 0	1, 1

The table presents the perceived payoffs for the two parties on a scale from 0 (least desirable) to 5 (most desirable). As you can see from this table, the union has two alternatives. It can accept arbitration or go on strike. If it negotiates with the mayor for an arbitration board of its liking, its preference ranking is 3. This, however, is not the best option for the mayor, since she would prefer to take a tough stance against organized labor. In any case, she assigns this option a lukewarm 2.

From the union's perspective, the worst scenario is one in which the mayor refuses to negotiate and the union is forced to accept arbitration. This combination of strategies is valued as 0 by the union and 5 by the mayor.

The union may opt for a work stoppage. If this action brings a reluctant mayor to the negotiating table, it is the most preferred option for the union (4) and least preferred (0) for the mayor. Finally, if the union strikes and the mayor hangs tough in a high-risk game, both parties assign 1 to this option.

The rules of rational choice under uncertain conditions dictate that each player follow a **minimax** strategy, in which each chooses the strategy that minimizes his or her maximum loss or regret. From the perspective of the union, if it chooses to accept arbitration, its maximum loss is to be pinned to the mat by a tough mayor. Thus, for this option, its maximum regret position is 0. However, for the strike option, its worst possible outcome is 1. Hence, from the standpoint of the union, deciding to strike is superior to going for arbitration. Similarly, you can see that the mayor minimizes her maximum loss when she takes a strong position. Therefore, the only possible outcome of this confrontation is a strike by the garbage collectors while the mayor takes an intransigent posture.

This outcome, in the lower right-hand corner of the matrix, is called the solution of **Nash equilibrium,** after noted mathematician John Nash. This solution identifies an outcome from which neither player can gain by unilaterally switching to another strategy.[13] That is, if the mayor chooses to confront the labor union, the union does not gain by unilaterally switching to a compromise option of going for arbitration, since doing so would lower its payoff from 1 to 0. Similarly, if the union chooses to strike, the best option for the mayor is to project a firm position; otherwise, her own payoff would sink from 1 to 0.

The need for devising military strategies in the face of uncertainty has inspired much of the development of game theory. One of the textbook cases of game theory can be found in *Battle of the Bismarck Sea*.[14] In early 1943 the allies' counterattack on the Japanese navy was in full swing. By that time U.S. forces had gained a foothold on the island of New Guinea. The northern half of the island was controlled by the Japanese, while the allies controlled the southern part. Intelligence reports produced for Douglas MacArthur, the supreme commander of the allied forces, indicated that the Japanese were sending huge reinforcements for a major counterattack on the allies. General MacArthur ordered General George C. Kenney, commander of the allied air force, to challenge the Japanese convoy and inflict maximum possible damage. Figure 13.8 presents General Kenney's dilemma.

As you can see, the commander of the Japanese convoy had two options: he could take the northern route or the southern route. Therefore, Kenney also had the corresponding options of sending the bulk of his interceptor forces to the north or directing them to the south. His objective was to deliver the maximum possible damage to the Japanese convoy through relentless bombing. The weather report showed an approaching storm on the north side of the island. The storm would markedly reduce visibility and, consequently, the ability of the allied planes to locate and strafe enemy ships. General Kenney measured his payoff in terms of the expected number of days the allied air force would have to bomb the convoy as the allies headed west. The payoff matrix for the options open to the opposing commanders is shown in Table 13.6.

From General Kenney's standpoint, if he sent his forces up the northern route and the Japanese chose to sail to the north side of the island, since weather was expected to be poor, his pilots would be able to bomb the Japanese for just two days. However, if after flying north in the foul weather the allied bombers discovered that the Japanese had taken the southern route, they would still be able to bomb enemy ships for two days. In contrast, if Kenney sent his forces south, only to find out that the Japanese were on the other side of the island, the allies would have to be content with only one day's bombardment. But if they were lucky and found that the Japanese had taken the calmer waters of the southern route, they would be able to bomb the convoy for three days. We can show the situation facing General Kenney in terms of a decision tree (see Figure 13.9).

Figure 13.8   Strategies in Battle of the Bismarck Sea

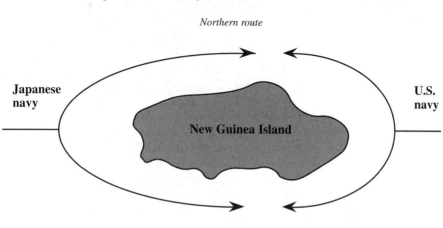

Northern route

Japanese navy

New Guinea Island

U.S. navy

Southern route

Table 13.6 Possible Days of Allied Bombing

Allied strategy	Japanese strategy	
	Sail north	Sail south
Search north	2 days of bombing	2 days of bombing
Search south	1 day of bombing	3 days of bombing

You can see from the decision tree that General Kenney's best option was to follow the northern route. Adopting the **minimax** strategy (by which you minimize your maximum regret—one day of bombing for the allies and three for the Japanese), Kenney realized that the worst he could do by flying south was to bomb the Japanese convoy for one day. However, if he sent his planes north, the worst outcome for him was to inflict two days of damage. Therefore, his **dominant strategy** was to fly north. That is, that strategy provided him with the highest payoff given what he expected the Japanese to do. Similarly, for the Japanese fleet, its worst fears would have been realized if it had taken the calm waters of the south and had been quickly discovered by the allies for a full three days of attack. Hence, this classic battle situation presented the game theorists with a textbook case of a Nash equilibrium. In reality, the Japanese sent their ships through the northern side. General Kenney also went north, and his planes delivered a devastating blow to Japanese aspirations in the Pacific with two days of incessant bombing.

Game Theory in Local Government Decision Making

The most often cited examples of the use of game theory involve strategic decisions in military operations or international relations. This powerful analytical technique may also be used to aid local government decision makers. We have

Figure 13.9 Decision Tree for Allied Strategy in Battle of the Bismarck Sea

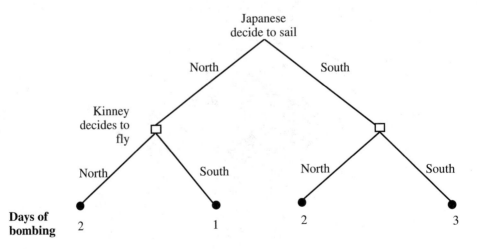

considered a hypothetical case of a city mayor confronting a labor union. In reality, local governments often face the prospect of strikes resulting from disputes with labor unions. Until about a decade ago, a universal ban prevented strikes by state and local government employees. For example, New York's Taylor law flatly prohibits strikes by public employees and prescribes forfeiture of tenure and double loss of pay for striking workers.[15] However, during the past decade this stance has softened somewhat. By the early 1990s about ten states permitted certain groups of government workers to strike under specific circumstances.

Needless to say, strikes or work slowdowns by public employees can cost cities millions of dollars. At the same time, a city can get into a financial bind by signing an overly generous pay package with the unions. In fact, many have blamed New York City's brush with bankruptcy in 1975 on politicians too eager to placate the demands of labor unions.[16] Strikes usually do not help the workers' union, either. Unions lose out in terms of public support and may even risk court-imposed sanctions and fines.

If the union and the city administration are not careful, they can get locked into a losing proposition. Such a situation is known as a **prisoner's dilemma**. The name comes from a game in which, due to a lack of mutual trust, understanding, and cooperation, both players must settle for a less than satisfactory resolution. Let us consider the following scenario, portrayed frequently on television in the police and courtroom dramas. You and your best friend have committed a crime, but no one saw you do it. The only way the district attorney can get a conviction is if either (or both) of you confess. Knowing this, the police have kept the two of you in different cells, with no possibility of communication. Your attorney tells you that you have two options: you can either confess or not confess. If you choose to confess, you will face two alternate scenarios. If your unrepentant, bull-headed friend does not confess, you will be rewarded with the witness protection plan while your friend languishes in jail for fifteen years. If, on the other hand, your weak and gutless friend decides to confess as well, both of you will draw five-year prison terms. If you decide not to confess and your friend betrays you, you end up with the fifteen-year prison term. However, if he turns out to be equally trustworthy, and remains steadfast in not confessing, the prosecution has no case, and both of you are acquitted.

What should you do? Before answering this question, let us consider the payoffs for each strategy (see Table 13.7). You can see in the matrix that *collectively* both of you will be better off by choosing not to confess. However, you will reach this desirable position (from both of your viewpoints) only if you trust each other.

Table 13.7 Prisoner's Dilemma

	Your friend's strategy	
Your strategy	*Confess*	*Do not confess*
Confess	5, 5	Witness protection, 15
Do not confess	15, witness protection	0, 0

Without trust, you will look at only two strategies: confess or do not confess. If you confess, the maximum risk is five years in prison. If you do not confess, the maximum risk is fifteen years in jail. Therefore, following the decision rule of minimizing your maximum loss (the minimax rule), you should choose to confess. Following the same rule, your friend will arrive at the same conclusion, leading to a joint confession and a five-year prison term for both of you. You may notice that in this case, confessing is the dominant strategy for both players.

In our Table 13.5 example, both the mayor and the union could have gone for a negotiated settlement in which both parties would have been better off. The labor union would have improved its position from 1 to 3 and the mayor, from 1 to 2.

Game theory, by providing insight into the dynamics of a conflict, can help the involved parties avoid the prisoner's dilemma. The reason why parties get locked in a prisoner's dilemma is that they do not trust each other. If the mayor and union had not been as mistrustful of one another, they could have found a mutually acceptable arbitration board. In many areas of decision making under uncertain conditions, an effort to develop trust can save everyone from being locked in an undesirable position.

The Golden Rules of Decision Making under Uncertainty

Identifying the optimal strategic moves in situations of uncertainty has been the subject of a great deal of academic discussion. Based on this lengthy discourse, we can offer four rules of advice.

RULE 1: LOOK AHEAD AND REASON BACK.   Successful strategies depend on conscious forward thinking. However, while planning, one must think about the possible reaction of the opponent and the opposing course of action. The old Native American adage of learning to walk a mile in someone else's moccasins has considerable validity. Putting yourself in your opponent's shoes requires you to draw lessons from past experience to anticipate where your moves ultimately will take you.

RULE 2: IF YOU HAVE A DOMINANT STRATEGY, PLAY IT.   It may not win you many friends, but if you have a dominant strategy, you must play it regardless of the situation. This rule is especially true in **zero-sum games,** in which the players' interests are strictly opposed and one player's gain is the other's loss. If we are playing poker, your win is my loss, and the total amount to be distributed is fixed. The confrontation between the mayor and the union may be construed as a zero-sum game. Everyone must play the dominant strategy and, inevitably, must choose the undesirable outcome—deadlock. However, given the absence of trust, by playing the dominant strategy, each party ensures that it will not be stuck in an even worse position.

RULE 3: SUCCESSIVELY ELIMINATE ALL DOMINATED STRATEGIES FROM CONSIDERATION.   If you have a number of possible alternatives, you should compare the outcomes and eliminate the dominated strategies. We followed this rule during our discussion of the decision tree. You may recall that by the process of elimination, we arrived at the most desirable strategy of building a levee and a floodwall. Proceeding in a similar way in your decision making may bring you to a unique alternative that is better than all others.

RULE 4: IN THE ABSENCE OF A UNIQUE DOMINANT STRATEGY, LOOK FOR AN EQUILIBRIUM. In the absence of a dominant strategy, settle for a point that represents the best response under the circumstances, given the players' positions. These circumstances can be quite complicated. Game theorists have pointed out that some situations may have more than one equilibrium position, or none at all. Since the discussion of these complicated scenarios is likely to take us beyond the scope of this book, for the sake of economy we will table these questions for now and will simply refer the more curious readers (and certainly the adventuresome) to other books and articles.[17]

STRATEGIES TO OVERCOME THE PRISONER'S DILEMMA

Uncertainty often causes us to take actions that are not in our best interest. This is true for individuals, organizations, and even for nations engaged in international strategic moves. Often people get locked into situations that offer poor solutions; however, given the circumstances, there seems to be no other way out.

You can see that following the rules of rational decision making under uncertainty can put you in an undesirable situation. We will discuss some ways of building trust and engineering cooperation in the next section. However, often in life we must proceed without trusting our adversaries. In international relations, nations get into wasteful arms races (even those that can least afford to do so). By engaging in destructive labor disputes, industries around the world have been forced to shut down, causing unemployment for workers and economic hardship and loss of capital for owners and management. Of course, many interpersonal disputes remain unresolved because of lack of trust.

However, trust is not developed in a vacuum. It can evolve only through the players' trustworthy actions. If I know an individual to be reliable, I can expect cooperative behavior in response to my cooperative gesture. However, this reciprocity of cooperative behavior can break down due to greed or fear. In our example of the prisoner's dilemma, I can truly win if my friend is made to believe that I will not confess—and then I turn star witness for the prosecution. If I pursue this strategy, I am guilty of greed. If I know that I can win with an unexpected defection, like all other swindlers and con artists, I will slowly develop trust and then defect at the most opportune time. Or I may defect out of fear. I may believe that you are about to break our bond of trust, so I may do it on my own. From violent ethnic strife in Eastern Europe and Africa to broken relationships between friends and relatives, life is full of examples of such defections, which result in suboptimal payoffs for the players.

Greed and fear can be minimized if there is an avenue for punishing defection. The Mafia in southern Italy was able to maintain its iron grip over society by using *olmert,* the universal code of silence. Regardless of the situation, a defector was sure to face the fearsome wrath of the organization. This code kept the system of organized crime going for years. In the United States the court system punishes breach of contract, as defined by clearly understood and vigorously enforced tort laws. If the players are aware of the costs of defection, and the costs are higher than the expected gains, they can be assured of a cooperative game.

However, in many cases, such enforced cooperation is not viable. A great deal of effort has gone into discerning the best strategies under complete uncertainty, when cooperation between two players cannot be guaranteed. In the early 1980s Robert Axelrod, a University of Michigan professor of political science, organized a tournament.[18] Game theorists from around the world submitted computer programs proposing strategies for dealing with uncertainty. These strategies were matched against one another in pairwise competition, in which each computer program was pitted against every other computer program. Each game was repeated 150 times. The strategies varied from nasty (defection on every move) to saintlike (cooperation regardless of the opponent's action), from simple techniques to highly complex systems of calculated cooperation and punitive defection. The game that received the highest number of points was one that was submitted by Anatol Rappaport, a professor of mathematics at the University of Toronto. This surprising winner followed a simple strategy, tit-for-tat. It started out by cooperating (that is, not confessing, in the language of our example). After this it simply repeated the last move of its opponent. In other words, if the opponent cooperated, tit-for-tat did the same. However, if the opponent defected, the strategy sought immediate retribution and defection. But if the opponent, having defected, went back to cooperation, it was quick to forgive and adopt a cooperative position.

Axelrod attributed the success of tit-for-tat to four desirable qualities: clarity, "niceness," provocability, and forgiveness. The rules of this strategy are simple and, therefore, *clear*. The strategy is *nice* in the sense that it does not defect unprovoked. Although it is quick to exact retribution for a breach of trust (*provocability*), it is equally quick to *forgive* and go back to the cooperating mode. Axelrod claimed great possibilities for tit-for-tat and saw through it the evolution of a cooperative system. During the period of the renewed cold war (after the "evil empire" speech by Ronald Reagan), this simple strategy symbolized for many the hope of a new trusting world order.

However, despite the early hopes for greatness, later scrutiny of tit-for-tat found damaging flaws in the universality of this strategy. First, tit-for-tat was the winner only on cumulative score; it could not beat any strategy in a pairwise game. The best it could do was to tie with the cooperative (saintly) games, or the games following a strategy close to its own, starting with cooperation. It won overall because, since it echoed the opponent, it always came close, regardless of strategy—a quality that could not be matched by any other strategy.

Tit-for-tat also suffers from some other serious flaws. Avinash Dixit and Barry Nalebuff point out that if two are playing this strategy and one defects by mistake, or the move is seen as a defection, tit-for-tat will kick in and the two will not be able to extricate themselves from an ever-lasting cycle of retribution. Instead of tit-for-tat, Dixit and Nalebuff suggest a more forgiving strategy.

OTHER STRATEGIES: TRUST AND BARGAINING

It is obvious that no one would want to get mired in a game of "getting even." Mahatma Gandhi often quipped that the strategy of "a tooth for a tooth and an eye for an eye" ultimately leaves both the contenders toothless and blind. Across the United States a great deal of academic energy is being devoted to finding ways to resolve seemingly intractable disputes. The key to the resolution of conflict lies in developing trust. When trust is lacking, participants need external enforcement of compliance through the imposition of costs for noncompliance, and as always in a conflict situation, they should rely on bargaining. In their widely read book *Getting to Yes*, Roger Fisher and William Ury of the Harvard Negotiation Project spell out a number of strategies to achieve agreement in disputes.[19] Although these strategies make for extremely useful and lively debates—and I strongly recommend that you become familiar with them—their full discussion falls outside the scope of this book.

I leave you with a final word of caution. Because of the very nature of disputes, not all of them have peaceful resolutions. For many different reasons, the contenders may deem open hostility to be more desirable than a negotiated compromise. In such cases, the only outcome is continuing conflict.

Key Words

Actions (p. 334)

Collectively exhaustive (p. 336)

Decision tree (p. 334)

Dominant strategy (p. 348)

Expected payoff (p. 333)

Game theory (p. 343)

Minimax strategy (p. 346)

Mutually exclusive (p. 336)

Nash equilibrium (p. 346)

Outcomes (p. 334)

Prisoner's dilemma (p. 349)

Risk (p. 331)

Risk averse (p. 342)

Risk lover (p. 343)

Risk neutral (p. 342)

Uncertainty (p. 331)

Zero-sum games (p. 350)

Exercises

1. What is an expected payoff? How does the concept of expected payoff help analyze a situation of uncertainty? In this context, explain "dominant strategy" and the minimax rule.

2. What is a zero-sum game? With an appropriate example, explain how conflict arises in the area of resource allocation (resulting from a public policy) because of a zero-sum situation.

3. What is a prisoner's dilemma? What are its outcomes for the participants? How can it be prevented in real life?

4. In July the parks and recreation department in your town wants to organize an exhibition of local arts and crafts. The department is considering whether to hold the exhibit inside the downtown sports arena or outside in its open-air parking lot. However, the problem is that while planning the location of the exhibition, the planners face uncertainty about the weather. The weather bureau reports that there is only a 20 percent chance of rain. If the town holds the event inside the

sports arena, after paying for the use of the facility, it expects to break even if it rains. If it does not rain, the town will make a profit of $15,000 from the event. On the other hand, if the exhibition is held outdoors, it can be either a great success or a real failure, depending on the weather. If it does not rain, the town will make a tidy profit of $35,000, but if it rains, it stands to lose $10,000. Draw a decision tree and explain the options open to the decision makers. What would be your recommendation?

5. Your town is located on the shores of the Atlantic Ocean, directly in the line of devastating hurricanes. You are evaluating a policy to invest $10 million in emergency preparedness. It is estimated that the chance that a moderate to strong hurricane (categories 2 and 3) will come your way next year is 30 percent. The chance of being hit by a devastating category 4 hurricane is 5 percent. Right now, without this additional preparation, the town can handle small tropical storms without much problem or property loss. If there is a category 2 or 3 hurricane, however, the estimated loss will be about $15 million, and for a fierce category 4, the estimated property loss could rise as high as $50 million.

The financial administration department estimates that with the $10 million invested, the town will be able to withstand a strong hurricane of category 2 or 3 with a minimum damage of $5 million. Even if there is a giant hurricane of category 4, the damage estimate goes no higher than $20 million. Should the town invest the money in disaster preparedness? Draw the decision tree and write a report explaining your recommendation.

6. Suppose you are an aide to the governor of your state. Due to a much publicized story of a mentally deranged person killing a number of innocent victims in a crowded restaurant with an automatic weapon, the governor is considering a proposal to ban all sales of automatic guns within state borders. This issue is emotionally charged, and the governor is keenly aware of the political cost of an unpopular decision.

Facing this controversial problem, the governor sees three options: to do nothing, to propose a mild law banning the sale of a few such weapons, or to establish a commission. If the governor does nothing, there would be a political cost, to which the governor's advisors assign a value of –3. If a mild ban is unilaterally imposed, it will cause a net loss of popularity, valued at –2. On the other hand, if an independent commission is set up, the governor may be able to circumvent this lose-lose situation. However, the governor has no control over the recommendations of an independent commission. The commission may come up with a "do nothing" recommendation, which would absolve the governor for not doing anything (value = 0). Another possibility is that the commission will recommend a mild ban, or it could suggest a strict ban on the ownership of automatic weapons. The governor, however, retains the right to go along with the commission or to reject its recommendations. If the commission recommends a mild ban, the governor can accept it for a political payoff of +3, or he may reject it and do nothing for a small loss of –1 (the commission has taken the edge off the governor's inaction).

A real problem may arise if the commission recommends a radical plan of gun control. If the governor accepts it, he will be hit for a loss of –10, but if he rejects the plan, he will incur a loss of –4. The probability that the commission, which will have broad-based support, will recommend doing nothing is 0.3, the chance that it will suggest a mild ban is 0.5, and the chance that it will support a strict gun control measure is 0.2. If you are a political analyst for the governor, what will be your recommendation and why?

7. Many social conflicts arise when rival factions place themselves in a prisoner's dilemma situation. With an appropriate example, discuss the prisoner's dilemma, pointing out the reasons for the intractability of problems and suggesting some possible measures that may help generate cooperation among the parties involved.

Notes

1. Frank Knight, *Risk, Uncertainty, and Profit* (Boston: Houghton Mifflin, 1921).
2. Over the years, authors have altered the definitions of "risk" and "uncertainty" proposed by Knight. You may come across a definition of risk that describes it as associated with the project itself, whereas uncertainty is thought to relate to the overall environment. However, in a delightful work on the subject, Young Back Choi argues for the original definitions of these terms. Following Choi, I stick to Knight's definitions of risk and uncertainty. See Choi's *Paradigms and Conventions: Uncertainty, Decision Making, and Entrepreneurship* (Ann Arbor: University of Michigan Press, 1993).
3. Choi. *Paradigms and Conventions,* 13–16.
4. Dipak K. Gupta, "Economics and Collective Identity: Explaining Collective Action," in *The Expansion of Economics and Other Disciplines: Toward an Inclusive Social Science,* ed. Shoshana Grossbard-Sechtman (Armonk, N.Y.: M.E. Sharpe, 2001). A number of eminent economists have broken ranks with the traditional view of utility maximization. See George Akerlof and Rachel E. Kranton, "Economics and Identity," *The Quarterly Journal of Economics* 115: 715–754; Timur Kuran, "Ethnic Norms and Their Transformation through Reputation Cascades," *Journal of Legal Studies* 27, pt. 2 (1998): 623–659; Amartya K. Sen, "Goals, Commitment, and Identity," *Journal of Law, Economics, and Organization* 1 (fall 1985): 341–355; and Howard Margolis, *Selfishness, Altruism, and Rationality* (Cambridge: Cambridge University Press, 1982).
5. Harvey Leibenstein, "The Prisoner's Dilemma in the Invisible Hand: An Analysis of Inter-firm Productivity," *American Economic Review: Papers and Proceedings* 72 (1982): 822–823.
6. Choi, *Paradigms and Conventions,* 15–16.
7. Arthur M. Silverstein, *Pure Politics and Impure Science: The Swine Flu Affair* (Baltimore: Johns Hopkins University Press, 1981). Also see Richard E. Neustadt and Harvey V. Fineberg, *The Swine Flu Affair: Decision-making on a Slippery Disease* (Washington, D.C.: Department of Health, Education, and Welfare, 1978).
8. For an actual study of the probability of flood damage, see *Flood Proofing: How to Evaluate Your Options: Decision Tree* (Fort Belvoir, Va.: U.S. Army Corps of Engineers, National Flood Proofing Committee, 1995).
9. For an informative, highly entertaining explanation of game theory, see Avinash Dixit and Barry Nalebuff, *Thinking Strategically* (New York: W.W. Norton, 1991).
10. David Krep, *Game Theory and Economic Modeling* (Oxford: Oxford University Press, 1990). Also see Paul Kemperer, "Multimarket Oligopoly: Strategic Substitutes and Complements," *Journal of Political Economy* 93 (1985): 488–511.
11. Roger Fisher and William Ury, *Getting to Yes* (New York: Penguin Books, 1981). Also see Howard Raiffa, *The Art and Science of Negotiation* (Cambridge: Harvard University Press, 1982).
12. *Newsweek* magazine, in reviewing *Getting to Yes* (see note 11), called the book "a coherent 'win-win' negotiation which, if it takes hold, may help convert the Age of Me to the Era of We." Quoted on the book's back cover.

13. Bruce Bueno de Mesquita, *Principles of International Politics: People's Power, Preferences, and Perceptions* (Washington, D.C.: CQ Press, 2000), 48.

14. For an excellent discussion of the importance of game theory, see John L. Casti, *Five Golden Rules: Great Theories of 20th-Century Mathematics—and Why They Matter* (New York: Wiley, 1996).

15. Robert J. Thornton, "Unions and Collective Bargaining," in *Management Policies in Local Government Finance*, ed. J. Richard Aronson and Eli Schwartz (Washington, D.C.: International City/County Management Association, 1996), 418.

16. "The Talk of the Town: Message to Rudy," *The New Yorker,* May 15, 1995, 36.

17. For a discussion of multiple equilibrium, see John C. Harsanyi, "Advances in Understanding Rational Behavior," in *Foundational Problems in the Special Sciences,* ed. R.E. Butts and J. Hintikka (Dordecht, Holland: D. Reidel, 1977). For an example of this kind of situation and its resolution, see Frank C. Zagare, "Rationality and Deterrence," *World Politics,* January 1990, 238–260. Again, for the most readable explanation, see Dixit and Nalebuff, *Thinking Strategically.*

18. For the results of this tournament, see Robert Axelrod, *The Evolution of Cooperation* (New York: Basic Books, 1984).

19. Fisher and Ury, *Getting to Yes.*

14

CHOOSING THE
BEST ALTERNATIVE:
COST-BENEFIT ANALYSIS

Y our city is considering acquiring a parcel of vacant land near the center of the city to develop a new convention center with a hotel complex. Your job, as a policy analyst, is to evaluate the proposal and send your recommendation to the city council. The question is, of course, how to go about it.

It is obvious that you will recommend the project if the benefits outweigh the costs. When we make a decision, any decision, we consciously or unconsciously evaluate its potential benefits and costs. In fact, this evaluation process is so fundamental to human cognition that many economists have equated it with the very notion of human rationality.[1] Economists argue that when individuals make a decision, even an emotional one, they have a good sense of the benefits and costs of their actions. How do we choose our mates in marriage? Poets and authors of romantic novels claim that love is blind—anyone can fall in love with anyone else without following any definite pattern of behavior. Yet statistical data show that marriage partners tend to match each other's "endowments" (age, looks, wealth, education, social standing, and so forth). That is, their actual preferences reveal a "rational choice" based loosely on the economic notion of **cost-benefit analysis.**[2] Thus, you will probably not be surprised that this chapter on cost-benefit analysis mirrors the chapter on critical thinking (see chapter 4). Cost-benefit analysis, which emphasizes monetary evaluation, provides critical thinking with a more formal structure. I mentioned that the techniques of statistics and operations research greatly aid the process of thinking critically. Hence, because cost-benefit analysis draws on all these tools, I am discussing it at the very end of our discussion of analytical techniques.

In sum, the fundamental principles of cost-benefit analysis are the following:

- *When considering a single project, accept it if its benefits are greater than the costs.*
- *When considering alternative projects, choose the one that gives you the highest benefits in relation to the costs.*

In our convention center example, we should go ahead with the project if its benefits are greater than its costs. Similarly, we should evaluate alternative uses for the land (for example, a new public library, a public park, or a shopping mall) in regard to their respective benefits and costs and choose the one that gives us the highest benefit relative to the costs.

If you recommend building a new convention center, how much should the city pay for it? Those who derive their livelihood from the tourist industry may benefit more than those who do not. Thus, those in the former group may be willing to pay more for it than others. If the total amount that the city is willing to pay (reflecting the total utility of the project to the stakeholders) is greater than the cost of the project, then it is worth undertaking. This total amount is known in economic terms as the **consumer surplus** (see chapter 4). Therefore, this question goes to the heart of cost-benefit analysis. However, the more we look into the issue, the more complicated it becomes. To fully appreciate the complexity of the problem, we start with the process of conducting a cost-benefit analysis.

Similar to the familiar process of critical thinking, the process of conducting a cost-benefit analysis is as follows:

1. Define the goal(s) of the project.
2. Identify the alternatives.
3. Make an exhaustive list of all benefits and costs, present and future.
4. Estimate and express benefits and costs in monetary terms.
5. Forecast the future streams of benefits and costs, if needed.
6. Choose the alternative with the largest benefit in comparison with the cost.

Let us now discuss in detail each of these six steps. This powerful analytical tool can be used to evaluate almost every social decision. And, as you will see from our discussion, its thoroughness (which is directly linked to the cost of the study) has to be matched against the importance of the project. If we want to evaluate a proposal for a neighborhood park, we may want to devote a modest amount of time and effort. In contrast, the evaluation for the construction of an atomic power plant, which may affect the health and welfare of hundreds of thousands of residents in the region, would require a much greater degree of precision.

SOCIAL VERSUS PRIVATE COST-BENEFIT ANALYSIS

Before getting to the steps mentioned above, we should briefly discuss the various ramifications for the public versus the private sector. An example may clarify the distinction. An analyst friend, who works for a small neighboring town, called me to say that he was disappointed. The town was negotiating with a national retail chain store to locate within its boundaries. After months of negotiation, the store decided to locate in a more affluent medium-size city next door. Because my friend's town was coming out of a long fiscal slump and the store would have given it a significant boost, he complained, "Didn't the management of the retail chain know how much social good they could have achieved by choosing to locate here?"

Indeed, if you considered the positive externalities of this relocation decision, you might have agreed with him. However, from the standpoint of the retail chain, the private net benefit was the only calculation that counted. This difference in perception explains the distinction between private and public cost-benefit analysis. Every project, large or small, contains social benefits and costs. Retail stores generate employment, produce sales and income tax, and may even increase property values in the surrounding areas. In contrast, they may also create traffic congestion and pollution. While conducting cost-benefit analysis for a public project, we must take into account these **positive** and **negative externalities;** because private firms are not rewarded for the positive externalities that they generate in the community, nor penalized for negative externalities (unless their actions cause a lawsuit), they do not consider them in their cost-benefit calculations.

DEFINING GOALS

The first task of a cost-benefit analysis is to identify the goals of the project. The clearer the goals are, the easier it will be for an analyst to select the best course of action for achieving them. In chapter 4, I demonstrated the importance of defining the goals of projects. When evaluating the convention center proposal, we must determine whose goals to maximize, the city's, the county's, or the convention center authorities'. We also need to know the goals of the project. We may identify as a goal an increase in tax revenue, urban renewal (as a result of the new convention center), or the enhanced image of the city. Elected representatives may set the goals, or we may determine the wishes of the stakeholders through surveys and focus groups.

IDENTIFYING ALTERNATIVES

The second step toward preparing a cost-benefit analysis is to identify the alternatives. Typically, when there are not many identifiable alternatives, we evaluate a project against the option of doing nothing. However, if there are other feasible uses of the site, such as a new public library, a park, or a shopping mall, we should consider them in our analysis.

LISTING COSTS AND BENEFITS OF THE ALTERNATIVES

After selecting the alternatives, one should make as exhaustive a list as possible of the costs and benefits of the various alternatives. It may be useful to use the scheme shown in Figure 14.1 to delineate costs and benefits. They can be broadly classified into two categories: **direct** and **indirect.** The direct costs and benefits are those that are associated directly with the project itself. The indirect costs and benefits are those that affect the surrounding community but do not show up in the ledger of the project.

In our convention center example, the revenues from the new facilities are considered to be the direct benefits, and the construction costs are the direct costs of the project. However, beyond these benefits and costs are the externalities of the proposed project. Thus, the generation of economic activities, such as increased business for the surrounding areas, is to be counted as its indirect benefit. The increased activities, however, may create factors that are detrimental to the city, such as increased traffic, pollution, or crime. These are the social or indirect costs of the project.

Not all costs and benefits are measurable in monetary terms. Many costs and benefits are primarily qualitative in nature, and as such, cannot be readily expressed in dollars and cents. For example, a beautiful convention center can produce the intangible benefit of newfound pride in the city. Its construction can

Figure 14.1   Classification of Costs and Benefits

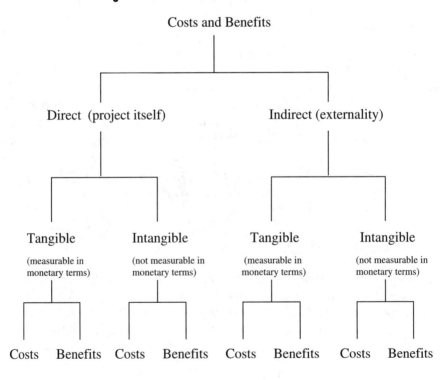

bring about a change in attitude in the city's citizens. In contrast, such negative conditions as environmental hazards brought about by the construction of the hotel and convention center would constitute part of its social costs. These are the **intangible costs and benefits** of a project. Analysts should be as comprehensive as possible in enumerating the costs and benefits of a public project, both intangible and tangible. I present a list of possible tangible and intangible costs and benefits in Table 14.1.

ESTIMATION AND VALUATION OF BENEFITS AND COSTS

One of the most difficult problems of conducting a cost-benefit analysis is that many of the benefits and costs may not be measurable in monetary terms. Another problem is that if they are to be accrued in the future, they must be estimated. It is not enough to state that the construction of a new convention center would increase revenue for the city. We need to come up with a reasonable estimate of how much additional revenue there would be.

A convention center would draw groups of people from outside the region for business meetings. The proposed center would provide large rooms for various

Table 14.1 Benefits and Costs of Convention Center

Benefits				Costs			
Direct		Indirect		Direct		Indirect	
Tangible	Intangible	Tangible	Intangible	Tangible	Intangible	Tangible	Intangible
Revenues from the convention center	Appearance of the new facility	Increased business for the surrounding areas	Increased civic and community pride	Construction expenses and other related costs	Appearance of structure	Increased costs to the business as a result of traffic congestion	Increased urban congestion, traffic jams
		Higher property, sales, and transient occupancy taxes for the city		Cost of acquiring land	Reduced property values for some neighborhoods		Increased crime and pollution
		Increased property values for some neighborhoods					Environmental degradation
							Displacement of the poor from the neighborhood

gatherings as well as hotel space for convention participants and their guests. Suppose that city hotels can accommodate 300,000 guests per year. The new convention center would increase this capacity to 350,000. The average cost of renting a room in the city is $50, but the increased supply of rooms would reduce this cost to $45 (see Figure 14.2).

You may recall our discussion of consumer surplus from chapter 2. We illustrate this concept in Figure 14.2, in which the demand curve for hotel rooms (D) is shown as a downward sloping heavy line. Suppose that before construction of the convention center, the supply curve was vertical line S, which gave us an equilibrium occupancy rate of 300,000 rooms at an average room cost per room of $50. At that point, the triangle abc represented the total benefit, or consumer surplus. As a result of the convention center, the supply increased to S', with an equilibrium room occupancy rate of 350,000 and an average rental rate of $45. As you can see, this increase in supply and reduction in price have allowed 50,000 extra guests to visit the city. This new situation has enlarged the area of total consumer surplus to the triangle aef.

Of the total consumer surplus represented by triangle aef, the part described by triangle abc is not new. However, the convention center project has in fact created two new areas of consumer surplus, the rectangle cbdf and the triangle bde. Rectangle cbdf is an added surplus to consumers. That is, as a result of the reduced price of lodging in the city, the gain to consumers is a dollar-for-dollar loss to producers—the hotel and motel owners who had to lower their rates to fill the additional capacity. Rectangle cbdf illustrates what microeconomists call the

Figure 14.2 Consumer Surplus and Social Benefits

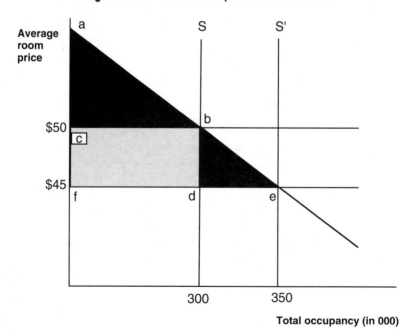

pecuniary effect, which occurs when a change in the welfare of one group of individuals comes at the expense of some other group. Since the gains of the gainers exactly match the loss of the losers, for the society as a whole there is no change in welfare, unless we want to value one group's gain differently from the other group's loss. In that case, society must make a value judgment about the redistribution of income. We will discuss this issue later in the chapter.

Returning to the Figure 14.2, we see that the true additional consumer surplus is represented by triangle bde, the area of **net social benefit**. Using the Pythagorean theorem, we can calculate the area of triangle bde as

$$\frac{height \times width}{2} = \frac{(\$50 - \$45) \times 50,000}{2} = \$125,000$$

Thus, the net gain in consumer surplus to the city is $125,000. Let us suppose that the project has been financed with municipal bonds. The bonds cost city taxpayers $75,000 per year. Therefore, the net gain to the city is $50,000, the difference between the gain in consumer surplus and the cost of servicing the loan ($125,000 − $75,000 = $50,000).

The preceding problem was an easy one to solve. In real life, calculations of costs and benefits are rarely as simple as those in our example. Table 14.1 gives you an idea of the different kinds of costs and benefits that have to be estimated and translated into monetary terms.

One of the most important aspects of conducting a cost-benefit analysis is the valuation of intangibles, which are not bought and sold in the market. Yet for the sake of comparison, an analyst must ascribe monetary values to these items. Let us consider a few examples.

Can We Put a Price Tag on the Intangibles of Life?

How would you value the life of a human being, or the risk of injury that could result in physical disfigurement, or irreparable damage to the environment? Putting a value on such matters evokes controversy, yet it has become a routine matter. For example, when a jury hands down an award for pain and suffering, loss of face, disability, or loss of life, it is imputing a value to the most intangible aspects of life. The case of *State of Alaska versus Exxon Corporation*, resulting from an oil spill in the pristine and ecologically fragile Prince William Sound, is an example of putting a specific monetary value on the loss of habitat. Therefore, it is indeed legitimate and necessary to consider ways of imputing monetary value to these intangibles while conducting a cost-benefit analysis.

For instance, our large construction project carries the possibility of accidents resulting in severe injuries and even death. In such circumstances, it is essential to include the costs of such accidents. There are several methods for calculating these costs: the **face value of life insurance, discounted future earnings,** and **required compensation.** The face value of life insurance measures the monetary worth of one's life by the amount of one's life insurance policy. However, people buy insurance for many different reasons (for example, to some it is a form of forced saving), and as such their purchase may have little to do with their perception of the value of their own lives. The discounted future earnings approach is often used in court cases. Thus, a person's life is worth the discounted value of future income. The future earnings are discounted because a dollar in the future is worth less in today's money. But since it evaluates life by one's earning potential, this approach under-values the lives of those individuals whose talents are not sold in the market or who have stopped earning money. Therefore, it will fail to place much value on home-makers, retirees, and people with disabilities who cannot work.

The market valuation of life does not ask the crucial question of how the worker involved perceives how much of the added risk is compensated by the income dif-ferential. The answer would imply how much an individual believes his or her life to be worth. There are people whose jobs carry no risk of death (for example, ele-mentary school teachers, bank clerks), whereas the jobs of others carry an inordi-nate amount of risk (for example, fire fighters, members of a bomb squad). There-fore, if we take an individual's education, age, experience, and other relevant factors of earning determination as constant, we will arrive at a larger payment for the risky jobs to compensate those workers for their added risk. The calculation of this margin of compensation for risk is called the required compensation princi-ple. This is an important issue, and many economists have attempted to estimate the size of this margin. From their studies it seems that this value varies from a lower boundary of $2.5 million to $5 million in 1988 constant dollars. This value turns out to be, on average, five to ten times the value of life calculated under the discounted future earnings principle.[3]

As you can imagine, the imputing of a very high value for human life would make many projects less than economically viable. Therefore, you may think of these numbers as quite excessive, until you realize that the individual who took this job might not have been totally aware of the risk involved. This is particularly true in the high-technology field; for example, workers whose job was sealing radi-ation chambers in the construction of an atomic power plant complained that they were not adequately apprised of the risk by management. Even individuals who are aware of risk may not have the bargaining power to gain adequate mone-tary protection against the loss of life. Finally, this measure does not take into account the externalities of such a loss. The death of an individual can destroy a family and cause irreparable damage to the welfare of those who were dependent on this person for financial and emotional security. In light of these kinds of exter-nalities, the U.S. military often exempted an only son from the draft, or two broth-ers from serving on the same ship.

As technology improves we come to realize the deleterious effects of sub-stances such as asbestos, whose risks most people were not aware of until only a few years ago. In December 2000 the Environmental Protection Agency (EPA) announced its decision to clean up a dangerous chemical, PCB, from the waters of the upper Hudson River by dredging 2.65 million cubic yards of sediment along a forty-mile stretch. The General Electric Company had discharged an estimated 1.1 million pounds of PCBs into the river before 1977 from capacitor plants in Fort

Edward and Hudson Falls, about forty miles north of Albany. As a result, the EPA claimed that a two-hundred-mile stretch of the river down to New York City was contaminated. The project would cost GE an estimated $460 million. However, the effects of PCBs were not previously known and therefore they were not banned before 1977.[4]

An example may help you understand the differences among the three methods of valuing a life. Suppose an innocent thirty-five-year-old schoolteacher is killed by the police during a high-speed car chase. Pursuing a suspect, the police cruiser goes through a red light and crashes into the teacher's car. The city is asked to pay compensation for this loss of life. Assume that the young man was earning $35,000 a year and had purchased a life insurance policy worth $150,000. According to the face value of life insurance method, the city will be liable for $150,000. However, if we assume that the young man would have lived for another thirty years and earned his current salary, his lifetime earnings discounted at a 6 percent rate turn out to be $201,022.19 (see the discussion of present value later in this chapter). In contrast, since he was not in a hazardous job, the required compensation method would estimate the value of his life in the several millions.

Since valuation of most of the intangibles in life is often highly subjective, the numbers can vary, climbing to absurd amounts. In 1991, two years after the Exxon ship *Valdez* had spilled oil, causing extensive environmental damage in Alaska, the Exxon Corporation agreed to settle criminal and civil complaints brought by Alaska and the federal government for $1.25 billion. Yet within a relatively short period, a study commissioned by the state and federal governments put the damage to the ecology at $15 billion.[5]

Indeed, as a society we may at times place extremely high prices on projects. If a project threatens a species with extinction or destroys a place of national interest or veneration, then we may assume that the cost of its destruction is too high for any conceivable monetary compensation. To prevent the extinction of spotted owls, the U.S. government declared a moratorium on logging in Oregon in 1991.

How Can We Measure Future Loss or Gain?

The prospect of future loss poses one of the most difficult obstacles to public projects. In popular terminology, this is the dreaded NIMBY (Not In My Backyard) factor, which community groups can effectively use to stop construction of projects that have widespread indirect benefits but impose specific costs on a certain community. Thus, while the construction of a new airport may prove to be a boon to a region's economy, the question remains as to which community will have to live with the noise and increased traffic. Although small in proportion to the total gain to the region, the cost of increased noise can have disastrous effects on property values in nearby neighborhoods.

The analyst is often faced with estimating a loss of property value that has not yet occurred. This estimate can typically be carried out using a causal regression model, discussed in chapter 12. We can form a regression model in which the price of property will be a function of changes (Δ) in:

$$\text{Price} = f\Delta \text{ (Noise, Pollution, Travel Time, Other factors)} \qquad (14.1)$$

In this case, we hypothesize that the price of property will depend on the altered levels of noise (measured in decibels) and pollution (measured by various standardized emission units), which will have a negative effect on the price. A decrease in travel time (measured in terms of minutes to the airport), in contrast, is likely to increase the price. Other factors include the property's size, location, view, and so forth. For the model we can take these factors as given because the construction of the airport will not change them.

Taking a cross section of city properties, we can estimate the relevant coefficients for noise, pollution, and travel time. The coefficients for each term measure the impact on the dependent variable of a one-unit change in the independent variable. By multiplying the estimated coefficients with the expected change in that variable as a result of airport construction, we can estimate the total loss to the property. Suppose our regression coefficient for the effect of noise on the price of property turns out to be –$5,000. This would mean that a one-unit increase in decibel level would reduce the price of a piece of property by $5,000. Suppose the environmental impact statement estimates that the new airport would add five decibels to the already existing noise level of a particular neighborhood. Then we can estimate the loss of property value for that neighborhood to be –$5,000 $\times$ 5 = –$25,000. Other coefficients can be used in a similar manner to measure the total impact the new airport would have on property value.

This kind of estimation poses many problems. The property owners are likely to dispute the results, because the estimates certainly will not cover all the costs associated with increased noise and other kinds of pollution (such as the effect on the physical and psychological health of the residents). It is interesting to note that frequently there exists an asymmetry in information between the gainers and losers of large public projects. In some instances a small group of potential losers tends to know and care about its losses a lot more than the larger group of potential gainers. In such cases, well-organized groups are often able to stop a project through political protests or obstructive legal actions. Conversely, in other cases, where the potential for individual gains are strong, a handful of powerful interest groups are able to get approval for a project that may inflict costs on a wide segment of the society.

It should be obvious by now that inferring the value of nonmarketable items is not an easy task and often creates controversy. Yet as an analyst you may have to estimate the value of time saved as a result of a traffic diversion or the emotional cost of destroying a community to build a freeway through it. You have to approach such matters boldly but with caution. For example, a recent report suggested that the construction of high-occupancy vehicle lanes (the highway lanes set aside for vehicles carrying more than a certain number of passengers) on the perennially clogged Atlanta freeways reduced commuting time by fifteen minutes. You may be tempted to put a value on the time saved by multiplying it by the average wages of the commuters multiplied by their number, until you realize that the time saved is not likely to increase the commuters' working hours. Instead the fifteen minutes, which would have been spent sitting in a traffic jam, will now be spent pursuing enjoyable activities that carry no commercial value. You may instead consider the amount of gasoline saved by having to run the car engine for fifteen minutes and then calculate the money saved by commuters. In addition, you may look for the environmental benefits of reduced auto exhaust emissions.

In the previous pages we discussed the problems of putting monetary values on nonmarketable items. If you find items that are simply not translatable in money, you may do well not to overstretch your imagination. As we have seen, unless you are careful, the valuing of nonmarketables can quickly veer toward the ridiculous. Therefore, in such cases, an analyst should report accurately the intangible effects of the proposed project so political decision makers can make an informed decision.

INTRODUCTION OF TIME: PRESENT VALUE ANALYSIS

In the preceding example of the convention center, we have a relatively simple choice to make based on a one-time, lump sum net benefit. However, the benefits and costs of most projects do not occur at one time. Instead, they come in over a period of time. This inclusion of time adds one more dimension to our problem.

To begin with, a dollar received a number of years down the road may not be worth as much as a dollar already in our pockets. I am always reminded of a local television commercial for an annuity program. The announcer asks viewers to join a "millionaires' club." If a young adult saves a certain amount of money per month, then at the end of nearly thirty-five years this individual will receive $1 million from the annuity. Of course, during the dreamy announcement part of this commercial, the camera lens pans over all the trappings that are commonly associated with the lives of millionaires—a fancy home, a limousine parked in the driveway, and so on. Ask yourself though, Would a million dollars thirty-five years from now be worth a million dollars in today's money? Obviously, the answer is that the two amounts of money are not equal. But the question of the difference between a dollar in my pocket today and one in the future can be answered only if we understand the process of discounting.

To explain the process of discounting, I must first explain the process of compounding. Suppose I have invested $100 in a certificate of deposit, maturing at the end of the year, at a 10 percent interest rate. At the end of the year, I will receive $110. Thus, $100 invested at 10 percent interest for a year will yield $100 $\times$ (1 + 0.1), or $110.

The preceding formulation is perfectly obvious. If I keep this investment one more year at the compounding interest rate of 10 percent, then at the end of the second year I will get back not another $10, but $11, because I will earn interest on the previous year's interest. Therefore, at the end of the second year, I will receive $110 $\times$ (1 + 0.1), or $121. By inserting into the preceding equation the formula by which we obtained the result of $110, we get $100 $\times$ (1 + 0.1) $\times$ (1 + 0.1), or $121, which can be rewritten as $100 $\times$ $(1 + .1)^2$ = $121.

If you are observant, you will note that keeping the money for *two* years requires us to multiply the original amount of money invested by 1 plus the interest rate

(10 percent, or 0.1 in this case), the quantity raised to the power of two. Therefore, if I had kept the money for three years, the exponent of the term within the parentheses would have to be raised to three. Then, by extending this logic, we can generalize by stating that the original investment of P_0 amount invested at r percent rate of interest for n number of years will give us P_n amount of money:

$$P_n = P_0 \times \left(1 + r\right)^n \tag{14.2}$$

where P_n = principal amount at the end of the nth period
$\quad\quad P_0$ = original principal amount at period 0
$\quad\quad r$ = rate of interest

Using a calculator, we can determine that $155, invested at a 6.5 percent rate for seventeen years, would yield $155 $\times$ $(1.065)^{17}$, or $452.14. This is the formula for the computation of compound interest. This formula, therefore, tells you how much a dollar invested today at a certain interest rate would be worth in the future.

In contrast, a dollar in the future may not be worth its full face value in today's currency; the forces of inflation, uncertainty, risk, and the plain fact that you would rather have your money now than at a later date may eat away much of its value. In other words, I may pose the question from the opposite direction: How much would a dollar be worth to you in the nth year in the future? In such a case, without compounding your initial investment, you would have to discount your future income. Let us take a specific example. Suppose I were to receive $100 a year from today. Since I will be getting it in the future, if I use a **discount rate** (which measures the intensity with which I want my money in the present) of 10 percent, then the $100 will be equal to

$$\frac{100}{1.1} = \$90.91$$

As in our previous example, if we are considering n years in the future, our future gain will have to be discounted by 1 plus the rate of discount, raised to the number of years we have to wait for the money. Thus, we can generalize the formula as

$$P_v = \frac{P_n}{\left(1 + r\right)^n} \tag{14.3}$$

Going back to the example of the millionaires' club, we can see that if the discounting factor is 10 percent, then $1 million received thirty-five years from now will be equal to

$$\frac{\$1,000,000}{(1 + 0.1)^{35}} = \$35,584.10$$

Alas, in light of this analysis, it appears that the dream of $1 million has to be curtailed; the *present value* of $1 million received thirty-five years in the future is worth only about $35,000. With this amount, one certainly cannot expect all the trappings required for membership in a millionaires' club. This process is called **present value** analysis, by which we calculate the current or present value of a dollar to be gained in the future. We can use this formula to calculate the present value of a stream of benefits and costs to arrive at the net present value of a project. Notice that the larger the discount rate, the lower the present value of future dollars. If we were to discount a million dollars at a 15 percent rate, we would arrive at the paltry sum of $7,508.89 for the same time period.[6] You can see that as we increase the discount rate, the future dollars look smaller and smaller. As a result, gains to be made in the future look increasingly less attractive; similarly, the prospect of losses in the distant future looks less ominous. Therefore, the discount rate captures the strength of the desire to have money now as opposed to sometime in the future. This desire is called **time preference.**

The relationship between time preference and the discounted future value of a dollar is shown in Figure 14.3. In this figure, we have plotted this year's earnings on the horizontal axis and next year's earnings on the vertical axis. If we do not have a time preference, then we will be indifferent between $10 today or $10 next year. The line connecting $10 on the two axes shows an **indifference map** (we are indifferent between, or prefer equally, any two points along this line) with no time preference. However, if we discount the future earnings at a 10 percent rate, then to be on the same utility plane, we must earn $11 next year. If we have an even higher time preference, equal to a 15 percent rate of discount, unless we earn $11.50 in the following year, we would prefer to have $10 today.

Let us consider a concrete example. Suppose we are evaluating two projects with the streams of benefits and costs shown in Table 14.2. From this table, it is

Figure 14.3 Time Preference and Discount Rate

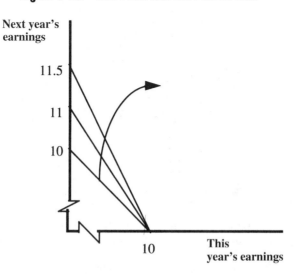

Table 14.2 Comparison of Costs and Benefits for Projects A and B

	Project A		Project B	
Year	Benefits	Costs	Benefits	Costs
0	0	30	15	5
1	0	15	15	5
2	0	10	15	5
3	10	5	15	10
4	20	5	15	10
5	120	5	15	15
Total	150	70	90	50

clear that Project A provides us with double the net benefit ($80) provided by Project B ($40).

So should we automatically choose Project A over B? If we were to jump to this conclusion, we would be remiss, since we would fail to consider that the increased net benefits of Project A come at a later stage in the project's life. Our choice between the two projects will depend on the strength of our time preference—the willingness to wait for future returns. Therefore, to compare the two projects on a level ground, we must translate these future streams of benefits and costs into their present values. The formula is written as

$$PV = \sum_{t=0}^{n} \frac{(B_t - C_t)}{(1+r)^t} \qquad (14.4)$$

where PV = present value of the project,
B_t is the benefit, and
C_t is the cost at t.

We can open up this expression and write

$$PV = \frac{(B_0 - C_0)}{(1+r)^0} + \frac{(B_1 - C_1)}{(1+r)^1} + \frac{(B_2 - C_2)}{(1+r)^2} + \frac{(B_3 - C_3)}{(1+r)^3} + \cdots \cdots \frac{(B_n - C_n)}{(1+r)^n}$$

Since any number raised to the power 0 is equal to 1, the expression can be written as

$$PV = (B_0 - C_0) + \frac{(B_1 - C_1)}{(1+r)^1} + \frac{(B_2 - C_2)}{(1+r)^2} + \frac{(B_3 - C_3)}{(1+r)^3} + \cdots \cdots \frac{(B_n - C_n)}{(1+r)^n}$$

You may notice that the 0th year's net benefits are not discounted. This makes eminent sense because the current year's dollar is equal to its face value and, hence, does not need to be discounted.

If we are willing to wait (that is, it does not matter to us whether we receive our payments today or tomorrow), our time preference is said to be nil. In such a situation, we discount the future stream of net benefits with a zero discount rate and, therefore, do not discount at all. Thus, if we do not have any time preference, the net benefits for Projects A and B are $80 and $40. In contrast, suppose we do have a definite time preference, and we want to evaluate the future stream of net benefits for the two projects at a 10 percent discount rate. In such a case, we can write the present values of Project A (PV_A) and Project B (PV_B), discounted at 10 percent, as[7]

$$PV_A = (0-30) + \frac{0-15}{(1+.1)} + \frac{0-10}{(1+.1)^2} + \frac{10-5}{(1+.1)^3} + \frac{20-5}{(1+.1)^4} + \frac{120-5}{(1+.1)^5}$$

$$= -30 - 13.64 - 8.26 + 3.76 + 10.25 + 71.41 = 33.52$$

$$PV_B = (15-5) + \frac{15-5}{1+.1} + \frac{15-5}{(1+.1)^2} + \frac{15-10}{(1+.1)^3} + \frac{15-10}{(1+.1)^4} + \frac{15-15}{(1+.1)^5}$$

$$= 10 + 9.09 + 8.26 + 3.76 + 3.41 + 0 = 34.52$$

From the preceding calculation, we can see that discounted at a 10 percent rate, Project A is less preferable than Project B because it carries a lower present value. We can also see that the present value of the two projects will depend on the rate of discount, which determines their relative desirability. We have plotted the present values as functions of the rate of discount in Figure 14.4. From this figure, it can be seen that the two projects become equally desirable at a discount rate slightly less than 10 percent. For discount rates below 10 percent, Project A is preferable to B, but the relative desirability changes for discount rates of 10 percent and above. This change reflects how Project A's benefits come at the end of the project life. In contrast, Project B yields positive net benefits from its inception. Therefore, if we can afford to wait (and have a small discount rate), we would prefer Project A. However, if we are in a hurry to get back the returns on investment (and, therefore, have a stronger time preference), we should choose Project B.

Finally, if the present value is negative (as Project A is for a discount rate close to 24 percent), we should reject the project.

Choice of Time Horizon

The choice of an appropriate **time horizon** is of crucial importance for a cost-benefit analysis. The relative desirability of a project is intrinsically connected to when a project ends. The length of a time period affects the desirability of long- and short-term projects. Many of the projects for drug interdiction are designed for short-term results. In these projects, drug use is considered primarily as a law-and-order problem, and efforts are made to lower the supply of illicit drugs by

Figure 14.4   Plot of Present Values as a Function of Discount Rates

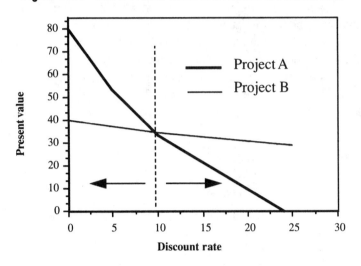

police action. In contrast, programs treating drug abuse are seen as long-term public health initiatives that require expenditure on education, rehabilitation, and employment opportunities. These demand-side efforts (trying to reduce the drug demand) offer longer-term solutions. So unless they are given longer time horizons, their impact on drug use will not be fully realized. Project desirability dependent on the choice of time horizon has been shown in Figure 14.5. You can see that before the critical point in time, T_n, the short-term project (Project I) yields higher net present value. However, beyond this point, the long-term project (Project II) becomes more attractive.

Choice of Discount Rate

The results shown in Figure 14.4 demonstrate how sensitive the assessment of a project's desirability can be to a change in the discount rate. Therefore, it is essential that we come up with the "correct" discount rate in evaluating a public project. In fact, the sensitivity of a public investment decision to the choice of discount rate was underscored by a proposed joint water project between Canada and the United States. Whereas the United States analysts, who used a lower discount rate, recommended the project, their Canadian counterparts, who used a higher discount rate, rejected it. There is little mention in the cost-benefit literature of how to choose the "appropriate" discount rate. A simple personal example may explain one of the reasons for this confusion. Suppose I am thinking of investing in a project that yields a certain amount of money over a period of time. While considering the desirability of this investment I may consider alternative ways to invest this money. I find out that the best return on available investment is 8 percent. In such a case, I would discount the future net benefits of the project at an 8 percent rate. If this discounting provides me with a positive net present value, I should invest;

Figure 14.5   The Effects of Choosing Time Horizon

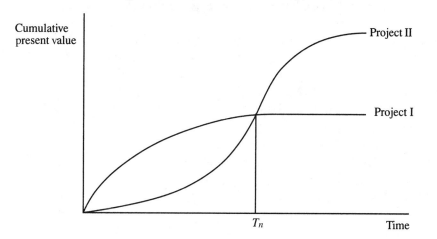

otherwise I should not. This process of considering alternative uses of money provides the opportunity cost, or the **shadow price,** of money. From the standpoint of a local government, the alternative use of money determines its opportunity cost. That is, if we did not invest in the convention center, we could use the money for some other projects important to the residents. Without full information on the opportunity cost of money, we may not be able to determine the appropriate discount rate.

However, the opportunity cost of money may not be the only guiding principle for investment. I may choose to discount my investment with a rate that reflects my own time preference. People may use many different rates of discount representing different time preferences. Thus, if I want my money right now (or, in other words, I have a strong time preference), I would use a very high discount rate. If, however, I have a long-term perspective, I would be willing to wait for a higher return in the future, in which case the rate of discount will be quite low. In fact, in an extreme case, my time preference can even be less than zero. Imagine that you are the dictator of a small but wealthy country. You have all the money you want for the present. However, what you do not have is security for the future—you may find yourself deposed by a coup or a revolution. In such a case, your discount rate can even be negative, and hence you will be willing to put your money in a Swiss or otherwise secret bank account, where the bank will charge you for the safe-keeping of your (presumably ill-gotten) assets and will not pay you interest. In other words, depending on my circumstances, it may be perfectly reasonable for me to use a discount rate different from the opportunity cost, in conformity with my personal time preference.

Similarly, in the case of the society, economists have argued back and forth regarding the optimum rate of discount on the basis of opportunity cost and **social time preference.** The proponents of opportunity cost for investment argue that government pays for its investments by taking money away from private citizens;

thus, unless the returns of these investments are at least equal to those of the private sector, it does not make any economic sense for the government to invest. According to this point of view, while evaluating a public project, the analyst should take into account the opportunity of alternative investment opportunity in the private sector, and hence discount the project by a rate equal to the private rate of return. Suppose that the U.S. space agency is proposing building a new kind of space vehicle, which will be able to deploy satellites with a greater degree of efficiency than do the existing space shuttles. Money for this project must be raised from private taxpayers. If the market is yielding 10 cents on a one dollar investment, unless it can be shown that the return from this project is going to be at least 10 percent (that is, the project carries a positive net present value when discounted at 10 percent), the project should not be undertaken.

This rule of discounting seems reasonable. However, upon further consideration, it turns out to be unsatisfactory. Problems arise because like all other markets, the capital market is characterized by various kinds of imperfections. For example, monopolies can significantly distort security prices.[8] Also, the government may face several political constraints in its investment decisions, which can make any comparison with the private sector invalid. Therefore, by looking at the vast and imperfect capital market, an analyst is likely to be confused about the "appropriate" rate of yield in the private sector.

The comparison of government rate of return with that in the private market is further complicated by the often ill-defined source of government revenue. Thus, if tax money comes out of the taxpayers' savings, the consideration of opportunity cost may be valid. However, if it comes from the money that was allocated by the taxpayer for consumption, the comparison would not make much sense. In addition, the source of government revenue is diverse. The government may get its money from taxes, tariffs, licenses and fees, or from selling bonds or government property. Not all of these moneys have the same opportunity cost, and it is impossible to pinpoint the exact source of the funding for a project.

Finally, the outputs of government projects may be intangibles and as such cannot be measured in monetary terms. Thus, it will be impossible to convert the benefits of subsidized school lunch programs into strict monetary units. Also, many government programs can generate long-term positive externalities, which are extremely difficult to measure. For example, the development of computer technology, to a large extent, has been a by-product of the space program. Yet, at the time of the inception of the program, nobody could have predicted this fortuitous outcome.

The recent literature in economics suggests the use of a discount rate that reflects the subjective time preference of society.[9] Unfortunately, the scholars who have spent a great deal of time contemplating the appropriate discount rate are unable to tell us exactly which number to use.[10] However, the insights derived from these discussions can at least point out the folly of using grossly inappropriate rates. Given the enormous complexity of our world, we may consider that benefit to be a giant step forward. In any case, the confusion about the correct discount rate is reflected in the practice of the highest federal agencies.

At the federal level the Office of Management and Budget (OMB), the General Accounting Office (GAO), and the Congressional Budget Office conduct discounting on a regular basis for capital expenditure programs, lease-purchase decisions, regulatory reviews, and sales of government assets. However, they use different discount rates.[11]

For example, the OMB, which determines rates for all executive agencies, typically uses a 10 percent discount rate, corrected for the rate of inflation, for all tax-financed projects. If an agency wants to use a different rate, it must justify its choice. Since lease-purchase projects are funded by government bond financing, they are evaluated at the Treasury Department borrowing rate with a maturity date corresponding to the projects' completion, plus 0.125 percent to cover the Federal Financing Bank's borrowing charge. Thus, a fifteen-year project is going to be discounted at the fifteen-year Treasury bond rate (say, currently at 4.75 percent) plus 0.125, or at 4.875 percent. In contrast, when a government asset is sold to nongovernmental entities, the OMB uses comparable private sector borrowing rates.

The GAO's use of a discount rate is based on the current yield of Treasury debt between one year and the life of the project. The GAO uses sensitivity analysis through different discount rates (see discussion of sensitivity analysis later in the chapter).

The Congressional Budget Office, like the OMB, uses an inflation-adjusted Treasury borrowing rate and then looks at the sensitivity of the project by adding or subtracting 2 percent from the chosen discount rate. Also, like the OMB, it uses private sector rates to evaluate asset sales.

Because there is no unanimity at the federal agency level, the state budget offices either follow the federal directives or use different rates. Local governments usually follow the state guidelines.

The Internal Rate of Return

Since it is so difficult to settle on a universally acceptable discount rate for public projects, a decision maker can often be tempted to use what is known as the **internal rate of return** for judging the desirability of a project. The internal rate of return is defined as *the rate of discount at which the present value of a project is equal to zero.* Thus, from Figure 14.4, you can see that the present value for the hypothetical Project A approaches zero at about 24 percent, which is its internal rate of return.[12]

The advantage of using an internal rate of return is that it reduces the decision maker's burden of having to make a choice based on a single discount rate. Instead, a project can be accepted if the returns are larger than what can be reasonably obtained in an alternative investment. Going back to our example, if the internal rate of return for a project is 24 percent, it is so much higher than what can be reasonably expected in other possible investments that a decision maker will be hard-pressed to reject it.

However, despite this intuitive appeal, the internal rate of return suffers from some important shortcomings. First, although the internal rate of return is useful in pointing out the desirability of a single project, it is ineffective when choosing between two or more. Second, depending on the configuration of streams of net benefits, projects can often have more than one internal rate of return, as shown in Figure 14.6.

Since there are two rates (5 percent and 20 percent) at which the present value of the project becomes equal to zero, our decision maker is likely to remain confused about the desirability of the project. Edith Stokey and Richard Zeckhauser note that the internal rate of return can point to the correct public policy decisions under some rather unrealistic circumstances, such as when there are no budgetary constraints, there are no comparisons with other alternative projects, and the stream of returns is first negative and then positive.[13]

CHOOSING THE BEST ALTERNATIVE

Sensitivity Analysis

After conducting the analysis, you may decide that you do not agree with your finding, or other experts in the field may disagree with you, or you may simply want to know how robust your finding is. In such cases, you may want to conduct a sensitivity analysis. This process allows analysts to change the assumptions underlying their analysis, estimate a different set of numbers, choose an alternative discount rate, and then see if there is a significant change in the outcome. Where there is a nonexistent market, you may impute monetary values based on a different set of criteria. Or you may look into alternative scenarios for estimating future streams of income. For example, you may consider the most plausible case,

Figure 14.6   The Internal Rate of Return

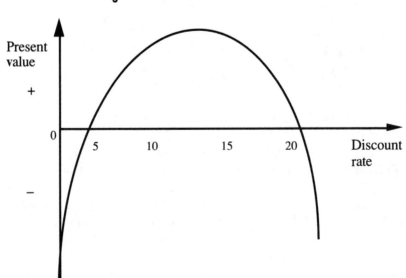

the most optimistic case, and the most pessimistic case, with their corresponding subjective probabilities. If the probability of a disastrous case scenario poses an unacceptable amount of risk, that risk should be made clear to the decision makers. Finally, the use of different discount rates can also be of tremendous help in understanding the strength of a particular project. In our hypothetical case shown in Figure 14.4, you can demonstrate that Project A is preferable up to a 10 percent discount rate, beyond which Project B becomes preferable. Such a demonstration of sensitivity strengthens the robustness of your argument more than choosing a single rate and then drawing a conclusion on the basis of it.

Cost-Benefit Ratio

When choosing among alternatives, you may want to consider the ratios between benefits and costs, instead of their difference. In many cases, the use of either of these two criteria will lead to the same conclusion. However, a difference in the scale of operation may bring about a conflict. Consider the problem shown in Table 14.3.

From this table, you can see that the sheer difference in the size of the two projects means that we are really comparing apples and oranges. Therefore, by using the ratio method we are apt to choose Project A, whereas by using the difference method we would have chosen Project B.

Cost-benefit ratio, however, is often thought of as the efficiency measure. It may be particularly useful when you are evaluating a set of projects with a fixed amount of funds available for them. Let us consider the following hypothetical example. Suppose your city is considering spending $10 million, raised through bond financing, to expand the public library system. Eight facilities are being proposed: one large facility at the center of the city and seven smaller facilities spread through various neighborhoods. Each one has different cost estimates. The purpose of a public library is making its facilities accessible to the residents of the city, so you have decided to use the projected circulation from each facility as the measure of each facility's benefit. Table 14.4 shows the various benefits and costs.[14]

If you add up the costs of all eight facilities, you will quickly find that the project would cost $18.25 million, far beyond the city's allocation of funds. Therefore, you may have to choose among these eight possibilities. In this case (Table 14.5), you may rearrange Table 14.4 according to the relative rates of efficiency, the cost-benefit ratio.

In this table, the column on cumulative cost tells us how much each facility would add to the total cost. Alas, reality often does not make the life of an analyst

Table 14.3 Contradictory Decision Based on Net Difference and Benefit-Cost Ratio

	Benefit	Cost	Net benefit	Benefit-cost ratio
Project A	10	3	+7	3.33
Project B	50	25	+25	2.00

Table 14.4   Costs and Benefits of Library Facilities

Location	Benefits (projected circulation per year—millions)	Costs ($ millions)	Benefit-cost Ratio
City center	15.00	7.50	2.000
Neighborhood A	3.00	0.75	4.000
Neighborhood B	1.75	0.50	3.500
Neighborhood C	0.95	0.76	1.250
Neighborhood D	2.10	0.66	3.182
Neighborhood E	6.50	1.78	3.652
Neighborhood F	8.30	5.10	1.627
Neighborhood G	3.90	1.20	3.250

easy. In this case, listing the sites based on their efficiency shows that the top five require $4.89 million. Adding the city center facility would mean going over the $10 million budget limit by $2.39 million. Therefore, you may decide to drop this one and include the next efficient site, Neighborhood F. In that case, the total expenditure comes to $9.99 million, serving 25.55 million readers.

As you can see, cost-benefit ratio served as a guide for our choice of the most efficient allocation of public funds. However, efficiency may not be the only consideration. For instance, the mayor may want the grandiose facility at the city's center for political reasons, or a more deprived neighborhood may be more deserving even though it does not show well on the measure of relative efficiency.

The Limits of Cost-Benefit Analysis: Redistribution of Income

The preceding discussion of cost-benefit analysis leaves out one important problem: Every government project creates winners and losers. How do you balance the gains against the losses? In a zero-sum society one group of individuals almost always comes out on top of some others. It is relatively easy to show the benefits of

Table 14.5   Costs and Benefits of Library Facilities

Location	Benefits (projected circulation per year—millions)	Costs ($ millions)	Benefit-cost ratio	Cumulative cost ($ millions)
Neighborhood A	3.00	0.75	4.000	0.75
Neighborhood E	6.50	1.78	3.652	2.53
Neighborhood B	1.75	0.50	3.500	3.03
Neighborhood G	3.90	1.20	3.250	4.23
Neighborhood D	2.10	0.66	3.182	4.89
City Center	15.00	7.50	2.000	12.39
Neighborhood F	8.30	5.10	1.627	17.49
Neighborhood C	0.95	0.76	1.250	18.25

massive highway construction in the United States. This was especially true during the 1950s, when the increased ease of transportation gave a tremendous boost to trade and commerce. Yet such construction did not come without a long list of those who were adversely affected by this development. Many small towns by the now abandoned but previously well-traversed roads were simply wiped out of existence; many communities lost their identities as the highways caused dislocation, isolation, and a general deterioration of neighborhoods. The trucking industry gained at the expense of a much more energy-efficient railroad industry; suburbs gained at the expense of downtown areas.

Yet as a reflection of the state of the art in social sciences and social philosophy, cost-benefit analysis is singularly unable to solve the problem of inevitably having winners and losers. I discussed the problem in chapter 4. Social philosophers have been grappling with the problem of determining distributive justice for centuries, with surprisingly few solutions. 1 can safely paraphrase Sir Winston Churchill to state that rarely in the entire field of social philosophy and social science have so many spent so much effort to produce so few results. The inability to address the question of redistribution not only remains the biggest challenge for cost-benefit analysis, but also truly exposes the intellectual poverty of our social philosophy.

Cost-Effectiveness Analysis

The basic principle of cost-benefit analysis is simple enough: Choose the alternative that gives you the maximum net benefit. However, in many cases of public expenditure the benefit schedule is ill defined or impossible to measure: The local fire department wants to buy fire engines that can accomplish more or less the same task as their current trucks; an organization is planning to purchase personal computers of similar capabilities to the ones they are now using. In such cases, if it is reasonable to hold that all the alternatives are substitutes, then we can assume that the benefit levels for all of them are equal and, hence, can be regarded as constant. Thus, we can choose the least expensive alternative.

Suppose, however, that money has been allocated to support an outreach program to teach children of homeless families, and proposals are being evaluated for choosing the best alternative. In this case, all the alternatives will spend the full allocation, so the costs are the same. For our comparison we need concern ourselves only with maximizing the benefits. In this circumstance we can use a truncated version of cost-benefit analysis. This is called **cost-effectiveness analysis.** The two simple rules for cost-effectiveness analysis are as follows:

1. If the benefits are the same, choose the alternative with the least cost.
2. If the costs are the same, choose the alternative with the most benefits.

Returning to the fire department example, two different makes of fire engines are under consideration. Both serve the same function, so we can concentrate on various aspects of costs of purchase and operation. Having done so, we can choose the one that is less expensive. Although the process seems simple enough, all the

A CASE IN POINT

Fitting Seat Belts in Texas School Buses[1]

The problem: In 1985 Texas was confounded by the problem that more adults and children were injured in school bus accidents (635 total in 1985) than in any of the previous eight years. Since Texas did not require school buses to be equipped with seat belts, only a very small fraction of the injured children (1.7 percent) were wearing them.

The goal: Evaluate the potential reduction in serious injury and death to the schoolchildren resulting from the installation of safety belts.

The alternatives: Install seat belts on all the school buses, or do nothing.

Assessment of costs and benefits: Avoidance of serious injuries to children (benefits) and the cost of refurbishing the existing school buses (costs). Imputing tangible values on intangible benefits was a bit trickier because data on the effectiveness of seat belts in the prevention of serious accidents were not available for school buses. Therefore, it was assumed that seat belt effectiveness in buses was the same as in automobiles, for which data were available. These data were used to calculate the percentage of preventable injuries. The severity of injuries was calculated by the Multiple Abbreviated Injury Scale (MAIS). The results are shown in the table.

Types of Injuries and Preventable Numbers for Texas, 1983–1985

Age and injury category	Number of accidents		Preventable fraction	No. of preventable cases
	Belted	Not belted		
MAIS 0: No injury	4	354		
5–14 years	3	297	0.00	0
15–18 years	1	57	0.00	0
MAIS 1: Minor injury	3	253		
5–14 years	2	212	0.00	0
15–18 years	1	41	0.00	0
MAIS 2: Moderate injury	1	150		
5–14 years	1	126	0.01	1
15–18 years	0	24	0.23	6
MAIS 3: Serious injury	0	91		
5–14 years	0	76	0.07	5
15–18 years	0	15	0.39	6
MAIS 4: Severe injury	0	37		
5–14 years	0	31	0.20	6
15–18 years	0	6	0.64	4
MAIS 5: Critical injury	0	32		
5–14 years	0	18	0.25	5
15–18 years	0	4	0.71	3
MAIS 6: Fatal injury (no fatal injuries were reported)				

Discount rate: A social discount rate of 6 percent was used to calculate the present value of net benefits over time.

Recommendations: The results indicate that the economic benefits from mandatory seat belts would not be cost effective for all the existing buses. However, mandatory seat belts could be cost effective for new buses.

Conclusion: This result is surprising given the widely accepted social benefits resulting from automobile seat belts. The authors explain this discrepancy by noting that the number of injuries per mile of school bus ride is significantly less than for automobiles. Also, the severity of injuries is much higher in autos. Second, since the injury victims are children, who do not start earning income for years (in contrast to an income-earning adult), the use of their discounted earning capability reduces the size of the benefits. Third, the indirect benefit that the habit of wearing seat belts may carry over to private automobiles, as the children learn to use them, was not included in the study. Finally, the study did not consider the cost effectiveness of requiring seat belts for only the newly acquired buses.

Note

1. Adapted from Charles E. Bagley and Andrea K. Biddie, "Cost-Benefit Analysis of Safety Belts in Texas School Buses," *Public Health Reports* 103 (September–October 1988): 479–488.

Discussion Points

1. How was cost-benefit analysis used in determining whether to fit seat belts on existing buses?
2. Do you agree with the study? If you were doing the analysis, would you have altered any of the assumptions? How do you think that might have changed the recommendation?

---

problems of a full-fledged cost-benefit analysis remain just as relevant. For a real-world application of the concepts discussed in this chapter, see "A Case in Point: Fitting Seat Belts in Texas School Buses."

Key Words

Consumer surplus (p. 358)

Cost-benefit analysis (p. 357)

Cost-effectiveness analysis (p. 379)

Direct costs and benefits (p. 360)

Discount rate (p. 368)

Discounted future earnings method (p. 363)

Face value of life insurance method (p. 363)

Indifference map (p. 369)

Indirect costs and benefits (p. 360)

Intangible costs and benefits (p. 361)

Internal rate of return (p. 375)

Negative externality (p. 359)

Net social benefit (p. 363)

Pecuniary effect (p. 363)

Positive externality (p. 359)

Present value (p. 369)

Required compensation principle (p. 363)

Shadow price (p. 373)

Social time preference (p. 373)

Time horizon (p. 371)

Time preference (p. 369)

Exercises

1. Suppose you are considering buying a new home or renting a bigger apartment. In a report, define your goal, the feasible set of alternatives, and the set of desirable attributes. Then, given your budgetary limitations, write a report describing the process by which you arrived at the optimum choice.

2. Consider a project in your city that proposes to increase the supply of any public good. Indicate the benefits and costs, pointing out the possible area of consumer surplus, the pecuniary effect, and the loss of producer surplus. You many also think of a project that proposes some new government regulation to bring social cost in line with private cost. Point out the area of possible dead weight loss in consumer surplus, the pecuniary effect, and the gain in producer surplus. Explain your choice of discount rate (you do not need to show any actual calculation of present value).

3. What is a social discount rate? Why is there so much confusion in defining the term "social discount rate"? Why is it important to determine this rate when calculating the relative desirability of a public project?

4. What is a cost-effectiveness study? How does it differ from a full cost-benefit analysis? Give examples of when it is more appropriate to use a cost-effectiveness analysis.

5. Calculate the net social benefit of the two projects in the table by evaluating them at 0, 5, 10, and 20 percent discount rates.

Year	Project A Benefits	Project A Costs	Project B Benefits	Project B Costs
0	10	10	0	55
1	15	10	5	25
2	20	10	15	25
3	30	10	50	15
4	20	10	65	15
5	10	10	95	15

6. Suppose your final answer in a popular game show was correct and you received $1 million. The show gives you two options: You can take your million dollars in a lump sum, or you can get $145,000 per year for the next twenty-two years. Within the framework of the present value analysis, which option would you choose and why? Explain your choice of discount rate. One more small matter of information: Whenever you take your prize money, you are subject to a tax of 40 percent.

7. A recent study has demonstrated the link between death rates and the amount of fine particulates less than 10 microns (one-thousandth of a millimeter) across.[15] These particulates come from cars, trucks, power plants, construction, and even agriculture. The study found that for each 10 micrograms of particles per cubic meter of air over a twenty-four-hour period, the death rate from all causes rose more than one-half of 1 percent. That is, in a large city in which one hundred people die each day, a rise in the particulate pollution of 20 micrograms per cubic meter can cause an additional death per day. During the study period, New York averaged 190.9 deaths per day. The corresponding figures for Los Angeles and Chicago were 148 and 113.9.

   Suppose you are an EPA analyst in charge of producing a position paper on a new pollution standard reflecting the new findings. How would you develop your study? Specifically what kinds of information would you seek to demonstrate the desirability of your proposal through a cost-benefit analysis?

Notes

1. This line of reasoning has a long history and a voluminous literature in economics. For a seminal explanation, see Gary S. Becker, *Economic Approach to Human Behavior* (Chicago: University of Chicago Press, 1976).
2. See Shoshana Grossbard-Shechtman, *On Economics of Marriage: A Theory of Marriage, Labor, and Divorce* (Boulder, Colo.: Westview Press, 1993), esp. 5–84.
3. For an excellent discussion of the required compensation principle, see Edward Gramlich, *A Guide to Benefit-Cost Analysis*, 2d ed. (Englewood Cliffs, N.J.: Prentice Hall, 1990), 67–70.
4. Kirk Johnson, "G.E. Facing Order to Remove Poisons from the Hudson," *New York Times,* December 6, 2000, A1.
5. "Secret Studies Put Spill Damage at $15 Billion," *Los Angeles Times,* October 8, 1991, 1.
6. You can calculate the present value by using a simple hand calculator. If you have a y^x button on your calculator, you can make the necessary calculation. For calculating the present value of $1 million thirty-five years later, at a discount rate of, say, 5 percent, punch in the numbers in the following sequence: $1,000,000 /(1.05 y^x 35) =. This sequence will give you the answer: $181,290.29.
7. You can calculate the net present value by using the Microsoft Excel program. However, if you do, you should know that Excel assumes that discounting starts at period 0. Therefore, in order to get the results in this book, you should start discounting from the second year on and then add the net present value of the initial year.
8. Recall the security exchange fraud during the late 1980s and early 1990s by the giant trading houses such as Drexel, Burnham and Lambert, and Solomon Brothers, which had a significant impact on the market. Similar irregularities in Japan caused widespread concern over the integrity of Japanese financial institutions.
9. See David F. Bradford, "The Choice of Discount Rate for Government Investments," in *Public Expenditure and Policy Analysis,* ed. Robert H. Haveman and Julius Margolis, 3d ed. (Boston: Houghton Mifflin, 1983), 129–144.
10. Edward Gramlich suggested that the social time preference for the federal government, corrected for inflation, in 1988 was about 4 percent for projects financed by tax revenue and 6 percent for those financed by bonds. See Gramlich, *A Guide to Benefit-Cost Analysis.*
11. John Mikesell, *Fiscal Administration: Analysis and Application for the Public Sector,* 5th ed. (Fort Worth, Texas: Harcourt Brace, 1999), 253.
12. By using Excel, you can calculate internal rate of return. For the example of Project A in Figure 14.4, the internal rate of return comes to about 23.7 percent.
13. Edith Stokey and Richard Zeckhauser, *Primer for Policy Analysis* (New York: Norton, 1978), 167.
14. You may notice here that although I have defined benefits in strict monetary terms, in this case we are using a nonmonetary measure. When a monetary measure is not feasible, and everyone can agree upon a readily available indicator of benefit, there is no harm in using such a nonmonetary index.
15. Jonathan N. Samet et al., "Fine Particulate Air Pollution and Mortality in 20 U.S. Cities, 1987–1994," *New England Journal of Medicine* 343 (December 14, 2000): 1742–1749.

THE "GOOD ENOUGH" POLICY ANALYST

Myy analyst friend looked dejected. Shaking her head, she told me that she had spent a great deal of time preparing an analysis on a particular issue. The results, based on a sophisticated mathematical model, clearly showed the "correct" course of action. Yet the politicians had rejected her recommendations and made an "obviously wrong decision." As I sympathized with my friend, I wondered if she should feel so dejected. Indeed, if you have spent a large amount of time on a project, it often is impossible to separate your emotions from the project itself. Her problem raises the question of what is the analyst's role in a public organization.

From the earliest days of organized society, rulers have sought the advice of shamans, sages, sorcerers, and, in recent days, social scientists. The wise men and women of the past predicted the outcomes of an uncertain future by interpreting dreams, reading tea leaves, or relying on other dubious methods. In this book I have presented the techniques of statistics and operations research, the tools of the trade for today's policy advisers. But are these professionals any better at analyzing complex matters of public policy with scientific objectivity than were their functional predecessors?[1]

As the influence of policy advisers has increased in the American political system, so has skepticism about their methods. The skeptics hail from many walks of intellectual life. In his famous book *The Rebel*, the French author Albert Camus argued, in effect, that human beings are not smart enough to be rational. Influential scholars such as Aaron Wildavsky and Charles Lindblom say that we should stop pretending that we can be objective in our analysis. Instead, we should embrace "ordinary knowledge." Others, like Robert Formaini, flatly claim that "scientifically-based (i.e., *justified*) public policy, a dream that has grown ever larger since the Enlightenment and that, perhaps, has reached its apogee toward the close of our century, is a myth, a theoretical illusion. It exists in our minds, our analyses, and our methods only because we seek to find it, and, typically, we find what we seek." [2]

In the debate between those who claim "objective rationality" in their public policy research, basing their conclusions on scientific analysis of data, and others who view statistical analysis as nothing more than mischievous manipulation of facts by clever liars, I take the middle ground. Along with a well-known jurist, I adopt an agnostic stance and ask, "Facts, what are facts?" In this book I have tried to show that almost every step of an objective analysis, from observation to conclusion, forces an analyst to make subjective judgments that can significantly alter the conclusion of a study. Yet this subjectiveness does not negate the overarching scientific method rooted deep in our long intellectual history. Thus, Nobel Prize–winning economist James Buchanan correctly points out that we pursue not the "logic of choice" but the "science of choice." Although we cannot know whether our analyses have given us the best solution, we must make sure that the process by which we have made our selection is objective. Therefore, as an analyst, your job is not so much to defend the outcome of your analysis as to justify the way in which you went about it.

At the beginning of the book I invoked the image of the fictional fiddler on the roof, who plays his music on the slippery rooftop, performing an amazing balancing act. As policy analysts we little resemble the white-cloaked scientists conducting dispassionate research in the seclusion of a laboratory. Rather, we are professionals attempting to balance the often-conflicting needs of society, politics, and economics. In particular, this work involves balancing the following competing interests:

- Ethics and efficiency
- Professionalism and personal biases
- Individual judgment and organizational needs
- Cost and accuracy
- Interests of clients and those of society

Therefore, we aim not at creating perfect analysts with perfect answers to complex social problems but at developing competent professionals, those with a thorough knowledge of quantitative tools and techniques and a balanced view of competing needs. That balanced view is the first and last qualification of the "good enough" public policy analyst.

Notes

1. For a recent discussion of the issue, see Dan Durning, "The Transition from Traditional to Postpositivist Policy Analysis: A Role for Q-Methodology," *Journal of Policy Analysis and Management* 18, no. 3 (1999): 389–410.
2. Quoted in Young Back Choi, *Paradigms and Conventions: Uncertainty, Decision Making, and Entrepreneurship* (Ann Arbor: University of Michigan Press, 1993), 5, fn. 11. See also Robert Formaini, *The Myth of Scientific Public Policy* (Bowling Green, Ohio: Social Philosophy and Policy Center; New Brunswick, N.J.: Transaction Publishers, 1990), 1.

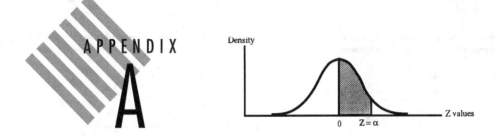

APPENDIX

A

Density

0   Z = α

Z values

Areas of the Standard Normal Distribution (the Z table)

Z	.00	.01	.02	.03	.04	.05	.06	.07	.08	.09
.0	.0000	.0040	.0080	.0120	.0160	.0199	.0239	.0279	.0319	.0359
.1	.0398	.0438	.0478	.0517	.0557	.0596	.0636	.0675	.0714	.0753
.2	.0793	.0832	.0871	.0910	.0948	.0987	.1026	.1064	.1103	.1141
.3	.1179	.1217	.1255	.1293	.1331	.1368	.1406	.1443	.1480	.1517
.4	.1554	.1591	.1628	.1664	.1700	.1736	.1772	.1808	.1844	.1879
.5	.1915	.1950	.1985	.2019	.2054	.2088	.2123	.2157	.2190	.2224
.6	.2257	.2291	.2324	.2357	.2389	.2422	.2454	.2486	.2517	.2549
.7	.2580	.2611	.2642	.2673	.2703	.2734	.2764	.2793	.2823	.2852
.8	.2881	.2910	.2939	.2967	.2995	.3023	.3051	.3078	.3106	.3133
.9	.3159	.3186	.3212	.3238	.3264	.3289	.3315	.3340	.3365	.3389
1.0	.3413	.3438	.3461	.3485	.3508	.3531	.3554	.3577	.3599	.3621
1.1	.3643	.3665	.3686	.3708	.3729	.3749	.3770	.3790	.3810	.3830
1.2	.3849	.3869	.3888	.3907	.3925	.3944	.3962	.3980	.3997	.4015
1.3	.4032	.4049	.4066	.4082	.4099	.4115	.4131	.4147	.4162	.4177
1.4	.4192	.4207	.4222	.4236	.4251	.4265	.4279	.4292	.4306	.4319
1.5	.4332	.4345	.4357	.4370	.4382	.4394	.4406	.4418	.4429	.4441
1.6	.4452	.4463	.4474	.4484	.4495	.4505	.4515	.4525	.4535	.4545
1.7	.4554	.4564	.4573	.4582	.4591	.4599	.4608	.4616	.4625	.4633
1.8	.4641	.4649	.4656	.4664	.4671	.4678	.4686	.4693	.4699	.4706
1.9	.4713	.4719	.4726	.4732	.4738	.4744	.4750	.4756	.4761	.4767
2.0	.4772	.4778	.4783	.4788	.4793	.4798	.4803	.4808	.4812	.4817
2.1	.4821	.4826	.4830	.4834	.4838	.4842	.4846	.4850	.4854	.4857
2.2	.4861	.4864	.4868	.4871	.4875	.4878	.4881	.4884	.4887	.4890
2.3	.4893	.4896	.4898	.4901	.4904	.4906	.4909	.4911	.4913	.4916
2.4	.4918	.4920	.4922	.4925	.4927	.4929	.4931	.4932	.4934	.4936
2.5	.4938	.4940	.4941	.4943	.4945	.4946	.4848	.4949	.4951	.4952
2.6	.4953	.4955	.4956	.4957	.4959	.4960	.4961	.4962	.4963	.4964
2.7	.4965	.4966	.4967	.4968	.4969	.4970	.4971	.4972	.4973	.4974
2.8	.4974	.4975	.4976	.4977	.4977	.4978	.4979	.4979	.4980	.4981
2.9	.4981	.4982	.4982	.4983	.4984	.4984	.4985	.4985	.4986	.4986
3.0	.4987	.4987	.4987	.4988	.4988	.4989	.4989	.4989	.4990	.4990
3.5	.4998	.4998	.4998	.4998	.4998	.4998	.4998	.4998	.4998	.4998

Note: Suppose you want to find the area under the standard normal curve between the values $Z = 0$ and $Z_\alpha = 1.77$. In that case, come down the first column of Z values and locate the row for $Z = 1.7$. Then move along this row and find the number corresponding to the column .07 (in effect, you just added 1.70 + .07 to get the value for 1.77). This number is .4616.

APPENDIX

B

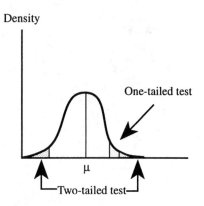

Density

One-tailed test

μ

Two-tailed test

Critical Values of the *t* Distribution

	Levels of Significance				
	One-Tailed Test				
	10%	5%	2.5%	1%	0.5%
Degrees	Two-Tailed Test				
of Freedom	20%	10%	5%	2%	1%
1	3.078	6.314	12.706	31.821	63.657
2	1.886	2.920	4.303	6.965	9.925
3	1.638	2.353	3.182	4.541	5.841
4	1.533	2.132	2.776	3.747	4.604
5	1.476	2.015	2.571	3.365	4.032
6	1.440	1.943	2.447	3.143	3.707
7	1.415	1.895	2.365	2.998	3.499
8	1.397	1.860	2.306	2.898	3.355
9	1.383	1.833	2.262	2.821	3.250
10	1.372	1.812	2.228	2.764	3.169
11	1.363	1.796	2.201	2.718	3.106
12	1.356	1.782	2.179	2.681	3.055
13	1.350	1.771	2.160	2.650	3.012
14	1.345	1.761	2.145	2.624	2.977
15	1.341	1.753	2.131	2.602	2.947
16	1.337	1.746	2.120	2.583	2.921
17	1.333	1.740	2.110	2.567	2.898
18	1.330	1.734	2.101	2.552	2.878
20	1.325	1.725	2.086	2.528	2.845
21	1.323	1.721	2.080	2.518	2.831
22	1.321	1.717	2.074	2.508	2.819
23	1.319	1.714	2.069	2.500	2.807
24	1.318	1.711	2.064	2.492	2.797
25	1.316	1.708	2.060	2.485	2.787
26	1.315	1.706	2.056	2.479	2.779
28	1.313	1.701	2.048	2.467	2.763
30	1.310	1.697	2.042	2.457	2.750
60	1.296	1.671	2.000	2.390	2.660
120	1.289	1.658	1.980	2.358	2.617
Infinity (normal distribution)	1.282	1.645	1.960	2.326	2.576

C

Critical Values of the F Statistic: 5 Percent Level of Significance

	v_1 = Degrees of Freedom for Numerator									
	1	2	3	4	5	6	7	8	10	20
1	161	200	216	225	230	234	237	239	242	248
2	18.5	19.0	19.2	19.2	19.2	19.3	19.4	19.4	19.4	19.4
3	10.1	9.55	9.28	9.12	9.01	8.94	8.89	8.85	8.79	8.66
4	7.71	6.94	6.59	6.39	6.26	6.16	6.09	6.04	5.96	5.80
5	6.61	5.79	5.41	5.19	5.05	4.95	4.88	4.82	4.74	4.56
6	5.99	5.14	4.76	4.53	4.39	4.28	4.21	4.15	4.06	3.87
7	5.59	4.74	4.35	4.12	3.97	3.87	3.79	3.73	3.64	3.44
8	5.32	4.46	4.07	3.84	3.69	3.58	3.50	3.44	3.35	3.15
9	5.12	4.26	3.86	3.63	3.48	3.37	3.29	3.23	3.14	2.94
10	4.96	4.10	3.71	3.48	3.33	3.22	3.14	3.07	2.98	2.77
11	4.84	3.98	3.59	3.36	3.20	3.09	3.01	2.95	2.85	2.65
12	4.75	3.89	3.49	3.26	3.11	3.00	2.91	2.85	2.75	2.54
13	4.67	3.81	3.41	3.18	3.03	2.92	2.83	2.77	2.67	2.46
14	4.60	3.74	3.34	3.11	2.96	2.85	2.76	2.70	2.60	2.39
15	4.54	3.68	3.29	3.06	2.90	2.79	2.71	2.64	2.54	2.33
16	4.49	3.63	3.24	3.01	2.85	2.74	2.66	2.59	2.49	2.28
17	4.45	3.59	3.20	2.96	2.81	2.70	2.61	2.55	2.45	2.23
18	4.41	3.55	3.16	2.93	2.77	2.66	2.58	2.51	2.41	2.19
19	4.38	3.52	3.13	2.90	2.74	2.63	2.54	2.48	2.38	2.16
20	4.35	3.49	3.10	2.87	2.71	2.60	2.51	2.45	2.35	2.12
21	4.32	3.47	3.07	2.84	2.68	2.57	2-49	2.42	2.32	2.10
22	4.30	3.44	3.05	2.82	2.66	2.55	2.46	2.40	2.30	2.07
23	4.28	3.42	3.03	2.80	2.64	2.53	2.44	2.37	2.27	2.05
24	4.26	3.40	3.01	2.78	2.62	2.51	2.42	2.36	2.25	2.03
25	4.24	3.39	2.99	2.76	2.60	2.49	2.40	2.34	2.24	2.10
30	4.17	3.32	2.92	2.69	2.53	2.42	2.33	2.27	2.16	1.93
60	4.00	3.23	2.84	2.61	2.45	2.34	2.25	2.18	2.08	1.84
120	3.92	3.07	2.68	2.45	2.29	2.18	2.09	2.02	1.91	1.66
infinity	3.84	3.00	2.60	2.37	2.21	2.10	2.01	1.94	1.83	1.57

v_2 = Degrees of Freedom for Denominator

Note: F-statistic is a joint probability distribution and measures statistical significance on the basis of two-sided hypotheses about more than one regression coefficient at a time. Unlike the *t* statistic, the *F* statistic is measured by two sets of degrees of freedom. v_1, the degrees of freedom for the numerator (the column values), is calculated by *K*, the number of restrictions (coefficients for the independent variables plus the intercept term) and the denominator (the row values) $v_2 = n - K - 1$, where *n* is the number of observations. Thus, if in an estimated equation there are 50 observations and 5 independent variables, then the numerator value (v_2) for the *F* statistic is 5 + 1 = 6, and the denominator value (v_2) is 50 − 5 − 1 = 44. Since we do not have the exact value corresponding to these degrees of freedom, approximate it with the closest number, which is $F(6,30) = 2.42$.

APPENDIX

D

Critical Values of the F Statistic: 1 Percent Level of Significance

		$v_1 = Degrees\ of\ Freedom\ for\ Numerator$								
	1	2	3	4	5	6	7	8	10	20
1	4052	5000	5403	5625	5764	5859	5928	5982	6056	6209
2	98.5	99.0	99.2	99.2	99.3	99.3	99.4	99.4	99.4	99.4
3	34.1	30.8	29.5	28.7	28.2	27.9	27.7	27.5	27.2	26.7
4	21.2	18.0	16.7	16.0	15.5	15.2	15.0	14.8	14.5	14.0
5	16.3	13.3	12.1	11.4	11.0	10.7	10.5	10.3	10.1	9.55
6	13.7	10.9	9.78	9.15	8.75	8.47	8.26	8.10	7.87	7.40
7	12.2	9.55	8.45	7.85	7.46	7.19	6.99	6.84	6.62	6.16
8	11.3	8.65	7.59	7.01	6.63	6.37	6.28	6.03	5.81	5.36
9	10.6	8.02	6.99	6.42	6.06	5.80	5.61	5.47	5.26	4.81
10	10.0	7.56	6.55	5.99	5.64	5.39	5.20	5.06	4.85	4.41
11	9.65	7.21	6.22	5.67	5.32	5.07	4.89	4.74	4.30	4.10
12	9.33	6.93	5.95	5.41	5.06	4.82	4.64	4.50	4.10	3.86
13	9.07	6.70	5.74	5.21	4.86	4.62	4.44	4.30	3.94	3.66
14	8.86	6.51	5.56	5.04	4.70	4.46	4.28	4.14	3.80	3.51
15	8.68	6.36	5.42	4.89	4.56	4.32	4.14	4.00	3.69	3.37
16	8.53	6.23	5.29	4.77	4.44	4.20	4.03	3.89	3.59	3.26
17	8.40	6.11	5.19	4.67	4.34	4.10	3.93	3.79	3.51	3.16
18	8.29	6.01	5.09	4.58	4.25	4.01	3.84	3.71	3.43	3.08
19	8.19	5.93	5.01	4.50	4.17	3.94	3.77	3.63	3.37	3.00
20	8.10	5.85	4.94	4.43	4.10	3.87	3.70	3.56	3.31	2.94
21	8.02	5.78	4.87	4.37	4.04	3.81	3.64	3.25	3.51	2.88
22	7.95	5.72	4.82	4.31	3.99	3.76	3.59	3.45	3.26	2.83
23	7.88	5:66	4.76	4.26	3.94	3.71	3.54	3.41	3.21	2.78
24	7.82	5.61	4.72	4.22	3.90	3.67	3.50	3.36	3.17	2.74
25	7.77	5.57	4.68	4.18	3.86	3.63	3.46	3.32	3.13	2.70
30	7.56	5.39	4.51	4.02	3.70	3.47	3.30	3.17	2.98	2.55
40	7.31	5.18	4.31	3.83	3.51	3.29	3.12	2.99	2.80	2.37
60	7.08	4.98	4.13	3.65	3.34	3.12	2.95	2.82	2.63	2.20
120	6.85	4.79	3.95	3.48	3.17	2.96	2.79	2.66	2.47	2.03
infinity	6.63	4.61	3.78	3.32	3.02	2.80	2.64	2.51	2.32	1.88

v_2 = Degrees of Freedom for Denominator

APPENDIX E

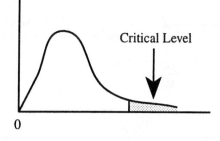

Critical Level

0

The Chi-Square Distribution

Degrees of Freedom	Level of Significance (Probability of a Value of at Least as Large as the Table Entry)			
	10%	*5%*	*2.5%*	*1%*
1	2.71	3.84	5.20	6.63
2	4.61	5.99	7.38	9.21
3	6.25	7.81	9.35	11.34
4	7.78	9.49	11.14	13.28
5	9.24	11.07	12.83	15.09
6	10.64	12.59	14.45	16.81
7	12.02	14.07	16.01	18.48
8	13.36	15.51	17.53	20.1
9	14.68	16.92	19.02	21.7
10	15.99	18.31	20.5	23.2
11	17.28	19.68	21.9	24.7
12	18.55	21.0	23.3	26.2
13	19.81	22.4	24.7	27.7
14	21.1	23.7	26.1	29.1
15	22.3	25.0	27.5	30.6
16	23.5	26.3	28.8	32.0
17	24.8	27.6	30.2	33.4
18	26.0	28.9	31.5	34.8
19	27.2	30.1	32.9	36.2
20	28.4	31.4	34.2	37.6

INDEX